ANNOTATED INSTRUCTOR'S EDITION

EXCELLING
in College

Strategies for Success & Reducing Stress

JEFFREY KOTTLER

California State University, Fullerton

Annotated Instructor's Edition Contributing Authors

MARY CARSTENS
Wayne State College

BARBARA DOYLE
Arkansas State University

SHANNON E. McCASLAND
Aims Community College

 **WADSWORTH**
CENGAGE Learning™

Australia • Brazil • Japan • Korea • Mexico • Singapore • Spain • United Kingdom • United States

Excelling in College: Strategies for Success & Reducing Stress

Jeffrey Kottler

Senior Publisher: Lyn Uhl

Senior Sponsoring Editor: Shani Fisher

Senior Development Editor:
 Julia Giannotti

Assistant Editor: Daisuke Yasutake

Editorial Assistant: Cat Salerno

Media Editor: Amy Gibbons

Senior Marketing Manager:
 Kirsten Stoller

Marketing Coordinator: Ryan Ahern

Marketing Communications Manager:
 Stacey Purviance

Content Project Manager:
 Susan Miscio

Senior Art Director: Pam Galbreath

Print Buyer: Julio Esperas

Senior Rights Acquisition Specialist,
 Image: Jennifer Meyer Dare

Production Service:
 Cadmus Communications

Text Designer: Henry Rachlin

Cover Designer: Yvo Riezebos

Cover Image: Graduates: © Kevin
 Dodge/Corbis Sky: © 2010
 Photos.com, a division of Getty
 images. All rights reserved.

Compositor:
 Cadmus Communications

For product information and technology assistance,
contact us at **Cengage Learning
Customer & Sales Support, 1-800-354-9706**

For permission to use material from this text or product,
submit all requests online at **www.cengage.com/permissions**
Further permissions questions can be emailed to
permissionrequest@cengage.com

Library of Congress Control Number: 2010926158

Student Edition:
ISBN-13: 978-1-4282-3120-7
ISBN-10: 1-4282-3120-X

Annotated Instructor's Edition:
ISBN-13: 978-0-495-79280-2
ISBN-10: 0-495-79280-2

Wadsworth
20 Channel Center Street
Boston, MA 02210
USA

Cengage Learning is a leading provider of customized learning solutions with office locations around the globe, including Singapore, the United Kingdom, Australia, Mexico, Brazil and Japan. Locate your local office at **international.cengage.com/region**

Cengage Learning products are represented in Canada by Nelson Education, Ltd.

For your course and learning solutions, visit **www.cengage.com**

Purchase any of our products at your local college store or at our preferred online store **www.cengagebrain.com**

Printed in the United States of America
1 2 3 4 5 6 7 14 13 12 11 10

TEAMup

TeamUP Faculty Programs

Our **TeamUP** program provides a range of services to help you implement new ideas and learning tools into your courses. Choose the level of support that works best for you, including:

- **Consultants** who understand your challenges and create a customized solution to meet your unique needs.
- **Trainers** who work with you and your students to fully utilize the power of your technology solutions.
- **Experts** in education who offer opportunities to explore new educational tools and ideas through peer-to-peer and professional insight.

To connect with your **TeamUP** Faculty Programs Consultant, call 1-800-528-8323 or visit www.cengage.com/teamup.

Free eSeminars to Reinvigorate Your Teaching

Convenient, cutting-edge, and practical, the Wadsworth **College Success eSeminar Series** offers opportunities for professional development right at your desk. Our experts present relevant topics ranging from learning styles and active learning strategies to motivation and raising expectations. Take advantage of this no-cost faculty development opportunity. Visit **www.cengage.com/tlc/collegesuccess** to access updated eSeminar schedules and archival presentations.

Custom Solutions: Your Course, Your Way

Let Cengage Learning Custom Solutions help create the perfect learning solution for your course. Add key information about your campus and resources, a campus photo, planner pages, or other content from our College Success programs into your student's copy of *Excelling in College*. Visit **custom.cengage.com** for more information.

Engaging. Trackable. Affordable.

College Success CourseMate

Interested in a simple way to *complement* your text and course content with study and practice materials? Cengage Learning's **College Success CourseMate** brings course concepts to life with interactive learning, study, and exam preparation tools that support the printed textbook. Watch student comprehension soar as your class works with the printed textbook and the textbook-specific website. **College Success CourseMate** goes beyond the book to deliver what you need!

College Success CourseMate includes:

Interactive Teaching and Learning Tools

Quizzes, Flashcards, Videos, an Online Stress Assessment, and more, enable students to prepare for class, review for tests, and address the needs of students' varied learning styles.

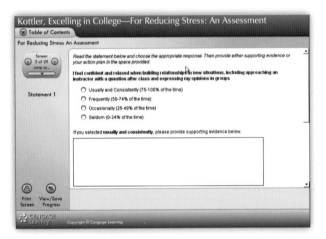

▲ *For Reducing Stress: An Assessment*

By taking this online assessment, students will have an honest and accurate profile of the situations and circumstances that cause them the most stress. Once they have a better idea of potential areas of stress, they can develop an action plan for dealing with those situations that matter the most.

Study Strategies

Students discuss what they find works best when studying, as well as mistakes they made that got them in trouble. (www.cengagebrain.com)

◀ *View It* Video Modules

The text's *View it* feature directs students to view online video modules where they can watch real students talking about the challenges, especially as they relate to stress, that they faced during their first year of college and how they dealt with them. Videos relating to stress-reduction techniques are also provided.

Interactive eBook

With the interactive eBook, students can take notes, highlight, search, and interact with embedded media specific to their book. Use it as a supplement to the printed text, or as a substitute—the choice is your students' with **CourseMate**.

Engagement Tracker

With **CourseMate**, you can use the Engagement Tracker to assess student preparation and engagement in your course. Use the tracking tools to see progress for the class as a whole or for individual students. Identify students at risk early in the course. Uncover which concepts are most difficult for your class. Monitor time on task with the resources you assign. Keep your students engaged.

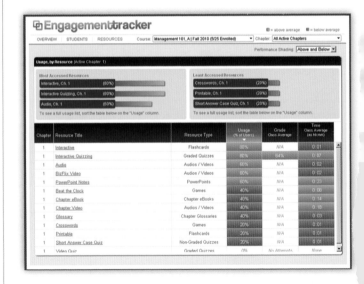

College Success Factors Index (CSFI) 2.0

www.cengage.com/success/csfi2

— Support students on their path to success
— Improve retention rates
— Validate your College Success program

The **College Success Factors Index** (CSFI) 2.0 is an **online survey** that students complete to assess their patterns of behavior and attitudes in 10 key areas that have been proven by research to affect student outcomes for success in higher education.

The **CSFI** is a perfect assessment tool for demonstrating the difference your College Success course makes in your students' academic success.

- As a **pre-course assessment**, the **CSFI** helps incoming students determine their strengths and areas   in which they need improvement, allowing you to tailor your course topics to meet their needs.
- An **Early Alert indicator** flags students who are the most at-risk of falling behind. This information enables instructors to intervene at the beginning of the semester to increase their students' likelihood of success—and improve retention rates.
- **Text-specific remediation** guides students to appropriate pages in their book for added support.
- Increased reporting functionality provides instructors with access to more information and data about their students.
- As a **post-test assessment**, it measures student progress and validates your College Success program.

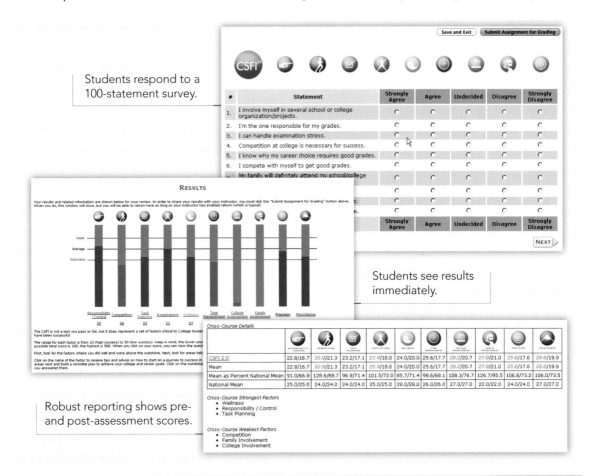

Students respond to a 100-statement survey.

Students see results immediately.

Robust reporting shows pre- and post-assessment scores.

Are your students stressed out?

Excelling in College offers a wealth of resources to help students not just survive but also thrive in their college environment.

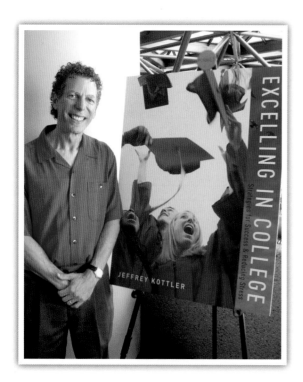

In surveys by the American College Health Association (2009) and the Cooperative Institutional Research Program (2009), half of all students reported feeling plagued by stress in the previous year. One-third found that there were times they were so overwhelmed that they could barely function on a daily basis.

—**Jeffrey A. Kottler,** *Ph.D., Professor of Counseling and of Freshman Programs, California State University-Fullerton*

Look **inside** for information about the resources, training, and support that accompany this exciting new text:
- College Success **CourseMate**
- **College Success Factors Index 2.0**
- **TeamUp** Faculty Programs
- …and more!

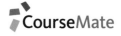

Brief Contents

Contents

CHAPTER 3 · MANAGING TIME AND SETTING GOALS 55

CHAPTER 4 · STRIVING FOR EXCELLENCE IN THE CLASSROOM 77

CHAPTER 7

WRITING PAPERS AND DOING PRESENTATIONS 155

CHAPTER 8

MAKING LIFESTYLE CHOICES 181

CHAPTER 9

THINKING CRITICALLY AND SOLVING PROBLEMS 207

CHAPTER 10 STRESS MANAGEMENT AND PREVENTION 229

CHAPTER 11 NEGOTIATING RELATIONSHIPS 251

CHAPTER

12

DIVERSITY AND APPRECIATING DIFFERENCES   273

CHAPTER

13

PLANNING FOR THE FUTURE   291

To The Student

Welcome to your new role and lifestyle, your new job, as a college student. These next years will be among the most exciting, interesting, stimulating, demanding, bewildering—and stressful—of your life. Whether you have just completed high school, or have years (or decades) of life experience, college life will expose you to a number of intellectual, emotional, social, physical, and moral challenges for which you may feel unprepared.

But here's the good news: this course and textbook will provide you with many of the ideas and skills you need to not just function reasonably well, but to actually excel in higher education and beyond. This will involve not just improving and mastering academic strategies about which you may already be quite familiar—things like taking notes, writing papers, studying for quizzes, taking tests, doing class presentations, and asking questions—but also managing the stress levels that can compromise your optimal performance and reduce your enjoyment of the college experience. Yes, you read that correctly: I am talking about learning to enjoy the ways you will be tested in a variety of settings, whether in the classroom, athletic fields, or social arena. Your success in these areas depends, to a large extent, not just on what you know and what you can do, but also how you can perform when you are being evaluated.

In surveys of students conducted for this book, the number one source of stress was related to financial concerns (most notably paying for college, especially during tough economic times). This was closely followed by students reporting that they are stressed about keeping up with assignments and doing well in classes. Clearly, it is not just a matter of being well prepared and having the necessary skills to succeed in college, but also being able to cope with daily pressures, juggle multiple tasks, manage time and priorities, and find ways to remain calm in the face of inevitable challenges.

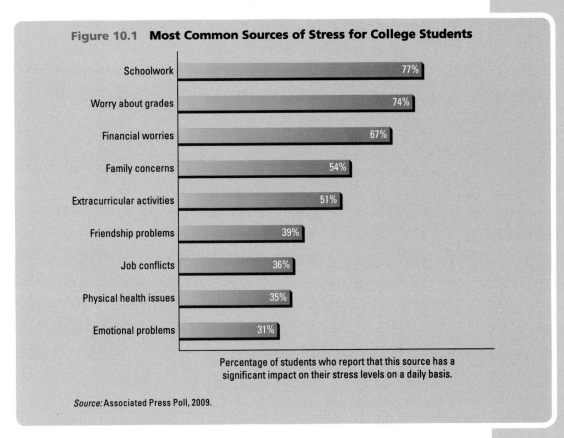

Figure 10.1 Most Common Sources of Stress for College Students

Percentage of students who report that this source has a significant impact on their stress levels on a daily basis.

Source: Associated Press Poll, 2009.

Throughout your college experience you will be called upon to operate under considerable pressure, whether that means taking pop quizzes and final exams, giving presentations and speeches, juggling academic work with social opportunities, or scoring a goal in front of a crowd. Far more often, however, you will be asked to think and respond in reasoned ways, to make considered arguments supported by evidence, and to put yourself on the line by expressing your opinions or even just approaching someone who interests you at a party. In these, and so many other challenges you will face, your heart will be pounding in your chest and that voice inside your head will be freaking you out with scare tactics. What a comfort it would be if you learned ways to manage—and even prevent—stress from compromising your ability to express yourself in the way you are most capable.

WHAT YOU WILL FIND IN THIS TEXT

In this course, you will be exposed to many of the skills you need to flourish not only in college, but in life. Look through the table of contents and you will see immediately how practical and relevant the topics are to your particular needs and interests:

Academic Skills can be applied right now to the variety of courses you are taking.

- Make the most of learning experiences and capitalize on the resources available to you (*Chapters 1 and 2*).
- Ask the right questions, actively listen, and take good notes while you're in the classroom (*Chapter 4*).
- Discover your personal styles for studying and learning (*Chapter 5*).
- Manage anxiety and learn new strategies for taking tests (*Chapter 6*).
- Learn how to write and speak effectively (*Chapter 7*).

Personal Skills help you learn more about yourself, including weaknesses, strengths, interests, abilities, and internal resources.

● Learn how to set priorities and goals and manage your time *(Chapter 3)*.

● Develop critical thinking skills and solve problems *(Chapter 9)*.

● Manage challenges related to your family, friends, romantic entanglements, fellow students, and faculty *(Chapter 11)*, and also to the overwhelming diversity of people with whom you will come into contact *(Chapter 12)*.

Life skills will serve you well in every other environment.

● Develop healthy lifestyle choices related to social and recreational activities, eating behavior, exercise, personal health, drugs and alcohol, and finances *(Chapter 8)*.

● Identify sources of stress that interfere with your performance and enjoyment of daily life, and learn ways to deal with adversity and pressure *(Chapter 10)*.

● **VIEW IT**

Study Strategies
Students discuss what they find works best when studying, as well as mistakes they made that got them in trouble. (www.cengagebrain.com)

© Cengage Learning

● Develop ideas for what you want to do and how you want to get there. Learn about career planning, ambitions, dreams, jobs, and life satisfaction *(Chapter 13)*.

There are a number of features in this text that are intended to help you to learn the concepts, practice the skills, and make the ideas part of the way you handle challenges in the future, whether they relate to academics, social situations, or any other aspect of your life.

● The "View It" feature directs you to view the online video modules where you can watch real students talking about the challenges they faced during their first year in college—especially as they relate to stress—and how they dealt with them.

● The "For Reducing Stress" feature offers strategies that you can apply to a variety of potentially stressful situations including taking tests, giving speeches, approaching someone who interests you, and dealing with conflict.

● "Student Voices" highlight real students talking about the realities of campus life, both the joys and the difficulties. As you read these brief stories, think about how they may compare with your own experiences.

FOR·REDUCING·STRESS

Take a Deep Breath

A little bit of stress before an exam actually *improves* your performance and concentration. But if you become too anxious, you can freeze and "forget" what you know and what you've prepared. There are several things you can do to reduce extreme anxiety related to an upcoming exam, but the most important thing besides being academically prepared is to feel psychologically ready for the challenge.

As anxious as you are to begin a test, first clear your mind of all distractions. Take a "cleansing breath," a deep, relaxing, meditative type of breath that feeds your brain maximum oxygen at the same time it helps you focus your attention. Do that now: Inhale as s-l-o-w-l-y as you can through your nose, expanding your lungs until your shoulders rise. Hold the breath for a count of three, then slowly—very slowly—exhale through your mouth.

Take another breath, this time concentrating so completely on the effort that you block out anything else in your mind.

It is absolutely critical that you let everything else in your life go while you are in performance mode. Regardless of what else is going on in your life—problems with love, money, friendship, family, whatever—put it aside until the test is over. Use the deep breathing as a way to get yourself into the "zone." Whenever you feel your attention wandering, breathe deeply to refocus.

Mimi:
Talking Out Loud

" For the longest time I didn't know how to study for a test. I would kind of guess that I knew the stuff because I had gone to class and taken some notes, so I would look over my notes and hope that was enough. Then, during the test I would actually blank out. I mean, if it was multiple choice I would end up doing the whole eeny-meeny-miny-moe thing, and if the test had essay questions, I would just fake my way through them. And my grades sucked, of course.

You know, it's totally true what they say about you learning more when you explain something to someone else. You know what I do now when I study? I talk out loud to myself. I pretend I'm teaching the stuff to someone and then I talk, talk, talk. I always remember everything really well if I do this. I know I look crazy, walking around the house and talking to myself, but it really works for me.

● The "For Reflection" and "For Reflection and Action" exercises found throughout each chapter help you personalize and apply the textbook concepts to your daily life. These activities can be used to practice new skills and make them a natural way that you deal with challenges.

6.1 FOR REFLECTION

Assessing Your Test-Taking Skills

Rate on a 1–5 scale how skilled you are at taking the following types of exams. If you have never encountered a particular exam before, leave it blank.

I Stink	Get Mostly C's and D's	Not Bad	Pretty Good	I Rock
1	2	3	4	5

Type of Test	Rating
Multiple choice	_____
True-false	_____
Fill-in-the-blank	_____
Short answer	_____
Essay	_____
Oral	_____
Take-home	_____
Matching	_____

Now that you've honestly admitted weaknesses, how are you going to get the help you need to improve your skills?

_____

_____

_____

EXCELLING ONLINE

College Success CourseMate brings course concepts to life with interactive learning, study, and exam preparation tools that support the printed textbook. Resources include:

- **View It: Student Voices and View It: Reducing Stress,** which show students talking about the challenges and stress they faced their first year in college and how they dealt with it all.

- **Video Skillbuilders**, which draw from popular topics covered in College Success courses. The Video Skillbuilders bring to life techniques that will help you to excel in college and beyond.

- **For Reducing Stress Assessment:** Managing and preventing stress begins with having a clear assessment of problem areas in which you feel most vulnerable. By taking this online assessment, you'll have an honest and accurate profile of the situations and circumstances which cause you the most stress. And once you have a better idea of potential areas of stress, you can develop an action plan for dealing with those situations that matter the most.

   The above resources can be found at: www.cengagebrain.com

Learn how to use these resources so they become part of your plan for excelling in college. This book, and this class, have been designed to help you navigate through the confusing maze of college life. The skills you will learn, the knowledge you will acquire, and the networking you will initiate will help you to adjust far more quickly and effectively than students who don't have these assets.

Preface

EXCELLING IN TEACHING COLLEGE SUCCESS

There is persuasive evidence that stress is the single most reported obstacle to academic success in college (Chronicle of Higher Education, 2009). This is true not only among students in general, but first-year students in particular. In surveys by the American College Health Association (2009) and the Cooperative Institutional Research Program (2009), half of all students reported feeling plagued by stress in the previous year. One-third found that there were times they were so overwhelmed that they could barely function on a daily basis.

Excelling in College recognizes the stress that students are under and offers a variety of ways (exercises, in-class activities, video demonstrations, and more) to help students manage these challenges in order to better maintain supportive relationships with family and friends and learn skills that can be internalized and practiced on a daily basis. In particular, students are helped to address their fears related to speaking up in class, approaching instructors, making new friends, performing under pressure, dealing with financial struggles, and making healthy lifestyle choices.

Right from the start, students can assess their stress by taking the online For Reducing Stress Assessment. Managing and preventing stress begins with having a clear assessment of problem areas in which students feel most vulnerable. By taking this online assessment, students will have an honest and accurate profile of the situations and circumstances that cause them the most stress. And once they have a better idea of potential areas of stress, they can develop an action plan for dealing with those situations that matter the most.

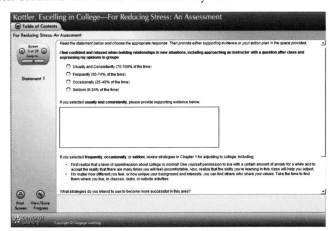

College Success can be a very difficult class to teach well. Instructors are faced with so much material to cover, so many ideas and skills to introduce within a limited timeframe, and so many student needs to address.

STUDENTS COME FROM A VARIETY OF BACKGROUNDS

More than ever, campus life has become increasingly diversified. This is not just the result of ethnic, religious, socioeconomic, and cultural diversity, but also a greater balance in gender and age. In tough economic times, an increasing number of adult learners are choosing to return to college for educational opportunities that were not available to them earlier in their lives.

Greater diversity creates increased stimulation in terms of life experiences, worldviews, and value systems, but also additional challenges in helping each voice to be heard and respected. More than ever, instructors need support and assistance to build classroom communities that are safe, cohesive, and open, leading to more open and honest discussions of important issues. In a sense, the atmosphere of the classroom and the relationships among the participants determines how deep explorations will go.

Whereas this text, like most others, provides the necessary content of the course requirements—providing important ideas related to study skills, test preparation, class performance, and so on—it also focuses on the process of learning that is so critical. Excelling in College is intentionally written in a personal and accessible style to make it easier for the instructor to raise difficult issues with a student population that is diverse in terms of its background and values. It is through the blending of traditional students, first-generation college students, and returning students, that a more realistic forum for learning is created, one that recognizes and responds to different learning styles, personal and professional goals, and value systems.

STUDENTS WANT TO BE ENGAGED AND ENTERTAINED, AS WELL AS INFORMED

Teaching is as much about relationships as it is the dissemination of content. When students feel that they are heard, understood, and respected, their motivation for and commitment to a class are far more likely to increase. This text, any text, should be designed as a supportive companion to the work that any instructor accomplishes in his or her own unique style.

Great pains have been taken to make this textbook package as accessible, fun, and interesting as possible for students. I am a psychologist who has long been interested in ways to make learning stick over the long haul. I am also a professional writer who has specialized in making books as "untextbookish" as possible, meaning that they (1) highlight stories, (2) teach practical skills, and (3) speak directly to students' hearts as well as their minds.

I have tried to strike a balance in this text between academic rigor and engaging prose. Students learn the importance of supporting ideas with research and sources, but they are also encouraged to find their own unique voices and express them with passion.

Suggestions for exploring the content in this textbook in your classroom are presented in this Annotated Instructors Edition, which has been contributed to by Jeffrey Kottler, Mary Carstens of Wayne State College, Barbara Doyle of Arkansas State College, and Shannon McCasland of Aims Community College. Annotations are broken up into a variety of different categories, allowing you to pick and choose what best fits the needs of your course. Categories include:

- Group Activities
- Classroom Discussions
- For Community College students
- Teaching Tips
- Reducing Stress

Students feel relief and validation that they are not alone in the challenges they face. Thousands of first-year students were interviewed across the country, in universities and colleges stretching from Hawaii to New Jersey and from Texas to Canada, from rural and urban community colleges to large research universities. Their honest disclosures and experiences are featured in "voices" that are inserted throughout the book, as well as in video excerpts that accompany the text. These confessions and well intended advice can be used to stimulate deeper exploration and class discussions, bringing some of the most difficult topics out into the open. I asked them questions: As they looked back on their first semesters in college, how do they reflect on the

Teaching Tip
Ask students to pick three dates for visiting with their professors and write these dates in their appointment books. Suggest they contact each professor one week before this date to verify an appointment time. During each visit, the student should get a course grade update and revisit the stated course goals, including the student's individual objectives. After each visit, have students journal what types of modifications are now required to their behaviors and/or attitudes to assure the successful completion of the course and attainment of the course goals.

mistakes they made and what have they learned? What are some of the "tricks of the trade" that they have found most valuable, passed on to them from previous generations of successful students? What are some things that students are most confused about and how have they managed to tackle these problems effectively? Each chapter contains several representative "voices" that highlight the concepts discussed. Students can access the videos on the CourseMate for College Success.

STUDENTS STRUGGLE WITH BALANCING ACADEMIC LIFE SKILLS WITH TIME PRESSURES

Coverage of academic skills includes helping students make the most of their learning experiences and providing them with the tools to capitalize on the resources available to them on campus. Excelling in the classroom by using time management, a variety of note taking strategies, and strong reading skills is critical but so is learning to think critically, do research, interact effectively with others, communicate well, and manage relationships. First year students, whether recent high school graduates or adults with their own families who are returning to school, must learn ways to negotiate all of the tasks required of them with the limited time available. Social, family, and peer influences exert additional pressures.

Excelling in college also involves mastering life skills that will serve students well in every other environment—at home, at work, in the community, in recreational activities, athletics, leisure pursuits, social situations, as well as the classroom. These include developing healthy lifestyle choices, time management strategies, interpersonal skills, stress reduction techniques, and solid critical thinking skills. Students will be required to make a number of moral and values choices during their first semester: decisions related to sex, drugs, and alcohol, as well as the ways they structure their eating and sleeping habits that are so critical for optimal functioning.

STUDENTS NEED WAYS TO PUT NEW SKILLS AND CONCEPTS INTO USE FOR ALL OF THEIR COURSES

One of the most challenging and frustrating things for any instructor is to help students not only acquire new knowledge and skills, but hold onto them and apply them long after the class has ended. So often students sell their books and discard their notes immediately after a semester has ended, clearing their minds before beginning the process anew. Yet so many of the ideas presented in this course are transferable skills that can be internalized and maintained in years to come.

Structured exercises, reflective activities, and action assignments are included in every chapter to help students personalize the concepts and begin applying the ideas on a daily basis. For instance, active listening skills not only help one succeed academically but also enhance all relationships. Knowledge about learning styles aids class and exam preparation but also provides a foundation for successful learning in the future. Cognitive self-talk strategies reduce test anxiety but also provide an antidote for emotional discomfort. Each and every chapter contains specific ways that students can take new ideas for improving their academic performance and apply them to social and other arenas that interest them the most:

● The "View It" feature directs readers to view the online video modules in which real students talk about the challenges faced during their first year in college—especially as they relate to stress—and how they dealt with them.

▶ VIEW IT

© Cengage Learning

Study Strategies
Students discuss what they find works best when studying, as well as mistakes they made that got them in trouble. (www.cengagebrain.com)

FOR · REDUCING · STRESS

Take a Deep Breath A little bit of stress before an exam actually *improves* your performance and concentration. But if you become too anxious, you can freeze and "forget" what you know and what you've prepared. There are several things you can do to reduce extreme anxiety related to an upcoming exam, but the most important thing besides being academically prepared is to feel psychologically ready for the challenge.

As anxious as you are to begin a test, first clear your mind of all distractions. Take a "cleansing breath," a deep, relaxing, meditative type of breath that feeds your brain maximum oxygen at the same time it helps you focus your attention. Do that now: Inhale as s-l-o-w-l-y as you can through your nose, expanding your lungs until your shoulders rise. Hold the breath for a count of three, then slowly—very slowly—exhale through your mouth.

Take another breath, this time concentrating so completely on the effort that you block out anything else in your mind.

It is absolutely critical that you let everything else in your life go while you are in performance mode. Regardless of what else is going on in your life—problems with love, money, friendship, family, whatever—put it aside until the test is over. Use the deep breathing as a way to get yourself into the "zone." Whenever you feel your attention wandering, breathe deeply to refocus.

- The "For Reducing Stress" feature offers strategies that students can apply to a variety of potentially stressful situations including taking tests, giving speeches, approaching someone who interests them, and dealing with conflict.

- "Student Voices" highlights real students talking about the realities of campus life, both the joys and the difficulties. As students read these brief stories, they are prompted to think about how they compare with their own experiences.

The "For Reflection" and "For Reflection and Action" exercises found throughout each chapter help students personalize and apply the textbook concepts to their daily life. These activities can be used to practice new skills and make them a natural way to deal with challenges.

Nadya:
Sitting in the Back

❝ So, there was this girl in one of my classes, she was a real pain. She was always talking and being loud and stuff like that. I like sitting in the back of the class, you know, with my back against the wall. She was sitting in the back, too. And she wouldn't shut up. The teacher totally ignored the people back there and he only paid attention to the people in front. You know, the smart kids.

I have a really hard time paying attention in class, especially if the class is kinda boring. Seriously, I have a pretty hard time concentrating and this girl was always, like, chatting and asking stupid questions. The worse thing is that the teacher didn't care, so this went on and on. Then, one day I decided that I needed to move if I wanted to learn anything in that class. I sat closer to the front of the room and it really helped me. I was able to pay attention because I didn't have anyone distracting me. Now I always sit close to the front row because none of the chatty people hang out there.

Students need resources to support their learning—and instructors need resources, too.

College Success CourseMate includes an interactive eBook, interactive teaching and learning tools including quizzes, flashcards, videos, and more, as well as Engagement Tracker, a first-of-its-kind tool that monitors student engagement in the course. Go to www.cengagebrain.com for more information.

Instructor resources include test items, PowerPoint slides, sample syllabi, and suggested teaching methods. The online video modules provide real-life demonstrations that can be used in class to stimulate discussion or outside of class as assignments to supplement and enliven discussions and lectures.

E-seminars have also been created by the author especially for the instructor to discuss best practices for working with first-year students. Check out the unique ways that social justice issues can be infused into the class and how to teach stress management techniques for the class. For more information on E-Seminars, visit the instructor website.

It's also important that we be honest and realistic at the outset. Just because there are resources and adjunct structures available doesn't mean that students are going to use them. In fact, the majority of students, even those with the best of intentions, may never bother to check out companion websites and demonstration videos that are designed to bring the content to life—unless their instructor assigns them! Perhaps students can get away with such negligence in other classes (although this is not recommended), but so much of the material in this class represents applied skills. There is no way that students can make these ideas part of their own behavior unless they actually practice them on a daily basis. Get your students started by assigning them activities from the College Success CourseMate, such as the videos or the For Reducing Stress Assessment.

ACKNOWLEDGMENTS

A book of this scope can never be conceived and produced by a single author. A number of instructors in the field, many of whom have been teaching this course for years, shared their expertise, feedback, and suggestions to help make this text so reality-based and reflective of what students—and instructors—need most. This book has gone through many sets of review by hundreds of experts from a variety of academic disciplines and student services, who offered many valuable suggestions and helped shape the present product. Nevertheless, I am solely responsible for the content.

Although my name is on the cover of this book, this was a collaborative project in which my editors Annie Todd, Shani Fisher, and Julia Giannotti were significant partners in the process. Special thanks also goes to senior marketing manager, Kirsten Stoller; assistant editor, Daisuke Yasutake; and editorial assistant Cat Salerno. I'd also like to thank Anne Talvacchio for her excellent work with production and Scott Rosen for his excellent expertise in selecting the gorgeous photos in the book.

I wish to acknowledge the following reviewers, who were especially helpful in providing feedback on various drafts of the manuscript:

Sandy Aguilar, Florida State College

Eunie Alsaker, Winona State University

Arne J. Anderson, College of DuPage

Cecile Davis Anderson, Pasadena City College

Valeria Becker, University of North Dakota

Gary Bennett, Brookline College

Susan T. Berry, Elizabethtown Community and Technical College

Kristi Bitz, Mayville State University

Matthew R. Blankenship, Western Illinois University

Jeff Bolles, University of North Carolina at Pembroke

Stewart Brewer, Dana College

Mark Canada, University of North Carolina at Pembroke

Mary Carstens, Wayne State College

Elizabeth Charrier, Sam Houston State University

Geoff Cohen, University of California, Riverside

Carrie L. Cokely, Curry College

Richard Conway, Nassau Community College

Allison Cumming-McCann, Springfield College

Lee Davis, University of South Carolina, Upstate

Barbara S. Doyle, Arkansas State University

Tony Enerva, University of Maine

Nancy Page Fernandez, California State University, Fullerton

Juan J. Flores, Folsom Lake College

Virginia D. Granda-Becker, University of Texas at El Paso

Carlond W. Gray, Florida State College at Jacksonville

Winona T. Hatcher, Aiken Technical College

Cathy Hoult, Monmouth University

Karon Jahn, University of Texas, Brownsville

Joel Jessen, Eastfield College

Gary G. John, Nassau Community College

Grace Johnson, California State University, Fullerton

Cathi Kadow, Purdue University Calumet

Ellen Katoll, Northern Illinois University

L. Dianne King, Anderson University

Joseph Kornoski, Montgomery County Community College

Arnold Korotkin, Montclair State University

Jennifer Krimmel, Pima Medical Institute

Karen Lang, Ivy Tech Community College of Indiana

Liz Largent, Oklahoma City Community College

Christopher Lau, Hutchinson Community College

Jean Layne, Blinn College

Lea Beth Lewis, California State University, Fullerton

Barbara M. Lujan, Lone Star College, Tomball

Diana Lurz, Rogers State University

Debbie McCarty, Metropolitan Community College, Maple Woods

Shannon E. McCasland, Aims Community College

Wendy McNeeley, Howard Payne University

Renae Messner, Miller-Motte Technical College

Paul Miller, California State University, Fullerton

Patricia A. Mills, College of Mount St. Joseph

Lisa Moore, Eastern Kentucky University

Kelly Morales, University of Texas Pan American

Amanda Nimetz, Midwestern State University

Christopher J. Olivera, University of California, Riverside

Stan Parker, Charleston Southern University

Patricia Parma, Palo Alto College

James C. Penven, Virginia Polytechnic Institute and State University

Sean Peters, The College of Saint Rose

Patrick Peyer, Rock Valley College

Carole Pfeffer, Florida Atlantic University

Laura M. Pipe, Florida Atlantic University

Terry Lee Rafter-Carles, Valencia Community College

Anthony Ragazzo, California State University, Fullerton

Virginia Reilly, Ocean County College

Charles Rhodes, Sonoma State University

Christine S. Ricks, Old Dominion University

Jennifer Rockwood, University of Toledo

Tara Ross, Keiser University

Kurt Schackmuth, Lewis University

Annamaria E. Shiplee, University of West Florida

Sarah Shutt, J. Sargeant Reynolds Community College

Rebecca Signore, Gwynedd-Mercy College
Phebe Simmons, Blinn College
Rebekah Smart, California State University, Fullerton
Elizabeth Stewart, City College of San Francisco
Crystal Thomas, University of South Alabama
Lynda Villanueva, Brazosport College
Kirk W. Voska, Rogers State University

Jodi Webb, Bowling Green State University
Kathie L. Wentworth, Trine University
Cheryl R. Wieseler, Luther College
Toni Woolfork-Barnes, Western Michigan University
Kathy Yorkshire, Prince George's Community College
Donna Younger, Oakton Community College

I'm grateful to Larissa Patton and Christine Tomasello for help interviewing students and collecting the "voices" that are found throughout the book, and to Chris Carlino for his interviewing and video filming effort.

The following professionals contributed ideas that were used in the book: Jennifer Cunningham, Sue Passalacqua, Jonathan Blake, David Leary, Dave Hart, Lee Gilbert, and Chuck Buck.

Several students also reviewed the book and made suggestions:

Angelina Allessi, California State University, Fullerton
Greg Arney, Berklee College of Music
Nicholas Cassidy, Tulane University
Jillian Chan, California State University, Fullerton
Wesley Chiu, University of Connecticut
Garrett Dickerson, Rensselaer Polytechnic Institute
Zephyr Doles, Temple University
Joachim Enriquez, California State University, Fullerton
Jenny Fan, California State University, Fullerton
Scott Feeley, California State University, Fullerton
Katherine Franz, California State University, Fullerton
Joey Garcia, California State University, Fullerton
Kevin Giang, California State University, Fullerton
Rafael Gutierrez, California State University, Fullerton
Colton Harker, California State University, Fullerton
Erica Holmes, California State University, Fullerton
Michael Huberman, College of Charleston
Marguerite Jones, California State University, Fullerton

Stefani Laci, California State University, Fullerton
Ryan McGovern, Emerson College
Rebecca Nelson, Smith College
Kyle O' Brien, University of Massachusetts
Moni Olusekun, University of Massachusetts
Spencer Riddle, California State University, Fullerton
Victoria Santana, California State University, Fullerton
Daniel Schweitzer, California State University, Fullerton
Trevor Spencer, California State University, Fullerton
Jessica St. Louis, Tufts University
Fengyi (Andy) Tang, University of California, San Diego
Cayla Tepper, University of Vermont
Rojay Wagner, University of Massachusetts
Laine Winokur, Mount Holyoke College
Kevin Wong, California State University, Fullerton
Ramses Yanez., California State University, Fullerton

Jeffrey Kottler,
Fullerton, California

Introduction

A Very Personal Introduction

Memories of my first year in college are so fresh that it seems as if they happened just a few years ago instead of decades. I had never been considered "college material," even though it was my parents' fondest wish that I might become the first in my family to last longer than a semester. I barely got out of high school with a C average, so the prospect of further education was not much of a target on my radar. On the other hand, the thought of working full time in the factory where I'd been working throughout my high school years was also not very attractive.

I was an apprentice working on huge printing presses that left my hands raw and my fingernails permanently stained from different colored inks. I watched the operators rush off to a bar during lunch breaks, down shots of whiskey with beer chasers, and then head back to the shop. I didn't want to follow this path. The prospect of going to college began to seem like a way out, a place I could hide for a few years and yet seem productive.

Even though my parents supported the idea of me attending college, I had few options for where I could attend. My grades were lousy. I didn't score well on the entrance exams. I had no extracurricular activities to my credit. In truth, I didn't have much going for me. And this was before the open admissions policies that are now in place at many colleges.

I later learned from the admissions officer that he decided to admit me on probation because I showed up for the interview without my parents. Although this streak of self-reliance impressed him a little, he also confided that he didn't think I'd last longer than a semester with my mediocre academic record. By the way, in case you are wondering how I know all this, fifteen years later I ended up as a professor at this same university with that same admissions counselor now my colleague.

As predicted, my first semester did not go particularly well. I was so poorly prepared for college life, had so little confidence in my abilities, and had such low expectations for what I could do that I continued my average performance. I realized that if I was going to make it through this experience with anything even remotely marketable as a degree, somehow I was going to have to buckle down and redefine myself as a scholar.

I borrowed money so I could live on campus, thinking that maybe this would help me to focus better, not to mention get me away from my family (but that's another story). I decided that I was tired of being viewed as a dummy, a no-talent, mediocre student who was lucky to scrape by. I wanted to be smart. I wanted to be one of those people who others go to when they want to know things. But I wasn't sure how to do this exactly. What does it take to be smart, anyway?

After sitting on the steps of the library for a few days between classes (I had yet to step inside), I studied students walking by trying to figure out who was smart. I figured that all I had to do was identify these people and then do what they were doing. The answer was pretty obvious: smart students walked around campus carrying books—lots of them, in fact. If that's what it took, I could do that, too!

I walked inside the library, a first big step, checked out an armload of books, and then walked around campus quite proud of my new image. Once I got them back to the room, I realized that smart people didn't just carry these volumes; they actually read them. Well, if that's what it took, I'd do that, too.

A funny thing happened after that. Once I started pretending I was smart, always walking around carrying (and reading) books, people started to treat me that way. They assumed I knew things. They asked me questions about what puzzled them; even more surprising, they listened to my answers. After a while, I kind of, sort of, maybe, a little bit, started to believe that perhaps I *did* have something going for me.

That was the beginning for me. If I'd had a class like the one you are taking now, it sure would have saved me a lot of trouble. I didn't know how to study or take tests very well. I didn't know I could write. I was too shy to speak up in class. And I sure couldn't manage my time very well.

I mention this brief introduction to my early college life to let you know that I'm qualified to write this book not just because I know the subject, but also because I was once so clueless about how to succeed. You've probably heard this before, but if I could do it, surely so can you.

Why This Class Is So Important

This might very well be the most important class you ever take in your life. Beyond what it can do to help you excel in college, most of the skills and methods introduced will be of immeasurable help in the job market, where you will be required to demonstrate similar skills in reading and retention of information, analytic reasoning, problem solving, interpersonal networking, persuasive communication, and performing under pressure. This one class can teach you what you need to know to flourish in almost any competitive environment.

A lot of research describes what best predicts success in college. It is no surprise that prior academic achievement makes a big difference, as does socioeconomic status. But these are things you can't control at this point in your life, just as you can't do much about your gender (women tend to do better) or age (older students are more successful). The variables that *are* within your control are your grades during your first year, which are good predictors of how you will do throughout your education

Lee:
Director of First-Year Programs Remembers His First Year of College

❝ My first semester didn't go very well at all. I went into my math final with a low D, yet somehow managed to get a B on the final and scraped by with a C– in the class. All of my other grades were C's with the exception (prophetically) of German, in which I got a B. My moment of revelation came during the winter break, when I realized that if I was going to be successful, I was going to have to study a lot harder and manage my time a lot better. (I was also working twenty hours a week in exchange for room and board.) I allowed myself a half hour of relaxation after dinner each night, and then hit the books for four to five solid hours. I started outlining chapters, rereading and rewriting my notes from class every day, and trying to get ahead in my texts. At the end of the spring semester, I had made the honor roll. I had already changed my mind about my major two times and finally decided I would stick with German, the one class I liked best. Neither of my parents had gone to college since they had worked in factories their whole lives, so they thought I was crazy, but they still supported my decision.

(although your grades usually improve as you gain more experience), as well as the preparation you receive in necessary skills (Ishler and Upcraft, 2005).

Second, considerable evidence shows that students who participate in a "survival skills" or "student success" course are far more likely to complete their studies, and do so in a timely and satisfying way. In addition, such students show significant gains in their academic skills, are far more likely to remain in college, demonstrate greater sensitivity and critical thinking, and are better equipped to deal with complex challenges (Engberg and Mayhew, 2007). They attain higher grade point averages their first year in college, performance that is maintained throughout their college careers (Lang, 2007). In addition, they are far more likely to have more meaningful relationships with faculty and fellow students (Goodman and Pascarella, 2006). However (and this is a big *however*), it has been shown that mere attendance in such a class does not make a big difference in terms of adjustment, satisfaction, and academic performance *unless* you are actively involved in meaningful activities that prepare you for success (Strayhorn, 2009).

Regardless of where your life path takes you, whether you remain in college for one semester or end up in graduate school, the skills you will learn from this book will make you not only a better student but also a better person. They will assist you in becoming more efficient and productive, although flourishing in life is not just about getting work done—it is about enjoying the process. It is about having fun. It is about finding meaning and purpose in what you are doing. And it is about making strong connections with others.

Making Learning Stick

This introduction to a new text and course should inspire you with promises of how exciting and wonderful this experience is going to be. This is where you hear about all the great things you will learn, how they will make your life in college so much easier, and how they will change your life and help you to bring about world peace (okay, maybe the last one is a stretch). It so happens that most of this is indeed true.

Group Activity
Put students into groups of three or four. Assign each group to a different aspect of college like classroom behavior, personal responsibility, or teacher behavior. Ask the groups to list the differences between high school and college that they have observed so far. Invite the small groups to share with the whole class, and then discuss differences of opinion.

0.1 FOR REFLECTION **AND ACTION**

How College Learning Is (or May Be) Different from High School

This is the first in a series of reflective exercises scattered throughout the chapters of this book that help you to personalize the content and remain actively involved in the learning process. You already know that it can be difficult to learn new concepts, much less recall things you have read, unless you find ways to make the material relevant to your interests.

In this section, you are being challenged to consider that most students are unprepared to succeed in college, largely because the environment and expectations are so different from those of high school. List below some of the most significant ways that the learning environment is different in college compared to what you were used to in high school.

1. _____ 5. _____

2. _____ 6. _____

3. _____ 7. _____

4. _____ 8. _____

Possible answers are listed at the end of this chapter.

Group Activity
Ask students to write their contact information on a note card, along with what they like to do for fun and what they hope to learn from the class. Collect the cards and, without providing names, share with the rest of the class samples of what students hope to learn.

However (and you knew this was coming), the reality is that many students don't take this course very seriously, nor do they devote the necessary time and effort it takes to master the skills that are introduced. They let themselves get distracted by other things. They don't make the class much of a priority because they don't see the value of what they're learning.

So here's the key: *Everything* included in this book and class is presented for a good reason, based on decades of experience and research about what it takes to succeed—and thrive—in college. I don't expect you to be absolutely enthusiastic about every unit, riveted by every chapter, and spellbound by each class; however, if you are patient and devote the work necessary to make the skills part of your own style, you *will* find that you can learn far more efficiently and effectively for the rest of your life.

One thing you already know about learning is that most of it doesn't stick. No matter how good the teacher was, or how interested you were in the subject, you can recall only a small fraction of the material that was covered. As you begin your college career, you should also be aware of the difference between learning things for a test or to attain a high grade versus mastering content and skills that are essential for you to succeed in life.

During those times when you learned a lot in a class and retained it over time, several conditions were likely operating. First of all, the material was of interest and direct relevance to you. You could see how investing the time and energy into the studies would pay off for you in the long run. Second, you were able to personalize and customize the content to fit your particular interests and needs. Third, you had opportunities to practice what you learned, to apply the skills to real-life situations. Finally, the content stuck with you because you found ways to actually use it on a regular basis.

Looking back on your high school career, consider how many classes impacted you in such an enduring way that you use the knowledge and skills on a weekly, if not daily, basis. Consider all the things you memorized, the concepts you studied, the books you read, and the classes you sat (or slept) through. How much of it stuck with you?

Not much.

College life is better in that you have more freedom to study what *you* want (within limits). The quality of instruction is often better, and the stimulation level is significantly improved. Nevertheless, you are going to struggle with the same challenges of retention that you have faced most of your life. It is really, really difficult to learn new things—and hold onto them.

During challenging or stressful times—whether taking a test, giving a speech, debating an argument, or climbing a rock face—you don't have much time to think before making quick, strategic, and intelligent decisions. For any learning to stick, you must internalize the concepts and practice the skills until they become a natural part of the way you function.

A lot of research discusses what leads to relatively permanent acquisition of new knowledge or skills. You won't be surprised to hear that *active learning* works far better than passive learning. In other words, sitting still in a classroom for more than a half hour at a time (no matter how interesting the material) isn't nearly as potent as having opportunities to engage actively with the concepts through discussion, group interaction, practice, immersion, or some other form of direct experience. Likewise, it is absolutely critical for retaining new knowledge and skills that *all* your senses are engaged. It is great to simulate your intellect, but even better if you can become

Voices of Three Different Students

" The "voices" of students are presented throughout the book talking about their experiences related to various topics. In some cases, they support particular ideas that have been introduced; in others, they present a counterpoint showing alternative realities.

* * * * *

I'm here, aren't I? That's something. I never shoulda been here in the first place. I'm from a small, farming town and nobody in my family ever went to college before. I'm the first. On top of that, the only reason I'm here is because I play basketball so they gave me a scholarship.

I'm pretty smart, but I didn't have the best preparation to compete with the folks here, at least in class and stuff. I miss my family terribly—and my friends, too. People are different around here. I'll pretty much just keep to myself until I can figure out what's going on. That's gonna take a while, I can tell, because I'm already pretty lost.

* * * * *

This isn't that different from high school for me since I live nearby. Maybe the classes are a little bigger and the campus is, too, but it's pretty much the same. I still have to work after school and I'll probably keep hanging out with my old friends. So I don't expect that much will be all that different. But maybe I'm kidding myself and I just don't know yet what I'm getting into.

* * * * *

With two young ones at home and being a single mother, everyone says I'm crazy to be going to school at a time like this. I look around here and I see kids who are ten years younger than me and I wonder what the hell I'm doing here too. I don't have any idea how I'm going to keep up on all the work with everything else I've got going. How am I going to find the time to study or go to class when my children get sick or something comes up at their school?

I see others like me, even much older, but I still don't think I fit in. Maybe that will take time. But for now I'm going to try to do my best.

---

involved emotionally, physically, and interpersonally. In other words, it isn't enough to merely read this material in a book or hear an instructor talk about it in class. You must also have opportunities to practice the skills and make the ideas your own.

In class, you will do a number of activities and exercises, including those contained within this text. These are not "supplemental" or "ancillary," meaning they are not secondary to the really important material; in fact, they are the *most* important part of your learning experience. If you really want to excel at speaking and writing, solving problems, managing your time effectively, resolving conflicts, becoming more persuasive and influential, reducing stress in your life, dealing with disappointments, finding a good job, and so on, you *must* devote considerable time and effort to practicing these skills.

It all comes down to motivation, doesn't it? If your instructor and this text can convince you that this class is worth your devotion, and you can persuade yourself of its value, you won't have to work that hard learning the material. Work can be defined as something that you *have* to do, whereas play is something that you *want* to do. It is entirely possible that you can make this class (and others) an exercise in play because you can readily see that your efforts will result in immediate personal and professional gains.

Classroom Discussion

Ask three students to read the voices aloud. Open it up to the class: Which voice, if any, most closely reflects your own feelings? What do you think are the chances for success in college for each different voice? What do you think these voices could do to improve their chances? What are some of the greatest sources of stress that might interfere with or sabotage your efforts to do well in college?

ANSWERS TO FOR REFLECTION 0.1

Significant ways that the learning environment is different in college from that in high school include:

- Bigger classes.
- Classes meet less often.
- Less emphasis on memorization.
- More emphasis on application of concepts to solve problems.
- Multiple viewpoints presented and less emphasis on "right" answers.
- More focus on critical thinking.
- Expectations are less clearly defined.
- Less structure and direction.
- A *lot* more reading and preparation required for class.
- The pace is faster.
- Teachers are less accessible.
- Some teachers may not speak English as clearly as you'd like.
- Fewer exams and evaluations.
- Less feedback from teachers on how you are doing.
- More outside distractions.
- The "curve" is a lot steeper because everyone is qualified.
- Grading is more stringent.
- More writing is required.
- Instructors don't necessarily take attendance.
- More use of technology and electronic media.
- More difficult to get extensions on late assignments.
- You plan your own day instead of it being planned for you.
- More teamwork and cooperative learning required (group projects).
- Zero tolerance for cheating or academic dishonesty.

Give yourself a pat on the back (or gold star) if you thought of some important differences other than those mentioned above.

The Nature of Life on a College Campus

KEY QUESTIONS

▶ **What are the values of a college education?**

▶ **What is the evidence that a college degree represents a solid investment, returning significant profits after a relatively short period of time?**

▶ **What is the principal "mission" of college education besides training for a career?**

▶ **How is wisdom different from knowledge?**

▶ **What are some of the normal fears and common apprehensions that are experienced by most college students?**

▶ **How are college students most often changed by their experience?**

▶ **Why is it generally not a good idea to give people advice?**

You are literally entering a whole new world, if not a universe. A college campus is like no other place on earth. It can be a bewildering environment, a confusing maze of buildings with names that don't often connect with what they actually do inside them. Various administrative offices are scattered in nooks and crannies, as if testing navigational skills. Colleges have their own rules and policies, many of which may strike you as incomprehensible.

Going to college for the first time is very much like traveling to a foreign land, with all the same predictable transition challenges: trying to make sense of the language, finding your way around, and making sense of the strange customs and rituals. Similar to a new immigrant, you are likely to feel adventurous and optimistic, but also recognize that you have relatively low status and little power, and are subject to an incomprehensible, bureaucratic, and political government (Chaskes, 1996).

As a college student you are likely to experience one-third less stress and depression than your friends who passed up higher education (Foreman, 2009), however, you are still in store for some difficult challenges. In fact, 85 percent of students report that they have difficulty managing the stress they experience in college and 60 percent say they sometimes feel so overwhelmed that they can't function well (Associated Press, 2009).

Group Activity

Break the class into small groups and ask each group to come up with a list of how college culture is different from the "cultures" of high school, work, or home. Examples include language (acronyms), peer group, age, cliques, values, group work, and schedules.

The good news is that this book, and this class, will help you navigate through the confusing maze of college life. The skills you will learn, the knowledge you will acquire, and the networking you will initiate will help you to adjust far more quickly and effectively than students who don't have the advantage of this support.

College Life and Its Inhabitants

As you look around the grounds of your new home for the next two, three, four, five, or even more years, you may be struck by the incongruity of two distinct groups of people. First are those who seem to be in a hurry. You can see them rushing to get wherever they have to be—and they look distracted, anxious, and tardy. They may be administrators wearing suits or dresses, faculty in jeans or khakis, or students on skateboards, bikes, or scooters; everyone running, walking briskly, or otherwise moving quickly to some destination. What they all seem to have in common is a sense of definite purpose.

In contrast, the second group seems to have absolutely nowhere to go. They are relaxing on the lawn, lying on a bench, chatting with friends, drinking a Coke or coffee, eating a snack, playing Frisbee, staring aimlessly toward the sky, or strolling along at an unhurried pace. They exude a serenity that you can't help but envy. Which leads to the question: Why are some students so rushed and harried, while others appear so calm and unhurried? The answer is related to how they have learned to manage their time effectively as well as their stress levels.

Of course, this brief snapshot of behavior does not necessarily represent the way people feel through the day, just at this particular moment. Maybe the guy you thought was running to class was really just getting some exercise. Perhaps the Frisbee thrower lost track of time and soon realized she was late for class, joining the harried group for the mad rush.

Indeed, a college campus is among the most tranquil, soothing, enlightened settings on our planet. The grounds are specifically designed to provide an atmosphere of heightened stimulation—not only of the intellect but also of your whole being. The architecture of the buildings conveys a sense of dignity and stature. The landscaping is planned to provide islands of solitude and social gatherings. The campus is indeed a

The college experience involves not only doing things but also reflecting on what you have done. Lectures, seminars, readings, discussions, homework, tests, research projects, and field experiences all provide you with concepts, theories, and skills that increase your knowledge. Ultimately, it is up to you to make sense of what you have studied, and to personalize it so that you can apply knowledge in meaningful ways.

Andersen Ross/Jupiter Images

world of its own, not so much a single "ivory tower" as an eclectic community devoted to pursuing knowledge and growth in all its various forms.

Variety of College Experiences

Keep in mind the incredibly diverse community of students around the nation, and the world, who are joining you on this journey. Institutions of higher learning are so different in every region and within each community. This diversity ranges from small colleges in rural areas to urban research centers, from community colleges to doctoral-granting institutions, each of them with their own unique strengths and resources.

Those who may be reading this text with you in colleges across the continent range from those living in a residential community on campus to commuters who live near the campus. Some of your fellow students are seventeen- or eighteen-year-olds and have just graduated high school, whereas others are returning students who have spent years, or decades, gaining life experience. Some students are living at home with their parents, and others with their own children. Although you all face similar challenges, each of you has particular needs that are a bit different from the rest.

Some of the content and sections in this book may not quite fit your situation or interests. That's fine—just make the needed adjustments in order to make the material more appropriate for your particular needs. For instance, in the following section on the purposes of college, you should consider that various institutions have very different missions: some to serve people in the local community; some to prepare students for advanced learning in four-year institutions; some focused on engineering, teacher education, or nursing; and some primarily geared for high-level research.

What Is College For, Anyway?

There are as many different purposes for attending college as there are individuals who attend them. Some are driven by ambition to prepare for a satisfying career or make a lot of money, whereas others are driven by much more subjective, personal quests. See if you recognize yourself in some of the statements below. Keep in mind that your own reasons probably involve several of these motives, plus others not even mentioned.

- "I don't know what I want to do with my life, so I wanted some time to sort things out."
- "I want to do big things with my life and know that I can't get very far without a degree."
- "I want to make a lot of money so I can buy the things I want."
- "I never really had a choice. My parents told me this was what I was going to do."
- "I recently lost my job and so I want to prepare for a new career."
- "At my high school, everyone goes to college. It's just something you do."
- "I didn't want to work in some crummy job."
- "I want to party and have fun."
- "I love learning and reading and studying new things. I want to be a smart person, wise and knowledgeable."
- "The neighborhood where I grew up is a dead end. This is my only way out."
- "My best friend was going, so I thought I should go too just so we could still hang out together."
- "I know what I want to do, so I need college and graduate school to get there."
- "I want to be a more cultured person."
- "I've played ball since I was a kid, so this is the next stop in my career to get the coaching and playing time I need."

Classroom Discussion
Open it up: What are your reasons for attending college? Which of your fellow students do you think have a better chance of success? Which may need to develop more direction? Which reasons are similar to your own motives for attending college?

Group Activity
Ask students to introduce themselves to five students they don't know in class and ask them their reasons for starting college. Emphasize that there are both public and private (more honest) reasons. Tally these reasons on the list here and/or add reasons at the bottom of the list if they are not listed. Based on their experiences so far in college, ask students to share what has happened or what they have learned in a class that is helping them to fulfill their goals for coming to college.

1.1 FOR REFLECTION

Motives for Attending College

What is the main reason you tell your family and friends why you are attending college?

_____

_____

_____

_____

If you are completely honest with yourself, what are more personal and private motives that have led you to college at this time?

_____

_____

_____

_____

- "I want to get promoted at work, and the company is paying for school anyway."

- "I want to be the first person in my family to ever go to college and graduate."

- "I just have to get away from home. My parents drive me crazy."

- "Now that my kids have left home, it is finally time for me to examine what I really want."

This is hardly an exhaustive list of reasons why people go to college but it provides a realistic cross-section of some possibilities. In fact, three-quarters of entering students disclose that their primary purpose is to prepare for a good career and earn a good income. This isn't a great leap of faith based on convincing evidence that a college graduate makes double the amount of money as a high school graduate, and literally millions more in their lifetimes (Day and Newburger, 2002). Even more impressive, a graduate degree will triple the income of a high school graduate (Baum, Payea, and Steele, 2006). So even with the high cost of tuition, and the sacrifices you may make to pay off the debt you accumulate with student loans, you are likely to recoup your investment within a relatively short period of time.

Did You Know?

Inserted within the preceding paragraph you will have noticed some names and dates in parentheses. These are called *citations* and they come in different styles, depending on the field you are in. The names and dates represent a particular referencing style that shows who wrote the work and when it was published. You will see these citations appear whenever a statement requires documentation or support. For example, you may think to yourself that the statement predicting income sounds great but you wonder where the data come from. Is this is a legitimate, reliable source? Maybe you want to check this out for yourself. Perhaps someday you will want to do your own research in an area and these citations provide you with starting points to investigate questions that interest you most.

Both of the citations in the paragraph can be found online, as well as in government reports. If you go to the reference section at the end of the book, and look up the name of the first author on the list, you will find the web address for you to consult the report yourself.

You will notice throughout this text, and others you will read in college, that the knowledge of a discipline is advanced by building on the work of those who came before us. It is important to acknowledge the research and efforts of others from whom our own ideas and propositions are derived.

College and University Missions

Although it is perfectly legitimate to hold very personal reasons (some you would not admit to most people) for attending college besides preparing for a job, you may find it surprising that universities were originally designed for more lofty goals. All colleges have mission statements that describe their primary objectives. Whereas any modern college would boast that it seeks to help students find a place for themselves in the world and secure productive and meaningful work, traditionally it would also have claimed that the main purpose of higher education was to pursue "truth." The majority of students agree, stating that they attend college to learn more about things that interest them.

Academics debate at considerable length as to whether such a thing as truth even exists (at least outside of mathematics) since this ideal is based on individual perceptions and cultural norms. But no one would dispute that college provides a unique opportunity to discover and pass along new knowledge.

You cannot contribute to making the world a better place in the future unless you know something about what has happened in the past, unless you are educated about the foundational knowledge that has been accumulated before you. This includes a review of contributions in as many disciplines as possible in the sciences, humanities, arts, social sciences, and professional fields. The whole idea is not only to expose you to what is already known, but also to stimulate your interest in making significant contributions to what is unknown.

There is a difference between training for a specific job and becoming enlightened as a citizen of the world. College is designed to provide both: to equip you with the basic skills and knowledge for career success, and also to expand your horizons about how history, science, and human behavior shape you and everyone else on the planet (see Table 1.1). It is designed to teach you how to reason and how to think. It is structured around the goals of broadening your interests and exposing you to a range of

Group Activity

Ask students to write a brief response to the following prompt: Identify two schools that each of them considered for postsecondary work. What did each school offer that made it unique? Why did they choose their current institution?

For Community College Students

Develop a list of possible mission statements including your institution's mission statement. Ask students to identify your college's mission statement and then engage them in a discussion about how the community college mission is different from or similar to that of four-year universities.

TABLE 1.1

What College Can Do for You

▶ Enable you to earn double the income that you would otherwise accrue with only a high school education.
▶ Introduce you to a network of intelligent, ambitious, and potentially successful friends.
▶ Teach you to work as part of a team.
▶ Expose you to subjects, books, and ideas that would otherwise be out of reach.
▶ Increase your knowledge of a wide range of disciplines.
▶ Teach you to be more flexible and adaptable when faced with new situations.
▶ Develop your appreciation for others from different backgrounds and points of view.
▶ Provide access to cutting-edge technology and research.
▶ Develop your internal resources for solving problems.
▶ Improve your tolerance for ambiguity and appreciation for complexity.
▶ Teach you how to think critically and reason intelligently.
▶ Help you to communicate more effectively in speech, writing, and conversations.
▶ Provide you with skills for making sound decisions.
▶ Offer experience in cooperative learning, as well as leadership.
▶ Expand your range of interests.
▶ Increase your confidence and self-esteem.
▶ Improve the quality of your life and lead to a longer life span.
▶ Help you to instill in your own children an appreciation and hunger for learning.
▶ Equip you with a credential that will prompt others to take you seriously and to qualify you for jobs you desire.
▶ Prepare you for graduate school or advanced training in a profession.
▶ Enable you to make significant contributions to your community and the world.
▶ Inspire you to initiate social change to improve the quality of life for others.
▶ Spark a lifelong love of learning.

Group Activity
Provide students with a list
of the general education
requirements for your
institution. Take a poll of the
class: Which are they most
excited about? Least excited?
Ask them to discuss their
reasons why.

possibilities. This is why the curriculum is specifically designed around not just a major but also general education courses, electives, and requirements that lead you on a journey of discovery.

You will hear complaints (and make them yourself) about the burden of taking required classes in which you have little interest. You may resent being forced to take organic chemistry, art history, Shakespeare, physical education, calculus, economics, a foreign language, statistics, or anything else that seems boring or overly challenging to you (including this class). But sound justifications support this educational plan that are not directly related to job training but to developing *wisdom*.

What Is Wisdom, and How Do You Get It?

Throughout the ages, philosophers, writers, scientists, and religious scholars have wrestled with the meaning of wisdom. Think of people who you consider "wise," and it's likely that they exude something more than merely being smart or "knowing stuff." Geniuses abound in every field, from physicists and entrepreneurs to car mechanics and sculptors, but such individuals are not necessarily wise, meaning that they truly understand themselves and the way the world works. The physicist may have a brilliant grasp of atomic particles, or the mechanic the mysterious workings of fuel injection systems, but that does not mean that they are what philosopher Immanuel Kant once described as having "an organized life." Poet Alfred Lord Tennyson once observed that wisdom is what lingers long after knowledge first arrived.

Attaining wisdom often requires sacrifice and even suffering on occasion. Several common themes embedded in the world's great myths and legends attest to this struggle, as identified by Joseph Campbell (1968), who spent a lifetime analyzing the folklore of cultures since ancient times. Whether Chinese proverbs, Eskimo tales, African Bushmen sacred narratives, Greek myths, *The Lord of the Rings*, the Harry Potter books, or the fairy tales of Hans Christian Andersen, the focus is a quest in which the heroes or heroines strive for wisdom, represented by the search for a sword, a ring, or the Holy Grail. They overcome trials and challenges, slay dragons, solve problems, and circumvent dangerous traps, but eventually (often with supernatural assistance from the likes of Merlin, Apollo, Dumbledore, a fairy godmother, Hermes, or an angel) the heroes cross a threshold, achieve the object of their desire, and resolve life's riddles along the way.

The college experience has all the elements of a full-fledged adventure in quest of wisdom. It certainly has obstacles to overcome and dragons to slay, most of which are internal demons. Conflict is inevitable. Antagonists will test you. Loneliness, stress, frustration, and feeling lost are all part of the journey.

In addition to the academic learning that takes place during college years, this time of transition promotes greater autonomy, independence, social competence, and separation from family (Reason, Terenzini, and Domingo, 2007). A certain amount of conflict is inevitable, especially for first-generation college students and those from cultures that are more interdependent and collectivist. Yet if you prepare yourself, if you build resources and learn the lay of the land, and if you persevere during times of doubt and trouble, you will accumulate greater knowledge and perhaps even the beginning of wisdom. What is important to remember is that you are not alone on this journey. Even though those around you may appear confident, the majority of first-year students feel just as clueless as you feel most of the time.

The People You Will Meet

Whereas high school tends to reinforce conventional stereotypes and cliques, college life is far more accepting of individual differences. If you like to go your own way, or

Justin Sullivan/Getty Images

Steve Jobs, the founder of Apple Computer, did not find college responsive enough to his interests and needs, nor did his counterpart Bill Gates, founder of Microsoft and one of the most successful entrepreneurs in history. Jobs felt scorn for the value of college—he had a plan to invent a new computing device and didn't care to put it on hold. Yet missing out on this special opportunity to pursue wisdom is something many college dropouts come to regret, in spite of financial success.

resent people being categorized according to some narrow dimension, you may find very good news that colleges and universities typically show much greater acceptance of diversity. On the other hand, you will find it much more challenging to make sense of who belongs where, and how you fit into the mix.

In high school, alliances were often formed based on race, ethnicity, religious affiliation, neighborhoods, social interests, athletic teams, and so on. College affiliations can be far more fluid and flexible. Now is a great opportunity to break free of the tendency to hang out with only those of your own kind, however you define that.

Actually, more than two dozen classifications (based on behavior rather than appearance alone) are described tongue in cheek on a website devoted to all things that students might wish to know but are afraid to ask (Askstudent, 2008). You may recognize the "one-hit wonder," who never, ever speaks in class until one day when he says something so brilliant and insightful it brings tears to everyone's eyes (but he never speaks again). The "babyface" looks *way* too young to be in college and is some kind of genius or something. The "lovebirds" can't keep their hands off one another. They sit together and pay attention only to themselves. The "answer machine" knows everything and is delighted to tell everyone how much she knows. The "sociable slacker" is charming, nice, and seemingly well adjusted but rarely shows up for class.

Well, you get the idea. The point is that on college campuses, there is room for almost *anyone*, and rarely is someone totally ostracized because of a little eccentricity. Diversity, in all its glory, is what makes college life so interesting, but it can also be a bit overwhelming and confusing to make sense of it all.

So-called nontraditional students, meaning those who are not beginning college full time right out of high school, are becoming the norm rather than the exception. One-third of undergraduate students today are working adults, and that figure is likely to increase in coming years (Giancola, Grawitch, and Borchert, 2009). More students are working full time and going to school at night. More students are married, have children, or are single parents. Students today are older than they used to be, taking time out for work, travel, family obligations, or life experience. And more diversity exists than ever in ethnicity, race, religion, gender, sexual orientation, and background.

Teaching Tip

Ask students to search the college website for social organizations, especially those related to their desired area of study. Tell them to identify two interesting campus organizations and answer the following: (1) What is the purpose of the organization? (2) When does the organization meet? (3) Where does the organization meet? and (4) who is the current president of the organization?

Classroom Discussion

Open it up: What advantages do traditional students have over nontraditionals? What advantages do nontraditional students have over traditionals?

For Community College Students
Community college and commuter students must be more deliberate about learning outside of the classroom. Ask students to pair up with a partner; have half of the pairs list the ways *not* to learn outside of the classroom (speak to no one, don't spend extra time on campus, resist study group participation, keep to oneself in class), and ask the other half to list the ways that promote learning outside of class.

Learning Inside and Outside the Classroom

Life on a college campus involves far more than what happens in your classes. In some important ways, the interactions, conversations, relationships, and experiences that occur *outside* of class are just as critical. These include not only extracurricular activities but also the kinds of informal connections you make with friends, instructors, and classmates.

Looking around, you will observe others who seem to adjust to college life almost effortlessly. They appear relaxed, comfortable, and totally at ease. Don't be fooled: Looks can be deceiving. Adjusting to any new environment, especially one as complex as a college campus, is fraught with difficulties. You are exploring new territory, and, when doing so, it always helps to have a map and guide. Think of this book and class as a kind of GPS, steering you with useful and (sometimes) secret tools for adjusting as smoothly as possible. Following are some suggestions to keep in mind.

Some of the Best Stuff Happens during Breaks

One key to unlocking the potential of college life is knowing that the most significant learning in college often takes place out of class. Don't take this as an excuse to skip your classes; on the contrary, your classroom experiences are specifically designed to stimulate the learning you do on your own. Lectures, discussions, and activities build a foundation of basic concepts, as do the readings and papers you are assigned. But useful knowledge, the kind that stays with you over time, is not secured merely by you hearing someone say it aloud. In order for learning to stick, you must find some way, somehow, to personalize the ideas—to make them *yours*.

Among college life's most stimulating aspects are personal interactions and friendships. Exposure to people representing very different interests and life experiences will impact you as much as anything you absorb in a classroom.

Ariel Skelley/Jupiter Images

James:
A Frustrated
Instructor

> I've been teaching in universities for a long time and yet I try to structure every class differently. This isn't just based on advances in my field, new research and theory, or new applications, but it's so things don't become stale for me. I figure that if I can remain excited and enthusiastic about what we are doing, that makes it easier for students.
>
> I've noticed that it has gotten more and more difficult to make learning stick, and the reason might surprise you: Cell phones are sabotaging what I do. I don't mean them ringing in class, although that is pretty annoying. What I am referring to is what happens during breaks. There used to be a time when students would actually talk to one another after class, or during scheduled breaks; now they whip out their phones and call, text, or e-mail their friends. I go out in the hallway and instead of seeing students intimately engaged with one another, talking about some provocative idea, arguing about what they just heard, or processing what they experienced, each one is having a conversation with someone who is somewhere else. That makes my job so much harder when students seem to just turn off their minds once the "official" meter stops running.

In a study conducted by a college professor who went back to school as a freshman to learn what it was really like, Rebekah Nathan (2005) interviewed students in her residence hall about what they learned most in college. The students estimated that anywhere from 65 to 90 percent of learning occurs *outside* of class, specifically in social activities, in informal conversations, and within intimate relationships.

Once class is over, or you take a break, that is when the internal learning process really begins. You question what you heard. You talk to classmates. You challenge and debate different positions. You convert the concepts to language that makes sense to you. You test the assumptions in places that matter the most to you. You may arrange an internship to apply new skills.

James, the frustrated instructor, comments about his challenge trying to keep students engaged in their learning because they often tune out the minute they walk out of class. You will learn as much from fellow students as you do from your instructors. It is rare to see any student taking notes on what another student says, either in class or out, yet some of the most intelligent things instructors hear come not from their own mouths but from those of students. You should know that perceptive instructors take their own notes in class, writing down insightful remarks from students that may lead to their own further growth and development.

Group Activity

Ask students to select one day in which they do not use their telephone between classes or at other free times during the academic day. Ask them to go up to three people that are isolating themselves with their cell phones. Instruct the students to introduce themselves, apologize for interrupting, but explain how they are trying to kick the phone habit. Suggest the student start a conversation by sharing information about the organizations or other groups on campus that they either are or intend to become involved in while at college. Ask students to report back to the class about their "cell phone–free" day.

1.2 FOR REFLECTION AND ACTION

Talking to People around You

As an experiment, resist the temptation to bring your cell phone or mobile device with you to classes for a single day. Have faith: The world will not end, and the worst that will happen is that you'll have several text and voice mail messages waiting for you when you return to your room.

Students Teach Their Instructors, Too

I didn't always understand the reciprocal influence that takes place between teachers and students until I worked in Latin America, where students routinely meet in coffee shops before, after, and sometimes *during* class to talk about issues that were raised. Many of my students viewed class time as the mere stimulus for their learning, which they believed would become solidified through their own conversations personalizing the content. Instead of talking to people you already know, use the time before and after class, as well as during breaks, to actually talk to people who are hanging around (not on their own cell phones).

Many important things you will learn in college will be taught by fellow students as well as instructors. Conversations with friends about what you are learning in class help you to personalize material, integrate ideas, and apply concepts to your own life.

© Istockphoto.com/Chris Schmidt

Group Activity

Ask students to put this into practice tonight: Take one new thing learned in any class today and teach it to a friend or family member. Come back to the next class period ready to discuss how it went. The goal is to demonstrate that you learn best what you teach.

For Community College Students

Regrettably, negative societal stereotypes still persist concerning community college attendance. Students who buy into these stereotypes feel inferior to their university counterparts. Break students into teams to write and present a "Letterman-esque" list of the top ten reasons it makes a lot of sense to go to a community college in terms of getting a better education.

From that experience onward, I realized that my job was not only to teach in the classroom, but also to stimulate learning *outside* of class. A wise instructor will provide plenty of raw material for when the real educational action begins: while arguing with yourself or someone else, while explaining something that happened in class to roommates or friends, and while thinking about some idea during a walk or drive.

Your instructors learn a lot from the feedback that you provide, both informally and on evaluations at the end of the semester. Good instructors, in particular, are always watching carefully to see what works best and what doesn't work at all, changing directions if a particular activity or strategy is not producing desired results.

Some Reasonable Fears and Apprehensions

If you aren't feeling a certain degree of apprehension about the transition to college, you aren't paying very close attention. It is perfectly understandable when beginning any new enterprise, especially one that is as overwhelming as college life, that you would experience a certain amount of dread, even anxiety.

It is normal to feel doubt about your decision (if it even *was* your choice) to attend college in the first place and to question whether you are going to the "right" institution. Expect that during the coming weeks, months, and years, you will encounter challenges that will test you in ways for which you feel unprepared. It is not unusual that students develop a number of stress symptoms, such as losing sleep, worrying a lot, and even feeling depressed at times.

Huge differences separate high school and college, and an even wider gulf looms for older, returning students who have been in the world of work for some time. Not only will you encounter adjustment difficulties but you should expect them. The college campus is an enriched environment, but one fraught with special rules and customs that may appear quite strange, especially to those who are among the first in their family to attend college (Pascarella, Wolniak, Pierson, and Terenzini, 2003). First-generation college students tend to work more hours, lack secondhand

Angie:
Talking about Fears

"I remember my first night at college. Move-in day was on a Sunday, but because I came from pretty far away, I moved in a day early. In the entire three-story dorm building, there were only two of us there that Saturday night. We spent the evening hanging out together, staying up until 4:00 A.M. talking in the common lounge. I can't say how grateful I was that we shared that experience. Even though we had only met that afternoon, we talked about everything—our excitement at being away from home, our anxiety about our classes, our fears about what college had in store for us. I knew in my head I wasn't the only one that was scared about college, but actually talking about it, putting it out in the open, made me feel lighter. I thought that talking about my fears would make them scarier, more intense, but the opposite happened. During our conversation that night, I realized how helpful it is to talk about problems, rather than pretend they don't exist. Talking about the fear was like a release of anxiety, and helped calm my mind. The next day, I was able to just relax and enjoy my first full day of college experiences.

knowledge about what they will encounter, hold unrealistic expectations, and take longer to complete their degrees (Dennis, Phinney, and Chuateco, 2005). Yet all students, regardless of background, age, and life experience, hold fears and apprehensions that may be quite legitimate.

"I Don't Belong Here"

In spite of how self-assured others might appear, *everyone* is uncomfortable in a new environment. The fact of the matter is that you *don't* yet belong to the campus community; you are a newcomer who doesn't yet know what is expected and how to fit in. Belongingness comes only with experience.

Not only is it normal to feel apprehensive about whether college in general, or this college in particular, is the best choice, but you should know that these feelings will not go away anytime soon. Can you really expect to enter a whole new world and think that you are going to effortlessly jump right in without a ripple of uneasiness or waves of self-doubt?

One of the remarkable aspects of college life is that a campus has enough different people around that eventually, with some effort and persistence, you will find others like yourself. No matter how much you may feel like an outsider, or how unique your background and interests, there are others who share your values. You just have to discover them where you live, and in classes, clubs, or outside activities.

"I'm Going to Flunk Out"

Fear of flunking out is common among new college students, although likely exaggerated. What you are really afraid of is not being adequately prepared to excel in this new, more demanding academic setting. Now this apprehension is well founded: You probably are not as prepared as you'd like to be.

Even those who were the most brilliant scholars in their high schools are now one of many others who earned that status back home. Almost every one of your peers is smart; furthermore, they know things that you do not. So what greatly increases your probability of success is making close connections with fellow students so that you can share resources and support one another.

It is not altogether bad to fear failure—at least within reasonable limits to the point you are not overwhelmed. Yet "failure" is a relative concept. Is it failure if you score below your expectations on a test, or merely a disappointment providing feedback on things you can do differently in the future? Is it failure when someone you like doesn't like you

Group Activity to Reduce Stress

Divide students into small groups to discuss the following: What is your biggest fear about college? Talk about these concerns and apprehensions in the most honest way possible. Share the small-group list with the full class and look for common factors. Talk about what skills they might need that would help them cope better with these fears.

▶ VIEW IT

© Cengage Learning

What Stresses You Out?

Students talk about their greatest sources of stress in college life, ranging from difficulty finding parking and family pressures to temptations related to drugs and sex. (www.cengagebrain.com)

Kiran:
Finding Strengths

"In high school I was a straight-A student. I always had the best grades in class, especially in my writing classes. So I was really disappointed when I realized that in college there were a lot of other people who could write even better than I could. Suddenly, I wasn't all that special anymore. I had relied on my writing skills all my life and I thought it would help me shine in college, just as it did in high school. I mean, I am a good writer and all, don't get me wrong, but I realized very quickly that I'd need to discover my other talents because there was a lot of competition out there.

It took me a while to figure out other things I could do well, but I did. Who knew I was really good with finance? I decided to take an elective class in business and I learned I could do that really well. As a matter of fact, I had the highest grades in that class! That's what's so cool about college; we have so much more stuff to learn and it's challenging, but it's also a pretty cool opportunity to find out other things we can do well and there is so much to choose from.

> Failure is often more a state of mind than of circumstance. During athletic contests, it isn't a matter of one person winning and everyone else losing, but rather of everyone striving for their personal best. Likewise, in academic and social arenas, if you don't do as well as you had hoped, this isn't failure but rather valuable feedback that you can use to make adjustments in how you perform in the future.

back, or is this merely a mismatch of interest? Is it failure when you try something and it doesn't work out, or just an intermediate step on your way to eventual success?

Success can be measured in ways other than passing classes or making the decision to continue your studies (Upcraft, Gardner, and Barefoot, 2005). Did you develop a sense of competence and greater confidence in your intellectual ability? Did you build new relationships and enjoy greater intimacy? Did you learn things that enhance the quality of your life? Did you get closer to deciding what you want to do with your life? Were you able to maintain a healthy lifestyle? Did you develop greater sensitivity toward others who are different from you? Did you develop a higher sense of morality and civic responsibility?

Jupiterimages

"People Won't Like Me and I Won't Make Friends"

It is true that some people really won't like you, as may have happened in the past. If you were expecting more upbeat reassurance, sorry to disappoint you. No matter how you present yourself in any social setting, some people will gravitate toward you, others will be indifferent, and still others will be turned off. It doesn't matter how much you try to please others, how you change your appearance or manner, and how carefully you try to figure out what others want: You will still annoy and disappoint some, while attracting others.

I feared rejection so much as a first-year college student that I could never muster the courage to initiate a conversation. There were girls I liked, but I felt too shy to approach them. During almost every Saturday of my junior high school years, I went to the mall with my best friend, supposedly to meet girls. During the course of fifty or more Saturdays in a row, not only did we not meet any girls but also we never even approached any! I was too afraid that a girl I liked might reject me. I had a breakthrough my first year of college when I finally realized that the worst thing that anyone could ever do to me was decline my invitation—and that was *nothing* compared to the ways I beat myself up for being so spineless.

Jack:
Partying Too Much

"Skipping classes can get you in a lot of trouble. I should know. I was put on academic probation after my first semester, and almost ended up dropping out of school because I partied way too much. I mean, a lot of people drink and hang out and have a good time in college. But for me, I lost control. First, I dropped a few classes so I had more time to catch up on sleep after staying up every night, so then I was a part-time student.

One day, I was sitting with a girlfriend I met freshman year. She was talking about her future, and how scared she was to graduate and have to work in a real job for the rest of her life. That's when I realized what was really at stake for me. All my friends were ahead of me and I was still screwing around trying to complete the core requirements, and not even doing well at that.

Finally, I told my parents what was really going on and they helped me to figure out a more realistic plan. I just wasn't cut out to go to school full time, so instead I took a few classes at a time. It took me three years longer than my friends to graduate, but hey, a few years later really didn't make much of a difference.

Many of the fears and apprehensions previously mentioned are not only normal but also quite reasonable responses when adapting to a foreign environment. Give yourself permission to live with a certain amount of anxiety for a while, and accept the reality that many times you will feel uncomfortable. No matter how much you prepare or how hard you try, you will also make lots of mistakes. After all, you don't know the rules. You will have trouble meeting certain expectations that you don't fully understand. These are the challenges that will transform you into someone who is more flexible and adaptable.

How College Will Change You

What you get out of college depends on what you are looking for. What do you say when people ask you about your goals, your major, or what you want to do with your education? One of the most common first inquiries by a new acquaintance is that magical question: "So, what's your major?" Whether you answer with a specific discipline or the more equivocal "undeclared," the person will nod sagely, as if what you said unlocked the secrets of your soul.

Consider that the average college student changes majors at least three times prior to graduation. Three times! That is an *average*, so for every engineering, pre-med, or teacher education major who absolutely knew what she wanted to do on her first day of school, and didn't waver until the very end, there is another student who changed fields five or more times. The very purpose of a college education is to expose you to things that you would never otherwise consider. You may begin your career intent on doing one thing, perhaps because of pressure at home or because of limited vision, but with every class you take, and every conversation you have with others, your perspective will broaden. You will find you enjoy subjects that never interested you before. Likewise, classes that you thought would be your passion turned out to be boring, although this might depend as much on who is teaching the class as on the subject.

Expanding your interests is only one of many other ways that college will impact you. Although you might imagine that during your task-focused effort to take classes, meet requirements, accumulate credits, and complete your degree, the main outcome would be expanded knowledge, in fact that is only a small part of what you will gain.

Teaching Tip

Suggest that each student choose one test, quiz, or assignment in which he or she failed to score at the expected level. Then, make an appointment with the professor of the course and ask him or her to help diagnose what concepts or learning principles the student didn't master on this particular test or quiz. The student should use this feedback to remediate this knowledge lapse and help prepare the way for future success in the course.

Group Activity to Reduce Stress

Conduct a "snowball fight" in class. Ask students to write their biggest fear or anxiety on a piece of paper (without their names). When everyone has written something on their paper, ask them to wad it up and throw it across room. All students should then pick up a ball of paper and report out what it says while the instructor writes the list on the board.

Dealing with Rejection

One of the most important ways to reduce stress is to acknowledge and deal with some of your ongoing fears. One common source of apprehension in college is the fear of rejection by others you approach or those you like, whether you are making new friends or building relationships with instructors. Think of a time recently when there was someone you wanted to approach or talk to, someone who you found interesting or attractive, and you hesitated to approach him or her, fearing that you would be rejected.

How did you feel about yourself not acting on your desire?

_____

_____

_____

What would it take for you to push yourself to respond differently in the future when there is someone you'd like to get to know better?

_____

_____

_____

What could you tell yourself if the person doesn't respond favorably?

_____

_____

_____

Examples of things you might tell yourself include the following:

1. You win a few, you lose a few. Oh well.

2. Just because this person didn't respond doesn't mean that I should give up. Who else can I approach?

3. What can I learn from that interaction that would increase the probability that the next time (or the time after that) will work out better?

4. People can decline my *invitation*, but that doesn't reject me as a *person*.

5. The only thing worse than feeling rejected is not ever taking the risk of reaching out to others.

Expanded Worldview

A "worldview" is an organized set of assumptions that is based on the unique lens through which you experience the world. It is influenced, in part, by your gender, cultural and ethnic background, and socioeconomic status, and a host of other variables that have helped to shape your perceptions. Regardless of where you were brought up—in a rural farming area, urban inner-city environment, affluent suburb, military base, commune, ghetto, or refugee camp—you will come into contact with others who are very different from you. Your interactions with instructors, class content, classmates, and extracurricular activities will broaden your perspective in a multitude of ways. Your political beliefs will change. Your values and priorities will evolve based on the people you meet and the reciprocal influence you have on one

Trent:
Finding Good Instructors

"One thing that I didn't catch on to for a while is that you never, ever pick a class by its title but by the instructor. I know that there are pre-reqs that you have to take, and GE [general education] courses, especially the first year or two, but still, you always have choices as to which section.

Probably the first priority, for me at least, is when the class is being offered. I never take a class before 9:00 in the morning or I'll end up skipping it a lot of times. I have other friends who won't take a class before noon, or who hate afternoon classes and only take them in the morning or evening.

Just as important is the instructor. I've had instructors who are simply amazing. I'd take anything they were teaching—well, unless it was at 8:00 in the morning or something. Seriously, you can get the scoop on who is really good from recommendations you find from trusted friends. I don't really trust websites much because only the angriest students take the time to write reviews because they didn't like their grade or something. I'm not saying you should totally ignore them, but I'd rather talk to students who've had the teacher before and find out stuff about how interesting the class is and how hard it is too.

another. While this is potentially very exciting, it is also stressful because family and friends you have known for a while will expect you to remain the same, the way you've always been.

Lifelong Friendships

Talk to graduates, and they will often admit that the people they are closest to are those they met in college. Even as you concentrate on your studies and career objectives, your relationships are what will remain most enduring. Just as the average college student changes majors several times, so do most people evolve in their careers. Yet the connections you forge with people you meet in classes, study groups, social functions, parties, athletic events, sports teams, and more informal settings will support you through not only your college years but often the rest of your life.

One college graduate, now a practicing lawyer, was studying photographs from his recent wedding and was surprised by what he observed:

I was so unhappy the first few months of my freshman year that I called my parents and told them to come and get me. I just didn't feel like I belonged there. I was lonely. I missed my friends. I just wanted to leave. But my parents told me I had to finish the first semester and then we'd talk about other options.

Out of desperation I started cruising the tables where the various clubs were recruiting new members and decided to join the rugby team, something I'd never done before. I don't think I'd ever seen a rugby game in my life. Anyway, now I look back at my wedding pictures and I see that all the guys who I'm still friends with after ten years, my best friends, I met my freshman year playing rugby.

Group Discussion

Open it up: What are your favorite qualities in instructors in college or in high school? What are their least favorite qualities? How do you make the best of classes taught by instructors whose styles you do not especially like?

▶ **VIEW IT**

© Cengage Learning

Being and Feeling Lost

Students talk about their first weeks on campus, how lost they felt, the challenges and stress they encountered, and how they adjusted to their first semester. One student summarizes the lesson she learned about taking initiative and reaching out to others: "If I didn't make it happen, I'd rot in my room before anyone found me." (www.cengagebrain.com)

For Community College Students
On a commuter campus, making friends looks much different: Lifelong friends can be made in class, in study groups, and through club or activity involvement.

You may indeed make lifelong friends during college, but this means that your relationships with family members and other friends will also change, requiring a degree of adjustment to keep those bonds healthy.

Tolerance for Ambiguity and Appreciation for Complexity

Rather than seeing things as simple and in black or white, college teaches you to adopt multiple lenses through which to view problems and the world at large. The most interesting questions don't have single, correct answers (in spite of that assumption on multiple-choice exams): What is the meaning of life? What is the path to world peace? Who would make the best leader? What does the future hold?

It is an interesting paradox (contradiction) that college life will lead to greater confusion rather than certainty. Education supplies you with the means by which to look at many different sides of a problem, to appreciate better its nuances, ambiguities, and complexities. Discussions you have in class and with friends will lead you to honor and respect different ways of addressing issues, all of which may be useful and valid. When you feel conflicted inside regarding a certain topic is when intellectual and emotional growth really occurs.

Curiosity

The purpose of most college courses is not to provide "answers" or all you need to know about a subject, but rather to stimulate you to learn more as well as to provide you with the skills to learn on your own. Literature classes will expose you to a selection of great books with the hope that you will feel motivated to read others independently. Statistics and research classes teach you the rudimentary skills of describing data, making predictions, testing hypotheses, and analyzing results, all with the intention that someday you will apply this to the unanswered questions that intrigue you the most. Art appreciation classes are not designed to expose you to all of the world's body of great art, but rather to stimulate your interest to seek out and investigate all kinds of art over the course of your lifetime. Social sciences expose you to classic studies and theories, not to fill you up with what scholars say, but rather to teach you how to understand behavior in your daily life. In each field, your curiosity may be piqued to the extent that you feel motivated to dig deeper. This will apply not just to academic subjects but also to your curiosity about any phenomenon that perplexes you.

Expertise

By the time you graduate from college, if not after your first year, you will feel an increased sense of competence in your ability to understand complex ideas and communicate your thoughts coherently and persuasively. Much of what you do in college is learn how to express yourself effectively, both verbally and in writing. Because you will receive lots of supervision and feedback on your work, your skills will improve significantly.

As has been mentioned, your expertise will extend far beyond the academic subjects to include very personal domains. Education isn't just about growing your intellect, but also about developing greater sensitivity in being able to interpret, express, and manage your feelings. This contributes to the development of confidence, self-esteem, and integrity. But be forewarned, it can also lead to confusion.

Michelle:
Losing Yourself

" I know that everyone tells freshmen to study and keep up with homework and don't skip classes, but I have learned something else that is also important: You have to hold on to who you are. I mean that there are so many students on campus and the place is so big and busy that it's easy to get lost—and lose yourself. I thought it would be easy to hold on to who I am, that nobody would care how I look or how I act. But during these last few months I've let myself float away. I just got caught up in the hustle and bustle of everything around here, and now I am not sure anymore who I am or what I really want. Everything is just so new and exciting that, before you know it, you're doing things you never thought you'd ever do. You've got to take a step back and ask yourself what is really important and not let yourself get caught up in what other people are doing. It's just so easy to be distracted. I've just learned the hard way that I've got to stop trying to be what everyone else thinks I should be and follow my own path. Fortunately it's not too late for me to fix some things but if I had waited much longer, I think I'd be in real trouble.

Good Advice You Won't Follow ... Until It Makes Sense

In theory, giving advice makes a lot of sense. Presume that the author of this book knows some things you don't, based on decades of experience, hundreds of interviews with first-year students, and familiarity with much of the research on what contributes most to student success. The author tells you what he knows. You follow the advice. And live happily ever after.

Unfortunately, giving advice is usually a miserable idea and a waste of time, mostly because people rarely follow what others tell them to do. When was the last time you felt lost, someone told you how to get "unstuck," and you actually did what was suggested? If you are like most others, you hate people telling you what to do so you don't do it.

When you tell someone what to do, you can expect one of two possible outcomes. The first possibility is that things work out miserably and the person blames you for the rest of your life. The friend gets an abortion, or has the baby, and her life becomes miserable. The guy you told to stay in school, or drop out, finds himself worse off than before and now hates you because that is far easier than blaming himself. And the girl who you told to stick out the relationship? She ended up being physically and emotionally abused. All your fault.

The only thing worse than giving bad advice is giving *good* advice. Yes, you read that correctly. Even if you should tell someone what to do and it works out extraordinarily well, what message has been communicated? You are telling that person that you know better than she or he does about how to live. In the future, when another problem comes up, she or he will have been trained to look for direction from outside rather than from inside. Dependency has been created.

So, where does that leave us? This whole class is based on giving good advice about how to flourish in college. Consider a compromise. Much of the material to follow happens to be tested in laboratories, research studies, and the life experiences of thousands of students. You have a right to be skeptical. Don't take anything at face value without checking it out for yourself. That is one of the most important things that college teaches you—to be a critical consumer of what you read and hear. Practice that here and now, and with the chapters that follow.

1.3 FOR REFLECTION

Create Your Own Advice

Most books for first-year college students provide a list of intelligent things that they should do in order to succeed. Pretend that you were hired to teach a class on this subject. What are five important things you would tell a new student to do in order to excel in this new environment?

1. _____

   _____

2. _____

   _____

3. _____

   _____

4. _____

   _____

5. _____

   _____

Possible answers are listed at the end of this chapter.

What is it that keeps you from following your own advice if you know these things are so important?

_____

_____

_____

SUMMARY

The first year of college is considered the foundation for everything that happens afterward. During this period, you will begin acquiring those attitudes, behaviors, skills, and habits that will help you to flourish in subsequent years. It is a time of intense, accelerated learning that sets the tone for everything that follows, not just in your academic accomplishments but also in your personal competence and social functioning (Reason, Terenzini, and Domingo, 2007).

Students who don't thrive in college, much less those who don't make it through the first year, were not successful in building sufficient support for themselves. They dropped out most often because of (1) conflicts with their jobs, (2) insufficient time to study and prepare for class, (3) poor advising, (4) financial problems, (5) pressure from family and friends, and (6) not feeling welcomed by faculty and staff (Franklin et al., 2002).

QUESTIONS FOR REVIEW AND FURTHER EXPLORATION

1. The chapter provided a list of the many values and functions of a college education. Which are the ones that apply most to you and your personal goals?

2. What are the reasons you think that college graduates make more money than those without a degree? Think beyond the obvious and identify aspects of the college experience that contribute to greater competence and productivity.

3. What are the reasons for providing citations to document statements made in this chapter or in any other professional paper?

4. What benefits accrue to a college graduate beyond training for a job or career?

5. Why do you think that attaining wisdom often involves a degree of sacrifice and suffering?

6. What does it mean that some of the most important learning occurs outside of class?

7. Novelist Len Deighton observed that if children did not fight with their parents, they would never leave home—and then the world would end. What do you think that means within the context of how interactions between college students and their parents change during this period of transition?

8. Beginning college students are often asked what they need help with the most. But how are you supposed to answer those questions if you have not yet been challenged in new areas? After this course and semester are over, you will have a much better sense of where your weaknesses lie. Nevertheless, what predictions would you make about where you are going to need the most assistance?

ANSWERS TO FOR REFLECTION 1.3

Possible advice for excelling in college includes:

- Get plenty of sleep.
- Don't skip classes.
- Don't procrastinate. Do all the assignments and homework well before the deadlines.
- Sit in the front of the class and become actively involved in discussions.
- Do the readings so you are prepared for class.
- Don't overschedule yourself with too many obligations.
- Create and build a support system of friends to study and hang out with.
- Don't let partying get out of hand. Limit indulgence in alcohol.
- Don't waste time in front of the TV or computer or on the phone.
- Don't get hopelessly in debt.

This is, of course, just a sampling of possible advice you could have generated. Because you came up with this yourself, rather than being told by some authority what to do, perhaps you'll feel more committed to actually following through on what you've developed.

Go to www.cengagebrain.com for an online quiz that will test your understanding of the chapter content.

Adjusting to Campus Life

KEY QUESTIONS

▸ What expectations do you hold for what you will accomplish during college? How do they compare to those of your family and mentors?

▸ What best predicts who will succeed in college and who is likely to fail?

▸ What are some examples of constructive and self-defeating attitudes that can help or hinder successful adjustment?

▸ Why do you suppose that one-third of first-year students either drop out or flunk out before the end of the second semester?

▸ Why would you want to ensure that you get the best guidance possible from your assigned advisor?

▸ What are the factors you would consider in planning a balanced course load?

Y ou can't make it on a college campus on your own. The environment resembles a maze. The rules and regulations are complex and often confusing. Others place demands on you constantly, and give you little room for excuses or pleas of ignorance. At various junctures, you are expected to know the requirements for prerequisites, major and minor concentrations, and graduation. Unless you are willing to ask for help and get expert assistance, you will flounder, if not self-destruct. And here's another difference from high school— nobody will seek you out to see how you are getting along. More than likely, no guidance counselor will closely follow your case. *You* are the one who must ask for assistance when you need it.

The good news is that the fees you pay to attend school cover not only the cost of instruction but also all the other student services that focus on your health, psychological, spiritual, financial, social, cultural, leisure, employment, and athletic needs.

For Community College Students
Student services are likely to be different in the community college setting.

PHOTO: Andersen Ross/Jupiter Images

Predicting Successful Adjustment

The transition to college life is considered among the most stressful adjustments you may ever experience. The changes that occur are both dramatic and rather sudden, possibly taking place at a time when other major changes are taking place in terms of your physical, emotional, intellectual, and moral development. In addition, all the usual and familiar support systems that you relied on during previous years are now obsolete, requiring that you find new ways to manage these stressful challenges. These stressors will take place in a number of different arenas, perhaps most of all in relationships with family, friends, classmates, roommates, and instructors, but also with regard to financial issues, academic performance, changing roles and expectations as an adult, and cultural confusion in a new environment with such diverse inhabitants (Howard et al., 2006).

Researchers have conducted a number of studies about what contributes most to a student's successful adjustment to the first year of college (Clark, 2005; Pascarella, Wolniak, Pierson, and Terenzini, 2003; Reason, Terenzini, and Domingo, 2007). Data were collected from both interviews and questionnaires, identifying those factors that best predict how well you will do. Many of the factors relate directly to the skills introduced in this book, while others are connected to the resources that you find and use on campus, as well as those within yourself. For each of these areas, note specific ways that you intend to capitalize on them. Think about what you can start doing right now to increase your chances for success.

Personal Characteristics

Certain traits are associated with doing well. Some people seem to have been born with them, but if you feel you are lacking, you're not out of luck. Many of these personal qualities can be developed with sufficient effort.

Logically, you might anticipate that having solid *motivation* is critical for doing well. It is okay to have some doubts at times, and to feel ambivalent about what you are doing, but drive goes a long way toward accomplishing goals, especially when the going gets tough. This leads to *persistence* as another important quality. It is inevitable that no matter how hard you try, how driven you feel, and how single-mindedly you pursue a goal, you are going to have setbacks. But what you do next during such times is what really determines ultimate success. If you become easily discouraged, tell yourself things are hopeless, and give up and refuse to ask for help, the outcome is not going to be pretty no matter how much talent and smarts you have.

Self-reliance is another important quality, especially when it is balanced with support from others. It is very good to be able to take care of yourself, trust your own judgment, and have the confidence that you can pretty much deal with things. Yet it is also important to understand the limits of your capabilities and to ask for help from those who are in the best position to deliver.

Expectations

Disappointments and poor performance often result from unrealistic expectations. Students who do best have an honest and realistic assessment of what lies ahead. It is important to have goals that are ambitious and important to you, but also within reach. It is also critical to examine the influence and pressure you feel to meet the expectations of others.

You are a delegate from your family. You are following not only your own ambitions but also the expectations that your teachers, parents, grandparents, and siblings have for you. Family "legacies" are historical issues from the past that you have inherited, whether you are aware of them or not. These have been passed on to you by your culture, religion, ethnic background, and ancestors. You have heard these messages growing up, and they have influenced your decision to attend college and

Classroom Discussion to Reduce Stress

Open it up: What has been your toughest adjustment to college life so far? When do you feel the most stress, and how does it show up? Examine your sleeping and eating patterns, and your social interactions. What advice will help this adjustment go more smoothly for you?

Group Activity

Break the class into dyads to discuss the biggest change in their lives or routines since beginning college.

Group Activity

Ask students to respond in their journals to the following prompt: What current class do you find least interesting? What would help you find or create some interest so you can complete the course successfully and enjoy it more?

For Community College Students

Be sensitive to students who didn't complete K–12 education and/or those who completed GED or alternative forms of high school diplomas.

Group Activity

The instructor can role-play as an employer looking at two graduates a few years down the road. Place two students in front of the room with the exact same résumés and transcripts (grades). The only difference between the two students' résumés is campus involvement (clubs, internships, work study job, etc.). Who gets the job?

where you have chosen to go. Throughout the next years, you will feel the pressure of these expectations and try to sort out which are truly your own goals.

Returning adult students live up to expectations for the future rather than the past. You might be attending college to show your children the value of education, not to mention the importance of reaching new goals. Regardless of how poor a student you might have been in high school, life experience and maturity provide additional resources that compensate for the enthusiasm and energy of youth.

Extracurricular Activities

Successful, large corporations have discovered that the best way to maximize their profits, as well as protect against catastrophic losses during volatile economic periods, is to diversify their interests. Thus the tobacco industry buys subsidiaries in food and manufacturing, oil companies invest in wind and solar energy, and automobile companies buy into technology firms. Likewise, the best way to protect yourself against extreme downtimes is to diversify your own interests.

Sometimes things won't be going well in class, at work, or in your social life. If you are invested in several different kinds of activities, then you are in a better place to find success and satisfaction from multiple sources. Much depends on your time availability, of course, not to mention your obligations to earn money, spend time with family, and other responsibilities, but it is still possible to become involved in many different extracurricular activities around campus.

Most students enter college with the intention of becoming actively involved in some athletic, social, civic, or other extracurricular activity. Yet one-third of students never made an effort to follow through on this intention, allowing themselves to be distracted by other things they considered more important (Kuh, 2007).

Group Activity

Ask students to construct a pie chart of their current weekly activities: work, class, study sessions, and various social and leisure activities. Determine the chart's proportions by the number of hours spent in each activity. Have students reflect in a journal entry: Do you have the right balance in your life for success? What changes might help assure the wise use of time to achieve desired college success?

Involvement in extracurricular activities such as an intramural sport, social or cultural group is important to developing your mind, body, and spirit. Finding diversified interests on campus helps you to feel productive, no matter how things are progressing in any single area.

Ian Walton/Getty Images

You can join clubs and intramural sports teams, and various cultural groups sponsor social and educational programs. Student government provides opportunities to become involved in social action projects or campus affairs. Student plays and musical ensembles are organized, not just for accomplished performers but also for those who just enjoy expressing themselves. Campus publications are always looking for new participants. Campus ministry provides religious and social activities. Service organizations give students direct experience in leadership or mentoring. Most departments and majors sponsor clubs. In addition, individual faculty are always looking for student assistants to help with their research projects. Just remember, it is important to set limits on what you can comfortably handle.

Relationships

One of the best predictors of healthy adjustment to college is the quality of relationships you develop with peers and friends, even more so than support you get from family (Friedlander, Reid, Shupack, and Cribbie, 2007). When you feel lost, you need people you can trust and rely on. The campus provides expert staff to assist you with specific problems and needs, however, peer support is just as important. That is how you discover that you aren't alone in your struggles.

Relationships are not going to come your way without making a concerted effort to initiate things yourself. This applies to potential study partners as much as to romantic connections. As fearful as you might be of rejection, and as shy and hesitant as you might feel, *you* are the one who is going to have to reach out to others. You can't wait for someone you like to approach you, or you may end up waiting an awfully long time. You can't expect instructors to initiate a private conversation; you have to schedule an appointment or make the first overture. And someone who interests you cannot read your mind unless you express that interest.

Self-Defeating Temptations

College life is largely about freedom. For students living away from home for the first time, the possibilities are dizzying and the temptations are numerous. Students who are commuting will also find opportunities to explore the boundaries of behavior, often to excess. Students who adjust well to college life are able to achieve some balance between temptations and the threat of overindulgence.

You think you know what is coming next—another scolding lecture about the dangers of drinking, frying your brain with drugs, promiscuous sex, violent and boorish behavior, or irresponsible choices and thoughtless actions. Well, let's skip that (for now) and simply acknowledge that you could do certain things, with virtually nobody around to stop you, that will get you in trouble—sometimes a lot of trouble from which you will find it difficult to recover.

Connie:
Becoming Someone Else

❝ I was a bit of a loner in high school. I suppose I got used to that. It wasn't that I liked spending so much time alone as I was afraid to be rejected.

Once I got to college, I decided that since nobody really knew who I was, or expected much from me one way or the other, I might as well pretend to be someone else. If that makes sense. What I mean is that I could pretend to be someone who had more confidence than I really felt. That gave me a push to walk up to people or talk to them in class. For the first time in my life, I didn't exactly feel popular but I was actually part of a group. I'm proud to say that this happened because of what I did to reinvent myself.

Adaptive Coping Skills

Students who do well in college possess skills that are lacking in those who flounder. Many of these habits and behaviors are part of this course, including skills related to finances, studying, test taking, dealing with stress, resolving conflict, and so on. Perhaps the most important skill of all is recognizing the areas in which you are most weak so that you can get help to improve your performance (see For Reflection 2.1).

Classroom Discussion

Open it up: Are you familiar with the resources on your campus? What are your responses to For Reflection and Action 2.1? What are the names and locations of available campus resources to assist with your weaker areas?

2.1 FOR REFLECTION

A Self-Assessment of Skills

Rate on a 1–10 scale your level of proficiency in the following skill areas that are associated with success in college. Be really honest!

1. I am proficient in keyboarding skills.
2. I have a background in basic computer skills.
3. I can use the Internet and e-mail and send attached files.
4. I know how to do research online.
5. I know how to find things I need in the library.
6. I have command of English grammar, punctuation, and spelling.
7. I know how to organize, construct, and write essays.
8. I have good preparation in high school mathematics.
9. I understand what I read and can read at a reasonable speed.
10. I have the discipline to complete tasks before deadlines.
11. I can listen attentively to lectures and take good notes.
12. I can communicate my opinions and ideas within groups.
13. I can work cooperatively in small groups.
14. I know how to prepare for and take various kinds of exams.
15. I am well organized in the ways I plan and spend my time.
16. I can interact with people from different backgrounds.
17. I can deal with disappointment and rejection.
18. I can carry on a conversation with most people.
19. I make good decisions that are in my best interest.
20. I can assert myself without appearing aggressive or hostile.
21. I can handle my finances and manage a budget.

Circle or highlight those items in which you rated yourself less than a 6.

Among the half-dozen or so skills that you identified as a weakness, what steps do you plan to take in order to improve functioning in these areas? If you don't know the answer, note how you intend to find out. Write the item numbers and your action plans below:

Getting to Know Your Academic Advisor

Teaching Tip
Assign your students to visit and interview their advisors during the first month of school. Have them plan out their questions ahead of time, or give them a list of questions you want them to ask. Have the students write a one-page summary of their meeting.

Group Activity
Split the class into three groups, and assign each group to do one of the following: (1) List student responsibilities in the advising relationship, (2) list advisor responsibilities in the advising relationship, and (3) list questions to take into an advising appointment.

Academic advising is handled differently by various institutions, yet most colleges assign each student to some mentor or advisor whose job is to help you plan your college career. In many four-year institutions, once you have declared a major, your academic department might assign someone to work with you who could be a member of the faculty, support staff, or a student assistant. Because most students don't know what they want to study during the first few years of college, your initial advisor may be assigned by the student services unit within the college. In community colleges, things are often handled a bit differently since many students plan on transferring to other institutions after they complete their first two years. In this case, the emphasis may be placed on two areas: (1) making sure that you take all the prerequisite classes you need and will transfer without difficulty, and (2) helping you settle on a major area of specialty based on these introductory classes.

Often advisors are overworked and overwhelmed. Sometimes they may operate in a mechanical manner, as if you are one more unit on the assembly line. They have been through the same conversations a thousand times, and answered the same questions over and over. Thus, as in any service profession, the quality of guidance may not be what you deserve. That is why *you* must be the one to make sure you get the guidance you need. This means being persistent in scheduling appointments and using the time to address your needs. One of the worst things you could try is negotiating the scheduling maze on your own, asking advice of classmates who may be as much in the dark as you are.

It is a great idea to study your college catalog, which may be published in the form of a book or is usually located online. This will give you the basic understanding you need to ask your advisor the most relevant, useful questions. Such knowledge will also help you to cross-check advice you are getting and expose you to a number of options that an advisor may not always present. Go online to see a sample list of questions you might want to ask your academic advisor.

VIEW IT

© Cengage Learning

Getting Help
Students talk about how advisors helped them clarify their academic plans and settle on areas to study. (www.cengagebrain.com)

Teaching Tip
Ask students to visit the campus career office to ascertain the following information: (1) What services are available to help them develop more self-understanding; and (2) how can this self-knowledge be applied to the process of choosing an appropriate major and career?

Developing an Academic Plan

You will likely take about forty college classes or so to complete a bachelor's degree, and half that many for an associate's degree (the exact number depends on your major, interests, and efficiency). Among these courses, about one-third are chosen for you and the rest will consist of those in your major, as well as others that interest you. Depending on which college you are attending, the required number of classes can vary considerably.

For first-year students, the college curriculum is often organized around general requirements that are called "core" or "general education" courses. Just as it sounds, these are the basic, introductory classes that wise minds believe that every student should explore. All colleges have requirements that you spend some time studying some aspect of science, mathematics, social science, literature, humanities, physical education, and so on. There may also be requirements that you take a certain number of classes in "life skills" that include things like conflict resolution, communication, stress management, and this present study of success skills.

Many of the classes you take your first year are considered *prerequisites* for more advanced study. This means that you can't take social psychology, for instance, without taking basic psychology first, or you can't study Shakespeare until after you've had a class in Western literature. This is like the arrangement in high school.

Major classes are those in your concentration area which provide the foundation for that academic discipline. You may be required to take a half-dozen (often more) classes that cover the full spectrum of content in your major area of study. All classes are numbered (100, 200, 300, etc.) in such a way that you can immediately figure out how advanced they are. Chemistry 101 may be a general introduction, 201 may be Chemical Computation, 301 Organic Chemistry, and 401 Atmospheric Chemistry. Consult your college catalog for more specific information (and see Figure 2.1 for a catalog excerpt).

Figure 2.1 Sample from College Catalog

The following is a sample course description from a college catalog that has to be decoded to be understood. The important features are highlighted, including the department abbreviation (AAS), the number of credits (3), and the requirements to take the course (sophomore standing and a *recommended* but not *required* anthropology course). This means you couldn't take this class as a first-year student ... unless you got special permission (which is sometimes possible from the instructor). Then there is a narrative description of what the course is all about.

African American Studies (AAS) 310: Peoples and Cultures of Africa. Cr: (3)
(Cross-listed with Anthropology). *Prereq: Soph. standing req.; Anthr 201 or 306 recommended.* Origins and distribution of peoples of Africa; geographical characteristics as related to culture types, including early civilizations; a comparative examination of economic, subsistence, language, social and political organization, and religious systems throughout the continent; change processes, the impact of colonialism, and the nature of contemporary African societies.

2.2 FOR REFLECTION

Choosing a Major

It might be too early to commit yourself to a major field of study, although it is never too early to consider options that appeal to you. Remember, regardless of which discipline attracts you most now, exposure to new fields is likely to influence a change in directions.

Below you will find a list of common majors. Circle all those (at least five) that initially interest you (even though you might not know what they involve).

Education	Engineering	Architecture	Management
Nursing	Sociology	Mathematics	Chemistry
Biology	Finance	Geology	Economics
Health	Psychology	English	Dance
Anthropology	Art/Graphic Design	Human Services	Journalism
Music	Health	Marketing	Communication
Computer Science	Social Work	Theater	Criminal Justice
History	Foreign Language	Accounting	Cultural Studies
Geography	Political Science	Physics	Gender Studies
Gerontology	Religion	Philosophy	Astronomy
Environmental Studies	Public Administration	Military Science	Automotive Technology
Medical Specialist	Paralegal	Hospitality	Graphic Design

Among the fields that you selected, what might they have in common?

_____

_____

_____

If you had to predict the future and pick the major you will end up with at graduation, what do you think that will be?

_____

_____

Julie:
Choosing a Major

" I was a business major originally. That was what my parents wanted me to do. That is what I always thought I wanted to do. That's why I went to college in the first place: to get a degree in finance or accounting or something useful like that to make money. I really resented that they made me take a bunch of other stupid courses like art history, astronomy, Shakespeare, and stuff that had nothing to do with my plans. But we had some choices within the social sciences, so I decided to take an anthropology class. The first thing I noticed was how different the students were in the room. I'm not sure if this makes sense, but they were more like me than the ones in my economics and business classes.

You think you know how this story ends—that I switched from business to anthro and lived happily ever after—but you'd be wrong. I did stick with business, but not because that's what my parents wanted, but because I liked the ways I learned to reason things through. But I ended up taking a bunch of electives in anthropology, too, just because I thought they were so interesting. Who knows? Maybe I'll end up going to grad school or something.

Finally, *electives* represent free choice. You are encouraged to study subjects that help to expand your knowledge and interests, often in areas you would never have considered before. Such classes often lead students to change majors based on their exposure to subjects in which they knew and understood little.

The number of electives you take depends on how much time and interest you have after fulfilling all the requirements for general education and your major. Students in engineering, nursing, education, and pre-med will have fewer options than those in liberal studies or humanities.

Rather than merely thinking of electives as "filler"—that is, courses that are scheduled at convenient times, or that round off your credit load—they have several important purposes (Minnick, 2008). Most of all, they present opportunities for you to find a major concentration for your studies, as well as a minor or secondary focus. They allow you to both satisfy the reality of preparing for a career you'll enjoy, plus explore other subjects of interest that could someday be useful as well.

Electives give you a certain flexibility as your interests change over time. When you take different electives, you are acting like the large multinational corporations that diversify their product lines to protect against changes in the marketplace. If sometime further down the line, you decide you don't want to pursue an initial field, then you already have a head start in other directions. In addition, electives exist to (1) help you develop new talents and skills, (2) broaden your knowledge, (3) provide life success skills, (4) increase awareness and sensitivity to different cultures and people, and (5) make learning fun by teaching things of great interest to you.

Choosing Courses

Your advisor is going to have definite ideas about which classes you should take. Pay attention to this advice, which is based on years of experience with other first-year students. Before you make a final decision to register for classes, however, you should consider several additional factors on your own.

Classmates

Having friends in class can be a mixed blessing. Learning is more fun when you are in the company of others you like and trust. Besides, it is frightening to go into a strange classroom without knowing a single soul. Yet whether signing up for classes with friends turns out to be a good decision depends on their priorities. If they are generally serious students, with good study habits if not some ability, this can be an excellent support system to nurture your own progress. But if they become a distraction or a lousy influence, your performance is going to suffer. "I was really bummed," one first-semester student confessed after realizing that none of his friends were signed up in his classes, "but it turned out to be the best thing for me because I got the chance to meet a lot of new people."

Balanced Course Load

Different subjects require different abilities and skills (learning styles are discussed in Chapter 5). Sometimes you will have a lot of writing to do. Large lecture classes often have multiple-choice examinations, while seminars will require that you contribute in class. Some classes are "performance oriented," meaning that you have to create something original, and in others you will have a somewhat passive role as a listener. Some subjects favor your "left brain," meaning that they access the logical, rational, analytical reasoning processes such as the subjects of mathematics, science, and philosophy. Other classes in the arts, drama, and humanities are more based in "right-brain" learning, meaning that they emphasize

Jae C. Hong/AP Photo

intuition and feeling over cognition. A simpler way to say this is that an acting class is going to require different abilities than one in geology.

Some classes will be relatively easy for you, and others extremely challenging (see Table 2.1 for a review of the types of classes). A good idea is to create a schedule that does not overload you in any one area and that maintains your interest throughout the semester. If one subject is particularly difficult for you (or has been in the past), balance that with another that plays toward your strengths. If one subject seems boring to you, pick another one as well that seems really interesting. If one class is going to have a very demanding workload, then balance it with another one that is less rigorous. Keep in mind, however, that classes that seem easy at first because they don't require you to do things you prefer to avoid may have other demands that will test you in other ways.

Time

If you don't go to class, and you don't concentrate while you are there, not much is going to sink in. Your grades are going to suffer as well.

You know your own sleep cycle and when you function at your best. For some students, this is in the morning, others in the afternoon, and still others in the evening. The good news is that most courses you will take the first year have multiple sections that are offered at all times of the day, from 7:00 in the morning to 7:00 at night. Depending on family and work obligations, extracurricular activities, how early you awake, how late you stay up, when you like to study, and when you can concentrate best, you can pick class times that are going to fit better with your style.

You never know what twists and turns your life will take. College electives could become passionate hobbies for life. President Barack Obama loves basketball and former President Bill Clinton is an avid jazz musician. Basketball player Shaquille O'Neal diversified his life in professional sports by singing in a band.

Group Activity

Ask students to reflect on their current academic schedule. Ask them to identify how each course differs from the others in terms of teaching style and the learning activities that are required. Ask students to comment on how these differences affect the appeal of this course.

> ### TABLE 2.1
>
> ## Types of Classes
>
> ▸ **Large lecture classes**. These auditorium-style formats may have a hundred or more students and emphasize reading assignments and listening to lectures. Your learning is often assessed through objective-type (multiple-choice) examinations.
>
> ▸ **Large lecture classes with accompanying section meetings**. In addition to the scheduled lectures, you may also attend small discussion sessions taught by graduate assistants. These may be ungraded, but attendance is required. You are given opportunities to ask questions, apply concepts, and complete group exercises.
>
> ▸ **Laboratories**. Science, engineering, nursing, and other disciplines may offer lecture classes that are accompanied by weekly laboratories in which you experiment or practice what was introduced that week. Mastery of laboratory skills is assessed through performance evaluations.
>
> ▸ **Distance learning**. Many colleges offer sections of classes (including this one) via the Internet, with or without scheduled meetings on campus or at satellite centers. Although this might sound like an easy alternative, such courses can be more challenging because they require more self-directed learning.
>
> ▸ **Field studies**. Some classes (education, social work, human services, nursing, etc.) include field observations in which you spend time on site learning about the everyday realities of professional practice. You are often required to write papers describing what you learned.
>
> ▸ **Seminars**. These are smaller classes, often ten to thirty students, in which the emphasis is on discussing ideas and personalizing material. Usually research or reaction papers are required.
>
> ▸ **Independent studies**. Later in your college career, you may be able to negotiate an individualized course with an instructor that caters to your interests in a much more focused and intense way. This self-directed, collaborative learning plan could involve completing a research project, working through a reading list, or becoming involved in community service. Often a major paper, or several papers, is required.
>
> ▸ **Service learning**. Most colleges offer extended immersion experiences for students to volunteer their time working in the community. The whole course may be spent in the field, keeping notes, and then writing a paper about your experience.

For Community College Students

For some students, there are no choices: They must work around part-time or full-time jobs and family responsibilities. Emphasize that college is like having yet another part- or full-time job depending on the number of credits taken. Discuss with them the formula of one credit = two to three hours of homework.

If you have trouble getting up in the mornings, and don't fully regain consciousness until midmorning, you would be crazy to sign up for 8:00 A.M. classes. If your friends or roommates entice you with things to do in the evenings or if you have family obligations, it would be very unwise to take 7:00 P.M. classes.

You will also be tempted to plan an "efficient" schedule, one in which you might try to load all your classes on Tuesdays and Thursdays, or Mondays and Wednesdays. Whereas later in your college career, you can indeed concentrate classes to provide large blocks of discretionary time, it is more important your first year that you set a steady pace. This means building breaks into your day so that you can recover, replenish your energy, regain your concentration, complete assignments, do your reading, and prepare for the next class.

In looking at the comparison between two sample schedules in Figure 2.2, at first you might admire the ambition of the second student who loaded all his classes on two days so he could free himself up to work more hours and have time for snowboarding. But examining the schedule further, you'll notice that he barely has time to eat anything, much less catch his breath. He runs from one class to the next, probably grabbing food from snack machines along the way. He can barely make the transition from one subject to the next. Needless to say, school is a grind for him even if he has

Figure 2.2 Comparison between Two Schedules—One Strategic and the Other Insane

	10:00–10:50 a.m.	11:30 a.m.–12:45 p.m.	1:00–1:50 p.m.	2:00–4:00 p.m.
Mon	Student Success		Bio	Bio Lab
Tues		English		Sociology
Wed	Student Success		Bio	
Th		English		Sociology
Fri	Student Success		Bio	

	8:00–9:15 a.m.	9:30–10:45 a.m.	11:30 a.m.–12:45 p.m.	2:00–4:00 p.m.	4:00–6:45 p.m.
Tues	Student Success	English	Bio	Bio Lab	Sociology
Th	Student Success	English	Bio		

managed to compress everything into two days. It is inconceivable that he is going to do very well in all of his classes.

Work schedules or long commutes may limit your options for spacing classes with as much time as you might prefer. Within the demands of your commitments, however, try to give yourself some time between classes so you can regroup from one before jumping in to the next.

Instructors

The college curriculum may be organized around courses and disciplines, but what often makes or breaks your interest in any subject is the quality of instruction. Some teachers you've had in the past were boring, mean, or clueless, and others were so charismatic that you'd study anything with them. Some classes, even in subjects you love, were tedious largely because the teachers could not engage you. Other classes riveted you, not because of the subject area as much as the passion, commitment, and expertise of the teacher. And you have also had teachers in the past who were hard, demanding, and perhaps even difficult at times, but you knew they really cared about you, so you gave them the benefit of the doubt.

Some of your college instructors will be absolutely brilliant, and others will be somewhat less than inspiring. First-year students complain most about instructors who are difficult to understand, perhaps because of their accents, choice of language, or pace of speech (too fast). They also don't like instructors who are boring, who are perceived as unfair in their grading policies, who don't seem to care about students, or who are out of touch with the realities of daily life. Interestingly, students least mind instructors who are extremely demanding and challenging, as long as they feel they are learning things that are important and useful.

One of the things you will find different about college life is that you actually get to "grade" your instructors at the end of the semester, providing them with feedback on what you liked best and least. You will be asked to share your opinion about their

Nick: Being Challenged in Class

"There's this one instructor who everyone complains about in the beginning because he's so hard and everything. He has about a zillion books on his syllabus, way more than anyone can afford or would ever buy anyway. He's kind of scary too, at least at first, because he's so serious—and I guess intimidating. The guy is so smart.

The interesting thing is—and I've heard this every semester that I'd been avoiding his class—that about halfway through the semester, students stop complaining about him and they start raving about how much they've learned and all. They work their butts off. They're always studying. But in the end, they say it's worth all the stress and work.

By the time I took his class, I thought I knew what I was in for, and had resigned myself that I'd be lucky to get a B. I never studied so hard for any class as I did for that one, but you know what? It's been two years, and I still use stuff that I learned almost every day. He taught me how to think differently about things, and I never could have done that without him pushing me.

Teaching Tip to Reduce Stress

Ask students to identify which current instructor causes them the most stress or confusion, then make an appointment to talk with that professor in his or her office. This will be challenging, as students will likely give excuses for why this isn't feasible. Once the visit is scheduled, ask students to look for clues in dialogue and the office's physical evidence as to what excites this professor. Ask students to identify some common interests and to reflect on anything the professor says or does that fascinates them.

level of expertise, preparedness for class, accessibility, grading policies, and interest in students, and how meaningfully the course was structured. These data are often quite useful to instructors in adapting the ways they teach; it is often quite critical for their future promotions.

In some cases, you may not be able to avoid taking a particular instructor because limited sections are available or your preferred section is already full. In such instances, you will have to make the best of the situation. Such is life: You don't always get what you want.

If you do some preliminary research by talking to your advisor, accessing student evaluation data, and also consulting with other students who are ahead of you, you can often discover which instructors are best for your learning style. The tough part is being able to locate people who have completed classes that you are planning to take. Websites such as www.ratemyprofessors.com and www.professorperformance.com provide some data as well. A word of warning, however: Often the students who take the time to provide feedback on websites want revenge for perceived injustices (usually because they got a disappointing grade), so make sure that you gather information from multiple sources so you can make an informed decision.

Meeting with an academic advisor on a regular basis is critical. Utilizing other student services on campus will also help you get the most from your college experience.

Interests

Just because there are required courses your first year doesn't mean that you have to study things that don't interest you. In fact, it is really, really important that you select courses that intrigue and stimulate you so that you don't become discouraged. Make sure you give yourself at least one "gift" class that you think you'll really look forward to, because of the subject matter, the reputation of the instructor, or the predicted activities in the class.

For Community College Students
Be aware that lower-level remedial students may not be able to take a "gift" class for several semesters due to college prep requirements. Nevertheless, there are still fun classes that can be scheduled in areas of interest.

 2.3 FOR REFLECTION

What Interests You Most?

Although students often select electives based on how conveniently they fit into their schedules, consider thoughtfully the privilege you have in college to study things that intrigue you and make you a more well-rounded, informed, inquisitive person, regardless of how they relate to preparing for a career.

● **What are your strengths?** It is often enjoyable to study subjects that play into your existing talents and skills, such as aptitude for languages, math, writing, or performance. *What are favorite subjects that you feel strong in, those in which you wish to develop greater expertise?*

_____

_____

_____

● **What are your weaknesses?** You may feel a temptation to avoid courses in areas that you have struggled with in the past. People tell themselves they are just not good at math or writing or public speaking or whatever. College gives you an opportunity to retry areas that have caused you difficulty. In a sense, you can redefine yourself by turning weaknesses into strengths, or at least competencies. *Which subjects frighten you a bit, but are ones you might like to conquer if you could build up the courage?*

_____

_____

_____

● **What might you like to explore?** You know next to nothing about so many subjects, perhaps because you never had the opportunity or time to study them before. These can include rather specialized subjects (quantum physics, cultural anthropology, or Impressionist art) or obscure ones (postmodern philosophy, artificial intelligence, or history of the Peloponnesian Wars), as well as introductory courses for which you'd be eligible your first year or two. *Review the class schedule this semester, and write down at least a dozen options you'd consider for the future.*

_____

_____

_____

The college curriculum may appear to you like a supersized menu from which you are force-fed all these requirements. Yet the whole objective of higher education is to help you to pursue your current interests, as well as to expand your tastes in new areas. Perhaps the best way for you to narrow down the overwhelming assortment of career choices is to experiment taking classes in areas that will either help you to eliminate a major or explore it a bit further.

Resources on Campus

During your orientation, if not during the first weeks of school, you were most likely besieged by various groups wanting you to join their ranks. Each table you passed tried to recruit you to become part of an academic department, religious organization, fraternity or sorority, or club. Other stations vied for your attention to sign up for credit cards or phone service, or to buy computers or products. All the signs, advertising, and marketing pitches became overwhelming.

Sorting out bad, good, better, and best is easier with an expert guiding hand. In addition to your academic advisor, many other student services on campus exist solely to assist you. A significant part of the tuition and fees you pay goes to support various student services on campus, those offices that deal with your health, finances, social and cultural enrichment, and athletics, among other things. In spite of the tremendous investment in these resources, almost one-half of first-year students never consult with the financial-advising, academic-tutoring, or career-planning units (Kuh, 2007).

First-Year Programs

The department in charge of organizing classes such as this one can be called by different names—such as "Freshman Programs," "Student Success," or "First-Year Student Services"—but in any manifestation, it exists to help you make a successful adjustment to college. Research studies have demonstrated consistently that such organized programs reduce dropout rates and improve the performance—and well-being—of new students.

This department may offer a number of other support services for you as a first-year student. It can provide academic advising, social activities, skills training, and even a space to study. During your orientation the staff likely introduced you to the variety of services they provide. As mentioned, only a very small percentage of students ever take advantage of this support. This is particularly disappointing because the staff are experts in helping first-year students to make successful adjustments.

Library and Technology Services

In Chapters 5 through 7 on academic skills, you'll read about the importance of learning basic research strategies in books, journals, media, and the Internet. This will be absolutely imperative for you when writing papers, working on projects, doing presentations, and simply pursuing areas of interest. As part of this class, or new student orientation, you will be introduced to the library facilities and services available to you. Either through this orientation or on your own, make certain you know how to do the following before you get too far into your classes:

● How to log in to your library via the Internet and do a basic search for materials

● How the "stacks" of books, journals, and media are organized, and where they are located

● How to use the "search" functions of the library to locate materials by subject, author, and title

● How to check out books and other materials (and how long you can keep them)

● How to order materials through interlibrary loan if they are not available on your campus

● How to find materials that have been placed "on reserve" by your instructors

● How to consult with a librarian for help with research projects

Financial Aid

If you have major concerns about financing your education, you are certainly not alone. Two-thirds of college students express apprehension, if not panic, about how they are going to support themselves throughout college, much less deal with student loan debt (Higher Education Research Institute, 2006). Half of students report they will probably not have enough money to graduate (Chronicle of Higher Education, 2008).

You have many options for financing your education, including low-interest student loans, scholarships, grants, and other subsidies. These financial aid packages are offered on the federal, state, and local levels. If you investigate the options, with the assistance of the appropriate office on campus, you will be amazed at the opportunities that are available to help support you.

Before you apply for any financial aid program, *carefully* read the instructions regarding qualifications and requirements. Many applications are rejected immediately because the student did not qualify in the first place or did not provide the information requested. It is always a good idea to ask someone to review your work, preferably someone within the financial aid office. If an essay or narrative explanation is required, have someone help you edit the prose to make sure it is perfect. Check to see that you have included all required documentation. Apply early and often—the more options you have, the better.

Teaching Tip
Ask students to develop a financial aid folder. Instruct students to keep copies of all documents related to financial aid applications and awards, and take this folder to all financial aid meetings. As an extension, encourage students to know their assigned financial aid counselor or develop a professional relationship with such a counselor in the campus financial aid office. Encourage students to talk with this counselor each time a financial aid issue arises.

Services for Resident and Commuter Students

At some local colleges, all students commute on a daily basis; at other institutions, half or more of the student body live on campus. Within U.S. institutions, 80 percent of college students commute to school every day. Students who live within a fifty-mile radius of their college have special needs and interests that are distinctly different from those who live in the residence halls (only the most obvious of which is hunting for convenient parking).

Being close to family and friends in your community provides one kind of support, but also presents some challenges in that it may be more difficult for you to fully immerse yourself in campus life. You likely have commitments at home, at work, and with lifelong friends that limit time available to participate in extracurricular and social activities.

Most colleges offer services for both residents and commuters that help each group find a place that is comfortable and appropriate. For instance, it has been found that the more cohesive the residence hall atmosphere is (meaning the residents show a lot of trusting, positive interactions and closeness), and the more students personalize their rooms with decorations and improvements, the more likely that there will be successful adjustment.

Likewise, it is just as important for commuters (who are the vast majority of college students throughout the world) to find a group of people with whom they share similar interests who can share information and provide ongoing support. So much

Classroom Discussion
Open it up: What do you see as the advantages and disadvantages of on-campus living versus commuting?

One of the best predictors of successful adaptation to college the first year is if a student, whether resident or commuter, is part of a cohesive group of like-minded friends who offer support and respect.

Jupiterimages

interaction now takes place through technologies such as the web and the Internet that commuter students crave face-to-face relationships with other students, staff, and instructors (Krause, 2007). With large, impersonal classes, online communications, and hectic driving schedules accompanied by parking frustrations, it is even more important for commuters to have varied face-to-face social involvements within their time constraints. One student from a study conducted in Australia summarized what a blessing it felt like to be part of a group that could cover for him: "Despite this year being one of the hardest of my life, it's been bearable because I have friends who I study with" (Krause, 2007, p. 37). Go to www.cengagebrain.com for more ways for commuter students to become involved in campus life.

Counseling and Psychological Services

Many (if not most) students experience stress, depression, anxiety, loneliness, or relationship difficulties at some point in their college careers. Counseling, support

Mitch:
Finding Hope

❝ I never would have gone to the counseling center unless I was absolutely falling apart—which I was. My girlfriend ended our relationship and I went a little nuts. I just got so depressed I couldn't function. I stopped going to classes. I couldn't think straight. I even thought of killing myself; I would have done it too if I could have figured out a way—but I didn't have the guts to follow through.

So I saw this lady at the counseling center and I don't think I'm exaggerating when I say she saved my life. I mean I was desperate. I could barely crawl out of bed. My family was worried. My friends were freaked out. And nobody could do anything. I was just feeling so sorry for myself.

It wasn't like she told me anything I didn't already know. Or it seems that way. But she really listened to me like nobody else had before. She gave me hope. She convinced me that I could get better. It's weird but she didn't really tell me what to do as much as she had faith in me. That's what helped me to have faith in myself.

groups, and stress management workshops help you to deal with the inevitable challenges that will arise.

The counseling center on campus (if you have one) offers a range of services that will likely meet your needs, including individual counseling, support groups, and workshops on different subjects. When and why might you decide to make an appointment or sign up for a group? This could span the range from relatively minor adjustment issues that are leading to anxious or disturbing feelings to more severe emotional problems that make it difficult for you to function. Common problems that students face include drug and alcohol habits, conflicts with family or roommates, sexual difficulties, grief reactions, anger management, difficulties concentrating, eating disorders, confusion or uncertainty about the future, or difficulty making important decisions.

Student Disability Services

This office provides support, guidance, and advocacy for students with disabilities who face additional challenges in their college success. This includes those with physical disabilities, as well as those with learning disabilities and mental impairments.

For those who qualify, based on a thorough assessment by staff, a number of services are offered depending on individual needs. Students may negotiate accommodations with instructors for exams, homework, readings, and writing assignments. Sign language interpreters or assistive technology and computer software can be provided. Handicapped parking can be arranged. Advisors within the office act as guidance specialists, providing counseling, support, and encouragement in adjusting to the demands of college life.

Service Learning

The same percentage of students (67 percent) who are worried about their own finances also express a major interest in helping others who are experiencing difficulties. In public colleges, the percentage is even higher, with three-quarters of students stating that devoting themselves to some type of service is an "essential" personal goal (Higher Education Research Institute, 2006).

Some colleges have offices that specialize in organizing, placing, and supervising students in the community who are working in various internships, field activities, and social justice projects. As you are well aware, developing knowledge and expertise in an area happens not just in a classroom, but also through real-life experiences. You will have many opportunities in college to volunteer your time, take field courses for credit, or become involved in projects that help marginalized or disadvantaged people. For applied majors like education, business, nursing, and human services, "field placements" enable you to work in real jobs under close supervision.

You are probably well aware that a college degree does not guarantee employment; just as important is work experience in the outside world. Participating in a service project in the community not only helps to make a difference in the lives of those who are less fortunate, but also provides you with marketable experience, demonstrates commitment, and develops reality-based skills. Even though such efforts are time-consuming in the already hectic schedules of first-year students, service learning has been found to have a huge positive impact on developing leadership skills, building friendships, and increasing confidence (Erickson, Peters, and Strommer, 2006).

Beyond what volunteer and service activities can do to gain valuable real-life experience and therefore enhance a résumé, today campuses and communities are witnessing a renewed spirit to devoting time and energy toward promoting social justice and human rights. This means (1) challenging inequities like racism, sexism,

Group Activity

Lead a discussion about what qualifies as a "disability." Ask students to share ways they have felt disabled in some way during their lives. For those with documented disabilities, ask them to journal about their rights and responsibilities as a disabled student. Encourage students to develop a professional relationship with their disability services counselor and to have frequent meetings to review progress being made.

Teaching Tip

Encourage students to keep a calendar or yearly planner to record service work completed throughout the year, including the organizational affiliation, the type of service provided, and the dates and hours of service. Instruct students to keep these yearly calendars as reference in developing future résumés.

Pivotal learning moments frequently occur outside the classroom, especially when you volunteer on behalf of people who are marginalized or disadvantaged such as helping at a food bank. Service learning projects in the community can be organized as part of a class, as an independent study, or through the appropriate office on campus. You can also search for such opportunities on your own just because it feels good to help others who are struggling or less fortunate.

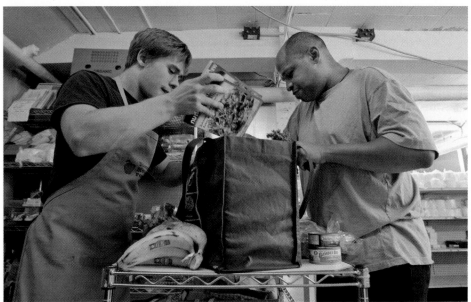

AP Photo/Elaine Thompson

and other prejudices; (2) advocating on behalf of those who are marginalized and oppressed; (3) empowering those who have historically been without a voice; and (4) taking action and volunteering your time and commitment to make a difference with those who need it the most (Kottler and Marriner, 2009).

Intramural and Club Sports

In high school, there were only two levels of participation in sports activities, both of which were very competitive: varsity or junior varsity. In college, besides the most competitive-level teams for student athletes, you can join a number of organized "club" sports for those who just want to enjoy their favorite physical activities without feeling pressured to perform at the highest levels. Some leagues are organized for high-level competition, while others are merely for enjoyment.

The range of options at most colleges is absolutely staggering, including everything from soccer, basketball, and baseball to flag football, fencing, table tennis, rock climbing, and Ultimate Frisbee. Intramural leagues are offered at various levels of proficiency, as well as instruction for those who wish to learn a new sport.

Students join club sports for a variety of reasons: (1) They always wanted to play in high school but never got the chance, (2) they want to relive past glories, (3) they want to meet new people who share common interests, (4) they want to stay physically active and maintain fitness, (5) they want to control their weight, (6) they enjoy competition, (7) they want to learn a new activity as an outside interest, and (8) they want to feel connected and part of a group. Most intramural and club sports are designed in such a way that almost everyone can be involved on some level.

Multicultural Affairs

This aspect of campus life organizes activities on behalf of various cultural, ethnic, gender, racial, and other historically underserved student groups. There may, for instance, be groups for African American, Latino, Chinese, Middle Eastern, Native American, and gay and lesbian students, and for a dozen other minorities.

The goals are to provide support and networking for students from marginalized groups, and educate the campus community about issues of significance. Activities may be organized to celebrate Martin Luther King, Jr. Day or Cesar Chavez Day. Prominent speakers may be invited on campus to discuss important cultural themes. Seminars may be offered that help students to develop greater sensitivity toward diversity issues.

International Student Support

This office assists students from other countries with their adjustment challenges. It provides guidance on visa requirements, housing, language training, introduction to university life and regional culture, and ongoing support—and for good reason: When researchers asked international students to describe their first year of college abroad, the majority used terms like "horrible," "scary," and "nerve-racking" (Andrade, 2005).

International students try to adapt to life not only on a college campus, but also in a whole new country. English may be a second, or even third, language; much of the time they may only understand about half of what they read and hear in class, guessing at the rest and possibly ending up with distorted translations. They may not understand many of the expressions and slang of their classmates. They may not be familiar with the customs that seem second nature to those who are born or raised in North America. They may be reminded of how different they are from others around them and may feel incredibly homesick and often bewildered by what they see going on around them.

When you encounter international students in your classes, extracurricular activities, residence halls, or the student union, make a special effort to reach out to them. Just consider how you would feel going to school in a strange country, without your family and friends nearby, trying to deal with academic stress while learning in a non-native language.

Studying Abroad

Most colleges offer programs in which you can study in another country for a semester or an academic year. In this increasingly global community, new professionals are expected to develop greater flexibility in working with colleagues in other countries. Spending time abroad helps you to develop new perspectives at the same time you are increasing your foreign language fluency. Although the experiences often involve a lot of sacrifices (financial and otherwise) and present a number of challenges, students often report that nothing in their lives has ever been more influential in shaping their values and broadening their views of the world.

Interestingly, the most memorable travel stories are often the ones in which you faced some adversity. Only after safely returning do your stories sound amusing, rather than portraying the very real confusion, apprehension, and discomfort you may have been feeling at the time.

Sagun:
Being an Immigrant

"I'm a foreign student, what they call an international student. I had never taken college-level classes here in the U.S. When I decided to go to school, everything was really confusing and I was completely lost. I didn't know anyone. The classes were completely different from what I was used to back home. I didn't want to ask too many questions because I was afraid of sounding ignorant. I always pretend to know more than I do. When people ask me if I understand, I just nod my head.

Meredith: A Semester Abroad

" I remember the day I was about to leave for a semester abroad in Spain. I was crying hysterically and draped dramatically over my suitcase. I was so frustrated that I could not fit everything I wanted to take into my large suitcase and duffle bag. The fears and anxieties about the months ahead tumbled out of me. My parents encouraged me to calm down by rethinking all of the reasons I was going abroad: to explore a new culture and to make connections with other American students and Spaniards, and of course to improve my Spanish skills.

As it turned out, I learned a lot of things during this semester, many of which had nothing to do with improving my Spanish language skills. I made unforgettable friendships with the other students in my program and with my host "family," a seventy-five-year-old widow. I learned and became more comfortable with being spontaneous, a necessity for realizing the full opportunities of living in a place for only a few months. Probably most importantly, I developed a lot more confidence in myself and my ability to deal with new situations.

During a semester I spent studying abroad, I now recall with fond memories the exciting places I visited, the adventures I experienced, the pride I felt in becoming conversant in another language, and the things I learned about myself and how people live in another country. Yet when I look back through the journal I kept during that time, I see how disoriented and lonely I felt much of the time. So be forewarned that if you decide to explore the possibility of studying abroad at some time (usually during your junior year), you will stretch yourself in ways you never imagined were possible.

Women's Center

Although the focus of such a center is on the special needs of women, often there may be a broadened emphasis on gender differences. Men, as well, have unique needs and interests. Such a center often sponsors programs and dialogues to help students, staff, and faculty become more respectful and sensitive to how gender affects relationships and communication.

College life involves exploration of the influence of culture, gender, socioeconomic background, ethnicity, and personal values on personal choices and opportunities. Consider how your life in the present, and plans for the future, might be different if you were the opposite gender, or a member of a different religion or race.

©Istockphoto.com/Chris Schmidt

Diversifying Your Life

Make college life more satisfying and stress free by capitalizing on the support services that can address your weaknesses, feed your interests, and diversify your life. That way, when one aspect of your life isn't going well, you can excel and find satisfaction in other areas.

In spite of all the resources on campus, most students don't access the services available to them. They say they are too busy or didn't know their options. Which resources presented in this chapter seem most relevant to your particular needs and interests, and how would they relieve your stress?

_____

_____

_____

_____

_____

Workshops, support groups, discussion groups, seminars, and information sessions are often offered through the women's center that focus on gender and related subjects. The center also acts as an advocate on behalf of women who experience harassment, discrimination, or sexual assault. Integral to the mission of some centers is to provide internships that allow students to explore issues more deeply. Interns are offered experiences that help them develop confidence, manage emotions, develop autonomy, establish their identity, and have better interpersonal relationships.

Religious Life

Many religious groups offer educational programs, spiritual guidance, and worship services. Every college campus has groups of various denominations and religious traditions that help students to explore the meaning of faith and spirituality in their lives. "Faith" means developing a sense of trust in someone or something bigger than yourself, a grounding in a set of values that guide your behavior and form your character (Braskamp, Trautvetter, and Ward, 2006). The focus of such programs is often on developing moral character and increasing religious commitment, but community service might also play an important role.

Given that being a first-year college student is often a rather self-centered stage of life in which so much of your energy and thought are about *you*, religious or spiritual involvement can help balance attention toward something much bigger than yourself. This is not just a Higher Power, but also the larger world. Joining Campus Crusade, one new student said, made a huge difference in his adjustment on campus: "That got me out meeting new people, which isn't easy for me. I also felt like I was doing some good for other people."

Knowing that religious activities must compete with hundreds of other campus groups vying for your interest, a big part of religious life is socially centered. Attending religious services may be part of the agenda, but just as critical are organized sessions that foster intellectual and social development. Leading spiritual figures may present lectures on campus. Seminars may explore spiritual issues related to finding meaning in life. For international students, in particular, religious activities provide a semifamiliar structure within an alien world, one that they often credit for their successful adjustment (Andrade, 2005).

Fraternity and Sorority Life

Group Activity
Lead a class discussion on the benefits and liabilities of the "Greek" system in college. Emphasize the importance of keeping a good balance in activities associated with Greek involvement. For freshmen, talk extensively about the need for balance during the "rush" and "pledge" periods.

Many colleges offer various "Greek" organizations that are dedicated to social and community programs. Students join a fraternity or sorority not only to feel part of a "tribe," but also to feel like they have a home.

The decision about whether to join a fraternity or sorority is an important one. Your choice may be based on your particular needs and interests, as well as how active such organizations are on your campus. Some universities have up to seventy-five different options available, while other campuses prohibit their presence altogether, feeling they can lead to exclusivity and elitism.

Committing to one social group has both pros and cons. On the one hand, you inherit a group of friends and have immediate structure to your social life, as well as develop a nationwide network of professionals who can help you in the future. On the other hand, some students find this very restrictive. Sometimes it makes sense to wait a semester before making a decision, since joining a Greek organization can be both stressful and time consuming.

Other Extracurricular Activities

This final category includes everything else that would be offered on campus for students to enrich social, cultural, physical, and intellectual growth outside the classroom. Depending on your campus, there can be anywhere from a few dozen to hundreds of clubs for you to join. And if you don't find a club of interest that appeals to you, you can start your own!

Media outlets on campus provide opportunities for students to gain experience in radio, television, or the web. The drama and music departments have productions going on at all times that are open to nonmajors to participate in. The campus recreation center provides outdoor activities and fitness programs. Many colleges have leadership institutes that organize programming for those who are interested in serving within student government or wish to develop leadership skills in their chosen fields.

SUMMARY

College life consists of a complex mix of academic, social, recreational, and extracurricular activities that together form an experience that is both stimulating and overwhelming. The first year of college is among the most stressful times of life, requiring you to find support systems along the way in order to succeed, much less to flourish. Located throughout campus are dozens, if not hundreds, of resources, offices, and opportunities that are designed to help support you. To give yourself the best chance to excel in college, make a concerted effort to reach out to classmates and instructors, and assertively seek out assistance from advisors and other student services staff.

QUESTIONS FOR REVIEW AND FURTHER EXPLORATION

1. If students who fully intend to participate in extracurricular activities do not follow through, why do you suppose they change their minds?

2. Bring to mind your classroom with everyone sitting around you. Between one-quarter and one-third of your classmates may drop out or flunk out before they finish the first year. Half of those who begin college will never graduate. Some of the most common reasons why first-year students drop or flunk out of school are that they (1) are unprepared for college life (academically, socially, culturally), (2) had financial problems, (3) did not feel campus was welcoming, and (4) experienced family problems. What are some other reasons you can think of for why a motivated student with the best of intentions (that is, someone like you), would not graduate college?

3. Why is it that the quality of relationships on campus best predicts success and satisfaction in college?

4. If you, or a friend, were feeling depressed, lonely, anxious, or troubled about something, and you (or your friend) couldn't work things out on your own, what do you think are the most common excuses given for not seeking help from a counselor?

5. Among the resources that were reviewed in this chapter, which ones do you resolve to check out during the next few weeks? How can you arrange a campus tour of facilities and resources that are still unfamiliar to you?

Go to www.cengagebrain.com for an online quiz that will test your understanding of the chapter content.

Managing Time and Setting Goals

KEY QUESTIONS

▶ **What are potential problems with setting goals that are too ambitious, or too modest?**

▶ **What does it mean for goals to be meaningful?**

▶ **Why should goals be as specific as possible?**

▶ **What are the disadvantages of being too goal oriented?**

▶ **What are the most common ways that time is wasted, meaning that it is not used productively or for enjoyment?**

▶ **What are the effects of juggling multiple tasks at the same time?**

▶ **How do stress and worry actually sabotage your attempt to reach desired goals?**

▶ **What are the payoffs of procrastination?**

▶ **What are the best ways to overcome the tendency to procrastinate?**

This is one of the chapters that introduces strategies that will be useful to you way beyond college. Throughout much of your life, you will struggle with setting goals and priorities, as well as organizing and structuring your time to complete all your tasks and commitments. No matter what your age and stage in life, you will never have enough time to complete everything you'd like to get done. That requires making tough decisions about what is most important to you, and then devoting the time and energy to making those things happen. It also involves considerable self-discipline to stay on track despite a multitude of other distractions, temptations, and sources of stress you will face. The American College Health Association (2009) found stress to be the single most reported obstacle to academic success in college students. Two-thirds of students reported feeling "very sad." In addition, in a survey of 250,000 first-time freshmen, half of them reported that they felt "overwhelming anxiety" during the previous year (Higher Education Research Institute, 2009). One-third of students felt so depressed or stressed that they found it difficult to function on a daily basis.

Before you read in later chapters about strategies for flourishing in the classroom and elsewhere on campus, it is first critical that you have a handle on how you manage your time and deal with the inevitable stress you face in having far more to do than you can possibly accomplish in the limited time available.

Group Activity

Conduct a continuum exercise (students who "strongly agree" on one side of the room, and "strongly disagree" on the other side of the room) for three to four statements. Examples: I am balancing my work, school, and social life well right now; I am struggling to keep up with college; I expect to spend at least four hours a day studying in college; I feel overwhelmed by my schoolwork; I spend two hours or more a day on the computer recreationally, video gaming, or watching TV or movies.

For Community College Students

Is the nature of stress different for community college students than for their university peers? Conduct a class discussion about their stressors.

Formulating Priorities and Goals

This chapter is featured very early in this book because it is so critical for everything that happens afterward. Yogi Berra, the baseball player and philosopher with unusual syntax, once observed that if you don't know where you are going, you might wind up someplace else. The idea is that without plans for the future, you won't end up where you want to be. Of course, as a first-year student, you have every right not to know what you want to do with your life and where you'd like to end up: One purpose of college is to help you explore options and make preliminary choices.

You can save yourself a lot of time and energy if, over the next few years, you give serious consideration to what is most important to you and what you want to do with your life. Avoid the myth, however, that you are supposed to come up with some ambitious, detailed life plan and then follow it until the end of the rainbow. Things happen that are unexpected and unforeseen. Events in the world will alter the landscape. Opportunities will come your way that you never would have considered before. Friendships and networking will open up other possibilities. Your priorities and values will evolve as you gain new experiences and are exposed to other options. Anything you plan now will likely shift as you learn new things, develop new skills, and grow in new directions. In fact, it is imperative that you remain open to these changes.

In spite of the best strategic planning and goal setting, unexpected things happen that provide both opportunities and necessary readjustments. Goals must be continually updated in light of new skills you develop, new options that emerge, and new feedback you get regarding your performance.

This doesn't mean that it isn't important to plan for the future; rather, whatever plans you make should be fluid and flexible. In any successful business, the leader creates a detailed plan to secure financing, conduct market research, build a product line, and arrange sales distribution, but then remains open to the demands and preferences of customers. In football, the quarterback calls a play in the huddle but often changes it once he sees what the other team is doing at the line of scrimmage. Likewise, you can make all the plans you want for the future but you have to be ready and able to change them as circumstances—and you—change.

Setting Goals

Of the following two different views of setting goals, which perspective do you most agree with?

1. Unless you set goals that may seem improbable, you can never attain your highest potential.

2. Nothing else condemns a person to failure like setting objectives that are out of reach.

Actually, both have some merit, don't they?

It *is* important to push yourself to go beyond what you think you can handle (or what others tell you can be done). That is what leads you to achieve goals that are ambitious and fulfill high expectations for yourself. Most significant contributions to science, art, and the humanities were accomplished by those who did what was perceived as impossible.

Yet it is also important not to set yourself up for failure by committing to goals that are unrealistic. It can be quite discouraging to declare that you are going to do something that is way beyond what is possible, at least at that time. For instance, Molly heard someone speak about a new weight-loss program that really fired her up. At the end of the meeting, everyone was supposed to say out loud how much weight they would lose during the week. Feeling so inspired, Molly yelled out "Five pounds!" and then basked in the applause. Keep in mind that she hadn't lost *any* weight in the previous six months, but now she declared that in one short week she'd knock off a big chunk. Molly starved herself every day, determined to meet her goal, but when it came time to weigh herself, she'd lost "only" three pounds. This is actually a remarkable accomplishment, yet she felt like she'd failed because she didn't meet her declared objective. After that, she gave up.

Clearly, it isn't enough to just envision something you want to do; write it down or tell someone, and then accomplish it. If reaching goals were that easy, you would almost always get what you want. The reality is that most goals are not reached—or at least not immediately, as people slip back into old patterns of laziness.

Most people are not very skilled at setting goals for themselves. They don't take the time to plan what it is *they* want most rather than what others want for them. When they do declare goals, they are often stated so generally that it becomes difficult to tell if they are ever reached. And often they are structured in a way that isn't that relevant to what people say they want most. Here are some guidelines to keep in mind for setting goals that are important to you.

Thinking Short Term and Long Term

What is it that you want ultimately? And what are some objectives that you can reach along the way to get you closer to the final goal?

In the long term, you may want to get at least a B+ in a chemistry class, but that is not likely to happen unless you also structure short-term goals along the way: (1) Study chemistry a minimum of two hours every Monday, Wednesday, and Sunday afternoons; (2) make appointments to meet with a tutor in the chemistry department each week; (3) organize a study group to meet before and after each biweekly quiz and review questions; and (4) meet with the instructor at least twice during the semester to ask for extra work you can do.

Make Sure the Goals Are Meaningful

It doesn't do you much good to declare goals just for the sake of reaching them, if they aren't really that important to you in the first place. Many people spend their whole lives pursuing goals that were never really theirs in the first place, but rather imposed on them by family, friends, mentors, teachers, and others who believed they knew what was best.

Lots of people in your life have strong opinions about what you should be doing and how you should be doing it. They aren't shy about telling you what to do, either. Yet you aren't going to be very committed to accomplishing goals established by outside pressure. And who wants to wake up one day, years in the

Group Activity

Ask students to reflect on their academic goals for each course this semester. Have them determine three specific things they will have to do to reach their goals. (See the chemistry discussion above.)

3.1 FOR REFLECTION

Setting Goals for the Future

Effective goals should be

- **Specific:** Say *what* you will do, *when* you will do it, *with whom* you will do it, and *how often* you will do it.
- **Significant:** They should be important to you and have direct relevance to what you value most for yourself and your future.
- **Attainable:** They should be realistic enough that you are almost certain you can accomplish what you declare.
- **Measurable:** The goals should be stated in such a way that you can determine whether you reached them or not.

What is a goal that you wish to accomplish by the end of the semester?

_____

_____

_____

_____

What is a goal that you wish to accomplish by the time you graduate college?

_____

_____

_____

_____

Signature _____   Date _____

Witness _____

future, and discover that everything you fought so hard for wasn't really much of a priority in the first place? Focus on what is important to you, and base your goals on those values.

Be Very Specific

Exactly *what* are you going to do? *How many times* are you going to do it? *When* are you going to do it? *With whom* are you going to do it? *Where* are you going to do it?

Cassie says that she doesn't like that she is so shy and quiet. That is always how she had been in high school. Among her friends and family, that is how everyone expected her to be. During the rare times when she tried to speak her mind at home,

Symphonie/Jupiter Images

Most students lack skills at setting realistic, attainable goals, picking either something that is out of reach or something so general that having reached it is difficult to determine. Besides setting goals that are specific and manageable, publicly declare to others your intentions so you feel accountable to follow through. That is why in For Reflection 3.1, you are asked to sign your contract and have it witnessed.

she was told in no uncertain terms that she was being disrespectful and "not yourself." But now at college, she sees a wonderful opportunity to invent someone quite new—a more outspoken person who says what she thinks without terror of being shut down. So Cassie declares as her goal, "I'm going to try to be more assertive in the future."

What are the problems with Cassie's commitment? You can take a cue from the heading that it is far too general. She is going to *try* to be more assertive? What does *that* mean? How will she know if she ever reached her goal? If she tried inside her head? If she opens her mouth to talk in class but no words come out, does that count as reaching her goal?

Cassie should restructure her goal to become more assertive in far more specific terms that allow her to measure progress: "In my seminar class that meets twice a week, I'm going to find some reason to speak for at least one minute in each class. That could mean asking a question, answering a question, expressing an opinion, or making a comment. But one way or the other, I will make my voice heard each and every class period. Since there are only eleven students in the class, that should be realistic, although so far I haven't talked yet at all."

Structure Attainable Objectives

In Cassie's case, she acknowledges that even speaking up in class for one minute each time may be more than she can handle, given that she hasn't yet spoken at all. She also has a long track record of remaining passive and withdrawn, as much as she would like to alter this pattern. So ideally it might be even better for her to start out with a smaller, more manageable goal of speaking up one time each week for one minute, then building from there. As presently constructed, if for some reason the instructor decides to lecture one entire period, or an outside speaker takes up all the time, she will have to concede defeat. Better that she plan for contingencies she can't control so that no matter what happens, she can absolutely guarantee results.

Although it is important that your goals be ambitious and set high standards, make certain that they are realistic and that you are absolutely positive that you can reach them. If you aren't sure, start out with modest expectations until you build confidence.

Teaching Tip
Ask students to pick three dates for visiting with their professors and write these dates in their appointment books. Suggest they contact each professor one week before this date to verify an appointment time. During each visit, the student should get a course grade update and revisit the stated course goals, including the student's individual objectives. After each visit, have students journal what types of modifications are now required to their behaviors and/or attitudes to assure the successful completion of the course and attainment of the course goals.

Set Deadlines

What are you going to do by what date? It is crucial that you can measure whether you accomplished your objectives. Too often, goals are established in such a way that it is difficult to tell if you reach them. Compare the following:

Indeterminate Goals	Specific Deadlines
I'm going to complete my lit essay before the deadline.	I'm going to complete a first draft of the essay by November 1, get feedback within three days, and complete the final draft November 12, three days before it is due.
Sometime soon, I'm going to ask that guy I like to do something with me.	When I see that guy I like in class tomorrow, I'm going to find a way to talk to him and make plans to get together. If it doesn't work out for tomorrow for some reason, I'll do it for sure on Thursday.
I want to spend more time with my friends.	This weekend, I'm going to save the whole day on Sunday just to hang out with my friends.
I need to work out more and get some exercise in the next few months so I can fit into my clothes for the wedding coming up.	I'm going to make an exercise plan that begins tomorrow morning. At least three days this week, and every week thereafter, I'm going to work out for at least thirty minutes.

Build In Rewards and Punishments

In spite of your best intentions, you are going to need some incentives to stay on course. There must be consequences for failing to follow through on commitments, as well as encouragement when you do what you say you'll do.

Rewards include giving yourself things you enjoy or removing something you don't like. For example, Ty has been trying to reduce his impulsive spending. He made a commitment to stay within a strict budget for a week. His reward for doing so is that he allows himself discretionary spending of $20 on something frivolous. If, however, Ty does not stay within his stated budget, he has promised to confide to his parents that his finances are out of control and accept outside intervention to help him. This would be both humiliating and painful to admit, so much so that he vows he will stay on course to avoid this consequence.

Write It Down

It is always a good idea to hold yourself accountable for what you decide to do. You can do this in a journal or, better yet, on a piece of paper posted on your desk or refrigerator where you have to see it frequently as a reminder. Better still, construct a formal contract stating what you will do, including contingencies (see Table 3.1).

3.2 FOR REFLECTION

Setting Short-Term and Long-Term Goals

In several areas of your life, you might set goals to increase satisfaction, enjoyment, and productivity. These can include (1) improving relationships with people you know (or would like to know better); (2) changing the ways you approach your schoolwork and studying; (3) making lifestyle changes related to your eating, sleep, exercise, and leisure activities; and (4) reducing some self-defeating habits that are interfering with your performance. Think about these four domains as you declare goals that will improve the quality of your life.

Things I will do every day	Things I will do each week
Something I will do in the next year	**Something I vow to do before I die**

People don't often follow through on their goal commitments or stick with the changes for very long. Make a copy of this page, or tear it out of the book, and post it in a prominent place. Talk to others about what you intend to do as a way to increase motivation and the likelihood of following through.

Organizing and Structuring Time

Group Activity

As a class assignment, ask students to write all of their assignment due dates and exam dates in either a planner or a monthly calendar. Ask students to evaluate which weeks will be their busiest. Have the class discuss strategies to help each other get everything completed.

Group Activity to Reduce Stress

Discuss the importance of time scheduling. Emphasize that study time must be scheduled just like work or class period hours. Instruct students to write a time schedule for the following academic week, with a written statement outlining how they determined that this was a realistic amount of time for studying. Ask students to follow this study plan for a week. Students should write in their journal if they committed to this time management plan. How did following the plan help their academic progress and grades in each course?

It is one thing to make plans for the future and quite another to make them a reality. Every day, people entertain fantasies—win the lottery, inherit a fortune, start a business, star in a movie, write a best-selling novel, discover a miracle cure, meet their dream mate, attain an A in class—and most of them never happen. It isn't always a lack of enthusiasm for the dream that cancels its realization, but rather a lack of time management. It isn't enough to have plans for the future if they are not prioritized in such a way that you can accomplish them within your limited time and resources.

Time is a limited commodity. You can't slow it or bank it. You will never have enough of it to do everything you might wish. It will always be a matter of making choices (see Figure 3.1). You had planned to spend a few hours reviewing notes and reading a chapter in your text, but a friend calls with concert tickets. You want to play softball on an intramural team, but the practices conflict with a meeting at work. You want to watch Sunday afternoon football, but you've also got a big test on Monday morning. You want to sign up for a computer technology session, but the times conflict with your class schedule. You need to write a paper for your U.S history class, but you have to drive your child to soccer practice. You have to write a paper for one class, but also find the time to study for another. And oh yeah, your roommate just walked in and is trying to persuade you to go to a party for a little while: "We'll just check it out. Don't worry. You'll be back in an hour."

There will never be enough hours in the day to do everything you want. And you better get used to it because that's the way most people in our culture now live their lives. Furthermore, many important things are outside your control (traffic, weather, technological or mechanical problems, illness, deadlines, and other people), so you are left to manage those things within your power. Most of all, this refers to the attitude you choose, and the commitments and decisions you make, as well as how you use the limited time available to you.

In studies of how first-year college students spend their time, among those who drank alcohol (70 percent of freshmen) only about eight hours per week were devoted to studies, which is less than the amount of time they spent drinking (ten hours) (Outside the Classroom, 2009). When exercising (five hours per week), online activities (four hours), and socializing (three hours) are added to the mix, plus family and work obligations, you can easily see how quickly available time is consumed.

Figure 3.1   Where Time Goes in a Typical Day in the Life of a College Student

Sleeping	7 hours
Watching television	1½ hours
Surfing online	3½ hours
Listening to music	2½ hours
Talking on the phone	2 hours
Sitting in class	3 hours
Eating	2 hours
Working	2 hours
Studying	3 hours
TOTAL	**26½ HOURS!**

Source: Wesch (2008).

It isn't just the number of hours you spend studying that matters (recommended minimum of twenty hours each week), but also the quality of that time spent reviewing material. When you are distracted, diverted, or doing several things at the same time, learning is less likely to stick. Your job is to find or create an environment that is free of distractions and allows you to concentrate fully on what you are doing.

Construct a Schedule

If you don't already have one, you *must* get yourself a daily or weekly calendar to write down your class schedule, appointments, commitments, and when all your assignments are due. It also helps to fill in blocks of time when you will study, plus social activities. It doesn't matter whether you prefer a digital scheduler (PDA), a calendar on your phone, or a weekly planner that you write in, but you have to find a system that works best for you.

Second, you are going to need a running "to do" list of things that must be completed by the end of the day and/or week (see Figure 3.2). This includes assignments, errands, exercise workouts, calls to return, and other tasks. Check off or delete each

Figure 3.2 Example of a To Do List

TASK TO COMPLETE	IMPORTANCE	COMPLETED
Call Mom back and tell her to check on things.	**	X
Call Stephanie and ask about assignment.	*	
Read ~~fifty~~ pages in novel for lit class.	***	
Get some food.	***	X
Buy coffeemaker for room.	*	
Make appt. with librarian to get help on paper.	**	
Stop by bookstore to see if text is in yet.	*	
Study for quiz in Calculus.	***	X
Go to exercise class.	**	X
Tape Emmy Awards.	**	
Download new CD.	*	

item as you complete it. This creates a great sense of accomplishment, even for the little things.

Where Do You Waste Time?

For Community College Students

Commuter and nontraditional students' schedules will vary greatly from this example with many more hours dedicated to working and/or family time.

If you feel as if you don't have enough time to complete everything you want to during the day, it helps to get a handle on exactly what you do with your time from the moment you wake up until the moment you go to sleep. You can keep track of your time in a typical day by recording what you are doing within every fifteen-minute segment. Go online to find a blank schedule form to get you started.

Trent took the time (unfortunately while in class) to record everything he did from the time he awoke until arriving in class. Because he had been puzzled as to why he never seemed to have time to get things done, he decided to try this experiment. After examining the various time segments, he noticed that activities that should have taken just a few minutes (getting dressed, cleaning his room, and reviewing his notes for class) ended up

3.3 FOR REFLECTION

Wasting Time

The concept of "wasting" time is one of personal judgment: what *you* consider time that was frittered away doing things that were not especially important or enjoyable. For example, watching the news to get an idea of what is going on in the world, a documentary that is educational, or a favorite weekly show can be time well spent. But sitting mindlessly in front of the screen watching reruns for hours probably doesn't qualify.

Make your own determination of what things you do, or don't do, that habitually waste time. If you aren't sure what they might be, do your own time analysis of fifteen-minute segments during a typical day.

List the biggest culprits below:

1. _____

_____

2. _____

_____

3. _____

_____

4. _____

_____

5. _____

_____

What adjustments are you prepared to make to eliminate some of these time wasters and create more opportunities to do the things that matter most?

_____

_____

_____

Wasting Time through Worry

Needless worry and concern over things you can't control accounts for a lot of wasted time. You may spend time obsessing constantly about an upcoming exam, reliving previous conversations that bother you, wallowing in past events you wish you could change, and rehearsing things you could have said or done differently. Yet none of these efforts can change what already happened. There is a big difference between worrying about things you can't control and planning strategically for upcoming tests, assignments, and events that can be prepared for effectively.

What are some things that you have spent time worrying and obsessing about that are beyond your control?

_____

_____

Instead of worrying about matters that you can't change, consider several alternative ways that you can channel your energy into preparing better for the challenges you face:

1. Pay close attention to your particular style of worrying. What do you most frequently say to yourself inside your head? Examine carefully and logically the extent to which you are distorting or exaggerating the situation.

2. Sort out what is within your power to change and what is not. For instance, no matter how annoying and frustrating it might be, generally you can't control other people's behavior, nor can you do much about the weather, the economy, or bureaucratic rules. You can, however, change your attitude and responses to such things.

3. Ask yourself what you are "enjoying" as a result of fruitless worry (versus constructive planning). Oftentimes, it can be a distraction or give you a false sense of power that worrying about something may somehow prevent it from happening.

4. Take specific actions to prepare for the anticipated event, then move on to something else that feels productive or fun.

5. Consider making adjustments in the way you schedule your time to free up more opportunities to get the tasks done that most concern you.

taking much longer because he would do them while watching television or messing around with his music playlists. His next step, much harder, is to exercise the restraint to change those patterns.

Time is wasted for a number of reasons, but mostly because it isn't valued. You often act as if you have all the time in the world, as if it is unlimited. What you don't do today, you can always do tomorrow. And if it doesn't get done, so what? It probably wasn't that important in the first place.

Time is most often wasted because students are disorganized and allow themselves to become distracted by interruptions and annoyances. Other culprits include spending excessive time on the phone, instant messaging, going online, playing video games, or watching television. Playing with Facebook, MySpace, and other networking sites may not feel like a waste of time, but such activities can easily become addictive and excessive. Partying or sleeping too much can also eat up hours of discretionary time.

Time isn't squandered if you are truly enjoying what you are doing, it isn't done to excess, and it doesn't interfere with being productive. Ultimately, *you* are the one who has to make choices about what is worthwhile and what is not. For instance, daydreaming is not necessarily a "waste" of time (unless excessive) since it often leads

Teaching Tip

Ask students to identify their biggest time wasters. How do they think they can control them? Assign them to attack one time waster they would like to reduce. Have them spend the week keeping track of their success in reducing time spent on that activity, and then report back to the class.

to creativity, mental rehearsal, problem solving, stress reduction, and preparation for challenges you will face (Glausiusz, 2009).

Do One Thing at a Time

What do you think is the effect of juggling multiple tasks at the same time? You are catching up on a reading assignment with your book perched on your lap and your earphones playing music. A television is on in the background. You look up for a moment to check out somebody walking by. Eyes back to the book. Your phone rings, so with the best of intentions you answer and tell the friend you'll call back later. Ping. An instant message is on your computer sitting in front of you. That reminds you to check your e-mail, and while you're at it you might as well log on to Facebook to see what's happening. Oh yeah: Back to your reading. Then a text message captures your attention—an invitation to join some friends. But you're determined to finish your work. You turn a page of the book, but then realize you didn't really digest the page you'd been staring at for the previous ten minutes.

Between text messages, instant messages, e-mail, phone calls, web surfing, and the constant accessibility of computers, BlackBerries, iPhones, iPads, Kindles, and hand-held devices, life has become a juggling act in which you attend to three, four, even five different things at the same time, giving none of them more than partial attention. Nowadays, the average worker spends eleven minutes on any given task before facing an interruption (Mark, Gudith, and Klocke, 2008). Then it takes about the same amount of time to get back to the task with focused concentration. The consequences of all these interruptions and multitasking are an overload of information, overstimulation, impaired concentration, and significantly increased stress. People have almost no time any longer for leisurely, reflective, or creative thinking (Bailey, 2009). In addition, so-called multitasking, in which you think you are accomplishing several things simultaneously, is really just rapidly switching back and forth between activities, completing none of them with the focus and attention they deserve (Morioka, 2009).

When was the last time you just sat quietly and did absolutely *nothing*? No television, music, phone, or computer? When is the last time you studied for an hour, even a half hour, with not a single interruption or distraction?

Alain Shroder/Jupiter Images

© Cengage Learning

VIEW IT

Organizing Time

Students talk about how much they benefited from using structured planners and a "to do list" to stay on top of all their assignments, meet deadlines, and still allow time for fun. (www.cengagebrain.com)

Group Activity to Reduce Stress

Try it! Assign students to do absolutely *nothing* for ten minutes tonight. This means sitting in a dark room or in a private place outside, with no music, phone, distractions, or interruptions. Their only job is to sit there and do nothing. Ask them to report back to small groups about their experiences and realizations. What was most challenging about the assignment? What did they enjoy most? How can they bring more focused downtime into their lives to reduce stress and clear their minds?

Note the difference between "wasting" time, that is, engaging in activities that don't feel all that satisfying or enjoyable (especially when important tasks need to be completed), and taking time out to relax and replenish your energy.

Alison:
Scheduling Time

" Oh, college was a tough adjustment for me because I've been out of school for so many years, one of those so-called returning students, which just means I'm old. I was trying to figure out what classes I needed. I didn't have any friends on campus, and I still had to deal with work and my family. The classes are totally different from what I remember from high school. And you go in with all these expectations, like it's supposed to be great for you and you're finally learning what you want to learn, but it's not like that right away. It's a lot of work and you have to take some of those same boring classes you took in high school, like math and writing, except now they are even tougher.

Nobody ever tells you what college is really like, so you go in thinking it will be this magical, fun thing, but it's tough. I had trouble managing everything I had to do without always falling behind in everything. It took me a while, but once I got my routine down, things got easier. It's all a matter of realizing that you'll need to do the work to get through it and figuring out how you're going to get the work done. I scheduled my studying times and I went to study groups before midterms and finals. I found that it helped me a lot if I did it this way, otherwise I got distracted by other stuff and my schoolwork never got done.

Managing your time doesn't refer to how long you spend on a task, but rather how productively you use that time. As challenging as it might be, the single most important strategy for making the most of limited time is to devote more focused concentration on one thing at a time. You are far better off spending even fifteen minutes reviewing a chapter in silence and solitude than you are "reading" for an hour with constant and multiple interruptions.

Note: If while reading these words you are engaged in multiple tasks at the same time, try a simple experiment. For ten minutes, move away from a computer, television, or other visual and sound distractions. Turn off your phone—and don't just put it on "vibrate," you'll hear it buzz. Find a quiet place where you are sure not to be interrupted during these few minutes while you read. Compare the quality of your concentration and retention of the material to when you were simultaneously doing so many things at the same time. With the productive time you just spent, *now* you can go back to something else that is more enjoyable.

Classroom Discussion
Open it up: What are the best ways you have found to reduce interruptions as you study?

Procrastination

This subject must be important—it gets its own section, even if you think it is more of the same. Procrastination can be defined as avoiding decisions or putting off tasks to the point that it becomes detrimental to your welfare and personal effectiveness. It leads to bigger and bigger problems over time, falling further behind, and slipping into a chronic pattern of following Mark Twain's advice: "Never put off till tomorrow what you can do the day after tomorrow."

Among all the reasons for students failing to live up to commitments or complete declared goals, procrastination is at the top of the list. Rather than a single choice to avoid a task, over time it becomes a pattern of living, a way of conducting your business. Procrastination begins by avoiding something that doesn't seem all that interesting or may require too much effort; eventually, it becomes a way of life that is self-reinforcing. In most cases, procrastination results from impulsive decisions to put off tasks that don't need to be done for a long time and focus instead on things that immediately attract your attention—but may not accomplish your goals.

Group Activity
Ask small groups to brainstorm a list of when procrastination is necessary. (Hint: Almost never. This is a trick question.) Yet ... ask them to find exceptions to this statement: occasional situations when procrastination can provide reflective time; postpone or eliminate tasks that may not, in fact, be useful; or bring attention to unresolved issues.

The Payoffs of Procrastination

Classroom Discussion

Open it up: Have you ever thought of procrastination as having payoffs? What payoffs do you get from procrastination? How might the idea of "benefits" help you to better understand other behaviors which get you in trouble?

Procrastination, like many habits in life, is difficult to change once it becomes entrenched and comfortable. Putting things off, even with the apparent negative side effects, actually presents some advantages. Unless you understand what it is you most "enjoy" from this seemingly bad habit, you won't have much success changing it.

It is more than a little interesting to understand why people neglect to do things that they *say* are really important to them.

- **I really wanted to get it done, but I guess I just forgot.** How do you forget something that you really want to do?

- **I meant to do it, but I got distracted.** This is another way of saying that the distraction was seen as more important.

- **I don't know why I didn't do it. I just couldn't find the time.** It's not difficult to "find" time for things that mean the most.

Each of these statements, or any other possible excuses for procrastination, could mask underlying reasons besides plain laziness. In other words, whenever you engage in self-defeating or self-sabotaging behavior (like chronic procrastination), you often gain some hidden benefit. These *secondary gains*, or disguised advantages, continue to reinforce even obviously destructive behaviors precisely because they are useful in some way (see For Reflection 3.4).

3.4 FOR REFLECTION

Secondary Gains of Procrastination

Tammy is on academic probation after her first semester in college. Although she is a capable student with a successful academic track record, her grades were marginal because she turned in so many assignments late.

"I just don't know what happened, but I just kept putting things off until it was too late. I've never been like this before, but now I just can't seem to get things done on time no matter what I try. I keep putting them off, then thinking I'd get to it eventually, but something always seemed to come up, and I'd be late again. I hate this. I really do. But I don't know why I do it."

Let's assume that although Tammy says she doesn't like procrastinating, she actually benefits from the behavior. What are some of the secondary gains that could accrue to someone like Tammy who procrastinates consistently?

_____

_____

_____

_____

_____

Possible answers are listed at the end of this chapter.

Most people who procrastinate, and continue to do so over time, are somehow "rewarded" for this behavior even though they may appear to suffer consequences such as lower grades. You may find status and power associated with doing things on your own terms, rather than those dictated by others. Also, in the words of one student, "It makes things exciting to get things done at the last minute. I kind of like the pressure."

Understanding the true motivation behind your procrastination is an important step in changing the pattern. You can make all the resolutions you want, learn all the strategies in the world, and tell everyone you know that you intend to be different, but nothing much will change as long as you enjoy the secondary gains from the behavior. Why change something that is working for you, even if it has a few annoying side effects?

The reason to do so is that eventually habitual procrastination is going to catch up with you, if it hasn't already. In the business or professional world, you can't ask your supervisor for an extension and expect that this will be routinely accepted. You must learn to deliver exactly what you promise, exactly when you say you will do it. Otherwise, you lose credibility and respect.

Group Activity

Ask students to journal concerning their procrastination habits. Have them make a list of things they didn't accomplish because of procrastination. This list can include academic and personal items. Ask students to develop a three-column chart. In the first column, list the incident of procrastination. In the second column, list the benefits that they received from procrastinating. In the third column, list the repercussions of the procrastination. Students should write a journal entry discussing this chart and any insights they might have gained on their procrastinating behavior.

3.5 FOR REFLECTION

Conquering Procrastination One Step at a Time

Identify a task, assignment, job, or unfinished business that you have been avoiding for some time, creating unnecessary stress in your life. This is something that you really want to get done and out of your life, but for some reason you haven't been able to muster the time, motivation, or commitment to get it done. Meanwhile, you continue to think about it more than you'd like.

_____

_____

_____

_____

What are some of the secondary gains you enjoy from this procrastination that might be keeping you from completing this? Consult some of the answers listed at the end of the chapter for For Reflection 3.4.

_____

_____

_____

_____

What do you resolve to do differently to get this one thing out of your hair?

_____

_____

_____

_____

Addiction to opium and impulsivity led poet Samuel Coleridge to continually frustrate most of the people in his life. Most of his famous poems, including "Kubla Kahn" and "The Rime of the Ancient Mariner," were never completed. Much of his other work ended up as fragments, making him one of the most accomplished procrastinators in history. Coleridge manifested many of the symptoms that afflict chronic procrastinators: (1) low self-confidence, (2) fear of failure, (3) impulsivity, and (4) a propensity toward boredom.

© Bettmann/CORBIS

Overcoming Inertia

Procrastination is usually situation specific. Almost nobody puts off tasks in *every* aspect of their lives, just those that they resent, dread, or feel ambivalent about. Let's say that you are ready to do something about some facet of your life in which you tend toward avoidance. Here are some things you can do.

● **Resist temptations.** An endless assortment of entertaining options may seem far more interesting than taking care of business. Developing willpower and persistence takes practice. You must learn how to postpone instant gratification to complete priority tasks first.

● **Remind yourself of the secondary gains you get from staying the same.** One way to ruin your enjoyment of these benefits is to make them more explicit. Getting away with a self-defeating cycle is harder once you realize what you are doing.

● **Use your "to do" lists and scheduler to plan for deadlines.** The value of scheduling your time on a daily, weekly, monthly, and semester-long basis is that you won't get caught by surprise.

● **Reduce distractions.** Remaining focused on a task is more difficult when you are constantly interrupted. Isolate yourself from the phone, e-mail, and other intrusions until after you have completed your work.

● **Prioritize what is most important.** The worst procrastinator still gets some things done, usually those that have value. Get in the habit of finishing your most dreaded chores and tasks before you allow yourself to do the things you most want to do.

● **Confront the boredom.** People resist doing things they find boring or uninteresting. If you are putting off a task because it is uninteresting to you, find a way to make it more exciting.

● **Reframe the task.** If you are avoiding something because it seems distasteful, either decide not to do it and free yourself of the obligation, or else change your attitude about it so you can find some redeeming value.

● **Break down the task into chunks.** Tasks that seem overwhelming (such as term papers and final exams) can be broken down into more manageable units.

● **Make a public announcement.** Commit yourself to others about your intentions, both to help yourself be accountable and to give fair warning that you don't want interruptions or distractions.

● **Confront your perfectionism.** One of the things that keeps some people back is not being willing to let something go because it is not good enough. While it is admirable to hold high expectations for yourself, you will never be able to meet all of your goals, especially some that may not be reasonable. You have to do the best job you possibly can, but *within the designated time limits.*

- **Think about all the time and energy that you waste.** If you added up all the time you spend (1) thinking about doing something, (2) making excuses for why you don't do it, (3) making promises and resolutions you don't keep, and (4) feeling guilt and remorse for your lapses, you could easily have finished everything on your plate and more.

- **Examine the context for avoidance.** Does it occur in all situations, or just those of a specific variety? Do you manage to get many things done on time, except in a few areas? What does that tell you? Perhaps you are avoiding something because it really isn't right for you.

- **Pay attention to the messages you are getting.** Procrastination represents reluctance. Treat that as feedback. If you have trouble completing assignments in one particular class, maybe that class is not right for you. If you can't manage to finish *any* of your assignments on time, maybe you don't really want to be in college at this time.

- **Hold yourself accountable.** You can't let yourself get away with irresponsibility. Your integrity is at stake. When you promise to do something, or sign a contract (which enrolling in a class involves), you must learn to follow through if you are ever going to be successful. Use rewards to reinforce completed tasks, but also have the courage to administer punishments (taking away something you like) when you don't complete commitments.

- **See a counselor.** If your procrastination is chronic and pervasive in your life, and you feel powerless to change the pattern, it's time to ask for help. The alternative is not only getting bad grades, or even flunking out, but also cementing bad habits that will follow you throughout your career.

SUMMARY

Balance isn't something you find or discover but rather something you create and initiate. Work will take over your life, and frankly, as important as school is, it isn't as important as other things like your health, friendships, and family.

With everything already said about making and scheduling time to get your studies and assignments done, and avoiding procrastination, please remember that you also need diversity in your life or you will burn out before your first year is over.

Having fun is, and should be, a major priority. Spending time with friends and those you love is absolutely imperative. Laughing, playing, and socializing are critical pieces of your college experience. You can enjoy them all that much more when your work is completed and the good times feel like a reward for a job well done.

QUESTIONS FOR REVIEW AND FURTHER EXPLORATION

1. One point made in the chapter is that effective goals should be realistic, specific, and meaningful. What else is critical to increase the probability of completing them?

2. What is an example in which you tried to reach a goal you thought was important but ultimately failed? Which factors mentioned in the chapter most contributed to this disappointment?

3. Why would you deliberately try to have a setback or relapse after you've already made significant progress?

4. It was mentioned that procrastination can have certain benefits that make it difficult to change this behavior. Think of an example in your own life in which you "enjoyed" putting off a certain task because of the sense of drama it created, even though you might have paid a price for the neglect.

5. How do you determine whether your time is "wasted" or not?

6. What does it mean that anything really worth doing is usually difficult?

7. What are the ways that *you* most consistently waste time and avoid taking care of business?

ANSWERS TO FOR REFLECTION 3.4

Payoffs for procrastinating include:

- You avoid perceived or anticipated failure for as long as possible, postponing what you believe is inevitable disappointment.

- You have an excuse for not performing well: "Of course I could have done better if I'd really tried."

- You get sympathy and pity from others.

- You get others to bail you out.

- You can avoid doing things that you don't want to do.

- You get the thrill, excitement, and drama of working under pressure.

- You get to negotiate for extensions, enjoying attention and special privileges.

- You fail on your own terms, rather than on someone else's.

- With success comes additional responsibility, so you lower other people's expectations for you.

- You can thumb your nose at authority and act out to express your resentment or anger.

- You get to drive others crazy who seem more bothered by your behavior than you are.

- You can slow down the pace of something that you feel ambivalent about completing.

- You can give yourself more time to complete a task closer to your exacting, perfectionist standards.

- You can avoid doing other things you don't want to do because you can say that you are working under a nonnegotiable deadline.

- By defining yourself as a procrastinator, you can stay stuck and don't have to be responsible.

Go to www.cengagebrain.com for an online quiz that will test your understanding of the chapter content.

Striving for Excellence in the Classroom

KEY QUESTIONS

▶ What is most likely to lead to success and satisfaction in college?

▶ How can you best prepare for class?

▶ What is the difference between content and process in classes?

▶ What do instructors find most annoying about student behavior in class?

▶ What do students tend to dislike most about their instructors?

▶ How can you negotiate relationships with instructors you find difficult?

▶ Why is it so important to initiate informal contacts with instructors and what are ways you can do that effectively?

▶ What is the best way to process disappointing feedback?

▶ What is the difference between hearing and listening?

▶ What are ways you can listen more actively and effectively?

▶ Why is note taking so important, not only for academic success but also in the professional and business worlds?

Group Activity

To introduce this chapter's content, conduct a stand-up/sit-down or hand-raising exercise to poll the class on the following statements: "I have spoken in every class this semester," "I have read every word of all the syllabi for all my classes," and "I have visited with at least one of my instructors outside of class this semester."

There are things you can control—and things you can't. You have set reasonable and realistic goals for yourself this semester and academic year. You have done your best to plan and schedule your time to maximize productivity (and fun). Presumably you have also done your best to pick classes that not only fit your program but also reflect informed guidance from "experts" such as your academic advisor, data on instructor ratings, and recommendations from friends whose judgment you trust. Nevertheless, once you have decided to take a class—and stick with it after realizing exactly what you are in for—you should get the most from the experience.

This chapter covers several important skills (and they *are* skills that you learn and practice) to perform well in your classes, as well as enjoy the experience. These include listening attentively, taking notes on what you hear and observe, connecting with classmates and the instructor to clarify issues, responding actively in class, and generally making a positive impression in the college setting.

PHOTO: Andersen Ross/Jupiter Images

Strategies for the Classroom

Group Activity

As a warm-up for class, ask the students to compare differences in classroom behavior and expectations between high school and college. Ask them to talk about things they preferred in high school and things they like better at college.

These days, "classroom" is defined broadly since courses are structured in such a way that they can be offered in traditional on-campus settings, distance-learning formats, or a combination of the two. Your classroom experience might take place one, two, or three times each week, only at the beginning or end of the semester, at remote sites without the instructor physically present, or perhaps only via the Internet. Nevertheless, the skills and strategies presented in this chapter are easily adapted to the particular format that applies to your schedule.

Preparing for Class

You want to make sure you have necessary supplies in your book bag or backpack. Bring your books until your instructor tells you otherwise (even though they are heavy). You'll need at least two pens (inevitably one will stop working) and something you intend to write on, which could be looseleaf paper you intend to keep in binders, a notebook, or a laptop computer.

You will have read the assigned text material or outside readings (more on that in Chapter 5). You reviewed your notes from the previous classes. You checked out any online material that the instructor suggested you review. And you looked over the syllabus to make sure you have completed any assignments that are due.

Don't neglect to think about what you're going to wear. You want to strike the right balance—something casual and appropriate for the setting, but also an image that conveys who you are.

Teaching Tip

Encourage students to purchase a student planner. Ask them to do a quick review of all course syllabi and to make note of test dates, assignment due dates, and project dates for each course for the entire semester. Ask students to note the related textbook chapter(s) being discussed each week. They should also note the length of the chapters and give a personal estimation of the time required to read them. Encourage students to use this information to make realistic study plans for each week.

Don't Skip Class

One of the most dramatic differences between high school and college is that you are pretty much left on your own to attend classes as you like. If you are living in the residence halls, nobody will wake you up and bug you with annoying questions like "Aren't you supposed to be somewhere?" If you are living off campus with roommates,

Missing classes and failure to follow directions on the syllabus are the most common reasons why students do poorly in college. Although it is possible to get a good grade without attending class regularly, this means you have chosen not to learn much from the experience.

Image Source/Jupiter Images

or even if you are living at home with your family, no one is likely to monitor your schedule that closely. That's the good news. The bad news is that with all this freedom, when the alarm rings you may feel tempted to turn over and fall back to sleep instead of going to class. If you are living at home, there are even more temptations and reasons to skip class—a family member is sick, there are chores to do, there was an accident on the freeway, you are having car trouble, you need to work extra hours, or something along those lines.

You will meet people who brag that they hardly ever go to class and still manage to get good grades. In certain rare situations, that may indeed be possible—if the only objective is to get credit for a course and there is no interest in learning much of anything.

Study the Syllabus Very Carefully

How many times have you turned in assignments or papers, missed quizzes, or didn't prepare properly for exams because you didn't read the instructions carefully enough on the course syllabus? There is a reason why the instructor took the time to write down everything you need to know about the content and structure of the class, the requirements, and all the details regarding schedule, readings, and assignments.

A syllabus not only is an outline for what to expect, but also holds within it information about what the instructor values most. Sometimes this will be stated clearly ("The most important goal of this class is …"), but more often you may need to figure this out by reading between the lines. Instructors may tell you exactly how they intend to evaluate your performance and what is weighted most in the assignments. They may tell you which readings are most important. In some cases, they may tell you exactly what you need to do to earn a particular grade. Yet every semester instructors write over and over on the assignments, "Please review the syllabus."

A syllabus is a kind of contract between you and the instructor, stating what the instructor will do, what you will do, and how you will both be held accountable. It is usually constructed as follows:

Instructor information. You will see not only the location of the instructor's office and contact information, but also office hours. These are the times that you can always find the instructor around, although it is likely that other appointments can be scheduled if those times don't work for you.

Overview. Instructors often write a brief introduction to the course, talking about their intentions and goals, as well as what they see as most significant. Here you can find the best evidence for what the course is really about. There may be ten sections of the same class, all with identical objectives and assignments, but each instructor takes a different approach and has a different teaching style.

Textbooks. Listed are *required texts* that everyone must read and *supplementary readings* that are designed to enhance understanding. Think of the latter as extra credit. If you want to study some topic in more depth, or if you want your assignments and papers to reflect more advanced content, then the additional readings are useful. Even though textbooks can often be incredibly expensive, it is highly advisable that you purchase your own copies of the basic text(s).

Course objectives. These state the goals of the course and what you will learn. They are often written in language that satisfies accreditation agencies so you have to sort through them to find what is relevant to you. Often the goals will include (1) *factual knowledge* of the discipline (information, basic concepts, and terms—things that can be tested on multiple-choice exams), (2) *conceptual knowledge* that covers the major theories and approaches of the subject matter (often evaluated through essay exams), and (3) *applied knowledge* that helps you to solve problems or examine case examples (learned through laboratory assignments, field studies, and writing papers).

Classroom Discussion

Open it up: Where do you keep your syllabi for your classes? Has anyone misplaced or thrown away a syllabus? If you are a second-semester or second-year student, what do you have to say about the importance of a syllabus?

Group Activity

Give small groups a syllabus from a class they may take in the future or ask them to pull out a syllabus from a class they are taking currently. Ask them to find all of the bulleted items on this page and the next, write the answers, and share any surprises with the entire class.

Marylee:
Check the Syllabus

" First-semester students often have these huge classes—they're like cities they're so big. The professor can't even see me where I sit much less know if I'm there or not. And they don't tell you stuff like they do in high school about when things are due. It is so important to read the class syllabus every week and see what assignments and readings we're supposed to get done. I showed up to class and there was a reaction paper due and I had no clue about that. I was so mad at the teacher for not reminding us, but it was my fault for not checking. It's going to kill my grade probably but I hope I learned a lesson.

Assignments. Read this section carefully. *Very* carefully. Follow the instructions to the letter in completing the assignments. Pay close attention to the due dates because turning in assignments even one day late can lower your grade. Assignments take many different forms—not only quizzes, exams, and papers but also group projects, homework, library research, journals, class presentations, class exercises, field research, laboratory work, experiments, case studies, and class participation.

Evaluation criteria. These spell out how your final grade will be calculated. Grading criteria for individual assignments may also be defined. Some instructors use a system of points in which each exercise, quiz, test, or paper is worth a certain number of points that can be added up to determine your final grade.

Attendance policy. How many classes can you miss before it affects your grade? How many minutes can you arrive late or leave early and not have it count as an absence? Are late assignments accepted, and if so, how is your grade affected?

Classroom Discussion
Open it up: What are the attendance policies in your current classes? What is the policy in this class?

Academic integrity. This states the university policy about plagiarism, cheating, or otherwise not behaving in an ethical manner.

Contract. Some syllabi will have a list of rules for everyone to abide by, including items related to harassment, civility, students with disabilities, and misconduct. There will also be explanations for last dates to drop a class, what qualifies for an "Incomplete," and how makeup work can be completed.

Class behavior. This refers to school or instructor policies about food or drink in class, dress codes, computer use, and turning off cell phones.

Class schedule. The schedule lists the dates, topics, and assigned reading for each class session.

Teaching Tip
Encourage students to make an appointment to visit each course professor during the first three weeks of each semester. The main objective of the visit should be to develop a connection: to help the professor get to know and remember the student as a person, and to help the student humanize the professor. If students seem reluctant, brainstorm reasons they might use for this appointment (clarify an assignment, volunteer to do research, question a point raised in class, share an idea). Discuss techniques for determining office hours and requesting a specific appointment time. Role-play with students how to use the appointment to introduce themselves to the professor and help the professor understand their individual background and needs.

Reading Your Instructors

There are many ways to classify instructors—as good or bad, easy or hard, boring or interesting, for example. There are those you like and those you don't. Apart from their personalities, they have different teaching styles that reflect their academic discipline, temperament, and values. An instructor who teaches anatomy is going to approach things differently than one who teaches acting or social work. Even within the same field, there are tremendous differences in how people teach. And it is your job to figure out, as soon as possible, exactly who you are dealing with, what is valued most, and what you are expected to do.

Just as your instructors are sizing you up to see what you're made of, you need to do the same with them. This isn't just a matter of figuring out what they want and giving it to them—that's more about seeking approval than it is about learning. Adjusting your learning style to fit the unique demands of each class and instructor teaches you exactly the same strategy that will help you succeed in any job with multiple supervisors.

It is often difficult to generalize, but you can assume that those who teach math and hard sciences will employ different teaching methods and styles than those in the performing arts. Likewise, those who teach history may go about classroom instruction differently than those who teach nursing or education or business. Still, even with all this variation in subject matter, you can read your instructors with regard to several traits.

Content versus process. Some instructors believe that the most important aspect of learning is to master the content of the class—the facts, theories, concepts, and research—while others see significant learning taking place on a more interpersonal level. The former would be inclined to lecture, while the latter would lead discussions and structure small group work.

Lecture versus discussion. Most classes can be organized according to whether they are a lecture or seminar. Some instructors like to talk and will easily fill every available minute; others prefer class interaction and will do things to stimulate discussion. Depending on how many students are in the class, the layout of the room (auditorium versus movable desks or chairs), and how the instructor responds to interruptions and comments, you can easily deduce what type you are dealing with. Of course, some classes include both components, which is probably ideal.

Dramatic versus low key. Some instructors are naturally entertaining. They see teaching as a type of performance, recognizing that unless they can command and maintain your attention, you aren't going to learn much. They try to be unpredictable, interject humor whenever possible, and keep you on your toes with stimulating stories and anecdotes. Others have a "softer" style, one that is more direct and stable, and also easier to count on.

Flexible versus firm. Some instructors have rather strong opinions about matters, whether regarding issues in their field or the "proper" way to complete assignments. Others thrive on different ways of doing things, are open to ideas that directly conflict with their own, and welcome such differences of opinion. At times, each of these styles can be frustrating for students who might wish for more or less structure.

Classroom Discussion

After reading the section Reading Your Instructors, open it up: Describe some of the different types of instructors you currently have. Which types do you like best? (Be sure to point out the differences of opinion found in your classroom.)

Somos/Veer/Jupiter Images

Instructors have very different styles. Some, like the one pictured here, are wildly enthusiastic and dramatic in their presentations. They see teaching as a performance and do their best to entertain you while you're learning. Others may be soft-spoken and low-key, inclined to a more straightforward lecturing style, or prefer a lot of interaction in class. Regardless of the subject matter, it will be one of your most important challenges to adapt to the different approaches of each instructor, valuing what each has to offer in a unique way.

Reach Out to Classmates

As mentioned in Chapter 1, there is a myth that most learning occurs unidirectionally, from instructor to student. In fact, it is through discussions and informal conversations with classmates, friends, and family that you truly begin to integrate what you are learning.

It is over coffee, in the student lounge, during breaks, and even at parties and social functions that you really make sense of what you are learning in classes. This is especially true for commuting students who profit most from interactions that keep them connected to campus life and help them build a sense of community. During these conversations, you are explaining things in your own words, translating concepts into ideas that are personally meaningful, and sharing different perceptions of what you hear and understand. You are also building friendships based on common struggles.

Apart from these informal conversations, you would also be wise to link up with several different people in every class who can share resources with you. They can cover for you during that rare instance when you miss class. You can form study groups together. Just as importantly, they help to make the impersonal classroom feel like more of a learning community. You walk in the room and feel a sense of comfort over time, not only because the environment becomes more familiar but also because you have built a circle of friends.

You are the one who must reach out to classmates. If you expect others to take the first step, you could be in for a long wait. Accept the reality that not everyone you approach is going to be responsive or interested. If they aren't interested in hanging out with you, this is not a rejection but merely a choice. There could be a multitude of reasons that have nothing to do with you. But keep trying to reach out to classmates until you find at least a few others with whom you can collaborate, if not socialize.

Sit toward the Front

This is a tough one. Many students want to become invisible. They take a seat in the back and keep their heads down. Indeed, if you don't want to be noticed, sit as far away from the instructor as you can. Arrive on time. Look attentive (but not *too* attentive because it might encourage an invitation to speak). All this has the distinct advantage of minimizing risk so you are less likely to be called on. But is that what you really want—to be ignored and treated as if you don't exist?

Sitting in the front of the room, no matter how self-conscious this might make you feel, keeps you more actively engaged in what is going on. The closer you are to the front, the more visual cues are available, such as outlines, diagrams, equations, or photos that might be projected or written. The more you are able to maintain eye contact with the instructor, the easier it will be to remain involved and attentive.

Nadya:
Sitting in the Back

" So, there was this girl in one of my classes, she was a real pain. She was always talking and being loud and stuff like that. I like sitting in the back of the class, you know, with my back against the wall. She was sitting in the back, too. And she wouldn't shut up. The teacher totally ignored the people back there and he only paid attention to the people in front. You know, the smart kids.

I have a really hard time paying attention in class, especially if the class is kinda boring. Seriously, I have a pretty hard time concentrating and this girl was always, like, chatting and asking stupid questions. The worse thing is that the teacher didn't care, so this went on and on. Then, one day I decided that I needed to move if I wanted to learn anything in that class. I sat closer to the front of the room and it really helped me. I was able to pay attention because I didn't have anyone distracting me. Now I always sit close to the front row because none of the chatty people hang out there.

Whisson/Jordan/Jupiter Images

Sit in the back of the room, or next to a group of friends, at your peril. As comforting as it may seem to create your own sense of private space in the classroom, surrounded by those you trust, it is much easier to become distracted and lose much of what is going on. Physical distance from the instructor also creates a barrier.

Even if you aren't going to take this advice to sit near the front, never, *ever* sit in the back few rows. Not only is it more difficult to hear and see what is going on, but also there are far greater temptations to distract you. You also give the impression to your instructor that you may not be a serious student.

Taking Online Classes

You should still sit "in the front," figuratively speaking, when taking online classes. This means having a "presence" in the online group discussions, blogs, or postings, or at actual class meetings in remote sites. When you are not physically present in the room with the instructor and your classmates, it is even more critical to adopt active-learning strategies since there are even greater distractions. At the same time you are listening to a podcast, you could be bathing your children (or yourself). While watching streaming video, you could be sitting in your pajamas, talking on the phone, listening to music, and/or glancing at the television. A party could be raging in your room while you are sending e-mails. So it takes greater discipline to remain focused.

Some students (and instructors) absolutely love online courses and distance learning because they appreciate the greater flexibility and opportunity to work at their own pace, at times of their choosing, and at convenient locations. They avoid parking and traffic congestion, avoid commuting time, and save money on gas. Learning can be enhanced through individual concentration when students are able and willing to create a study environment free of distractions (such as family, friends, and work responsibilities) and intrusions (like phone calls, e-mail, and interruptions).

On the other hand (and you knew there would be another hand), distance learning can be an isolating and lonely experience. You don't usually receive feedback as quickly as you do when you are in the same room with people. You don't have the kind of intimate, face-to-face contact that often occurs in classrooms, and especially in the informal gatherings that occur before and afterward. As such, oral communication skills are often neglected in favor of written work that can become the sole basis for evaluation.

Teaching Tip

Students enrolled in online courses through a college or university close to their home or dorm should be encouraged to make an appointment to visit the attending professor for the course. Emphasize that building a relationship with online professors is just as important as building a relationship with traditional-delivery professors. If it is impossible for students to physically visit with their professors, suggest that they e-mail or Skype with the professor to share information about themselves as a learner, discuss their individual needs, and build a good rapport.

Asking Questions in Class

Every instructor will request, if not beg, you to ask questions in class. Such behavior demonstrates interest and curiosity, and often leads things in new directions that everyone may find stimulating. However, there are few things that teachers (and other classmates) find more annoying than questions that are self-indulgent, distracting, or incoherent (see Table 4.1 for other things that instructors find most annoying). *Classroom civility* is also an important concept to keep in mind, meaning that you demonstrate respect, sensitivity, and caring in the ways you interact with others, including questions that you ask.

Getting Over Your Fears

Because you don't wish to appear annoying or stupid, it is natural to feel a degree of reluctance to ask publicly about what you don't understand. The assumption is often that everyone else in the room understands what is happening—except *you*. Interestingly, this is often not the case. You can easily test this by noticing how grateful you feel when someone in class asks a question that you were thinking of as well.

For Community College Students
On a community college campus where older, nontraditional students are often taking classes, remind traditionally aged students not to assume that older students will do all the talking.

Group Activity
As a counterbalance to this list of the most annoying behaviors, ask groups to brainstorm five to seven things they think *impress* instructors the most.

Classroom Discussion
Open it up: What do you personally find annoying about your instructors? What is most annoying about your fellow students within the classroom? What are some ways you might be able to help yourself deal with these annoyances?

Teaching Tip
Assign students to contact their instructors in person or by e-mail to learn what they find most annoying about their students. Discuss any differences found between their answers and those found in the table.

TABLE 4.1

What Many Instructors Find Most Annoying

▶ Showing up late for class. This is not only rude and disruptive but also displays a lack of consideration for others.

▶ Leaving class early. Regardless of what you have planned that you believe is more important, this behavior communicates you don't value the class.

▶ Sleeping, yawning, repeatedly looking at your watch, or otherwise appearing to be less than absolutely captivated by what is going on.

▶ Listening to music, reading a magazine or paper, shopping online, instant messaging, or otherwise communicating that you are not fully present.

▶ Ringing cell phones. No excuses make up for the lapse of forgetting to turn off your phone.

▶ Answering the ringing cell phone and saying you'll call back later.

▶ Asking questions that are not related to the present focus and that distract from where the instructor was heading.

▶ Asking a question or making a comment that is rambling and attention seeking.

▶ Asking any of the following questions: "Will this be on the test?" "Do we have to read the whole chapter?" or "Can I turn in my paper late?"

▶ Not doing the assigned reading, and then avoiding responsibility for the neglect by making excuses.

▶ Repeatedly dominating discussions, interrupting the instructor or others, or grandstanding.

▶ Disagreeing with an instructor in a tone or style that is disrespectful.

▶ Talking to classmates in a voice loud enough that others can hear.

▶ Challenging a grade you received in a way that attacks the instructor's credibility or expertise (i.e., implying "You don't know what the hell you're doing").

▶ Sending e-mails that are excessive, are poorly written, or demonstrate a lack of courtesy.

▶ Eating or drinking in class, especially if it makes noise.

Speaking Up in Class

Asking a question or making a comment in class is challenging for some students. There is normal anxiety and fear of making a mistake, looking foolish, or being judged. This, of course, inhibits you from saying out loud the things you really think are important or stops you from asking the questions that would help you understand the material better.

The only way to get over your fear is to force yourself to break out of your usual pattern of sitting silently, never even considering that you would ever say or ask anything unless you were called on to do so. Make a commitment right here, right now, to speak up and ask one question or make one comment in a class in which you have previously been quiet. Plan ahead of time what you might want to say or ask, and write it down as a reference.

Do this *one time* and you will have taken a significant step to reduce your stress about speaking up in the future.

It is normal to be apprehensive about asking a question, especially in a large class. It is not only prudent but also wise to watch a few others wade into the water first with their own inquiries. Assuming that nobody else has already drowned in shame or been bitten by a shark, it is a reasonable assumption that it might be safe for you as well. But by all means, begin with a question that you have already rehearsed or even written down ahead of time. It is also possible to check out your uncertainty first with other classmates you trust—if several don't understand the same point, it is a safe bet that there are others just as confused.

Some students don't even consider the possibility of *ever* asking a question in class: "Are you kidding? I would never talk in a class that big!" It is just not part of the behavioral options they allow themselves. In fact, half of all students admit that they didn't ask a single question during their freshman year (Higher Education Research Institute, 2008). This is all the more remarkable considering that you are paying for the service of making learning personally relevant and comprehensible to you.

Speaking in class, whether you are asking a question, making a comment, disagreeing with something that someone said, debating points you consider neglected (or wrong), or just making a brief observation, is an important life skill. Fear—of judgment and criticism, of looking foolish or stupid, or of making a mistake—is what inhibits you most from speaking your mind or asking about what you most wish to know.

Yet nervousness is part of the ride. If you go on a roller coaster, you expect to feel churned up; that is what you pay for. Likewise, asking questions or making comments in class is supposed to make you feel a bit anxious. This is a good thing (within reason). It means that you are excited. It means you care enough to open your mouth. And it means you are pushing yourself to take risks.

If one purpose of college is to help you to stretch yourself in new ways, to experiment with new behavior, and to try alternative ways of being, then redefining yourself as someone who asks questions is a great place to begin. It is not that hard to think of something simple you could ask, with minimum risk, just to get your feet wet.

Asking Good Questions

The best questions are those that voice concerns shared by other students. They are universal rather than meeting only your needs (the latter are best asked privately). And they lead to clarification or deeper exploration of a topic. Examples might include "What is an example of that?" or "How is this connected to what we talked about last week?" or "I'm wondering how we might apply this concept?"

Teaching Tip

Emphasize the importance of reading textbook chapters before attending class, especially a lecture-based course. Ask students to prepare a list of five questions on the textbook material they have read for that week and to make a commitment to ask at least one of these questions in class in the coming week. Advanced reading of the textbook not only develops a schema for understanding the lecture but also helps students develop well-thought-out questions for class discussion and build confidence in themselves as informed learners. As a follow-up, ask students to report back on the questions they asked in class. Discuss the reaction of the professor, how the student felt, and any reactions from their peers. Discuss the perceptions of both the professor and classmates of the individual student and the self-perceptions of the student in regard to his or her learning.

Classroom Discussion to Reduce Stress

Open it up: How often do you speak up in class? Do you feel that you are discussing enough? If not, what keeps you from participating more often? What are some of the things you say to yourself inside your head that prevent you from speaking what's on your mind? Examples might be "People will think I'm stupid," "I'm probably the only one who doesn't understand," and "It doesn't matter anyway."

Thuy:
Overcoming Shyness

" I'm kinda shy. Okay, I'm really, really shy. I just don't like to talk in class. That's just not the way I am. In my culture, [Vietnamese] girls are supposed to be quiet. I know in this country that this is different, but still, that is a value in my family.

When I first started going to school here, I saw other students speak their minds, even other Asian women from countries like mine. But I just couldn't bring myself to say anything, even when I knew the answer, or when there was something I didn't understand.

There was another friend of mine with the same problem and we both wanted to change this, so we made a deal with each other. We both agreed that in our next class, each of us would promise to ask one question about something we planned ahead of time. I spent way too much time thinking about this, but I found something in the reading that I knew I could ask about. When the time came, I was so nervous. My heart was pounding. When I started to ask it, nobody could even hear me—the teacher asked me to talk louder. But finally I got it out. I was still so nervous I didn't even hear the answer. But I did it! That was the first time and now I'm not so afraid.... Well, maybe still a little.

Good questions are those that are:

- Relevant to what is being presented or discussed at the time: "Could you give us an example of that?"

- Reflective, meaning they stimulate deeper thinking and conversation: "When is resorting to violence a moral choice?"

- Provocative: "Why are blonde hair and blue eyes considered so attractive in our culture?"

- Stimulating: "What would it mean if this was *not* the case?"

- Applicable: "How could that apply to constructing a bridge?"

- Respectfully challenging: "What is the rationale for including that?"

Apart from these examples, good questions are often a matter of timing and appropriateness. Ask yourself whether what you are about to ask is likely to deepen or clarify the discussion. Look around the room for nonverbal cues to see if others are puzzled, lost, frustrated, or feeling what you are experiencing.

What to Do When You Get Called On in Class

If you were paying attention, and know the answer or have an opinion, by all means, express yourself. But do so concisely, without babbling or rambling. Make your point and sit down—nobody likes a monopolizer or show-off. While humor is often appreciated, be

Myra:
A Professor Describes "Good" Questions

" I love the questions that make me think. I've been teaching this class for so many years that, truthfully, I bore myself. I hate being on autopilot going through the same material, talking about the same examples, telling the same stories that I've told a hundred times before. So when a student asks me a good question, the kind I've not considered before or that forces me to rethink something, I just get so energized. A lot of the ideas I've gotten for research studies have come from these questions, from students asking me things that I hadn't considered before. That's the best part of my job in that I keep learning.

careful not to come across as a smart-ass. Speak in a voice loud enough for everyone in the room to hear or you will be directed to repeat yourself and talk louder.

But what do you do when you were lost in your own thoughts, occupied in the throes of a wild fantasy, or have absolutely no clue what is being asked, much less how to respond?

You could fake it and try to bluff your way through, but then you risk looking even worse than inattentive. Everyone in the room can relate to the experience of drifting away or not knowing what is going on. You may feel embarrassed, but there is really no shame in this (unless it happens repeatedly because you are never prepared). Saying directly that you don't know is difficult to admit, but most instructors will have mercy. Take this as a warning to pay closer attention, or do more preparation, the next time.

What to Do When You Get Left Behind

There is no shame in feeling lost. In most cases, if you are not following what is going on, there are others in the same position. Most instructors are grateful for feedback that they are moving too quickly or that they are not being understood (depending on how it is presented to them).

In some cases, such as a chronic problem of not understanding the instructor because he or she speaks too quickly, has a difficult accent, moves at a pace that is too fast, seems disorganized, or uses words you don't understand, it is best to meet privately and share your concerns. Since saying that he or she is essentially incomprehensible could be threatening for an instructor to hear, you want to handle this diplomatically and sensitively. One rule of thumb is that instead of saying, "you" as in "*You* have a bad accent," "*You* talk too fast," or "*You're* disorganized," it is best to use what is called an *"I" message*. This is a way of communicating in which *you* are the one who "owns" the problem. This means that instead of blaming the teacher (or anyone else), you acknowledge that you are the one with the problem and need help with it: "I am struggling with understanding the material in class and would appreciate if you would work with me on this."

A situation just like this arose with a student taking a math class. "The professor was so hard to understand because of her accent. Besides that, she was talking about math, which is a foreign language to me anyway. I was so lost and confused. I wanted to say something to her but I just kept my mouth shut. Then somebody in class asked her if she could slow down, and it has been so much better since then." Instructors really want—really *need*—feedback from you about what is working and what is not. If you can communicate observations and suggestions in a way that is perceived as respectful and helpful, you are far more likely to get the outcome you want.

What to Do When You're Bored

Note that this heading doesn't say what to do *if* you are bored in class; it isn't a matter of *whether* this will happen, but *how often*. In surveys of college freshmen, between 40 and 50 percent confess that they are frequently bored in class (Higher Education Research Institute, 2009). Of course, this is probably no surprise to you. In addition, your expectations of being entertained or engaged in class may already be so low that you just accept tedium as a normal part of your educational experience. You have always been forced to take classes that you have little interest in and have had to listen to teachers drone on about things that you don't find even remotely interesting or relevant to your life.

The reality is that as many as half the classes you take in college may not be particularly engaging for you, either because of the subject matter, the instructor, or your particular attitude and mood. Whereas you can't do much to change the

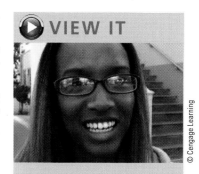

VIEW IT

Mistakes That Were Made
Students talk about the price they paid for skipping classes, not paying attention, and falling asleep in class. (www.cengagebrain.com)

© Cengage Learning

Teaching Tip
Discuss the importance of acknowledging learning difficulties immediately when a student first experiences a problem, and of seeking the professor's input into ways to overcome the problem. A visit with the professor should be scheduled immediately to help diagnose the problem and seek referrals or recommendations on interventions to overcome the problem.

Classroom Discussion
Open it up: What strategies have you used to stay engaged and involved in class?

content or the teaching style, you have loads of options to alter your approach to the class and subject matter. Here are a few examples suggested by successful students ready to graduate:

● "I always try to make a game out of a class I don't like, you know, like find some way to create a challenge for me. I had one instructor who spoke in an accent I couldn't understand and I decided to make it my mission to become fluent in his speaking style. I got so caught up in this little game of mine that I would sometimes pay more attention to how he was talking than what he was really saying. But it made coming to class more fun."

● "Once I decided to go to law school, I knew I couldn't afford to let my grades slip in a single class. I had to take classes like geology and economics, which really aren't my thing but I was determined to do well in them. It made things a little more interesting for me to concentrate on doing as well as I could even though I didn't care about the subject."

● "Maybe I don't get as much sleep as I need—well, I'm sure that's true. So when I'm in class, if the instructor is dull then I just start to nod off; I can't help it. I realized that I had to do something to stay awake, so I forced myself to take lots and lots of notes, practically writing down everything that was said, even though most of it was gibberish. But at least that kept me involved some way."

Boredom in class isn't an issue of *what if*, but of *how often*. Finding ways to become more engaged is a skill that will serve you well in the future when you must attend meetings or gatherings that are less than riveting. Rather than withdrawing or pouting, challenge yourself to connect with what is going on. Meeting with instructors also helps to create personal relationships that can foster understanding, curiosity, and commitment.

© Bill Aron/PhotoEdit Inc.

● "I guess what made the biggest difference was realizing how much the class costs, money I can't really afford. If I'm paying for this class, then by God I want to get something for my money. So if I felt that a class was a waste, I'd take it upon myself to find something of value. I also found that going to meet the instructor and talk to him or her really helps, because then there's a relationship and the person becomes more interesting."

One theme prevalent in these examples is how important it is for you to take responsibility for your own experience. Even if you feel that a class is boring or you don't like the instructor's style, remember that you will frequently be asked in life to do things that don't interest you. Rather than just complain about the situation, *you* need to figure out a way to become more actively engaged.

Interactions with Instructors

In an ideal world, everyone would be just like you. They would value the same things that you do. They would do things the way you prefer. They would agree with you 100 percent of the time. Alas, you have no doubt encountered people in all walks of life who are not only very different from you, but who are very difficult to deal with. They may be stubborn, arrogant, manipulative, controlling, mean-spirited, or incompetent or their personal style may be incompatible with your own.

It will come as no surprise, then, that some of your instructors you will adore, some will be tolerable, and some will be very challenging for you to be around. Students generally agree about which instructors are most difficult (see Table 4.2), but students may disagree on which ones they prefer based on (1) the student's personality, (2) his or her learning style, and (3) the instructor's teaching style. As you will learn in Chapter 5, there is often a mismatch between the individual style in which a student learns and the way an instructor presents the material. For example, if you are a so-called visual learner—which means you learn best by seeing things in action, watching demonstrations, and observing slides and films—but the instructor relies exclusively on auditory methods such as lecturing, you may have a hard time in that class.

Teaching Tip
Assign students to interview an instructor. Have the students develop questions in class, and then send the students out on their own to conduct the interviews and then write a one-page summary of their interviews.

TABLE 4.2

What Students Dislike Most about Their Instructors

▶ Requiring textbooks or readings but failing to use them.

▶ Assigning excessive work without appreciation for students' other responsibilities and commitments.

▶ Keeping the class past the scheduled time for it to end.

▶ Making students feel stupid or inadequate when they ask questions or make comments in class.

▶ Giving tests that don't evaluate what was actually presented in class or in the readings.

▶ Being too general about how students will be evaluated and about what will be covered on exams.

▶ Assigning busy work just to fill up the class time.

▶ Speaking in English that is difficult to understand (because of accents, obscure vocabularies, or speaking too fast).

▶ Presenting disorganized lectures.

▶ Misinforming students about important due dates or requirements for an assignment.

▶ Failing to provide practical examples or ways that material can be applied.

▶ Being boring; showing little passion and enthusiasm.

Source: Based on a study by Malikow (2007).

Students respond to individual instructors in different ways. Someone who you find overly demanding and rigid will be seen by others as having appropriately high standards. Another whose sense of humor you quite enjoy may be viewed by others as silly.

Much of your enjoyment of college in general, and any class in particular, relates directly to the relationships you have with your instructors. Good relationships with instructors mean that you feel a degree of respect for what they know and can do. You trust their judgment and believe they have your best interests at heart. You want to learn the things that they teach and find their classes interesting. You also feel respected, engaged, and safe in their presence.

Working with Instructors You Find to Be Difficult

Most misunderstandings arise from a lack of understanding about the other person's position. Perceiving an instructor to be particularly annoying, frightening, or frustrating, happens not only because of what he or she does (or does not do) but also how you interpret this behavior. Even with an open mind, generous attitude, and tremendous flexibility, you are still going to encounter instructors who will give you a hard time. They might feel you deserve it. Or, more likely than not, they won't even realize that they are doing or saying things that create problems for you. That is why it is up to you to do something about the situation if it bothers you enough.

Change your attitude. The first, and probably easiest, thing you can do is choose to approach the class and the instructor differently. Try thinking of the problem in such a way that you don't take it so seriously—or so personally. Unquestionably, the instructor has the power in the relationship, not only the power to grade you poorly and to evaluate your performance negatively, but also to oppress you as a function of greater experience and authority. Although educational institutions provide advocates and a judicial process to protect student rights, you would be wise to avoid escalating any conflict except where moral, ethical, and justice issues may compel you to stand up for something you consider important.

Change your approach to the class. For instructors who are disorganized, who speak with an accent you don't understand easily, or who present too much information at one time, you can adjust not only your attitude but also your approach. For example, if the instructor has a difficult accent, you can record the class and listen to it again until you learn the speech rhythms. If the lecture wanders all over the place, you can take notes according to the chaotic sequence and then reorganize your notes afterward. If the instructor doesn't respond to e-mails, try the phone or personal visits, or brief consultations before or after class. If the teacher seems intimidating or inaccessible, make an appointment to meet during office hours so you can talk about your concerns and improve the relationship.

Change your relationship. Difficult instructors are often those who you understand the least. Misunderstandings arise because certain expectations are not being met. In one sense, there are no difficult instructors; there are only those with whom you experience difficulty. In other words, a difficult instructor (or person) is a judgment by you that certain behavior is annoying or frustrating. And perhaps most others would agree with you. Nevertheless, it is within your power to redefine an unsatisfactory relationship by changing the way you look at it even if you can't do much to control how others behave.

Find an Excuse to Talk to the Instructor

One of the best predictors of success in college and the likelihood of graduating is the quantity (number of interactions) and quality (intimate, personal, supportive, and respectful) of informal relationships with faculty *outside of class* (Kuh, Kinzie, Schuh,

Felipe:
Visiting
an Instructor

" It took the longest time for me to work up the nerve to go see this one instructor. I really liked her. But she always seemed so busy, so I figured she wouldn't have much time for me. I know they have office hours and all, but still, they've got all that stuff they do. I just didn't want to intrude.

When she showed up, I was standing outside her door reading things on her bulletin board. At first, I wasn't going to say anything, but right away she invited me in. The weird thing is that she didn't even ask me what I wanted, or what I was there for. I had made up some reason to ask her a question, but really I just wanted to talk to her and get to know her better. She's just so interesting. You know what I mean?

Anyway, she seemed like she was actually glad to see me, so we talked for a few minutes and she invited me to come back again some time. Which I did. I plan to take another class from her in the spring. It will be great to take a class from a teacher who I already know and feel comfortable with.

and Whitt, 2005). Yet instructors in college can be quite intimidating, far more so than in high school. They are certainly less accessible. You don't find them sitting in "homerooms" between classes. They might show up only a few minutes before class begins, and hurry off as soon as it ends. Solving the mystery of where they go and tracking them down can be a real challenge since they may not be found in their offices except during appointed hours.

If instructors seem to be invisible outside of class, and harried when you see them, you're right: They are pretty busy with various academic commitments. They attend lots of meetings and have other responsibilities. Research projects require them to be working in laboratories or libraries. Keeping up on the latest advances in their fields calls for continuous reading. They spend enormous amounts of time in front of their computers (in their offices, homes, or laptops on the go) responding to e-mail. And preparing for classes, of course, demands considerable effort.

With all that said, most instructors are impressed rather than annoyed when students take the time to make an appointment or stop in during office hours. This is especially the case when students want to talk about ideas rather than just get clarification about assignments. As anxious as you feel about grades, how papers and tests will be evaluated, and what exactly is required, ideas are what college is really all about. If you can construct some reason to talk to an instructor about a concept, theory, or idea that was presented in class or your readings, you will most often have his or her undivided attention.

What are some reasons you might visit an instructor in person to strike up a conversation or begin a more personal dialogue?

For Community College Students

On a two-year campus, one-on-one academic interaction with an instructor might take a different form. For example, students could be supplemental instruction leaders, academic tutors, or work-study employees in an academic department.

- Ask a question about something that happened in class, especially one that addresses an issue you sense the instructor has a strong interest in.

- Ask a *penetrating* question about something in the reading, one that demonstrates your insight.

- Request suggestions for additional readings in a particular area that strikes your interest.

- Share an article you found that is related to a topic discussed in class.

- Talk about the possibility of selecting this subject as a major and what might be involved.

- Volunteer to assist in a research project that the instructor might be working on.

Approximately 25 percent of college students get involved in research projects with an instructor outside of class. Some colleges require every student to collaborate with a mentor since this has been frequently reported to be a highlight of the college experience. Not only was students' knowledge deepened, but such capstone projects led to close relationships with instructors and opened up new opportunities for careers or graduate school (Kuh et al., 2005).

- Share an example from your life or experience that illustrates a concept or idea presented in class.

- Find out what else the instructor is teaching in the future, demonstrating your special interest.

- Discuss ways you could go deeper into an assignment, or take it in a slightly different direction, that would involve more initiative and commitment.

Keep in mind that most students come to talk to instructors to (1) ask for clarification about an assignment, (2) offer an excuse for why something won't be done on time, or (3) argue a grade that was believed to be unfair. It's not that these aren't legitimate reasons for an office visit, just remember that instructors especially appreciate students who show genuine interest in the class.

Processing Feedback

Take a deep breath. This next subject is a touchy one. You get your first paper or test back and ... the grade is not what you expect. Remember that college is a *lot* more competitive than high school. Often a grading curve is operating so that only a certain number of students get A's or B's. Even those who had been straight-A students until this point will often notice a significant drop in their usual perfect grades.

Thomas Rodriguez/Jupiter Images

Sandy: Hearing Feedback

"So I get this paper back and all I can see are these thick, black scribbles everywhere. At first I was just mad. I've always been a good writer. Teachers always told me that. I took AP English and even a creative writing class. But then I see this paper and it looks like a disaster. I didn't use the right referencing style. I didn't give an overview. I didn't have a summary. A few of my paragraphs were too long. By the time I got to the last page, I expected a C or something. It's not that my grade was so bad (B+) but just that I seemed to screw up so bad. I was just so depressed.

But then I started rereading the comments again and I was amazed that she was so willing to spend so much time reading the paper so carefully. I have another class where I got my paper back and there was like nothing on it at all. Just a grade. I wondered if the teacher even read it. So by comparison, I was starting to feel grateful that this instructor was willing to be so helpful. After I calmed down, I realized that the things she pointed out weren't just nitpicking as I thought at first; she was really trying to teach me how to write better."

First-year students are at the bottom rung of the ladder in terms of academic skills. That's what this course is all about: to quickly get you up to speed. But it will take time and practice before you regain the confidence you may have felt in high school or in the workplace where you had the system pretty much figured out.

At some point during your first semester, you are going to get back an assignment and feel sorely disappointed with the grade attached. Even more than the grade, the comments may strike you as harsh and critical. It is hard not to take them personally.

Once you calm down and accept that you didn't perform as perfectly as you had hoped, *now* is the time to learn from the experience and process the feedback constructively. The goal is to note systematically what you did wrong and what you can improve, and resolve to do better next time. Based on your assessment, take constructive action:

- If you aren't sure where you went astray, consult with the instructor.

- If you are told that you have problems with your writing skills, don't wait one day longer to get some help from the writing center on campus.

- If you think you might have some kind of learning or reading problem that interferes with your comprehension, get a free assessment done at the disability office.

- If you studied poorly or missed the important stuff, join a study group to help you prepare better next time.

The most important lesson when processing disappointing feedback is to avoid blaming your instructor (or anyone else) for the problem, as tempting as that might be. You have to take responsibility for your role in improvement, or you will feel even more helpless. After all, if you just write off the problem to a lousy teacher or an unfair grade, how is that helping you to learn and grow?

The reason you are in college in the first place is to improve your skills as a critical thinker, writer, speaker, and problem solver. If you were already perfect in all these areas, why attend classes in the first place?

Most importantly, give yourself a break. The worst grades that most students ever receive in college are during their first year when they are still learning the ropes. As long as you learn from your mistakes and work to improve your weaknesses (such as by applying the skills in this course), you will see steady and consistent improvement.

Teaching Tip

Emphasize the importance of reviewing after a test or quiz. Suggest that students should research why they got a particular item wrong on a test or quiz. The student should answer the following questions:

1. Why did I miss this question?
2. Did I not understand the concept being tested?
3. Did I not convey my true understanding of the concept in a way that was complete? (In other words, what did I leave out?)

After this self-diagnosis, the student should either spend more time reviewing the concepts tested on the missed questions, or seek immediate assistance through conference with the professor, learning labs, or learning assistance centers.

How to Listen in Class

You already know how to listen, right? You've been doing it your whole life. Actually, if you're like most people, you don't listen very well. Your mind wanders. You rehearse what you're going to say next. You multitask, dividing your attention between the person who is speaking and a half dozen other things you are juggling at the same time. Listening in an educational setting, however, calls for an entirely different level of effort in that the primary object is to *remember* what you hear.

Focus Attention

Take a journey into the mind of a typical student, and you might hear something like this:

> The hippocampus enhances memory function? What the hell does THAT mean? Reminds me of hippopotamus. Like that guy sitting over there. What's HIS story anyway? What's he carry a skateboard for anyway if he never rides it? Oh yeah, got to remember to get my car fixed. I wonder what's wrong with it, making that weird sound when I stop at lights?
>
> Now he's talking about adrenoreceptors enhancing alpha-receptor sensitivity. Screw it, I'm totally lost now! Why's that girl in front of me writing so fast? Crap, we're going to have a quiz on this, I know it. I'm still trying to remember the damn cranial nerves—optic, vagus, abducens, glossopharyngeal—I love that one, love the way it rolls off the tongue.
>
> What's he talking about now, about cortisol effects? Okay, I'll study this stuff later. Maybe I can get that girl's notes. She seems smart. Kind of cute, too. Hey, asking her for notes would be a great excuse to meet her....

Your mind meanders constantly, nowhere more than in class when (1) you are worried about something, (2) you are anticipating something important, (3) you are upset about something that happened that you can't let go of, (4) you are distracted by someone in class who you like (or don't like), (5) the content doesn't interest you in the least, (6) the level of material is too basic and you already know most of it, (7) the level is way beyond you and you feel totally lost, (8) you're hungry, (9) you're tired, or (10) you're hungover.

So with all these obstacles and distractions, how on earth are you supposed to remember much of what you hear in class, especially when your motivation may be something less than ideal? You tend to lose most of what you have heard within twenty-four hours. And within two weeks? Forgetaboutit: You will have forgotten almost three-quarters of the content. Gone. *Adios.*

You will greatly improve the probability that you will be able to hold on to what you hear, even years later, if you engage as many different senses and parts of your brain as you can. This means that you can't just hear words and expect them to be long-lasting without stimulating visual senses as well as some form of movement or action, such as writing or talking about what you have heard.

During optimal conditions, the instructor will give you many opportunities to process the content, apply it to examples, and personalize it in ways that make sense

Group Activity

Assign each of five groups a different sense (smell, sight, hearing, touch, and taste) and ask them to determine one way to engage that sense to remember or study. Rotate the lists clockwise so that each group has the opportunity to add a different idea for each of the five senses.

to you. This might occur in small-group discussions, exercises, and activities. But even if that is not the case, you can still take steps on your own to listen more actively. There are some skills you can develop that will help you remember content, retrieve it more readily, and apply concepts in a variety of situations such as tests, quizzes, seminars, papers, and daily life.

Listen Actively

The average college student can pay attention in class for about twenty minutes without checking out. And this is at the very *beginning* of class. As class progresses, the amount of time diminishes to less than five minutes (Middledorf and Kalish, 1996). Since most classes are two, three, or even six times that length, you've got your work cut out for you if you want to remain attentive. Ideally, your instructors will alternate the kinds of things you do in class so there are a variety of activities to maintain your interest—brief lectures combined with discussion, group activities, role-playing simulations, films, cooperative learning, exercises, use of response technology (clickers), and so on. But often this will not be the case and you will be confined way beyond the twenty-minute attention span limit.

Passive learning—sitting back, waiting to be filled up with knowledge—doesn't stick. Involve more than one minimal part of your being to maximize the hours you spend in class.

Monitor when your attention wanders, and bring yourself back to class. It is perfectly natural that your mind drifts constantly in a hundred different directions. This is not a problem unless you "forget" to come back to the main event after a minute away. Identify the most consistent distractions, both internal and external. What prompts you to check out, go somewhere else, lapse into fantasy? When you "leave" class in your head, where do you go and why? Label these excursions. Watch for them as they intrude. Bring yourself back with some kind of mental cue, like picturing a school crossing guard holding up a stop sign or railroad crossing gates coming down.

Observe strong emotional reactions that you may experience. These include both positive reactions (like curiosity and excitement) and negative reactions (such as apprehension, anger, frustration, and resentment). What is being activated inside you, and what were the triggers?

Quiet your critical voice. Being critical in a constructive way is an important part of learning and advancing knowledge. Your job as a student is to be skeptical, to question things that don't make sense or that conflict with what you believe to be true. But sometimes that critical voice can be so strong that you decide to completely tune out what you are hearing because it is threatening in some way. Moderate your internal dialogue when it becomes so harshly judgmental that it prevents you from being open to new ideas. Maintain a constructively critical attitude in which you challenge ideas that don't make sense to you but don't tune out an instructor just because initially you don't like what he or she is saying. This could potentially be the growth edge for you.

Personalize the content as much as possible. Convert the material to your own language. Make links to what you already know. Figure out ways you could apply the ideas to your life in some way. Ask yourself (or talk to classmates) about what the content has to do with your own life.

Look for the big picture. Don't get lost in all the words. What is the main theme of the class? What is the most important thing that the instructor wants you to get from that particular lesson? If you asked the instructor to summarize the most significant points, what would he or she likely say? Among all the things that were talked about, what is your best guess about the material for which you will be held accountable? What would you predict will be on the test?

Teaching Tip

Following the logical sequence of a lecture can sometimes be difficult. An intervention that can help is for students to develop an outline of the textbook chapter before attending a lecture class on the topic. This outline should include all headings and subheadings in the chapter with a large space left blank between each entry. (If computers are allowed in the lecture, an outline document can be very effective.) As the professor gives the lecture, enter information under the appropriate heading or subheading on the outline. Leave space at the end of the outline (headed "Where does this fit?") for items discussed in the lecture that aren't easily located on the student's outline.

It isn't always easy to be attentive and fully focused in class. Your mind roams at will. Distractions are all around you, and inside you. Your stomach is grumbling. You can't stop stealing glances at the cute guy or girl a few rows over. You are worrying about stuff you have to get done later in the day. You are still upset about something that happened earlier. Yet, you need to put all that aside and engage yourself actively in the class. This means not just listening (or pretending to listen) but also concentrating on what is being said by the instructor and the other students, challenging your mind with new information and ideas, and asking questions in your notes—or, better yet, out loud.

Take good notes. In the next section, you will learn how writing while you listen can keep you more actively involved. Include not just what is being said but also questions you have for further exploration.

Keep a list of words, expressions, terms, and phrases that are unfamiliar to you. Most of the time when you read a word or expression you don't understand, you tend to skip it and move on. You can generally get away with this in daily life, but will find yourself handicapped in class when new terms are introduced that might represent key ideas.

Repeatedly summarize in your head, using your own words, what you are hearing and understanding. Talk to yourself. Talk to your instructor. Carry on a running dialogue.

Remind yourself about priorities and what's at stake. Realize that concentrating in class, especially a difficult or boring class, is good practice for developing self-discipline.

You have heard how listening deeply is much easier when you are actively engaged in the process. Talking about the material is preferred, and talking about it while it is being presented is ideal. That is the intention of seminar classes in which you are given plenty of opportunities to reflect on and discuss the content. But during lectures, you have to keep silent most of the time. This means that note taking—that is, writing down what you hear and converting ideas into accessible language—is absolutely critical.

How to Take Notes

Learning to take good notes is critical not only for doing well in class, but throughout the rest of your life. You are likely to attend meetings in future jobs in which you will be expected to remember key points and, in some cases, be evaluated on your ability to follow through on what was decided. You will have important conversations at work in which you must recall accurately and completely what was said, with sometimes dire consequences if you are mistaken. There are many times you will be required to read reports, articles, depositions, manuals, and records, and then later have to summarize what was in them. Frequently, you will take certain actions or initiate complex procedures, and then be expected to duplicate them or teach them to others. In each of these cases, note taking allows you to record and retrieve what you hear, what you learn, and what you do. There are few academic skills in college that are going to be more useful to you in later life.

Getting a head start on any note-taking assignment is always a good idea. In a business or organization setting, for example, an agenda is usually distributed ahead of time with a list of topics to be covered. This allows participants to prepare for the meeting, do research on selected topics that are of interest, and begin thinking about the items that will be covered. The same strategy holds true in classroom settings as well, where you have a syllabus that tells you what will be covered in any given class. Since you will have already studied the assigned reading for the day, you should have a good idea of what to expect. Most of the time, lectures or discussions are designed to augment what you've read rather than to repeat the same material.

Digital Vision./Jupiter Images

Dave & Les Jacobs/Jupiter Images

Whether in business, law, medicine, engineering, social services, education, or any other profession, it is absolutely essential to be highly skilled as a note taker. This means being able to efficiently and accurately record the most significant content of a meeting, conversation, or speech, and then retrieve the key points at a later time.

Handwritten Notes or a Laptop?

There are differences of opinion about which is more convenient, writing by hand or keyboarding on a computer. Even though you may be able to type faster than you can write, there may be some advantages to taking notes by hand. For one thing, you won't be tempted to surf the web as a distraction. For another, there are visual cues that may be evident in your handwriting, scribbles, jottings, drawings, and illustrations that help you to remember things.

It is important that you select writing instruments and paper that make the task of taking notes more fun and enjoyable. If using different color inks, markers, and pencils helps you to be more engaged, all the better. Some students like to use individual notebooks for each course; others prefer binders with hole-punched pages that can be updated or rewritten. Experiment until you find a system that works for you.

What to Write Down

Be selective about what you choose to record. How do you know what is most important? The easiest clue is when the instructor says things like "This is really important," "You might want to remember this," "Let me repeat that again," or the certain giveaway, "This will be on the test." There are other more subtle signs as well, such as when a particular point is repeated more than once, and when time is taken to spend considerable focus on one point, concept, or case. Notice during the pauses when the instructor refers to notes, a sure signal that whatever is coming next is considered important enough that he or she wrote it down.

Until you trust your own judgment, or have enough evidence that you are capturing the essential content, get together with a few classmates you respect (rather than just those you happen to like) and compare your notes. It is always an interesting exercise to find out what others picked up that you neglected, as well as things that you found important that were not noticed by others.

Develop a Shorthand System

Those who have done text messaging or sent abbreviated e-mail messages are already very familiar with the sort of shortcuts that are useful for saving time to communicate efficiently: NOYB (none of your business), OTTOMYH (off the top of my head), and IRMC (I rest my case).

You don't need to take a shorthand or note-hand course in order to develop shortcuts for recording words that are used most frequently. You can save a lot of time if you master only a dozen of the most common words in your writing vocabulary. Here are a few to get you started, most of which will already be familiar if you use text messaging:

and	&	except	✗	are	r
with	w/	where	wr	enough	enf
compare	cf	versus	vs	between	btwn
because	b/c	question	?	therefore	∴
you	u	without	w/o	when	wn
but	b	example	ex.	important	!

4.1 FOR REFLECTION

Note-Hand

Rewrite the sentence below using the note-hand symbols. Remember that learning sticks only if you become *actively* involved and practice.

I question what is important because you are with her a lot except when and where you are with me. Therefore, this is enough between us, without question.

_____

_____

_____

_____

Another version of shorthand is to write brief phrases that capture the essence of the points. For example, an instructor in a health class for medical personnel says the following in a lecture:

The problem with most diets and why they don't work is that they only focus on losing weight but not changing lifestyle choices. The goal is not just to lose weight but keep it off permanently. I remember one person I helped who had already lost thousands of pounds trying every diet she could find. They all worked—until she went off the diet. Unless the patient is prepared to keep doing the same things, relapses are inevitable. Furthermore, reducing food intake is only one part of the program. You must also include regular exercise to make the metabolism run more efficiently and help patients make better choices about how they spend their time and how they "medicate" their stress. After all, most people overeat not when they are hungry but when they are feeling anxious or depressed.

The notes for this brief segment of the lecture might look something like this:

Diets ≠ work. Short-term gains. Relapses common.

Programs: < food intake; better choices; exercise; long-term maintenance

Self-medicate depr. & anx. w/food

Draw Pictures

There is a difference between doodling and drawing pictures. In fact, if you doodle when you are supposed to be taking notes, it means you probably aren't paying close attention. You are actually defacing your notes in such a way that it will be harder to find what you are looking for when you review them.

But purposeful drawings, the kind that are intended to provide visual cues for spoken words, can be extremely useful. If the instructor takes the time to draw a diagram, illustration, or model on the board, or display it as a slide, you'd be wise to copy it if you have time. You can create your own visual summaries as well.

For instance, let's say you were listening to a talk about different kinds of stress and how they affect your performance and well-being. You are told that there is "bad" stress, the kind that inhibits you and throws you into panic. This is called *distress*. Then there is "good stress" that actually improves your performance during times of moderate pressure in which you feel prepared (such as being cheered on by friends when you are playing a sport). This is called *eustress*. Finally, there is *neustress*—stressful situations such as natural disasters, wars, or cultural changes that are neutral in terms of their direct impact on your daily life.

You want to take notes on this topic that are brief, efficient, and accurate, and that help you retrieve and remember the differences between these new terms. Perhaps you draw an illustration on a continuum that displays the three kinds of stress, with examples.

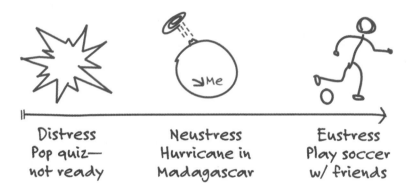

In about two lines in your notebook, you have summarized the three different kinds of stress, placed them on a continuum, and provided brief examples that will help you remember the differences when you see questions about them on the exam.

Experiment with Different Formats

There are whole books and courses on note taking that introduce several systems, some with columns, coded words, and features. Generally speaking, it is a good idea to leave plenty of space around your notes so that you can fill in details later. Some of the most popular methods such as the "Cornell system" (saving space on the bottom of each page for a summary of key points) or "block outlining" (using main headings with related details listed underneath) work especially well with fast-talkers or instructors who present overwhelming amounts of information. Go online to find examples of these formats of note taking.

One system that is particularly helpful is adapted from a research method used when transcribing and analyzing interviews. Essentially, you write only in the middle of the paper, leaving a column on the left for notes to yourself (called "memos") and a column on the right to insert major themes, subjects, and insights that you want to stand out for easy review. See Figure 4.1 for an example.

Group Activity

Go over the Cornell note-taking system in class. Then conduct a mini-lecture on any subject while the students use the Cornell system. After the lecture, compare the students' results. What notes did they write? What topics did they include in the "Main Ideas" column? How did they summarize the notes on the page? Did anyone use any abbreviations or pictures?

Figure 4.1   Example of One Format for Taking Notes

MEMOS	NOTES	HEADINGS
What r my fears?	Most fears irrational, based on myths.	Myths
Look for more recent exs	Incidences of common fears exaggerated.	Exs of irrational fear
	Workplace violence described in media as major threat to safety, yet incidence < 1/100,000.	Cases from Glassner's book
Source of data?	Violent crime reported in news as > 600% yet actually < 20% in last decade.	
	Plane crashes major fear yet odds of being killed < 1 in million.	

Regardless of your preferences and format, whether you write in paragraphs or short phrases, or adopt some standard system, you can add clear "markers" in the left margin to draw special attention to particular items:

? Don't understand

?? Totally lost. Push panic button. Get help!

! Important

!! Will be on the test for sure

* Commit to memory

...A Connected to earlier point, marked *A*

Get the Slides or Overheads

Many instructors will post their PowerPoint or overhead slides on the web, or distribute them as handouts. If that is not the case, be sure to record key points that were written on the board.

The ultimate goal of all these strategies is to create a record that allows you to (1) re-create what took place in class (including content and process, lecture and discussion), (2) be able to reconstruct the experience in such a way that you have ready access to the material, and (3) retrieve the most important content efficiently. This is where rewriting notes after class is so helpful because you can remove extraneous material, reorganize the content into more logical form, and also review the key points, which will help with remembering them later.

Review Notes on a Regular Basis

It won't do you much good to record material unless you periodically review it, linking what has been said in the past with what is currently being presented. Make it part of your standard operating procedure to get to class a few minutes early and reread the notes from the previous class period or two so that you have a better context for what will follow next.

Randy Faris/Corbis/Jupiter Images

When instructors take the time to go to the board and write something down, they do so for a reason—to emphasize points they consider significant. Take that as a cue to summarize or reproduce the figure, illustration, or list in your notes.

You are far more likely to remember and be able to apply the things you learn when you review the material frequently over a longer period of time rather than once before a test. Regular review increases the likelihood you can retrieve information stored in your brain when you most need it.

Transcribe Your Notes

If an instructor's lecture is perfectly organized, your notes may reflect this organization. But many times, a lecture may not follow the most logical pattern (at least according to your way of thinking) and your notes may be disjointed and disconnected, following the linear timeline of the instructor's presentation.

As soon as possible after a class is over, it is a good idea to transcribe the notes into a more coherent form. If you wrote them by hand, you can now summarize and rewrite them on a computer. You can reorganize the notes according to an outline with important headings. You can make connections between what happens in class and the assigned readings. Fill in details that you missed. Follow up on questions you might have about unfamiliar terms or concepts that eluded you. While the material is fresh, create some review questions to examine when the time comes to study for the exam.

Compare Your Notes to Those of Fellow Students

As a check of your comprehension, at some point compare what you wrote down to what others chose to record. Ask yourself several questions: What did you neglect that others found important? What did you include that others did not consider significant? What style of note taking did others use, and which of those styles might you like to use? This gives you some ideas for what you might do differently in the future.

What to Do When You Miss a Class

You know the benefits of going to class consistently. But in that rare instance when a meteor destroys your room or when you come down with bubonic plague, you will

For Community College Students

Since many community college and commuter students spend much of their college life in their cars, suggest that they transcribe notes verbally into a tape or digital recorder and then listen to the notes in the car, like an audiobook. A commuter student could also read the textbook chapter into a recording device and then listen to it later. This process engages several senses with the same material.

want to have access to reliable, accurate, and high-quality notes. You do not want to wait to until the meteor or plague strikes before arranging to collaborate with someone. Obviously, the quality of the notes depends solely on who takes them, so be selective about your choices rather than just picking people who might be convenient. It should become your personal mission during the first few weeks of any new class to make at least two friends in the room with whom you can exchange phone numbers and e-mail addresses. Then make a point to compare notes and get a feel for whether their note-taking skills meet your standards.

In some cases, lectures may be recorded and available for you to review at your leisure. Some students like to routinely record *all* their lecture classes (if acceptable to the instructor) so that they can listen to them again, especially before midterm or final exams. It is increasingly common that students will download lectures on their iPods and then listen to them while commuting to school or work.

SUMMARY

Developing excellence in classroom academic skills is something for which you are relatively unprepared. Since the demands of college are so much different from those of high school, you must expect a certain adjustment period during which you will learn new ways of preparing for class, listening actively, recording important information, and reviewing it to the point that the concepts become part of you. This takes patience and practice.

Excelling in the classroom, as in the rest of college life, depends to a large extent on the quality of relationships you develop with classmates and instructors. Initiate these connections yourself rather than wait for others to take the lead.

Regardless of how long you study, how much you prepare, and how hard you work, you must expect that learning new, more efficient ways of functioning will take time. However, mastering these skills will help you not only in the classroom but also in daily life. You will learn how to listen more carefully, to remember what you hear with greater recall and accuracy, and to apply the concepts to solve real-life problems. This is what makes college such great experience for any job you will hold in the future.

QUESTIONS FOR REVIEW AND FURTHER EXPLORATION

1. What do you think stops students from being more active and involved in class? How could this reluctance best be reduced?

2. What things would you put on a check-off list to prepare for each and every class?

3. Look at the syllabi for your current classes (including this one). With a more informed, critical eye, decode the most important cues and clues that the instructor included to help you get the best grade possible.

4. Students sometimes "pretend" to ask questions when they are really just expressing their opinions, making statements, or showing that they know something (in other words, they weren't really questions at all). Pay attention to the questions that students ask in your classes this week and consider how you might frame them differently. What should you keep in mind when asking "good" questions?

5. Imagine that you receive disappointing feedback on an assignment. What strategy would you adopt to learn from this experience so you can improve on future assignments?

6. Why do you tend to forget 75 percent of what you hear in class after two weeks?

7. Sometime this week you are likely to feel a class you are attending (barely) is boring or uninteresting. Instead of surrendering to this predicament and just checking out, what can you do to become more actively engaged?

> **Go to www.cengagebrain.com for an online quiz that will test your understanding of the chapter content.**

Studying, Learning, and Remembering: Personal Styles

KEY QUESTIONS

▶ In spite of good intentions, why don't most students follow through on their commitment to study the required hours each week?

▶ What should you consider when individualizing optimal study habits for yourself?

▶ What is your preferred learning style, and how might that guide the best way you can prepare for class?

▶ What's the difference between short-term and long-term memory, and how does this affect study strategies?

▶ What prevents memories and learning from sticking?

▶ What are some of the most effective techniques for memorizing large "chunks" of information or content?

▶ Why is cramming at the last minute so ineffective?

▶ What are the advantages of study groups?

Here's the rule of thumb: You are expected to spend about two hours per week studying for every hour you are in class. That includes reading assignments, reviewing notes, completing homework, doing research, preparing for exams, and working on class projects. If you are taking a full course load, that means you are in class ten to fifteen hours each week, so you are supposed to spend double that time working on your own. After all, most learning takes place outside the classroom.

Here's the reality: In spite of best intentions and ambitious goals, most students not only fail to meet the minimum recommended study hours, but also don't even meet their *own* expectations. In surveys of college students during their first and last years, the average student studies about thirteen hours per week compared to the twenty hours they set as a standard (National Surveys of Student Engagement, 2007). So that means that although you tell yourself that you will really buckle down and put in the time you need to do well in your classes, you will probably lose motivation along the way. Life intrudes. Distractions abound. Sometimes socializing and partying are a lot more attractive, or you have work and family commitments that take over. Consider yourself warned, probably not for the first time.

For Community College Students
Remind community college students that working a part-time or full-time job in addition to their classes may well mean they actually have *two* full-time jobs.

PHOTO: ©Istockphoto.com/Alberto L. Pomares G.

Teaching Tip

Ask students to write the number of hours they studied during the past week on a card, with no names. Total the hours and divide by the number of students to figure the class average. Ask students to discuss the number of hours studied and how they could increase their study time.

Classroom Discussion

Open it up: You are paying for this experience. Your expectations of yourself and your instructors should be high. In groups, calculate the cost of each class on a given day. For example, at $100 per credit a three-credit class costs $300; if it is held two days a week for a fifteen-week semester, the cost is $10 for each class. Would you throw $10 in the trash?

Teaching Tip

Ask students to identify where they do most of their studying. Have them analyze whether the location is already associated with another function (like the bed for sleeping or the kitchen table for eating). Discuss how mind-body reflexes are easily trained and become confused when you try to use a location for some purpose other than what you have been trained to use it for. Challenge students to develop a study location that signals to the body and mind that this is a study location.

This chapter is about your learning process, as well as how to best prepare for, study, and remember what you learn, whether in the classroom or on your own. Whether you are feeling confident or apprehensive about how well you think you will do in college, you should know that most first-year students are spectacularly unprepared for the realities they will face in their academic workloads (Kuh, 2007). High school existed on an altogether different academic planet in terms of its expectations and demands. That is why the strategies and skills contained in this chapter and Chapters 6 and 7 are so critical to helping you succeed, providing you with valuable information that is not likely part of your repertoire as well as advanced skills to help you build on what you already know.

Finding or Creating Study Space

Before we cover *why* you need to study, *when* to study, *how* to study, and *what* to study, we need to address *where* you will spend concentrated, uninterrupted time focused on your schoolwork. Chapter 3 on time management talked about why this is not as simple as it sounds. It can be quite challenging to find a place where you will probably not be distracted, where other people won't intrude and bother you, and where you are not tempted to divert your attention by socializing, watching TV, surfing the web, talking on the phone, getting up constantly, or staring into space.

You have a tremendous variety of options available for studying. Some students prefer the library because they like the relative quiet and being around other people who are pretty much minding their own business. Libraries have rules about not talking on the phone (and not talking—period) and other things that you can get away with in your own room.

Matt:
Being a Student Is a Job

"I went back to school later in life. After almost twenty-five years of a career, I was up for a change and decided college was the right path for me. Fortunately, I was able to quit working to go to school full time. At first I thought I was living in luxury, having much more free time than I was used to. Before long, however, I began falling behind in my classes. Though I had plenty of time outside of class to study, I wasn't using the time wisely. I was catching up on everything in my life except studying. By the time finals came around in my first semester, I was worried about failing some of my classes.

I decided to try a different tactic for the second semester. I began treating school like it was work. I would make schedules for studying and task lists for my assignments. I used the hours of the traditional workday, 8:00 to 5:00, because that was when my body and mind were programmed to work. It was tough to adhere to the schedule for the first few weeks, but eventually it became routine for me. I realized that just because I wasn't working didn't mean I didn't have a job to do.

Depending on the living situation, some students like to study in their rooms and have structured the environment in such a way that they have relative privacy. If you have a talkative or intrusive roommate, if your room is a party magnet, or if the phone keeps ringing or the computer pinging, these are less than ideal settings.

Returning and commuting students have their own challenges finding a suitable study space at home. Intrusions abound from family members who may constantly interrupt your attempts to concentrate. It will be up to you to "train" those you live with to understand your needs in terms of not only a space to work in but also the time to complete your work. When your parents, siblings, children, or roommates don't respect your space or time, it will be very difficult, if not impossible, for you to get much work done in that environment.

It doesn't really matter where you study if it works for you. And by "working," I am referring to high-quality time spent in focused concentration. It can take five minutes, or an hour, to read one page in a textbook, depending on what else is going on within you and around you. Yet any generalization made about absolute things to do, or not do, will have exceptions. Each of us is an individual, with unique tastes, preferences, and styles of learning. You have got to discover for yourself what works best—and the proof can be found in the results you obtain. If you aren't getting the grades you want, one possible reason could be where and how you are studying. If it's not working for you, then it's time to experiment with other options.

Naile Goelbasi/Getty Images

It is important to create a study environment that is quiet and free of distractions, but also keeps you alert and focused. Falling asleep with a book under your head doesn't count as quality study time.

5.1 FOR REFLECTION

Your Study Preferences

Most students have distinct preferences for how they like to study to best retain what they are learning. These characteristic styles can be roughly divided into *global* versus *analytic* processing styles (Dunn and Dunn, 1999; Dunn and Honigsfeld, 2008) and represent one example of how to distinguish what works best.

For each of the categories listed, make note of what works best for you:

	Global Style	**Analytic Style**
Lighting	___ Dimmed	___ Bright
Food	___ Snacks and drinks	___ None
Seating	___ Couch, bed, or floor	___ Table or desk with chair
Breaks	___ Frequent	___ None
Background	___ Music, TV, computer, and conversation	___ Quiet, no distractions

What Are the Best Approaches to Learning?

Human experience presents so many variations. People come in different sizes, shapes, and colors. We speak thousands of different languages, adapt successfully to live in hundreds of different environments and climates, and show so many different interests, abilities, and personalities. It should be no surprise, then, that everyone learns in different ways. You have friends who have no trouble at all memorizing the statistics of their favorite sports heroes but can't solve a math problem to save their lives. You know people who are absolutely brilliant at disassembling and rebuilding a mechanical device but can't seem to follow the simplest verbal directions. You see people in class who don't take any notes and yet seem to remember everything that the instructor said. Looking at your own life experiences, you know that in some situations you absolutely excel in learning something new but find other areas in which you struggle terribly. In part, this is based on the unique way that you tend to look at the world and process information. Research indicates clearly that you will perform much better in your classes, as well as learn and retain more information, when your preferred learning style matches the instructor's teaching style (Pascarella and Terenzini, 2005).

Learning styles can be classified in several different ways. For instance, students have distinct preferences for quiet versus stimulating classrooms, warm versus cool temperatures, dim versus bright lighting, morning versus afternoon classes, informal versus formal room arrangements, big versus small classes, lectures versus discussions, visual versus auditory information, and a host of other factors (Cutolo and Rochford, 2007). Also, student personalities, perceptual systems, and especially preferred ways that new information is processed, remembered, and accessed are all different. Rather than just one kind of intelligence, people actually have many forms of ability, each of which requires certain circumstances to function optimally.

Multiple Forms of Intelligence

In studies of extraordinarily intelligent and creative individuals (Gardner, 1993, 2006, 2009), researchers have consistently found that even the most brilliant individuals in their area of specialty are absolutely clueless when it comes to learning in some other areas. Not just one kind of creativity or intelligence exists, rather *multiple forms* play out in a variety of ways. You could be quite skilled at doing a crossword puzzle (linguistic intelligence) but you couldn't complete a jigsaw puzzle (visual-spatial intelligence) to win a million dollars. You might find that you learn best when working in small groups to discuss ideas (interpersonal intelligence) but can't concentrate or focus when working alone (intrapersonal intelligence). You might be really good at *sensing* what is going on in a situation but not nearly as comfortable following things in a logical-objective series of steps.

Your own experience confirms that everyone has strengths in which they can perform at the highest levels and other areas in which they can hardly function at all. Different types of ability can be reduced to fairly simple concepts that fit well with what you already know and can help you better understand and recognize them in yourself and others. If you were going to identify categories that describe the different ways that people are smart, you might come up with the following:

1. **Number-smart:** They have an easy grasp of all things quantitative.

2. **Word-smart:** They have a good vocabulary, speak well, and read fast, retaining much of what they've digested.

3. **People-smart:** They have lots of friends, get along with different kinds of people, and demonstrate a lot of sensitivity in their relationships.

4. **Self-smart:** They are very astute and aware of their own beliefs, needs, interests, and preferences.

This chapter will describe several other approaches to learning styles, but this is the big picture: Most people have preferences and distinct abilities to learn best in particular ways. Once you develop a clearer awareness of how you learn best, you can adapt study habits, assignments, and other tasks related to school or work so that you can operate from your strengths as often as possible.

Different Ways in Which People Learn

At least eight different kinds of intelligence access specialized parts of the brain that may be more highly developed in some individuals than in others (Gardner, 2006, 2009). Although you will recognize some of your strengths in these styles, you can learn to adapt assignments and studying to better suit the ways that you acquire and retain new information. Learning styles can be classified in a number of different ways. For instance, "Myers-Briggs classifications" divide people into those who are extraverts (outgoing) versus introverts (self-reflective), or those who operate as thinkers versus feelers. Another model, based on Gardner's theory described above, matches cognitive styles to the ways that students learn in the classroom (Armstrong, 2000).

Courtesy Everett Collection

Genius is usually domain specific, meaning that people tend to excel in one (or two) areas of specialty but are weaker in other areas. Sylvia Plath was one of the greatest poets of the twentieth century, a wordsmith who could create magical tapestries of language. Although nobody doubts that her linguistic intelligence was one in a million, her weaknesses in other areas led to tragic results: She was unable to make sense of her struggles (intrapersonal intelligence) or relate effectively to others (interpersonal intelligence). Plath struggled with mental illness and eventually committed suicide.

As you review these different categories, consider those that seem to fit best for you, as well as those that have been a struggle for you in the past (see Table 5.1).

Visual-Spatial: "I See What You're Saying." Think of people you know, or have heard of, who have unusual talent for learning things by seeing them. They are visual learners who have a special ability to function well in any realm that involves sight, images, and space. These are often artists and architects just like Picasso or Michelangelo, as well as graffiti artists and taggers like Ka-pow (aka Alex Alvarez), who once commented about his urge to express himself on the sides of buildings and bridges in Los Angeles: "Sometimes when I'm walking down the street and I see this bare wall, the urge hits me and, like, I just can't control it" (quoted in Buckley, 1994).

You know you're a visual learner when you have heightened sensitivity to visual images. You can easily remember scenes from movies and re-create them in your mind. You might excel at video or virtual reality games because of your ability to navigate through these visually rich worlds. You like to see things illustrated on slides, on the board, or in real-life demonstrations. You remember things better when they have been shown to you. Even when you try to access memory, you have an easier time *seeing* the things you've lived and learned.

If this sounds familiar (or, rather, you can *see* this point), you definitely want to make an effort to sit as close to the front of the room as possible. Not only does this give you complete access to whatever is written on the board or shown on slides or film, but also you can more easily burn into your memory visual images related to what the instructor has said and done. Sitting in front also allows you to reduce visual distractions, to which you would be more sensitive and easily diverted. Make

TABLE 5.1

Learning Styles

Visual-Spatial

I have a great sense of direction and rarely find myself lost.

I find that charts, diagrams, tables, and photos best help me to remember concepts.

I prefer to see or work with something rather than read or talk about it.

Logical-Mathematical

I've always enjoyed working with numbers and solving problems.

I like to figure out how things work and have a lot of patience with that.

Interpersonal

Whenever possible, I like to work with other people on assignments.

People tell me that I'm good at reading others' moods.

I have lots of close friends who trust me.

Bodily-Kinesthetic

I've always been good at sports, dance, and controlling my body.

I enjoy most kinds of physical activities.

I like to learn by doing or practicing something.

Verbal-Linguistic

I lose myself in books and love reading.

I like talking about ideas and playing with words.

I am good at communicating with others and expressing ideas.

Musical-Aural

When I hear something it is easy for me to remember it.

I have always had talent in being able to remember songs or melodies.

I express myself best through music.

Intrapersonal

I learn best by working on my own and enjoy going my own way.

I enjoy trying to figure myself out.

I think I know myself pretty well and what I want in life.

Naturalistic

I feel most comfortable when I am enjoying nature.

I've always enjoyed studying plants, bugs, animals, and the environment.

I am always aware of what is going on around me.

Group Activity

Break the class into eight groups. Assign each group one learning style and tell them they will have to teach the class about that style. They will need to brainstorm ideas and strategies within that learning style to increase classroom learning and study.

as many visual graphs, illustrations, and diagrams as you can to plot out material. Take as many notes as you can during lectures and readings, using different colors, print styles, and media to help create visual connections to the content. And as for the future, think about engineering, art, advertising, media, architecture, design, and any other possible careers that allow you to play into your visual strengths.

Verbal-Linguistic: "Let's Talk about It." Do you love to read? Do you have a talent for languages? Are you good at expressing yourself and persuading people to understand your point of view? Do you enjoy talking to people and have a good memory for remembering conversations and lectures? Would you say that you have a good vocabulary? Are you able to accurately repeat things that people have said to you? These are a few signals that verbal learning may be one of your strengths.

All good speakers and writers have the ability to learn in this way, as do actors who are able to memorize and reproduce scripts with excellent recall. This style relies most on words and language and is typical of traditional academic learning, which relies most on lectures and readings. Most of your instructors have this style as a strength because they are professional teachers—and it is good to realize this because you will need to increase

Becki:
Learning in the Right Situation

" I've never been good at math and have avoided it like the plague. It just never made good sense to me. Besides, nobody ever explained to me why it was useful to prove a theorem or move some variable from one side of an equation to the other. Who cares? I thought it was just something wrong with my brain that I couldn't understand this stuff that seems to come so easily to others.

But then we were required to take a math class in college, so I prepared myself for the worst—it was a statistics class with all this stuff about medians and standard deviations. The instructor set up the class so we could go at our own speed and retake tests as often as we liked until we mastered the material. I couldn't believe it, but I ended up with an A in the course. I got an A—can you believe it? So that got me thinking that maybe I can learn this stuff if I'm in the right situation. I'm even thinking about taking another stat class.

your proficiency if this is a weakness. Like all of the learning styles mentioned, you really can improve your skills in this area with determination and practice.

Careers to consider for those who love to work in this realm are anything that favors language—practicing law or journalism, being a translator, teaching, or politics.

Logical-Mathematical: "That Doesn't Make Sense." Logical thinkers like to reason through situations and reduce things to logical, practical scenarios. If this has been a strength of yours, then you have always enjoyed taking things apart and making sense of the way things work. You enjoyed math classes and did well in them. You like solving problems and do so in systematic ways. You enjoy puzzles and games that require reasoning and logic. Numbers are just another language in which you feel comfortable and fluent.

In most cases, you might naturally gravitate toward the sciences or mathematics, preferring classes and careers in science, logic, engineering, accounting, and computers. But when you take other classes in the humanities, the social sciences, the arts, and other disciplines, you will want to recognize the limitations of your preferred learning style as the *sole basis* for relating to information and other people. For instance, analyzing a poem, making sense of human behavior, appreciating a work of art, and talking to friends about their feelings don't necessarily lend themselves to logical analysis but rather rely on other modes of understanding (such as interpersonal, verbal, and visual) that might be exciting to explore.

Musical-Aural: "That Reminds Me of a Song." You can easily recognize if you have this learning style because it has been present as long as you can remember. You seem to have a natural ability to remember things that you hear versus remembering what you perceive with your other senses. You have always had an affinity for music, can remember the lyrics to songs you hear, and actually think in terms of chords and melodies. Your body is constantly moving to the sounds you hear around you, driven by an acute auditory sensitivity. Whether you prefer classical, hip hop, rap, country, jazz, rock, blues, gospel, reggae, musicals, or alternative genres, songs are constantly playing in your head. You gravitate toward interests that play into this learning style, although often it isn't possible.

Understanding, appreciating, and playing music reveal an underlying strength in appreciating patterns. All music has a structure and abides by certain rules that you have understood intuitively, if not systematically; in some ways, logic and mathematics influence how melodies and chords are structured.

Obviously, if this is a driving force in your life, then you will be attracted to opportunities that make music an important part of how you spend your time. Since you are required to take many classes in other disciplines, you should try to find ways to take advantage of your strength in aural learning, meaning your ability to hear things that others might miss. You will find recording lectures and listening to them to be especially useful as a study device to optimize your retention of information. Likewise, if you have never particularly enjoyed reading, listening to books on tape could be an appealing option.

Interpersonal: "I Really Feel for You." Throughout history, some remarkably influential individuals have capitalized on their abilities to connect with people in very persuasive, intimate ways. Consider the ways that Mahatma Gandhi, Nelson Mandela, and Franklin Roosevelt were able to persuade others to see their points of view. The same has been true for inspirational religious figures who have been able to connect with audiences because of their interpersonal learning skills, tuning in to what others want and need and responding to them so they feel heard and understood. This is also the hallmark of excellent teachers, counselors, clergy, nurses, doctors, and other helping professionals.

Have you noticed that people come to you with their problems or find you a compassionate and good listener? Do you enjoy having deep conversations and close intimacy with others? Do you find that you are able to see things from others' points of view? Are you able to build trust and openness in your relationships with others? Even if your answers are far less than positive to these questions, you can still significantly improve your learning curve in this area (see also Chapter 11). It so happens that, regardless of your major, the classes you take, or the career you pursue, interpersonal learning skills are going to be invaluable.

If this area is a particular strength, you will enjoy study groups and talking about ideas with others. This is especially true with respect to personalizing subject matter and figuring out ways to apply new ideas to improve your relationships with others. You will also find it meaningful to connect with your instructors outside of class and should make a special effort to talk to them during office hours or scheduled appointments. Since relationships are so important to you, the best learning may take place within the context of these connections.

Career options to consider would be described as "relational," meaning they involve working cooperatively with others. This could involve various aspects of management and sales, and helping fields like education, health, and counseling.

Intrapersonal: "I Need to Think about That." If you like learning on your own and enjoy solitude, if you tend to be self-reflective and introspective, intrapersonal learning could be your preference. You tend to be analytic and very much in touch with your inner processes—what you're thinking, sensing, and feeling. You may be perceived by others as quiet, even shy, but this is not strictly the case: You just enjoy working things out on your own. Your high degree of self-awareness is a definite strength in that you know where you stand on things, have a clear moral compass, and trust your instincts. On the other hand, you sometimes isolate yourself or avoid social interactions, which may limit opportunities for intimacy and networking.

As a learning style, you like to think about things you read and hear, reason them through, and form your own conclusions about their personal meaning. Keeping a journal would be especially useful to you in that you can record your thoughts and reactions to books you read, assignments you complete, lectures you hear, and films you watch. You probably also enjoy online discussions that give you a chance to express yourself with time to reflect on what others have said.

As far as career options, you might enjoy fields that encourage intrapersonal learning such as psychology, philosophy, religious studies, and almost any other field that allows you to do research.

Bodily-Kinesthetic: "I Want to Play with That." Movement is critical for this learning style, which is not well suited for traditional classroom learning that involves sitting passively in seats. You may be an athlete or have excellent physical coordination. You probably enjoy dancing, sports, acting, or activities that allow you to actually *do* things with your hands or body. You learn by movement, whether that involves your own body or manipulating objects through experimentation. You tend to be a person of action rather than reflection.

You often hear of people described as "brilliant" because of their intellect, yet geniuses also abound in physical intelligence and learning. Think of Michelle Kwan (ice skating) or LeBron James (basketball) as just a few examples of individuals who are extraordinarily skilled at body-based learning. Yet you don't have to be an athletic superstar to make the most of your own learning preference in this area. You would want to specialize in a career field that allows you to move around as much as possible instead of staying stuck in an office or behind a desk. This could involve anything from firefighting or law enforcement to dancing, acting, athletics, and construction. The important thing to keep in mind is that learning for you works best when it is concrete, literally "hands-on." As much as possible, seek out ways to learn that involve physical applications more than just listening or reading.

Naturalistic: "I'm Always Noticing Things around Me."
This last style of learning is just as it sounds—learning best in nature or the outside world. You may feel a special affinity for the natural world, including animals, plants, oceans, mountains, and most things in between. In the spirit of explorers and adventurers, or anyone who works in the field (anthropology, geology, botany, agriculture, environmental science, forestry, tourism, etc.), you are most attracted to the physical world and learn best in real-world settings. Internships, field trips, and service learning—anything that involves hands-on experience—are going to be preferred.

You are good at classifying and organizing things, sorting them into groups that make sense. Your superior organizing skills can be very useful in all the other things that you do.

The two most common teaching methods used in college classrooms rely primarily on auditory and visual learning styles, modes that don't necessarily match well with all students. During a lecture, some students take in information by *listening* to what the instructor says; others are *watching* the visual displays to understand the content; still others are not learning much at all because this style of teaching does not match their need for more active learning that involves experimentation, movement, or real-life applications. It is important to recognize the instruction style taking place in any class and then adapt your learning style accordingly, even if it is in an area of personal weakness.

Matching Learning Styles

Looking at the various kinds of intelligences and roughly matching them with corresponding learning styles, you will have noticed that a few of them fit you quite well. The challenge you face, however, is that most of the classes you take are designed around only a few of these modalities, perhaps those not within your strongest domains. The weaker you are as a student, or the less successful you are in your school performance, the more critical it is that you find ways to use your preferred learning style to master the content of a class. In fact, even just knowing the different learning styles can make a huge difference in the accommodations you might make (Cutolo and Rochford, 2007).

The first thing that will help you is the awareness that you may need to approach different subjects and classes with learning styles that best match the subject and situation—even if some are relatively awkward for you. At the same time, however, you can still be looking for ways to adapt the requirements of an assignment or class to best suit the way that *you* learn. Let's say, for instance, you've been given the task to learn a vocabulary list of Spanish verbs for a test next week. What would be the best way to approach this? The correct answer: *It depends on your learning style.* (You knew that.)

An interpersonal learning style would ideally work in small groups, in which you practice the verbs and test one another, and thereby support the learning. What would the learning style be for someone who best learns the verbs with associated

Group Activity
After reviewing all learning styles, ask students to get into groups based on their primary style and ask them to describe the challenges and opportunities this style has presented for them in college so far.

photographs? She places a photo of an airplane next to the verb *viajar* (to travel). Correct, this is visual-spatial.

What about someone who learns the list of verbs by examining their root prefixes and organizing them by "families"? He notices that the verb *volver* (to return) has the same Latin origins as *devolver* (to give back), *revolver* (to stir up), or *envolver* (to envelop). Logical-mathematical learning, right?

How about someone who looks at the list of verbs once, remembers it with perfect recall, and then goes out to a movie? Okay, a verbal-linguistic learning genius, and probably a future Spanish major.

The point is that you must figure out a way to study any subject, or work through any assignment, by (1) playing into your learning strengths, (2) compensating for your learning weaknesses, and (3) *employing a variety of different strategies* that access different senses and parts of your brain.

5.2 FOR REFLECTION

Best Study Practices

For the following learning styles, write down what you think would be preferred study strategies. Possible answers are listed at the end of this chapter.

Visual-Spatial	Verbal-Linguistic
Bodily-Kinesthetic	**Interpersonal**

Changes You Can Make When Things Aren't Working

In high school, you weren't often given much choice to consider what you want, what you like, and the best ways you prefer to work. In college, you are given much more freedom to make your own choices about the what and how of your education. You have choices about whether to investigate particular disciplines and individual courses within those fields. You can choose classes at particular times of day (or night), depending on your preferences and schedule. You can take large lecture classes if you respond well to aural learning (listening and taking notes). If you prefer learning through interaction and discussion, you can select seminars and classes that lend themselves to that modality. You can take classes online if you like going at your own pace and feel comfortable with technology. You can sign up for service learning and field experiences if you respond well to working outside the classroom. You can select instructors who match your preferred learning style, depending on their approach, personality, values, and interests. You can choose classes based on how students will be evaluated: written papers only, or multiple-choice exams, weekly quizzes, oral presentations, research projects, or performances. The point is that, until now, you may not have really considered what works best for you in terms of an optimal learning environment. Likewise, if you are not doing well in a class, one major reason may be because of a mismatch between how the experience is structured and how you learn best.

Once you have a better handle on your preferred learning styles (most students employ more than one), you can make better choices in the future about what will engage you most actively. In the meantime, if things aren't working for you this semester, or in a specific class, make an honest assessment of some things you can do differently to strengthen your skills. You can do a number of practical things:

1. If you aren't "getting" the material presented in class, record the lectures and listen to them several times.

2. If you are having trouble learning material on your own, join a study group to talk about the ideas.

3. If you find it difficult to focus, concentrate, and understand the essence of the content, change your study patterns so you read and review alone without distractions.

4. If you have trouble staying attentive in class, make yourself become more actively involved by taking lots of notes, drawing diagrams, summarizing what you hear and understand, and writing memos of things to follow up and question.

5. If you have trouble learning or memorizing terms, concepts, or ideas, engage more of your senses in the process. Don't just read the material but also write it, recite it, talk about it, act it out, role-play it, sing songs about it, and use flashcards, visualization, maps, photos, charts, diagrams, and mental lists—*anything* to involve your sight, hearing, touch, talk, and movement.

6. Personalize the content and make it *yours*. Own it. Translate the ideas into language and terms that make sense to you and apply to your life.

7. Use technology and campus support to help you with identified weaknesses. If you admit that you have trouble with writing or spelling, public speaking, memorizing, note taking, expressing yourself, or any other area, get some help. For most of my life, I told myself (and was told by my parents and teachers) that I was not good at math, that I just didn't have a brain for numbers. I believed this to such an extent that it limited the possibilities of what I could do. Only recently I decided I was tired of thinking of myself that way and got the help I needed to change this self-defeating belief.

8. Renegotiate terms: If you are having trouble staying on track with the content and assignments as currently constructed, consider renegotiating the requirements with the instructor. I recently had a student approach me because he has a learning disability that makes it difficult for him to write. He asked if he could cover the same topic but do so making a documentary film. The amount of work he put into the project was *way* more than what anyone else did, but he had so much fun and learned so much during the process that it was worth it to him.

Group Activity

Divide students into four or eight small groups. Assign each group a multiple intelligence or two. Ask the groups to come up with a learning activity for their assigned intelligence that would help a student memorize the system of classification in biology: kingdom, phylum, class, order, family, genus, and species. Have each group share their ideas with the rest of the class.

Teaching Tip

Following a discussion of learning preferences, emphasize to students that learning preference can be affected by the course content area and the teaching and testing style of an individual professor. Ask students to list their courses and determine the primary teaching styles being used by their instructors. Determine the best learning style to match those teaching styles and content areas.

Understanding How Memory Works

Apart from your preferred learning style, why do you remember some things yet forget other facts or experiences that seem a lot more significant? Why do you easily recall certain events like 9/11 when the World Trade Center towers fell, or your sixteenth birthday, but many other incidents of equal magnitude have long since faded? Why can you retrieve so easily the names of your favorite sports team and music group, but can't for the life of you remember those who are in your seminar class? Why are some things so hard for you to memorize, while others come so easily?

The brain is partitioned into specialized areas that function to hold onto certain information that you will only need for a brief period of time—*short-term memory*—and also critical data that will serve you over a much longer period of time. You guessed it: The second type is *long-term memory*. For instance, you learn the directions to get to a classmate's house, but forget the route if you don't return again soon. On the other hand, your usual route to school is so automatic that you barely have to think about it all—your car seems to function on autopilot because the memory is so well entrenched.

Short-term memories are designed to be wiped clean, to "delete the file" so to speak, as soon as you are done with them. This is efficient and makes space for additional data you may wish to store. After all, you don't want your mind cluttered with all the phone numbers you've ever dialed or every menu you've ever read. You want be selective about what you retain.

Depending on the complexity and difficulty of the subject matter you are studying, interruptions and distractions can sabotage any efforts spent trying to learn the material. It is generally better to study for shorter, more concentrated periods of time (one hour), and then give yourself a short break, rather than spend longer periods (several hours) lounging around and dabbling in the material.

© RubberBall/Alamy

How does your brain know whether to put a new piece of information in short-term or long-term storage? Except for certain exceptions like traumatic incidents that are burned permanently into your psyche, almost all new data start out in the temporary holding tank until you move them into long-term space, making temporary memories relatively enduring ones.

Based on your own experiences, what do you think prevents short-term learning from becoming long-term memories?

1. **Being interrupted.** If you are in the middle of gathering new information, like listening to someone give you a phone number, you are going to have trouble remembering it. That means that frequent interruptions during studying (like phone calls, instant messaging, and unplanned visits) will corrode the memories you are trying to create.

2. **Failure to rehearse.** One of the most effective cues for your brain to move data into long-term storage is when the data are repeated over and over again. This is a clear signal that this is information that will need to be retrieved over and over again. That's why learning new vocabulary words is facilitated by repeating them over and over again.

3. **Lack of practice or application.** Memories are enhanced if multiple parts of the brain are stimulated. You greatly increase the probability that you will remember something if you figure out many different ways to use and apply the information. To learn conversational phrases in a foreign language, you can try to memorize them by repeating them. But you will learn them more quickly if you use them in conversation, hear them repeated by others, and see them written down. The active learning methods in Chapter 4 related to remembering lecture material apply equally to studying on your own.

4. **Sensory overload.** Initially, the brain has a limited capacity for recognizing and welcoming new data. If I give you a phone number (without an area code), you can easily remember it, especially if you repeat it several times in your head. Seven digits, or seven pieces of information, are close to the limit of what most people can handle for initial exposure to new information. But if I add the area code, and perhaps an office extension at the end, increasing the number of digits to twelve or more, you are going to encounter some trouble unless you write it down right away. That is one reason why taking notes is so important when you are reading or listening to a lecture. It also explains why it is a good idea to learn information a little at a time until you commit it to memory.

5. **Isolated information.** When you are exposed to a bunch of new pieces of information, without logical connections, it is much harder to remember them. That is why memory aids are so crucial to help you group or "chunk" information into associations and categories that make greater sense and are thus easier to retrieve. When you were in junior high geography, you probably learned to memorize the names of the Great Lakes by using the acronym "HOMES," in which each letter refers to the first letter of Lakes Huron, Ontario, Michigan, Erie, and Superior. Generations of medical students have similarly learned the names of the optical nerves or the bones in the hand by using such methods.

Teaching Tip
Define the words "acronym" and "acrostic" for the students. Ask them to think of examples of acronyms and acrostics used for memorizing information.

6. **Lack of personal or emotional connection.** You tend to remember material with which you feel some kind of personal connection. When your studying is routine and dry, without any investment in the material, it is much harder to remember what you learned. You must have *direct experience* with new learning to make it part of you. That is why merely listening to lectures and reading chapters in text are not nearly enough to promote lasting effects unless *you* do something with the material.

7. **Stress interferes with memory and learning.** Although a little bit of pressure can actually enhance learning and increase performance, too much stress shuts

Blocking Annoyances

Understanding or memorizing new material is much more difficult when you are feeling annoyed or distracted by things around you, or within you. This underscores the importance of creating the right environment to optimize your studying, especially if retention is the key.

Although students have individual differences in terms of what they consider annoying or stressful, it is generally a good idea to maintain your focus while studying. You can do this, first of all, by working in a space in which sounds, sights, and intrusions are minimized. Second, turn off your phone to avoid repeated interruptions. Third, before you begin a study session, do whatever it takes to clear your mind—go for a walk, exercise, or practice deep breathing.

Group Activity

Brainstorm prime study spaces on campus. Where are your favorite places for studying on this campus? Any hidden gems you'd be willing to share?

down your capacity to process more than the most basic information. With the nervous system in overdrive, you are functioning in survival mode rather than making space for the "luxury" of learning something new.

Learning to Remember

You may think that people have either a good memory or a lousy one, and that's the end of the story; but remembering what you learn can be significantly improved with motivation, skills, and practice. You know people who can barely remember their own phone numbers yet still have an amazing capacity for remembering details of a song or a movie that escaped your notice. You have your own abilities to recall certain things while feeling helpless to remember others.

Among all the skills covered in this book, few are going to be more important to you throughout your life than learning to be a better "rememberer." Regardless of your job, you will constantly be called upon to memorize certain facts, recall critical information, and remember particular incidents. In a variety of social situations, you will want to remember people's names and significant details of their lives. You will want to remember meaningful scenes from books and movies so you can talk about them intelligently. You will wish to accurately re-create conversations you had to make sense of them afterward. Few life skills are more useful or important than remembering what you have experienced.

Commitment. It all begins with motivation. To remember new material, it takes a certain amount of energy and commitment. You can't just casually decide, "Gee, I'd like to know the names of all the capital cities, bones in the hand, or symbols for the elements in nature," and leave it at that. Such a task requires a major investment of time and practice. You have to really, really want to add something to your repertoire. And, generally speaking, doing it merely for a test is not enough.

Let's repeat that important point: If the only reason you are learning something is to get through an exam, then the material will stick with you for only a very brief time after the class is over (which might be fine with you). You will also encounter a lot more trouble trying to learn the material since it has no personal relevance or practical use in your life.

Classroom Discussion

Open it up: What are some possible reasons to learn more than just enough to pass your tests?

Since many of the courses you are taking, and will take in the future, are not really your choice but are requirements, you need to rally some motivation and relevance to make the learning task easier. This is not as difficult as you imagine. The key is to create some kind of challenge by making the assignment into a game, one with some enjoyable reward at the end. Recruiting a classmate, friend, or family member to join you in the activity makes it even more interesting.

Chris:
Creating a
Challenge

"I knew all along I was a business major. I also knew that I wanted to go into finance or investment banking. So it seemed stupid to me that I had to take this poetry class of the Romantic era. You know, Keats and Shelley and those dudes. If I tell you I have absolutely no interest in poetry, that's an understatement.

On top of that, the teacher sucked. She made us memorize parts of the poems and recite them in class. It was just awful. I could care less about this stuff, but our grade depended on how well we did on reciting these stupid poems.

It was my girlfriend who pointed out to me that this class wasn't just about poetry; it was an exercise to help my memory. That just clicked for me. I knew that in my business classes, I was going to have to memorize lots of other stuff related to economics, finance, accounting, all the rest. So I made this a challenge for myself to learn the darn poetry.

And you know what? I can't say I will ever buy a poetry book or anything, but I did start to appreciate some of the language. And I did manage to memorize a couple verses. You wanna hear it?

Create Associations. When you try to memorize something in isolation, it is much more difficult to retrieve it later; it gets lost in the swirling chaos of your brain. But if you can make a connection between new learning and something even tangentially related that you already know, it is much easier to access it. In the book *21* (and the movie of the same name), the author (Mezrich, 2002) describes how college students won millions of dollars playing blackjack in Las Vegas by developing a counting system that kept track of face cards, thereby allowing them to communicate to team members in code. If the deck was +9 they would say "cat" (as in nine lives), +11 was "football" (the number looks like goalposts), +17 was "magazine" (as in the teen publication), and so on. In each case, an association was created to match each number, allowing the students to easily remember the private language.

Professional comedians are faced with the challenge that all stage performers must master—how to remember their lines. In the case of comics, they must be able to speak for up to an hour in front of an audience, seamlessly moving from one story or joke to the next, often without notes. They get no cues from fellow actors and yet must talk nonstop in front of a live audience. How can they possibly memorize so much material that could involve up to twenty pages or more of content? They use *memory tags* that help them to build links from one story or idea to the next one.

Visual Images. In a study of why some people die and others survive when facing adversity in the wilderness, one intriguing finding was that even though people who were lost thought they knew the way back to where they started, and they stubbornly pressed forward into the unknown (Gonzales, 2003). It is also interesting that people who had all the equipment they needed to survive in their backpacks still perished because they weren't thinking clearly enough to use them. It turns out that taking visual "snapshots" of familiar cues along the way (landmarks, distinctive objects, geographical features) is the best way to prevent becoming lost.

Getting lost means that you can't find your way back to where you started, or to your intended destination. In wilderness areas that don't have obvious directional signs, survival is based on being able to "read" visual and sensory cues in the environment and recognize them well enough to find your way back. It takes years to become proficient in this skill, which is based primarily on developing the capacity for *visual memory*, that is, associating strong visual images with memory markers. So as you are walking in the woods and reach a crossroads where paths diverge, you have to associate the correct route with a strong visual image that you will recognize several hours later on your return trip.

Group Activity

Using an article from the campus newspaper, ask groups to try using the method of developing creative visual images described in For Reflection 5.3 to be able to memorize all the facts of the article.

When you are trying to remember difficult material that doesn't seem to stick, no matter how hard you try, it often helps to produce strong visualizations to bring the content alive. Imagine, for example, you are trying to memorize a speech for class but consistently get stuck somewhere in the middle where you lose the thread. It helps to break up the speech into several parts, linking them with visual markers (see For Reflection 5.3).

5.3 FOR REFLECTION

Visual Memory in Action

The following excerpt from a class presentation on musical genius Charles Mingus has several distinct parts. The student kept forgetting important parts of the speech and so decided to use visual links that would help her remember transitions from one part of the narrative to the next.

Charles Mingus was a great jazz composer and bass player who revolutionized the music scene in the 1960s by combining gospel, blues, classical, and jazz into a hybrid free jazz....

I see a hybrid car, a Prius, driving through the South, heading toward California.

In his early childhood, he suffered a lot of racism after moving from Texas to southern California. He wanted to become a classical musician, but such a position was out of the question for an African American at that time....

I think of a Beethoven symphony rising to a crescendo: The conductor gestures madly, and then accidentally smashes the first violinist with the wand.

Mingus had a terrible temper that would flare up without warning if one of his musicians missed a cue. One time he smashed a trumpet player in the mouth, knocking out his front teeth....

Mingus's temper reminds me of how spontaneous and improvisational he was. I see this picture of him laughing, holding his belly, but also everyone around him a little scared of what he might do next.

In Mingus's "Jazz Workshop," he forged new ground in jazz compositions, revolutionizing the way music was improvised....

I picture him playing the bass, a very low-sounding instrument. Low = depression.

Mingus struggled with depression at the height of his fame, and was eventually hospitalized. Throughout much of his life, he continued to experience severe mood swings....

Andrew Putler/Redferns/Getty Images

Chunking. Since it is difficult to hold onto more than seven units of information when you are trying to learn new material, one strategy is to reorganize the content into larger "chunks." In other words, instead of eating M&M's one at a time randomly, you consume them by handfuls of one color at a time.

Read the list of words below with the intention of remembering as many of them as you can:

Surfboard	Panda
Viola	Thirty-seven
Snow leopard	Timpani
Thirteen	Rutabaga
Carrot	Blue whale
Jupiter	Venus
Bicycle	Celery
Harpsichord	Broccoli
Eleven	Jaguar
Tennis racquet	Mercury
Lute	Five
Uranus	Football

Now cover the list and see how many of the words you can remember.

This time, consider the ways that these words could be "chunked" into categories according to what they have in common. Study the words again, but concentrate on remembering them in this context.

Prime Numbers	**Endangered Species**
Five	Snow leopard
Eleven	Panda
Thirteen	Blue whale
Thirty-seven	Jaguar

Sporting Equipment	**Musical Instruments**
Surfboard	Lute
Tennis racquet	Viola
Bicycle	Timpani
Football	Harpsichord

Vegetables	**Planets**
Rutabaga	Uranus
Celery	Mercury
Broccoli	Jupiter
Carrot	Venus

Cover the list of words again. Now check to see how many words you can remember.

The main idea behind this strategy is to invent your own "code" or group that helps you make logical links. It is much easier to remember six groupings than twenty-four unrelated items.

Group Activity

Ask students to pick a particular textbook chapter from one of their courses and make a list of the new vocabulary or key concepts presented in that chapter. Then have them categorize the list into three or four chunks based on topic division of the chapter. Ask students to discuss how chunking this list could impact their ability to remember the information.

Classroom Discussion
Open it up: Describe when you have rehearsed for an extracurricular activity, such as music or sports. How much did you practice? How did the practice pay off?

Rehearsal. Indeed, practice does make perfect, or at least longer memories. The more you repeat a piece of information, the longer it tends to stick with you, especially if you practice in multiple sittings over a longer period of time (Nelson, 2009). You can do this several ways, and even use all of them for difficult memory tasks.

Silent rehearsal is good, but often *reciting* aloud is even better. This gets you even more actively involved, stimulating the voice and ears, as well as the internal thinking. In fact, anything you do to become more active in the process helps you to retain what you are studying. *Writing* the material, as either notes or practice, activates other parts of the senses.

Role-playing involves actual behavior, which represents even greater active learning. This strategy lends itself particularly well to performance situations under pressure, such as giving a speech, doing a presentation, or preparing for a difficult conversation you are dreading.

Simulations are designed to re-create the conditions in which you will be expected to demonstrate what you have learned. If you are having an oral exam, you'd want to rehearse under circumstances similar to those in which you expect the test to occur. Practice is not enough, unless it is under realistic conditions.

Group Activity
Assign groups to create and present to class a mnemonic device for remembering the eight learning styles described earlier in this chapter.

Memory Devices. *Mnemonic* (derived from the Greek word for "memory") strategies are those that help you to code information so that you can find it when you need it. They can be created in many different forms, each of which cues you to remember things that would ordinarily be challenging.

For example, let's say you wanted to memorize the carpal bones in the hand, you could remember the catchy phrase "Some lovers try positions that they can't handle." The first letters of each word correspond with a small bone—schaphoid, lunate, triquetral, pisiform, trapezium, trapezoid, capitate, and hamate.

For those in mathematics who want to learn the correct sequence of operations, they use the sentence "Please excuse my dear Aunt Sally," in which each letter of the word refers to the corresponding order: parentheses, exponents, multiplication, division, addition, and subtraction.

Similar memory devices can help with almost anything you want to remember in most fields of study—and if you cannot find one, you can always invent one. The object of these strategies is to provide simple cues that help you access information that is stored in your brain.

How to Read

For Community College Students
Students in skills-based classes (occupational, remedial, or the like) may have different amounts of textbook and other reading requirements in class.

So, you think you already know how to read? Whatever you think you know about reading, and how to remember what you've read, is not nearly enough to prepare you for what you're going to encounter during a typical college semester. For one thing, your instructors don't compare notes about when assignments are due. During any given week, you might be assigned to read 50 or 100 pages—*in each class*. During a single week of midterm or final exams, you might be responsible for 1,000 or more pages of material in all your various classes. That doesn't include all the other assignments you have due, including projects, papers, research, and presentations. So you not only have to find a way to keep up with all your reading, but also actually learn the concepts and remember them several months later. In many cases, you will actually be expected to explain the ideas in your own words, and apply them to cases that you've never encountered before.

That requires a level of mastery that goes far beyond merely wading through chapters one at a time.

You can approach a reading assignment several different ways, whether it is to read an essay, book chapter, scholarly article, short story, or novel. Most strategies use what is known as the "SQ3R method," which provides a series of steps to follow:

1. *Scan* the material before you begin digesting it. Survey the main headings, charts, graphs, and tables, and bold or italicized type. Get an overview of the landscape you will be exploring.

2. *Question* what you need to know and what interests you most in the reading. Continually ask yourself questions (preferably writing them down) as you make your way through the content.

3. *Read* the whole thing from beginning to end, thinking of this as the first run-through of a script the way an actor might initially become familiar with a part.

4. *Recite* the material actively, making notes throughout to increase your comprehension and retention. This means taking lots of notes, including lists of important terms, unfamiliar words, significant points, main themes, possible questions on the exam, and ideas you want to hold onto for future use.

5. *Review* all of the above to commit the material to long-term storage. This means reviewing not only the text itself but also all your notes.

With this broad approach in mind—one that begins with an overview, then proceeds to detailed study and active engagement with the content, followed by a critical review—here are some other strategies to employ. For example, before you read further in this section about how to read, scan the headings and subheadings first; they alert you that you will be introduced to motivation, planning your reading, write while reading, and so on. Secondly, start formulating questions as you scan the headings, subheadings, tables, and illustrations. A few might immediately come to mind in this section: What does he mean by motivation being critical? Isn't "assigned reading" motivation enough? What sort of planning is really required just to read something? Why should I read in shorter, more concentrated sessions? As you might already notice, these questions build an attitude of curiosity that helps you to focus your interest once you read the content more carefully.

Motivation Is Critical

Considering that the purpose of academic reading isn't just to "consume" the pages (like a novel or story for amusement) but also to "digest" the material, you can take steps to improve the likelihood of actually remembering what you read and learning the concepts that are contained therein. You could probably guess what some of these logical actions might be (take notes, study what you've read, and so on), but just because you know them doesn't mean you actually use them.

You need to know the difference between *reading for enjoyment* versus *reading for comprehension and retention*. When you leaf through a magazine, breeze through a newspaper, or read a story, you usually don't care how much of it you remember; you are just enjoying the process. Yet for your college work, it is absolutely critical that you

Teaching Tip

Have students practice the SQ3R method with Chapter 6 of this text or with another textbook.

Teaching Tip

Call attention to the role of individual concentration or attention spans in developing realistic reading plans. During the first step in SQ3R, students are supposed to scan a chapter to determine its length and then break it into manageable reading units. To determine what "manageable" means for them, have students realistically ask themselves, "How many pages will *my* current attention span allow me to read in any given study session?" Students should then plan their reading schedules based on this assessment of time requirements.

Classroom Discussion

Open it up: How is the SQ3R approach different from the way you studied in high school? Why is this approach necessary? How can studying this way be useful?

VIEW IT

Study Strategies
Students discuss what they find works best when studying, as well as mistakes they made that got them in trouble. (www.cengagebrain.com)

are able to *fully understand* the ideas introduced, *recall* important concepts, and *apply* them to cases and situations. For that to happen, you will have to learn how to read far more effectively and critically.

Effective reading begins with motivation. This may sound rather obvious, but an important first step in becoming a better reader is convincing yourself that the reading assignment is a priority, enough so that you are prepared to invest your time and energy into not just reading it, but also *learning* what's inside. If you find that you don't feel particularly motivated to read an assignment (which is perfectly understandable), you have at least *pretend* to care. The readings were carefully selected by your instructor using a definite rationale. For some reason, he or she believes that it is worth your time and effort to know what is contained in the assignment. Give your instructor the benefit of the doubt and assume that if you devote sufficient time and effort, there will be an eventual payoff for you: If not right away, then in the self-discipline you learn to tackle future difficult assignments.

Plan Your Reading Sessions

When you open a book or begin a reading assignment, you may be tempted to just dive in and get the job done. Get through the requisite number of pages and then get on with the rest of your life. But you'll do a lot better if you plan carefully how to approach the material.

- **Know what you are reading for.** What is the goal? Will you be asked to discuss a case in class? Will you be expected to recall specific terms and concepts for a test? Will you be asked to analyze underlying themes? Clarify objectives before you begin the reading assignment.

- **How much time have you got?** You have to consider realistic factors, depending on how much reading is assigned, how much work you have in other classes, and how much time you have available. If you have a forty-page chapter to read the night before a quiz, that is a different task than taking a week to read, review, and study the same material.

- **How interested are you in the reading?** This shouldn't matter but it really does. Some reading assignments seem excruciatingly boring, while others are so interesting that you find it hard to tear yourself away. Alas, many assignments will not seem particularly attractive (at least until you get into them); these are the ones you are going to have to push yourself the most to complete.

- **How much does the instructor value the reading?** In some classes, you will wonder why you even bought the textbooks in the first place because the instructor rarely even mentions them. Other instructors will consider the reading so critical to mastery of the subject matter that the lectures are only designed to augment them.

- **Prepare to read.** Before you jump into a reading assignment, first review the headings and subheadings. Skim the visual aids that have been included (tables, charts, graphs, photos) as they are there to illustrate and reinforce the most important concepts. Review the focus questions at the beginning of the chapter and also those at the end. Review the list of terms, if appropriate, and look up those that are unfamiliar to you. *Now* you can actually begin reading the chapter.

● **Maintain concentration by planning shorter sessions.** A general guideline is to spend no more than one hour at any one time immersed in active reading before taking a short break and jumping back in. It is usually better to spend multiple brief sessions learning new material rather than long, extended ones. But this can vary depending on the subject matter and your interest in it (not to mention how well the book is written).

Write While You're Reading

Do you remember how important active learning is? Maybe you remember because you underlined and/or highlighted the phrase in this chapter and the one preceding it. Did you make this important point stand out?

Teaching Tip
Ask students to review this chapter and write a list of five things that caught their attention as they reviewed.

You can't just sit there and expect that the information you are reading is going to magically enter your brain and stay there until you might need it in the future. You have to find as many ways as possible to actively engage with the content. This book will cover strategies for doing that, but the first level of such engagement involves constantly assessing and analyzing what is most important and what is worth remembering. Furthermore, you want certain points to stand out more readily so you can focus on them during reviews.

Most of the time you are reading academic work, you should be holding a pen or pencil in your hand, plus have other writing instruments easily accessible. The particular system you use can depend on your artistic sense and the materials you prefer, but the simplest plan is to first underline important points that you want to draw your attention. These should be key concepts that you believe are central to the main thesis of a paragraph.

A second level of active engagement with the reading is to pay attention to words or terms that are unfamiliar to you. Each time you encounter a technical term that could be important, or a word that is not already part of your vocabulary, circle it so you can look it up in the dictionary. For instance, the section titled Bodily-Kinesthetic: "I Want to Play with That," uses the word "kinesthetic." If you don't already know that this means "related to the sense that detects bodily position, weight, or movement of the muscles, tendons, and joints," did you circle it to look up its meaning? Readers have a tendency to skip words they don't know and make assumptions about what they might mean. But this does not improve your vocabulary.

Third, and the most fun for those of you who like playing with color, is to use a highlighter to draw greater emphasis to main headings or subjects that you want to quickly recognize. Depending on your creativity, you can even use different color highlighters to emphasize various categories. Think of highlighting as doing the same thing that your textbook does with **bold type**: drawing your attention to certain subjects. Yet don't be overenthusiastic in your use of highlighter or you will become blinded by excessive color.

Fourth, and perhaps most important, is not just to identify things that you believe might be most important, but also to write your own comments, notes, and questions in the margins. This can also include your predictions for what might be included on the test or what might be discussed in class.

Teaching Tip
Discuss the role of highlighting in the learning process. All highlighting must be associated with a marginal mark that distinguishes *why* the information was important enough to highlight. As the student reads the textbook chapter, he or she should use a pen or pencil to make marginal marks or annotations for important information. Highlighting should only be completed after reading the entire chapter or a predetermined section of the chapter. Highlighting is *never* completed during the first reading of the chapter.

Reread What You've Read

The first time you read something through, it is new and foreign. The second (and subsequent) times you review the same content, you have some idea what to expect. You can organize things more coherently in your head. You know where things are going. You have a better grasp of the bigger picture and how the various pieces fall into place.

Since you have already looked up words and terms that you didn't understand during the first reading (right?), you can now comprehend details that eluded you before. Pay special attention to passages or paragraphs that you found especially difficult the

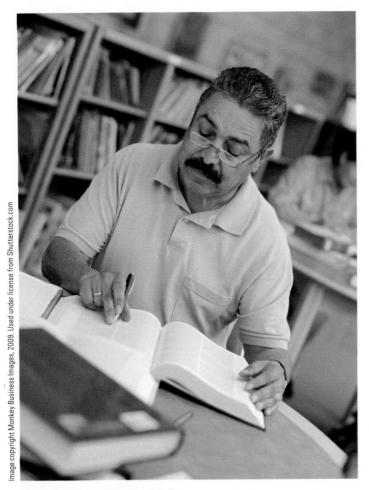

The key to remembering what you read is becoming *actively* involved with the content. This means *underlining* things that seem important, *highlighting* key terms, *taking notes* on ideas that are emphasized, *reflecting* on the relevance of the material, and *anticipating* how you might be tested.

first time. Maybe you only skimmed them because you didn't really understand what was being said. This time, don't skim them—use a notation system like [brackets] around the challenging paragraphs to signal that you need to investigate further what they are saying.

Repetition is what leads you to cement memories, especially if you are seeing and making new connections to what you have learned before.

Identify and Summarize Important Themes and Concepts

Based on your underlining, highlighting, and questions and comments you wrote in the margins, what are the most important themes that emerged in the reading? Ask yourself questions like "So what?" "What's the bottom line?" and "What is the author saying here?"

Use note cards to capture what you consider the most critical material. Compare your analysis and critical thinking to those of others in the class to make sure you got the most important information. Use these cards to help you review material and study the content for tests or discussions. Keep them handy for quick checks.

When constructing your study cards, include only the most basic information that captures the essence of ideas. You want to use them for quick review, like flash cards, except for reviewing concepts rather than memorizing terms. Imagine, for example, that you covered a chapter on gender differences in emotional expression and you want to remember the distinctions and influences that come into play (see Figure 5.1).

A critical part of remembering what you read is to make the content part of your own knowledge. You do this by personalizing the ideas, describing them in your own words. Better yet is to explain what you have read to others. Tell stories. Bring up the material in conversations. As much as possible, interact with the content in such a way that it becomes alive rather than just words on a page.

Figure 5.1   Sample Study Card

Gender differences in emotional crying influenced by—

Physiology: *size of tear ducts, limbic system, prolactin*

Evolution: *interpersonal sensitivity, emotional expressiveness*

Culture: *sex roles, outcomes, consequences*

Males cry for pride, sentimentality, disappointment, and joy.

Women cry for pity, sadness, frustration, shame, anger, and joy.

5.4 FOR REFLECTION

Talk about What You've Read

Sometime this week, when a friend or family member asks how school is going, rather than giving your standard one-word response such as "Fine" or "Okay" or even three words like "What you'd expect," use the opportunity to apply something from your reading. Explain some new idea or concept that you found interesting that week. Summarize what you learned in a chapter or class.

Note three new things you learned this week that others might find interesting.

1. _____
   _____

2. _____
   _____

3. _____
   _____

Critically Analyze Reading

Similar to the way you remain attentive in class, you should keep an open perspective to new ideas while also maintaining a critical mind-set. When you encounter some piece of research or information that strikes you as odd, or isn't consistent with what you already know, don't reject it out of hand. Rather, ask yourself several critical questions that will help you analyze the material at a deeper level:

- Who says? What is the source for this statement, and is this a credible authority?

- Where is the evidence? What is this based on? How solid are the evidence and assumptions upon which this is based?

- What is the source? Was it published in an article in the *Journal of the American Medical Association* or in *Us Weekly*?

You are not looking to refute what you read, or to discard ideas you don't like or understand, or those that conflict with your current values. Instead you are seeking a deeper level of understanding which will help you to better internalize the material.

When You're Frustrated or Stuck

It is inevitable that sometimes you want to throw one of your books out the window. You've read the same page three times and it still doesn't make sense. Even worse, you've decided that you just don't care. It all seems stupid and not worth your time or further effort. You're about to give up.

Don't.

This is the point when real learning takes place. There will be many other times in your life when you are given an assignment that seems impossible to tackle. Your supervisor at work will tell you to do something, and although you'll agree to do it, you

Teaching Tip

In a history or other fact-based class, have students use the professor-provided list of important people, events, or concepts to develop study cards. (If such a list is not provided, develop a list from the textbook chapters to be covered by the test.) These study cards should focus on "who, what, when, where, and why." Place the name, concept, or event on the front of the card. On the back of the card, answer each of the prompts—who, what, when, where, and why. These cards provide a portable, efficient study guide for each chapter.

don't have a clue what she really wants. You will find yourself repeatedly in situations *way* over your head, and you can't see a way out. You will frequently be asked to do things that are beyond your current abilities. This not only is the nature of life, but also represents some of the most important growth and learning you will ever experience.

So when you are frustrated because you can't seem to grasp what you are reading, or when the material seems too hard, this is a wonderful opportunity for you to build on your resources and patience, and push yourself to the next level of ability. Unlike a rock climber, sprinter, or other solo athlete, you don't have to rely only on your own strength and skill but can draw upon other resources at your disposal. You can consult with classmates, talk about the confusing material in a study group, and talk to your instructor. You can also select additional sources and readings that might explain the ideas in more accessible language.

Facing Special Challenges

Students who are non-native English speakers or who have learning disabilities face additional difficulties that make reading comprehension seem overwhelming. That is why your college has resources and offices set up to assist you with your assignments, providing ongoing training and support.

If you consistently have trouble reading, or remembering what you've read, it is worthwhile getting an assessment done. You have probably noticed, long before now, that you don't read as quickly as your friends, but perhaps you've never taken the time to check out what could be wrong. Consider several famous cases of scientists such as Delos Cosgrove, a heart surgeon and hospital administrator, and William Hewlett, cofounder of the Hewlett-Packard computer technology company, who were dyslexic and yet didn't realize the nature of their disability into well past college. Hewlett's dyslexia prevented him from being able to read all the way through school, so he learned to memorize everything through oral recitation. He became so frustrated that he eventually isolated himself in the solitude of the laboratory where he could learn and experiment on his own terms. A number of other famous individuals such as Winston Churchill, George Washington, Albert Einstein, Thomas Edison, and Alexander Graham Bell also struggled with learning disabilities.

Consult Other Sources

Here's an ambitious suggestion for those of you who are inspired to go above and beyond the call of duty. A textbook represents someone's attempt to describe and explain ideas. It is considered a *secondary source* rather than a *primary source* because it is not the original material but instead is the author's summary of it. In many cases, the author has made your job much easier because he or she has taken the time to study the original research, documents, artifacts, or sources, and then explain them in (hopefully) more digestible form. But in some instances, such reviews or descriptions lose the poetry, artistry, and detail of the original. For example, in the earlier Visual Images section, I mentioned research on wilderness survival about why some people live and others die. Maybe that intrigued you enough that you aren't satisfied with just my summary but want to read the book that I cited (Gonzales, 2003). And perhaps after reading the book, you will be motivated to examine the original studies that Gonzales cited to support his premises.

Readings may not always be chosen based on how comprehensible and accessible the prose might be, but rather on the expertise of the author. As you've already learned, just because someone is good at something doesn't mean that he or she can teach it well to others.

When you feel confused or frustrated with the way a topic is introduced or explained, go to the library or the Internet and consult with other sources that may describe the material a bit differently. In other cases, you might want to delve more deeply into a subject that is only touched on tangentially in your assigned reading.

Let's say the note card example (Figure 5.1) that summarized gender differences in crying behavior piqued your interest enough that you want to explore this subject further. This, in fact, is exactly what happened to me; there was a period of time in which I had stopped crying until a near-death experience while hiking in rugged mountains. After I had been rescued and revived, I began crying for the first time in many years, leading me to investigate the ways that men and women cry for different reasons and in different ways. I made a very personal connection with something I read, felt unsatisfied with the explanation, and so was motivated to go deeper.

5.5 FOR REFLECTION

Changing the Way You Study

Based on the strategies and suggestions presented thus far, what changes can you make in terms of the way you study? How can you improve the quality and quantity of work that you do?

_____

_____

_____

_____

_____

In addition to the ideas you wrote down, consider what you will do to follow through, including (1) making adjustments in creating a special, private work space; (2) reducing distractions (phone, computer, and interruptions); and (3) keeping an ongoing inventory of tasks that need to be completed by certain dates.

One of the most exciting parts of your education will involve similar journeys in which unanswered questions come to mind, prompted by something you read or heard in class. This motivates you to read further on a subject and perhaps someday even end up doing research on it yourself.

Studying in Groups

While there is something to be said for studying in solitude, minimizing interruptions, and focusing all concentration on the task at hand, study groups can make the experience a lot more fun. It all depends, of course, on the composition of the group. Get some slackers or partiers in the bunch, and you're in trouble. But if you join or create a study group that operates efficiently and productively, one that is composed of members who are compatible, cohesive, and productive, it can be the best way to learn (see Table 5.2 for suggestions about how to facilitate a study group).

In general, groups can be much more creative and productive than the work accomplished by any single individual for these reasons:

1. You can divide up different responsibilities and spread out the workload.

2. You can rely on the strengths and resources of many different perceptions and experiences.

3. Your interactions and discussions can deepen understanding.

4. You have the opportunity not just to read and memorize concepts, but also to apply them.

5. You can capitalize on the energy and diversity of perspectives.

6. You can test and drill each other to rehearse learned concepts.

7. Study groups parallel the way most work takes place in job settings in which cooperation is valued.

8. You build and enhance your social network.

9. You make learning more active and engaging, stimulating different parts of your brain.

10. You make learning more fun.

In summary, when you work in groups, whether in school or a work setting, you have the distinct advantage of being able to capitalize on multiple resources and utilize the collective talent, experience, and wisdom of many different people. Human beings were designed to function in groups, work collaboratively, and overcome the challenges of nature, predators, famine, disasters, and enemies by protecting one another's back and pooling time and energy for the benefit of the greater good.

TABLE 5.2

When Joining or Initiating a Study Group

- Be selective, *very* selective, about who is in your group.
- Include members who add something important to the group composition in terms of strengths and resources.
- Limit the size to a manageable number (less than five or six).
- Give consideration to the setting to make sure it is comfortable, yet private and free of interruptions.
- Set a consistent time each week to get together.
- Agree on ground rules that keep you efficient.
- Structure your time realistically; assign someone in charge of moving things along if you get stuck in one area for too long.
- Divide up work and responsibilities so you can cover more ground.
- Hold members accountable for their assignments.
- Share responsibility for leadership so everyone feels involved.
- Draw out quiet members and moderate talkative ones so participation is balanced and everyone feels valued and heard.
- Honor individual and cultural differences in terms of values, personality, and work style.
- Renegotiate membership if someone does not carry his or her weight (comes late, misses sessions, doesn't complete work, and/or detracts from goals).
- Take turns acting as a recorder, summarizing notes of what was discussed and distributing them to everyone.
- Compare notes that you have each taken in class, or on the texts, to make sure you have covered all the important material.
- Watch out for unintended plagiarism in which you copy others' work.
- Take time at the beginning and end for social interactions, but stay on task during the work session.
- Honestly assess how effective you are as a group; if there are problems, make some changes.
- Show these guidelines to members of your group, and negotiate agreement of the terms.

Zack:
On Not Liking Study
Groups

" I don't like study groups. People usually start talking about other things instead of studying. It's distracting. When I study, I like to read the book, take notes, and then type them up—this works for me. If I try to study with other people, then I can't do things the way I like because people have different ways of studying. Well, when I'm studying by myself, I don't have anyone to help me with stuff I don't understand, I know, but I can always call someone, like, if I get stuck or something. So, that's OK.

I'm pretty organized and I don't like to wait until the day before the test to study, you know? I like to start a week before to make sure I have time to review everything. I have a hard time remembering things. If I wait until the last minute, then I don't remember anything and I flunk the test. This used to happen to me all the time, before I started studying the way I do now.

SUMMARY

It isn't just how much time you put into studying that matters, but also how you organize yourself, your space, and the structures for concentrating and retaining what you read and learn. Studying in college is quite different from studying in high school: The material is more complex, the demands are higher, and you have more work than seems possible to complete in any given week. It is important to prioritize your tasks, as well as put into place some rituals and habits that you stick to no matter what.

All the techniques and strategies in this chapter will not mean very much if you don't find a way to make them part of your normal operating style. Studying alone has advantages, but it is also important that you join a study group to help support your efforts and share resources.

Ultimately, the skills related to reading for comprehension and retention, and remembering what you learn in class, are pretty similar to what it takes to succeed in any professional enterprise. You have to be able to discipline yourself and to focus on specific tasks that help you to resist interruptions and distractions. You also must develop ways to study that work for you, meaning that they produce the kind of results that demonstrate what you know and can do.

QUESTIONS FOR REVIEW AND FURTHER EXPLORATION

1. Review the way you read this chapter. Based on strategies introduced here, reread the chapter employing some of the strategies such as note taking, questioning, underlining, highlighting, summarizing, and other ways to engage actively with the material.

2. Imagine your ideal study space. Think about its location and features that would be most important to you. How is this image different from where you actually study now?

Group Activity
Present the "Red-Yellow-Green Lights" exercise to the class. Ask groups to list classroom or study behaviors they will stop (red light), continue (green light), and think further about (yellow light).

3. What learning styles would be best adapted for language classes as opposed to philosophy? What do you now understand about your own preferred learning styles that will guide how you should study?

4. Based on what you learned about memory and how it works, how can you maintain long-term storage of complex and challenging information?

5. What are the reasons why you don't remember things that you've read or learned (including the answer to this question)? What differences have you noticed between those times when you have no trouble remembering things versus when remembering something seems hopeless?

6. There were several strategies presented for increasing memory retention. What is an example of you how you have used (1) visual images, (2) chunking, (3) tags, and (4) rehearsal?

7. What do you resolve to *do* based on what you learned in this chapter? How will you hold yourself accountable if, and when, you "forget" about this commitment?

8. What have been the best learning experiences you've ever had in school? What made them so satisfying and enjoyable? Did you learn with friends, on your own, or with an inspirational teacher? Did you use your creativity, or perhaps something else? What do these past experiences tell you about the ways you prefer to learn?

ANSWERS TO FOR REFLECTION 5.2

Preferred study strategies for the following learning styles include:

Visual-Spatial

- Plan to take classes and instructors who are more dynamic and visual.

- Use charts, maps, graphs, photos, and flowcharts to organize and summarize content.

- Use a highlighter (different colors) to emphasize important content.

- Take photos of the instructor's notes on the board when class is over.

- Draw pictures, doodles, and diagrams to capture ideas and content.

- Summarize content in PowerPoint slides with visual images.

- When trying to remember facts or content, access visual memories that are linked.

Verbal-Linguistic

- Take lots of notes in lectures and when reading assignments.

- Read other original and secondary sources that have direct links to the content. Take notes.

- Check out related websites that provide additional information and make links to what you have learned.

- Keep a list of new words and terms you have learned.

- Meet with the instructor to get other recommended sources you can consult.

- Predict exam questions and write out your responses.

- Listen to books on tape.

Bodily-Kinesthetic

- Put ideas into action by testing them out as much as possible.

- Ask instructors for realistic examples of concepts presented.

- As much as possible, engage all of your senses to remember new ideas.

- Rehearse presentations; take practice tests in simulated conditions.

- Work in the field as much as possible to see ideas in action.

- Take classes that involve hands-on experiences, experiments, field trips, and service learning.

- Keep moving as much as possible—walk around while you study. Change locations frequently.

- Find other people like you, and work together in your preferred style.

- Take lots of brief breaks when you find your attention wandering.

Interpersonal

- Meet with instructors to talk about assignments.

- Work in study groups.

- Talk about ideas to friends, roommates, and family.

- Test new concepts and ideas in relationships.

- Work with partners to prepare you for exams and quiz you.

- Ask for feedback from classmates, friends, and instructors.

- Speak up in class as much as possible to talk about concepts.

- Meet with a librarian to talk about research projects.

- Network, text, and e-mail classmates to talk about class assignments together.

- Teach and explain what you've been learning to others who are interested.

> **Go to www.cengagebrain.com for an online quiz that will test your understanding of the chapter content.**

Performing under Pressure: Taking Tests

KEY QUESTIONS

▸ **How would you study differently for a multiple-choice exam than you would for an essay exam?**

▸ **What's the best way to approach a multiple-choice question to give yourself the best shot at getting the correct answer?**

▸ **What are the most common mistakes that students make when taking tests?**

▸ **What are some things you can do to manage your stress related to taking a test?**

▸ **What should you do *after* the test is over? (Hint: The wrong answer is to celebrate.)**

▸ **What should you do if you don't do as well on an exam as you hoped?**

Group Activity
Divide students into small groups. Ask each group to create five to seven test questions for Chapter 6, including multiple-choice, true-false, fill-in-the-blank, and short-answer ones. Create a quiz from them, and give it during the next class period. Ask the students to critique the questions to improve them.

Vladimir Horowitz is considered to be the greatest pianist of the twentieth century, a virtuoso blessed with extended fingers and a low wrist, allowing him to play the most challenging pieces of music ever written. His mastery of articulation, phrasing, and tone has never been duplicated. Yet with all his ability and experience, he was paralyzed by performance anxiety when the time came to appear in concert. In a few instances, he was so anxious that he had to be physically pushed onstage. At one point, his stage fright became so bad that he stopped playing in public for twelve years until he regained his confidence. And you thought you had trouble?

Performing under pressure is a constant in college life, just as it will be when you graduate. In whatever job you choose, and whatever circumstances you find yourself, you will face deadlines, performance evaluations, and stressful assignments that seem like they are beyond your capability. You may be called upon to explain complex ideas in front of large groups. You may be challenged to defend yourself or an idea in heated arguments or tense negotiations. You may face adversity in a multitude of situations.

The good news is that college will prepare you to perform under pressure. Whether you act onstage, give a speech in class, participate in a public debate, take a final exam that determines your course grade, or write a paper that features your critical thinking and ability to synthesize ideas, you will be called upon to demonstrate your abilities. Just as an actor studies her lines, prepares her part, rehearses continuously, gets coaching, and responds to directing, so can you develop skills and strategies that will improve your own performance.

Teaching Tip
If your campus offers free tutoring services, assign the students to visit a tutor. Give the students questions to ask, or have the class create questions. Have students meet with at least one tutor and ask their questions. Ask students to write a short paper on what their experience with the tutor was like.

Classroom Discussion
Open it up: How do you typically prepare for exams? When do you begin to study? How long do you study? As you go through the chapter, write down at least five suggestions for ways to improve the way you study for tests.

PHOTO: Ben Hider/Getty Images

Preparing for Exams

There are two parts to a performance under pressure. The first involves preparation and rehearsal, and the second is the actual event. What appears effortless and easy to those in an audience is the result of endless hours of practice on the part of a performer. Athletes spend up to eight hours each day training for upcoming events: drilling, practicing, rehearsing, visualizing, and testing themselves, all to ensure that they have done everything they can to deal with whatever might arise. If you consider preparing for a test in the same manner that actors practice their lines or athletes practice their skills, you may find greater success in your mastery of course material.

How Good a Test-Taker Are You?

Some people come to college quite skilled at taking tests. They knocked the socks off their SAT or ACT scores. They thrive under pressure and appear to relish exam time as an opportunity to show what they can do. It seems so easy for them to do well on tests, and then even report, "I hardly studied. The test was a breeze anyway, don't you think?"

You nod your head in agreement, thinking to yourself, "You've got to be kidding! That test was ridiculously difficult." And now panic sets in because if this person is telling the truth—even though you have some doubts—then you're in far more trouble than you thought.

It is time to do an honest assessment of your test-taking skills. This will help you to concentrate your efforts to develop better abilities in taking essay, fill-in-the-blank, short-answer, multiple-choice, true-false, oral, or take-home exams. Each of these forms of testing requires a different set of skills and different preparation.

Instructors prefer one kind of test over others for a variety of reasons—whether they are testing recall of facts, recognition of concepts, application of principles, resolution of problems, critical thinking, or case analysis, or just whether it is less time-consuming for them to grade a particular type of test. Nobody is equally good at all these evaluation methods. Remember what you learned in Chapter 5 about learning styles? Someone might be a whiz at objective-type exams (like multiple choice or true-false) but struggle while organizing his thoughts for essay or oral exams. Another student can easily pull together facts, terms, and concepts to support a theory or position, but has trouble choosing just one right answer to a question. Still another student treats multiple-choice questions like a game, playing detective to figure out clues, and can easily decode the mysteries.

Employing Multiple Learning Styles

In preparing for any exam, you want to use *multiple* strategies for rehearsal that access as many learning styles as possible. This means not only

Taking a test is a lot like playing professional sports. As much as you train and work out, practice skills, anticipate situations, and rehearse under various conditions, you still must think on your feet, improvise according to changing circumstances, and remain flexible when you encounter something unexpected.

Jim Rogash/Getty Images

6.1 FOR REFLECTION

Assessing Your Test-Taking Skills

Rate on a 1–5 scale how skilled you are at taking the following types of exams. If you have never encountered a particular exam before, leave it blank.

I Stink	Get Mostly C's and D's	Not Bad	Pretty Good	I Rock
1	2	3	4	5

Type of Test	Rating
Multiple choice	_____
True-false	_____
Fill-in-the-blank	_____
Short answer	_____
Essay	_____
Oral	_____
Take-home	_____
Matching	_____

Now that you've honestly admitted weaknesses, how are you going to get the help you need to improve your skills?

_____

_____

_____

playing into your preferred domain that was discussed in Chapter 5, but also employing alternatives that give you more options for remembering what you learned and demonstrating this on tests. The object is to utilize as many of your senses as possible.

Imagine, for example, that you were going to take an exam in an economics class, which is not your strong suit or a major area of interest. The content of the lectures and readings is complex and challenging, and you know that you have trouble grasping the material, learning the technical terms, and applying the concepts in case examples. What would you do to prepare for a midterm exam that covers a whole half-semester of content? The answer, as you already know, is to rely on multiple learning styles.

Begin with reading and then rereading assigned chapters, capitalizing on verbal learning. Review your lecture notes, paying particular attention to the graphs, charts, and summary tables that were provided. Related to this visual-learning style, study the handouts that were provided both online and in class. Use flash cards to memorize the technical terms, studying them visually and repeating them out loud as aural learning. Go to the website for strategies for creating flashcards that can help you study. Work in study groups (interpersonal learning) and on your own (intrapersonal)

For Community College Students

Many community college students began their college career with a test—an assessment test required after being admitted. Ask students to reflect on their experiences with that test.

Classroom Discussion

Open it up: Share with the group your best and worst types of test questions. What do you like or dislike about them? What hints do you have from your experience about how to do better on your favorite types?

to summarize and chart the most important concepts (logical) and apply them to case examples (kinesthetic).

Text Anxiety

Before we get to the specifics of how to best prepare for an exam, you should know that poor performance is related not just to material you missed, but also to your state of mind. In any situation where you are being evaluated, it is absolutely critical that you remain calm and in control. In Chapter 10, we will explore at length the sources of stress, how to prevent them as much as possible, and how to manage them effectively. But anxiety related to test performance deserves its own special section because it is so common.

It is perfectly normal to feel a degree of apprehension, even anxiety, prior to and during an important examination. After all, there is a lot at stake. A moderate degree of such stress can actually be helpful in focusing concentration and inspiring greater effort. Yet when the anxiety feels overwhelming to the point that it interferes with recall and performance, then you are indeed in trouble.

There are several factors that contribute to test anxiety, some of them entirely reasonable and others that are gross exaggerations of reality. For example, if you feel unprepared or lack confidence in your ability to do well, it makes sense that you would feel a certain dread. But if you have studied well, prepared to the best of your ability, know the content, and still can't get it together during the exam, forgetting much of what you know, then you've got a serious problem. Fortunately, it is one that responds to help.

Some students (estimated to be as high as 25 percent) experience test anxiety almost every time they take an exam, no matter what the subject or how much they prepared. They can perform extraordinarily well during practice tests or study sessions, but become paralyzed during the actual examination. They can't remember things. They can't think straight. And to make matters far worse, they panic to the point that they lose control.

Often the first step to overcoming text anxiety is to identify its source. Are you putting too much pressure on yourself? Have you had bad experiences in the past that you fear will recur no matter what you do? Are you not getting enough sleep? Are you drinking too much caffeine? Among the worst offenders is negative "self-talk" or internal dialogue that is self-defeating. Examples might sound something like this:

- "I'll blow it. I always blow it. This time will be no different."

- "If I flunk this test, my life is practically over. I might as well give up."

- "No matter how hard I try, it will never be enough."

- "The test will probably be unfair anyway. I probably studied the wrong stuff."

When you think such negative, disastrous thoughts to yourself, you program yourself for defeat. Test anxiety, like so many conditions of debilitating stress, is caused as much by what you do to yourself inside as by any challenges you face outside.

How do you know if you have test anxiety beyond what is normal, perhaps requiring treatment at the counseling center? Consider these questions:

- Do you lose sleep and/or your appetite worrying about an exam days ahead of time?

- Do you get stomachaches, headaches, or other physical problems anticipating an exam?

- Do you try to calm your nerves with alcohol or drugs because you can't control your anxiety?

- Have you frozen several times in the past while taking tests, to the point that you couldn't remember material that you were certain you knew?

- Have your test grades been way below what you think they should be, given how much preparation you've done?

- Are you filled with negative, self-defeating thoughts that become obsessive?

- Do you feel overwhelmed and depressed about your prospects of doing well on an exam?

There are several effective strategies for dealing with test anxiety or any sources of stress, which are covered in Chapter 10. Many of them involve learning relaxation methods and ways of counteracting defeatist thinking. The best "cure" for text anxiety is to keep things in perspective. In spite of the way things may feel, it is literally not the end of the world if you don't do as well as hoped.

Much performance-related anxiety, when taking a test or in any other pressure situation, is the result of "disasterizing" thoughts in which you imagine the worst. A few of the most effective ways to manage stress, whether in school or for the rest of your life, involve deep breathing to calm yourself and talking to yourself in gentle, measured ways. Both strategies are described in Chapter 10 and require practice over time.

You can significantly reduce anxiety related to exams, and improve your score, by taking practice tests in simulated conditions. This is a big part of test preparatory courses for college and graduate school admission. If possible, even arrange to take a practice test in the same room where your class meets. The more realistic the practice session, the better prepared you will be for the actual test.

Tactics for Test Readiness

Studying for an exam doesn't work very well unless you are strategic about the way you go about it. This is no different than interviewing for a job—you can't just show up and expect to impress anyone unless you know something about the job and what is expected. With test preparation, structure your studying according to what kind of test you are taking, what kind of material is being studied, and what you predict will be covered.

Your course syllabus is a good starting point for anticipating what kind of test will be offered and what material will be evaluated. But this isn't the only source of intelligence about what to expect. Assuming you have been taking good notes in class and your readings, you should already have a list of probable test question topics. Your ability to predict such things will become more accurate as you practice comparing what you anticipated with what actually occurred.

If you can find someone who had the course previously, especially with this same teacher, find out as much as you can about the test style and construction. How many questions will be on the exam? What specific areas will it cover? Will the test cover only a certain number of chapters or time period, or is it cumulative? How much time will you have to complete it? Are you penalized for making wrong choices? How will it be graded? Who will grade it? How much does it count toward your final grade? Keep in mind that your sources may not have the most current and reliable information since instructors often change their tests each year, or even the ways they teach their classes.

FOR · REDUCING · STRESS

Dealing with Difficult Situations

Normally, how do you cope with stressful circumstances? Some people rise to the occasion and thrive, while others just surrender. Some allow negative thoughts to take over, become impatient and frustrated, or resort to tension reducers (food, drugs, alcohol, and escape activities). Still others become angry at themselves or others. What is your usual pattern?

Think of a recent instance–other than taking a test–in which you had to deal with an extremely stressful situation and managed to maintain a degree of calmness and control, allowing you to function well. This could have occurred while playing sports or a game, during a debate or argument, or in some other kind of interpersonal conflict. What helped you the most in that circumstance that would be valuable to you during tests or other academic performances?

Teaching Tip

Ask students to choose an upcoming test in any subject and develop their own test on material they think might be covered. Suggest that they take this self-made test under the same time constraints as the normal testing situation. Grading the test should help diagnose problem areas that need additional study and test preparation.

It doesn't hurt to ask the instructor if there are tests from previous semesters available, on reserve in the library, online, or in the instructor's office. Many textbooks, including this one, have sample questions available on the companion website that are drawn from the exact same pool as those on the actual exam. Study the way the questions are constructed. Are they reasonably clear and straightforward, or tricky and complex? Do the questions require you to recall facts? Apply concepts? Recognize correct names and dates? Theorize based on principles that were introduced? Are the questions detailed and specific, or do they tend toward generalities?

You should gather information not only about the test, but also on your own testing style based on the practice tests you've taken so far. Where do you make mistakes? In what areas are you weakest?

The best way to prepare for an upcoming test is under the same conditions that you would expect for the actual examination. That is one reason why actors conduct dress rehearsals before a live performance or why athletes simulate game conditions as much as possible when they practice.

Jupiterimages

Showing What You Know

To do your best, you have to feel comfortable in the setting. No matter where you usually sit during class, pick a spot for the test that is going to be free of distractions (like friends who might bother you, or classmates who are unusually attractive). By this time, you have already scoped out the environment, so you know to avoid seats with poor lighting or sections of the room that are too cold or warm. Lay out the materials you need, including a watch, at least one extra pen (or pencil for Scantron answer sheets), or, if you are using a computer, an extra battery or plug and cord. The last thing in the world you want is to be in the "zone" and find yourself without a way to express your brilliance.

Some instructors will allow you to use notes or books during a test. This is a mixed blessing because you can waste a lot of time looking up some piece of information if you aren't exactly sure where it is. Bring only those materials that you are familiar with, and make sure you can find what you need when you need it.

Usually before the test begins, the instructor or assistant will give you additional instructions or clarification on some points. Think of this like a waiter telling you about specials of the day that aren't on the menu. You may hear some very valuable advice—*if* you are listening (which many students are not because they have already started racing through the test). The instructor may tell you, for instance, not to guess unless you are pretty certain because wrong answers count against you. Or you may be encouraged to guess because your score is based solely on the number of right answers.

Read the instructions slowly and carefully. Read them one more time just to be sure that you didn't misread something, or miss some critical piece of information. If you aren't perfectly clear about what is expected, raise your hand or go up to the front to get clarification.

Take a deep breath to help clear your mind and relax. Now you can begin....

Visual Ideas/Nora Pelaez/Jupiter Images

When feeling anxious before or during an exam—or any challenging performance—it helps to practice deep breathing while bringing to mind a visual image that totally calms you. Imagine yourself sitting on this beach, with the sun warming away all tension, the cool sand between your toes, and the sound of the waves rhythmically hitting the shore. If you practice deep breathing while focusing on this scene, or another one that works for you, you will feel an immediate reduction of stress. But it takes practice to use this skill under pressure—when you need it most.

Strategies for Multiple-Choice Tests

Like any evaluation experience in life, there are secrets to the game. The following are several tried-and-true tactics.

- **Pace yourself.** Keep an eye on the clock so that you don't run out of time.

- **Allocate your time according to point values.** With any kind of exam, the best strategy is one in which you invest the most time and effort in the questions that count the most. Don't waste a lot of time on a question worth one point when there are others that represent a higher portion of your grade.

- **Do the easy questions first.** These are the ones where you immediately know the right answer, or have full confidence in your choice. Move on. Don't second-guess yourself.

- **Read the whole question before answering.** Every student flubs a few questions on every test because the question was misinterpreted or not read clearly. It doesn't do you much good to know the right answer to the wrong question.

Take a Deep Breath

A little bit of stress before an exam actually *improves* your performance and concentration. But if you become too anxious, you can freeze and "forget" what you know and what you've prepared. There are several things you can do to reduce extreme anxiety related to an upcoming exam, but the most important thing besides being academically prepared is to feel psychologically ready for the challenge.

As anxious as you are to begin a test, first clear your mind of all distractions. Take a "cleansing breath," a deep, relaxing, meditative type of breath that feeds your brain maximum oxygen at the same time it helps you focus your attention. Do that now: Inhale as s-l-o-w-l-y as you can through your nose, expanding your lungs until your shoulders rise. Hold the breath for a count of three, then slowly—very slowly—exhale through your mouth.

Take another breath, this time concentrating so completely on the effort that you block out anything else in your mind.

It is absolutely critical that you let everything else in your life go while you are in performance mode. Regardless of what else is going on in your life—problems with love, money, friendship, family, whatever—put it aside until the test is over. Use the deep breathing as a way to get yourself into the "zone." Whenever you feel your attention wandering, breathe deeply to refocus.

- **Write in the margins.** If it is allowed, write notes to yourself in the margin of the test booklet, such as reminders of key points or markers of questions to return to later if there is time.

- **Decode the questions.** Most multiple-choice questions are constructed with one right answer, one that is close, and two or three that are clearly wrong. If you're stuck, narrow down the two best choices, then make your best guess. Don't dwell on it. You've done the best you can. Move on. If you have time later, you can go back and reconsider an alternative choice.

- **Make the questions easier.** Convert each possible answer into a true-false question: If you choose this answer, does it make the question true or false?

- **When you don't know the answer, play the odds.** Jokes included as choices are always wrong. Longer answers are more often correct than the shortest ones. When the answer is a number, more often the right one is not the largest or smallest one. When two answers are very similar, that is a clue that one of them is probably the correct one. When an answer has "always" or "never" in it, it is often wrong. If an answer has a typo or unfamiliar word, it is probably wrong. Remember, these are just probabilities (but instructors know them, too).

- **Read *all* the choices before selecting the best one.** There is often more than one reasonable answer. Your job is to pick the *best* one, a task that you can't complete until you review all the options.

- **Mark the questions that confound you.** Don't spend too much time on any one question. Put a mark next to those that give you trouble or require more thought, or those for which you are still uncertain about the best choice. Time permitting, go back to them later.

- **Don't assume there are "trick" questions.** Instructors don't intentionally play games to try to fool you. In most cases, they want you to do well because it makes them feel better about their teaching. If a question looks "tricky," make sure that you aren't reading more into it than was intended.

● **If you don't know the answer, guess.** Assuming you don't lose points for wrong answers, trust your intuition when all else fails, especially if you've been able to eliminate one or two choices.

● **Remember to look for clues from one question that might help you answer another.** You may find information presented in one question on the test that will help you answer another question.

● **Control your frustration.** There are always a few questions on every test that seem stupid, unfair, or just downright confusing. Don't get flustered. Take another cleansing breath. Mark the question for later analysis. If there is time, ask for clarification. Otherwise, make your best guess and move on.

● **Take mini-breaks.** Whenever your attention wanders or you lose concentration, stretch for a minute, and take another cleansing breath.

● **Don't let your eyes wander.** Being caught cheating will ruin not only your day, but possibly your life. Whether intentionally or not, if you look like you are checking out someone else's work, you can be found guilty of academic dishonesty. This can result in anything from flunking the exam to being kicked out of the college.

Strategies for True-False Tests

True-false tests might seem easier than multiple choice or matching because you only have to choose between two alternatives. That's the good news. The bad news is that it is sometimes tricky to determine whether a statement is correct or incorrect, even if you have some knowledge of that subject.

In addition to some of the strategies mentioned earlier, such as not leaving any questions blank, there are several other things to keep in mind when taking a true-false test.

1. True or false: When you don't know the answer to a true-false question, you should mark it false. Correct answer: False.

    As a general probability, there are usually more true answers because it is more challenging to write false ones that appear true.

2. With that said, look for *any* excuse to mark as false what might appear to be a true statement. Remember, this is a test not only of what you know, but also of your ability to examine details. These questions have all kinds of *extreme modifiers* included in them like "never," "always," "all," "none," "best," and "worst."

Mimi:
Talking Out Loud

" For the longest time I didn't know how to study for a test. I would kind of guess that I knew the stuff because I had gone to class and taken some notes, so I would look over my notes and hope that was enough. Then, during the test I would actually blank out. I mean, if it was multiple choice I would end up doing the whole eeny-meeny-miny-moe thing, and if the test had essay questions, I would just fake my way through them. And my grades sucked, of course.

You know, it's totally true what they say about you learning more when you explain something to someone else. You know what I do now when I study? I talk out loud to myself. I pretend I'm teaching the stuff to someone and then I talk, talk, talk. I always remember everything really well if I do this. I know I look crazy, walking around the house and talking to myself, but it really works for me.

Radius Images/Jupiter Images

When taking exams, it is sometimes a good idea to play your hunch when you can't decide on the correct answer. However, when you review questions that you aren't sure about, don't be afraid to change your answer after consideration. A number of studies have found that when students changed their answers on multiple-choice questions, half the time they went from the wrong answer to a right one and only 25 percent of the time did they change from the correct answer to an incorrect one (the other 25 percent changed from one wrong answer to another) (Kruger, Wirtz, and Miller, 2005).

True or false: *Every* student should reduce stress by participating in an exercise program that involves at least three days of aerobic activity.

Every student? No exceptions? What about someone with chronic heart problems? There are almost always exceptions (notice the "almost always," which is a *qualifier* and signifies that the statement is more likely to be true).

Qualifying words in statements include "usually," "almost always," "sometimes," "many," "might," "majority," "most," "frequently," and "often." Statements are more likely (again, notice the qualifier) to be correct when they are stated in conditional terms: *Most* students should participate in aerobic exercise.

3. Many statements have two parts that include something that is true, and then a reason that it may be false: "True-false tests are easy for instructors to grade [true] because students do better on them than multiple-choice or essay exams [false]." Make sure that *everything* in the statement is true—dates, names, conditions, examples, and reasons.

4. Decode the double negatives. Sometimes when reading a question, you get the impression it is written in a foreign language. You read it over several times and still can't figure out what is being said:

   It is not abnormal to feel some degree of anxiety when taking a true-false test.

   The "not abnormal" has to be converted to "normal" before you can figure out whether it is true or false. Whenever you see "not" paired up with another negative word like illogical, illegal, unhelpful, or uncommon, they cancel each other out to make a positive statement.

Strategies for Matching Tests

Matching is the same game as multiple choice but with different rules. Matching tests are also recognition rather than recall—all the correct answers are in front of you if you can identify what they are. You don't have to rely as much on memory, but rather must recognize connections between items.

As with every test, read the instructions carefully to determine what the rules are and how they apply. Among the following strategies for matching tests, the first and most important determination is whether you can use an item only once or more than once. The latter is more difficult since you are not eliminating choices as you use them.

1. Assuming that the items on one side are the same number as those on the other, and that each item is paired only once, cross off each alternative as you match it.

2. Do the easy ones first. This allows you to eliminate as many options as possible before you attack the more challenging items.

3. Resist the impulse to match items as soon as you recognize a connection. Make sure that you go all the way through the list of choices for each item as there are likely to be several possible options.

4. Unlike true-false and multiple-choice tests, be careful about guessing when you don't know the correct response. If you make one wrong match, this can lead to several others that follow from the miscalculation.

Strategies for Essay Tests

Objective questions ask you to either recognize (multiple choice, true-false) or recall (short answer, fill-in-the-blank) a correct answer. Essay questions are easier in the sense that you have the opportunity to show the breadth of what you know in your own "voice," but they are also more challenging in that they require a deeper understanding of the content. You are asked not just to recognize or repeat what you've read or heard, but also to *apply* it in some way. You are required to think critically, to draw connections between points, and to make a case for your own interpretations of concepts. Compare the multiple-choice and essay questions in Figure 6.1.

Teaching Tip

Take this opportunity to review and discuss your campus academic honesty policy.

Teaching Tip

Ask students to reflect on an upcoming test that will feature essay questions. Ask them to carefully review their course notes, looking for clues to repeated or emphasized areas. Next, they should develop a list of key topics, prepare practice essay questions on these topics, and practice answering them under the same time conditions as in the actual course. Students should grade each practice essay by comparing its completeness to the list of key items. Instructors can use the textbook as a reference for expansion on the concept.

Figure 6.1 Comparison between Multiple-Choice and Essay Questions

Multiple-Choice Question	**Essay Question**
When preparing for an exam, you should consider a. how the questions are written. b. what material will be covered. c. how much time will be allocated to complete it. d. all of the above.	What are the most important things to consider when preparing for an examination? Based on those factors, which ones do you think are most critical, and why? Support your answer with examples and evidence.

Students usually have strong preferences for one type of test over another. Almost nobody excels in all forms of evaluation because of relative strengths and weaknesses. So take heart that if you struggle doing well on one kind of test, there are other options for you to demonstrate what you've learned. After your first year, you can even select classes (and majors) based on your strengths as well as your interests.

There are basically two kinds of essay exams, so it is important to find out ahead of time which variety to prepare for. There are "recall" essay questions in which you summarize material that you've studied, and there are "analytic" questions in which you respond critically, synthesizing information and applying it to cases, problems, or situations (see Figure 6.2). Determine whether you are expected to simply spit back what you have learned, or go much deeper into critical analysis.

Figure 6.2 Comparison between Recall and Analytic Essay Questions

Recall Essay Question	**Analytic Essay Question**
What were the main causes of the American Civil War?	Using the American Civil War as an example, discuss how current problems in the Middle East are similar to and different from those issues that were disputed between the Union and the Confederacy.

Unlike a multiple-choice exam, where you can get away with merely recognizing the correct answer when you see it, essay questions demand that you have the information you need at your disposal. This means that you have to do your best to predict the questions you might encounter. You can do this by getting direction from the instructor, the text, previous exams, students who have had the class before, and your study group.

Among the list of possible questions you've anticipated, pick a few of them that you are most confident will be on the test. Write out responses to those questions in a practice session and get some feedback on how well you did and what you could do to improve. This is another excellent excuse to make an appointment to see your instructor for some guidance and critical input.

6.2 FOR REFLECTION

Predicting Essay Questions

What are some essay questions that you could predict might be asked on the material covered in this chapter so far?

_____

_____

_____

_____

_____

Now compare your questions to those that are listed at the end of this chapter.

Teaching Tip

Provide students with a list of words commonly used in essay questions, such as "compare," "contrast," and "trace," along with their definitions.

Group Activity

Arrange small groups. Put all twelve bulleted items under "Strategies for Essay Tests" on separate pieces of paper, and give a set to each group. Ask students to list the strategies in order of time and/or importance.

Here are some more suggestions to consider when you take an essay exam.

- **Read the instructions carefully to identify what is really wanted.** Students often write beautiful essays—well constructed, detailed, articulate, and persuasive—but don't answer the question asked. What are you being asked to do? *Discuss* a point? *Compare* points of view? *Summarize* concepts? *Analyze* a case? *Express* your opinion? *Justify* a position? *Interpret* the meaning of something? Pay close attention to the task you are assigned.

- **Think before you write.** Jot down a quick plan and outline of the main points you want to cover. Use scratch paper if available, or the margins of the test.

- **Budget your time.** Students frequently make the mistake of running out of time by getting carried away with one question that they really liked, while neglecting the others. Consider the relative point values of each question if they don't all count the same. Figure out how much time you can allocate for each question, and stick with it.

- **Never leave questions blank.** With essay tests, you *can* fake it and usually get at least partial credit. If you can't answer exactly what the question asks, then discuss something that is at least tangentially related. You'll often get a few "mercy" points for trying.

● **Organize your responses so they read coherently.** When writing essay answers, giving speeches, or writing papers, it is absolutely critical that you plan carefully what you want to say.

● **Be brief and to the point.** Longer answers are not necessarily better. In fact, they tend to be more rambling and disorganized. The instructor is looking for evidence that you "get it," that you have included the required points. Don't drift off the assigned topic just to add unrelated information that you wanted to say.

● **Answer all parts of the question.** Some essay questions contain multiple parts, for example: (1) Describe the most important things to consider when studying for a test, (2) include examples comparing different strategies for essay versus objective exams, and (3) why do you think that many students don't follow best practices?

● **Use supporting examples.** It isn't enough to make a statement in your essay answer, unless you can support it with some kind of evidence. In a comparison question, if you make the claim that one thing is better or different than the other, prove it with an example.

● **Spelling counts.** One source of anxiety for some students, especially if they don't yet have solid writing skills, is that essay exams don't always allow time to edit answers. Good spelling, punctuation, and grammar *do* count in that they are part of your presentation style. Consider how *you* would grade an answer that was written as follows (even if the sentiment is technically correct):

> *Ive lerned that spaced studing werks better than massed practise.*

● **Include as many details as you can remember.** One way to fortify your answer, and establish your expertise, is with specifics about the content. Use whatever names, dates, and locations you can recall.

● **Reread and edit.** If there is time to write a rough draft, sketch one out before completing a final version. If time is limited, at least proofread what you've written, making last-minute corrections.

● **Don't leave early.** Whether for objective or essay tests, use *all* the time that you are given. Even if you sailed through the test and are absolutely dying to get the heck out of there, resist the temptation. Review your responses, especially with those questions that stumped you a bit. As a last exercise, make a prediction as to what you think your grade will be based on your own self-scoring.

▶ **VIEW IT**

© Cengage Learning

What You Learn from Failure
Students talk about their favorite ways to prepare for tests. One story reveals what you can learn when you do much worse than you expected. (www.cengagebrain.com)

Proving Yourself: Final Exams

One of the major differences between high school and college is that in some classes, you will have only a midterm and final exam upon which to determine your grade. Some classes have just a final exam—period. This puts even more pressure on you to make sure you do all you can to demonstrate what you've learned.

Depending on the department, subject, and instructor, a final exam could count for 20 percent, 50 percent, 75 percent, or even 110 percent (just checking to see if you are still paying attention) of your grade. Some classes permit you to skip a final altogether, although many first-year classes will more likely than not require this final rite of passage that assesses *everything* you have learned during the semester.

If you have been keeping up with the reading assignments, attending class regularly, completing the required work, and studying on a regular basis, you are already in good shape. Remember that the best way to store and retrieve learning is through frequent, shorter study periods over a longer period of time, rather than trying to cram everything into a few all-nighters.

Teaching Tip
Ask students to review the syllabus for each enrolled course, paying close attention to the significance of the final exam for the overall grade. Three weeks before the final, students should schedule an appointment with each course professor. Having prepared a concept list from lecture notes and textbook reading in advance, students should seek guidance from the professor in terms of the completeness of their list, and then plan appropriate review times as part of a weekly time management plan for studying during the final three weeks of the semester.

Most colleges separate final exams from regular class sessions, providing you with several study days to prepare for them. Generally, the final exam is scheduled over a several-hour period of time. If the schedule works out well for you, you might have only one exam per day.

Since fatigue has often set in by the end of the semester, not to mention being sick of a few of your classes, this is time to redouble your motivation and press on toward the end. It is the fourth quarter with two minutes left, and you've got the ball. You're tired, but the whole game is on the line. You could have played well all the way until this moment, but if you mess up now, most of what you've gained is lost.

If your grades in the class are less than stellar thus far, the final exam gives you a chance to redeem yourself, to sink the last shot at the buzzer and pull out a spectacular win from the jaws of defeat. And if you have been doing well in the class, you can enjoy a cushion that allows you to relax a little, but still press your advantage to the end.

There is no way to soft-pedal this: Final exams are serious business. You will notice that everything around campus changes in pace. The library is open for extended hours; 24-hour study areas are set up around campus. There is a hush in conversations, a frantic look in many students' eyes. It is time to pay for whatever you have done, or not done, all semester long. And many unfortunate students try to press their luck and hope they get away with having slacked off a good portion of the year. Even if a few are fortunate enough to pull a final out of the fire at the last minute, that is a terrible habit to get into that will eventually burn you in the end.

Final exam period is sacred, in a way. It brings an even more intense level of commitment and concentration to the job of being a student. To continue the basketball metaphor, it is playoff time now that the regular season is over. Every minute of preparation is worth ten times what it was earlier. This is a time to say "no" to every social invitation, to decline any diversion or distraction, to devote yourself single-mindedly to the exhilarating sprint at the end. That isn't to say that you should run yourself ragged, neglect your sleep and usual exercise routines, pig out on junk food, and obsess constantly about the upcoming tests. If anything, it is even more important that you take care of yourself leading up to this final championship match.

After the Test Is Over

Here is a question for you to consider: Once the test is over, which is the best course of action?

a. Take a long nap to catch up on all the sleep you missed while studying.

b. Put the experience behind you and forget it ever happened.

c. Start partying as soon as possible to celebrate.

d. Review your notes and study material to see how helpful they were.

Whereas choice "A" (taking a nap) could very well be a major priority, the single most important thing you can do immediately after an exam is to review your performance.

Learn from Your Mistakes

As much as you might like to relax or celebrate, the optimal time to learn from the test experience is immediately afterward while everything is still fresh in your mind. This has the added advantage of helping you to feel like you are doing something productive if the test was more difficult than you had hoped. Even just a half hour reviewing your study materials will give you loads of feedback on what you neglected and how you might prepare differently in the future.

The most important action you can take occurs immediately after the test is returned. This is when you need to spend the most time learning from your mistakes, reviewing every wrong answer, examining patterns in your errors, and setting goals for a revised strategy. Come up with an action plan to avoid similar mistakes on your next test. It is also a good idea to review all the questions since you probably guessed on a few of them. Unless this was a final exam, assume you will see similar questions again.

If you are working in a study group, schedule a session soon after the tests are returned so you can review them together. Decide what you will do differently, individually and as a group, to improve your performance.

Taking tests is a skill, based not only on what you know and how well you prepare, but also on the strategies you use to decode correct answers or present your points of view. Since you will likely take fifty or more tests in your college career, you would be well advised to devote considerable time and effort to learning a successful system. All of this begins with how you make adjustments after tests are returned.

How Answers Are Graded

There is no mystery as to how "objective" tests are graded—the instructor just adds up the number of correct points. But essay tests are "subjective," meaning they are open to some judgment on the part of the evaluator. It isn't just a matter of deciding that one response is "good" and the other is "lousy"; rather, criteria are applied to determine whether a given answer meets the expectations.

Some instructors will use a formal template in which they assign specific points for required components. This works well with recall essay exams in which you are asked to describe, say, five causes of Shia and Sunni conflict in Iraq (with one point for each correct reason listed). But with analytic questions, in which you are expected to write short essays arguing or critically examining a particular point of view, responses are graded similarly to full-length papers. Here are guidelines that instructors might use:

● Are the facts correct and the content accurate?

● Was the question answered completely and comprehensively?

● Were points supported with appropriate examples?

Somos/Veer/Jupiter Images

Think about test grades as useful feedback about what you know and understand, and what you need to work harder on. Throughout your life, you will receive such input from supervisors who will expect you to take this "advice" nondefensively and learn from it so that you don't repeat the same errors. After a test or paper is returned, the single most useful thing you can do is to review your mistakes, look up answers you didn't know, and study alternative ways you can approach assignments in the future.

● Is there evidence of insight into the problem or situation?

● Is the essay organized, well thought out, coherent, and logical?

● Is the point of view convincing and persuasive?

● What is the quality of the writing, including mechanics?

● What is the level of synthesis and understanding evident in the writing?

I'll grant that this is a lot to keep in mind. Yet with practice and perseverance, you will become skilled at accomplishing these tasks in your writing. The same standards will be required for papers you write in any class. Even more critically, these are also the criteria that are often used for evaluating reports you will write in future careers.

Unhappy about Your Grade?

Human beings have a natural tendency to blame others (or unforeseen circumstances) when things go wrong. It is absolutely the case that tests don't always assess what you've actually learned. Sometimes they aren't fair or well constructed. But that is just like other aspects of life that don't meet your preferences or expectations.

If you receive a grade that you feel is less than you deserve, your first reaction might very well be to externalize the problem, blaming an unfair test, a heartless instructor, or some distraction that was going on in your life or in the classroom at the time. You may even feel justified in going to the instructor to lodge your complaint. Before you indulge that inclination, however, consider the following points.

Students rarely visit their professors to talk about academic issues, or get help in better understanding the subject; more often than not, when students stop by office hours or after class, they come to complain about a grade. It isn't that instructors never make mistakes, or that grading is not subject to error, but before you consider challenging a grade, make a plan for how you are going to broach the subject so you don't appear hotheaded.

Appeals about your grade on a test can occur under the following circumstances:

1. There was a mistake adding up the number of points or calculating the correct grade. This is easy to check by simple math.

2. The grade you were assigned was not consistent with the appropriate number. You got an 82, for example, which according to the curve should have been a B, but you were given a C+.

3. A question was marked wrong that should have been marked correct. This is also very easy to confirm.

4. You were given credit for a question that should have been marked wrong. This possibility is included in case you want to take the moral high ground. By the way, there are no guarantees, but taking this path is often viewed by instructors as sufficiently righteous that you may be given credit anyway just for your honesty.

5. You don't feel you were given sufficient credit for a response on an essay exam. You are welcome to try arguing this one, but it's a long shot. Instructors are reluctant to change grades unless there is an *obvious* mistake that is not open to subjective opinion.

6. You believe a particular question on the test was unfair. This one is a difficult call. If you are one of many who complained about this question, it is possible the instructor could decide to discard it and give everyone credit. But if you are the only one complaining, you can come across as a grade-obsessed whiner.

If you do decide to question, complain, or argue about a grade, try to come across as assertive rather than aggressive and respectful rather than argumentative. To make your best case, don't try to talk to the instructor immediately after class (when things are so hectic and others are waiting in line). Instead, prepare to present the facts with support. And here is a key point—use a style that is calm and that will not be interpreted as threatening. Don't attack, blame, or find fault, or you will put the instructor in a defensive position, making it more difficult for him or her to see your side of things. Be as polite as possible during this encounter.

If, when all is said and done, you believe that you were treated unfairly or subject to bias, or that your grade was not appropriately assigned, you do have the option of taking an appeal further. Do your homework and consult the student handbook or catalog for specific details about how to appeal a grade. Schedule an appointment and prepare your case. Explain your interpretation clearly and concisely. This may involve talking to the department chair (who will likely require that you talk to the instructor about the issue first), and then following procedures that may involve the assistant dean or an appeals committee on campus. With each of these steps you take, there are consequences you will wish to consider. Make sure that you don't lose perspective on what is most important, as any action you take can be quite time-consuming.

Finally, apart from any grade-related concerns on a particular test, if you really want to improve your test performances, visit the instructor and tutoring center on campus to get feedback. You can review the mistakes you made with expert assistance and plan better in the future for how to prepare more effectively.

© Richard Hutchings/CORBIS

If your goal is to present the best possible case for appealing a grade, you would be well advised to remain calm, and not blame the test or attack the instructor, but rather politely and respectfully explain the rationale for your point of view.

SUMMARY

Taking tests is a skill—one that can be learned. Although some people seem to have a natural talent for doing well on exams, the rest of us have to work hard to master the tricks of the trade.

Although testing doesn't necessarily measure what you've learned in a class, it does form the basis for your evaluation. Some tests may not appear to be fair, but that is the reality of education in which performance is judged based on narrow criteria.

It is important to customize your preparation and studying to fit the unique requirements of the exam—whether it covers limited material or the whole semester, whether it requires recall or recognition, and whether it involves writing essays or recognizing correct answers. Regardless of the grade you receive, the key to improvement is learning from your mistakes.

QUESTIONS FOR REVIEW AND FURTHER EXPLORATION

1. What are the ways you would prepare differently for a multiple-choice, essay, or take-home exam?

2. What are some ways that you can best predict what questions will be on the exam? Look back through this chapter and make some calculated guesses about what questions you might be asked.

3. How does deep breathing operate to reduce stress and keep you focused when you are under pressure during an exam? Provide an example of what you have done in situations where you were under pressure to remain as calm and controlled as possible.

4. If you were an instructor, what are the reasons why you might use a recall versus analytic essay test?

5. Describe how you will review a returned test to maximize your performance on future exams.

6. It is inevitable that the grade you receive on an exam is not what you had hoped for or expected. What will you tell yourself about this disappointment to prevent feeling discouraged and instead renew efforts to learn from the experience?

ANSWERS TO FOR REFLECTION 6.2

Don't feel discouraged if you came up with different essay questions that might be asked on material covered in this chapter so far—maybe your questions are better than these. Each question is labeled as to whether it requires *recall* of facts or concepts, is *analytic* in nature, or is a combination of both.

1. How do studying for and taking tests in college prepare you for the realities in the world of work? **Recall question**

2. What are the two parts of performing under pressure? Give examples of how this applies to a favorite activity that you participate in on a regular basis. **Recall and analytic question**

3. How would you prepare differently for an essay exam than for a multiple-choice exam? **Recall question**

4. What are some ways to best predict questions that might be on a test? **Recall question**

5. What are some of the best strategies to apply when you don't know the answer to a multiple-choice question at first reading? **Recall question**

6. Based on your own test-taking experiences, what are some points in the text with which you disagree? Support your answer with evidence or examples. **Analytic question**

 Go to www.cengagebrain.com for an online quiz that will test your understanding of the chapter content.

CHAPTER 7

Writing Papers and Doing Presentations

KEY QUESTIONS

▶ **How do you construct the anatomy of a paper?**

▶ **What are the critical parts to include in every paper or presentation?**

▶ **How do you develop your unique writer's voice?**

▶ **What are some things to consider when e-mailing instructors?**

▶ **What are the different ways that you can research a topic to generate interesting, even new, information?**

▶ **What should you consider when evaluating the quality and accuracy of any research source?**

▶ **What are the most frequent errors that students make in their writing?**

▶ **How do you overcome fears and apprehensions related to giving presentations?**

▶ **What are the most common mistakes that students make when doing class presentations?**

For Community College Students
Keep in mind that extensive writing and speech or presentation classes may still be two to three semesters into the future for students in beginning-level remediation.

Group Activity
Divide a dry-erase board into two columns: writing papers and doing presentations. Ask members of the class to go to the board and write one word under each heading for how they feel about each topic (writing or presenting).

Writing papers and giving presentations demonstrate your mastery of a subject. Both involve skills that are absolutely critical in the job market because most careers require you to write coherent, convincing, and accurate reports, as well as speak persuasively. Whereas during your first year of college you may be in larger classes that evaluate your performance through tests, as you progress to more advanced study you will be increasingly asked to synthesize content into expanded written and verbal forms.

At some point during college you will write critical essays, research papers, term papers, and creative projects. You will give speeches, do group presentations, participate in debates, and speak up in classes and meetings. You are not expected to already be accomplished in these important skills, even if you have some experience. But by the time you graduate, effective writing and speaking will be among your most valuable assets.

PHOTO: amana productions inc/Getty Images

Writing Papers

Group Activity
Conduct a brainstorming session for possible topics for a paper. Give the students some sample parameters, such as length of the paper and subject of the course.

Although writing an excellent paper and giving an outstanding class presentation have some parallels and similarities, their forms are sufficiently different that they require alternate constructions. You are going to write hundreds of papers before you graduate, and perhaps thousands more in your lifetime on the job, so this is definitely something at which you want to become as skilled as possible. While the basics are covered here, you will have many other opportunities to develop your writing ability.

Word-Processing Software

You most likely have some working familiarity with Microsoft Word or a similar word-processing program; if not, then sign up for a course *immediately*. This is not an option but an absolute requirement to complete your work in college. Regardless of any reluctance you might feel, you can develop reasonable competence in a matter of hours.

You must learn how to create and save files (and save them in such a way that you can find them again), move text around using the Copy and Cut features, and highlight text (select it) to change the font, size, or color, or to **bold**, underline, or *italicize* it. You also need to paginate (assign page numbers) and use "headers," which are those summary titles at the top of pages.

Once you have the hang of the basics, more advanced skills will make your life much easier. For instance, in the Review menu is listed a Track Changes tool that allows someone like your instructor or ~~a friend~~ an editor to ~~change things~~ make suggestions in your document. You can then decide to accept or reject each of the changes one at a time, or perform the same operation with all of them. The Insert Comment function allows an editor to make an observation in the margin.

Anatomy of a Paper

Simply put, a paper, *any* paper, has a beginning, a middle, and an end (that *was* pretty simple, wasn't it?). You'd think that with such a basic outline, it shouldn't be that difficult to follow it. Yet instructors are often surprised at how often students neglect these basic elements.

An important rule for writing any document or paper (as well as oral presentation) is to

1. say what you are going to do,

2. do what you said,

3. say what you did.

Every paper should have a brief introduction in which you give an overview of what you will cover and what the reader can expect. Depending on the length of the paper, this can be a single paragraph for a brief assignment or a page or two for a longer one (twelve or more pages). This introduction should accomplish two major tasks: capture reader interest, and provide a preview of coming attractions. The example in Figure 7.1 demonstrates how two paragraphs can be used to set the agenda and tone for what follows.

The middle part of the paper is the guts of the document. Here you present your ideas, develop your theme, and provide examples and evidence to support your thesis. Although this sounds as if it is one continuous segment, ideally it should be subdivided into sections with headings. Notice how this very chapter uses headings to set apart topics that are distinct yet related to one another. The *first-level heading* earlier in this chapter is "Writing Papers." It is in bigger, bold type to signal this is a "major" topic. *Second-level headings* are also in bold type, and are usually set against the left

Figure 7.1 Example of an Introduction to a Paper

Cyber-Stalking on the Internet

According to a recent study conducted by the Department of Justice, an estimated 1 million women and a half-million men are victims of stalking. They are plagued by unrelenting pursuers who annoy and harass them, terrorize them, and in some cases even resort to violence, physical abuse, or murder. Like almost every other facet of life in this age of computers, the ability of stalkers to identify, locate, and harass their victims has been enhanced by the power of the Internet, spawning a new wave of crime.

This paper will review the ways that cyber-stalkers target their victims through chat rooms, message boards, discussion forums, and e-mail. Such stalkers lurk in the most unsuspecting forms on the Web and take on innocent roles that make them appear inviting, if not seductive. This paper will highlight some of the most common forms of abuse that take place, including (1) threats of blackmail or physical harm, (2) obscene e-mail, (3) spamming, (4) chat harassment or flaming, (5) leaving improper or abusive communications on message boards or in guest books, (6) sending electronic viruses, (7) sending unsolicited e-mail, and (8) electronic identity theft.

margin; "Anatomy of a Paper" is one such example. These sections break the major topic into its important components or steps. *Third-level headings* are used when a particular section needs even more detailed description or organization.

The main point to remember is that you want to make it easy for a reader to follow your train of thought by organizing the main body of the paper into sections that are logical, sequential, and descriptive.

Now comes the end of the paper, and this is where many students just give up— the paper just stops like a movie that was cut off in the middle. You must include some type of summary that wraps things up. Like the introduction, it can be just a few paragraphs, but it should (1) summarize what was presented, (2) synthesize the material in a meaningful way, (3) mention applications or future directions, and (4) end on a memorable note.

Figure 7.2 provides an example of such a closing section in a paper written about the ways that travel can change one's life. The goal, in three brief paragraphs, is to bring together the various themes that were introduced and then close with an inspiring ending. You would alter the tone and style according to whether this was a research paper in the social sciences, an essay for an English class, or for the unique demands of any other discipline. The important thing to remember, however, is to make sure your paper concludes with some sort of synthesis.

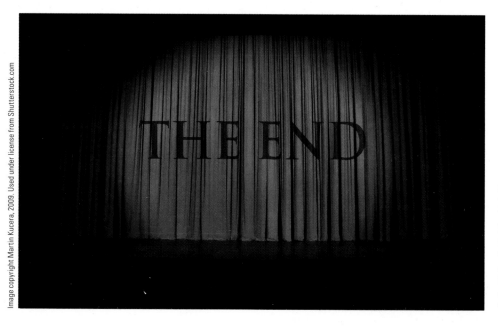

Papers should be structured in such a way that you introduce your subject and give an overview of the contents, present your main points, and then provide some kind of review or closure rather than just ending abruptly. It is usually a good idea to summarize key points or discuss what was learned from the assignment.

Figure 7.2   Example of a Closing to a Paper

Summary of How Travel Can Become Transformative

People often think of travel as being separate from their normal lives, a time-out that eventually ends once they return home. Yet all people are traveling every moment of their lives, whether they define it as a vacation or not. Wherever people may be, whoever they may be with, and whatever the circumstances, travel is a state of mind in which people pay close attention to where they are and what they're doing.

It isn't necessary to be in Tahiti or Madagascar to be transformed by a journey. Taking a trip, even an adventurous, unstructured one, is no guarantee that anyone will grow significantly and permanently as a result. Just getting out of bed in the morning in a particular way, facing the day with a spirit of adventure, encountering people with openness and flexibility, and pushing oneself to do things differently—this is what leads to personal growth.

While it is often easier to do this during a trip, away from usual influences and restrictions, these changes can take place anywhere someone chooses to make it happen. In fact, if travel teaches one important lesson it is that life is too short to limit one's freedom to mere vacations. Travel is not really an escape from normal life, nor is it a separate reality; rather, it acts as a reminder of what is possible to experience every waking moment of life. Only then will the changes endure.

Organization of Your Paper

Now that you have the introduction and summary taken care of, the next challenge is how to arrange the middle. As a useful beginning point for how to structure it, start with the standard format in most academic disciplines for completing a research paper:

1. **Statement of the problem.** This is a brief description of the issues, questions, hypothesis, or themes that will be addressed in the paper. This could be included as part of your introduction. Example: *This paper will examine the ways that stress and poor time management affect the quality of work for freshmen during their first semester.*

2. **Review of literature.** This is where you establish credibility that you are familiar with what has already been said on the subject. Any writer, scientist, journalist, or investigator can't hope to advance knowledge in a field unless he or she knows what has been done previously. In your last years of college, when you are doing more complete research papers, or even a thesis, you will be expected to do a fairly comprehensive review, but in the beginning you can often get away with including a few of the major sources.

3. **Methodology.** You describe what you did and how you did it so that someone reading your paper can replicate it if they want (this is a basic principle of science). In literature, arts, and humanities classes, you describe the methods you used to investigate, explore, or describe your topic.

4. **Results.** What did you discover? This is the fun part of the paper, but also the most challenging. Here you describe what you found and why you believe it is significant.

5. **Applications.** So what impact does what you described, explored, and analyzed have in the world? This part of the paper most clearly shows your ability to synthesize and make sense of your results. You can discuss implications as well as applications and case examples.

6. **Conclusions.** As discussed earlier, this summary brings closure to your paper.

Although this is a basic template for science and social science research papers, you can easily adapt this for many other class papers. You will want to work from an outline in which you list the most important points you want to make, under which are listed secondary points, supporting evidence, and case examples. Transitions are created to link the major points to one another. You don't want to stick in content that does not logically and sequentially flow from one point to the next. You are essentially telling a story that begins with a statement of purpose and ends with a synthesis of what you have explored or discovered.

Constructing the First Draft

There is no single "right" way to compose a paper. Some students like to work from outlines, following them sequentially from one point to the next. They list the main themes of each section, arguments, and important points, subpoints, supporting evidence, and so on. This is an excellent plan but not the only workable one.

Some writers just like to write. They start from the middle, or anywhere they feel like it, and just start producing prose. Rather than working according to a sequential plan, they prefer to write from the *inside out*. Both literally and figuratively, they prefer to write from the middle of the paper outward toward the edges and they also like to access their innermost thoughts before including other voices and sources. Because computers make it so easy to "cut and paste," the sequence of writing doesn't matter as long as you produce all the material you need and eventually insert it in the appropriate place in the outline. Any sections that are missing can be filled in later, along with transitions between them.

You may need to experiment to find the process that best helps you to express yourself fluently and articulately. Whatever you produce in this first draft is just that—an initial attempt to get the main ideas down. It is the editing and refining stage that follows next that turns jumbled writing into polished prose.

Writing Style and Personal Prose

Depending on the class, and your eventual major, you will learn to write according to the standards of your discipline. If you hope to enter a corporate setting, you'll learn to write in the language and style that are appropriate for business. The same is true for those of you who will learn to write lesson plans in education, committee reports for public agencies, technical reports for engineering, poetry and short stories for English, or the appropriate style for journalism, media and television, or science, law, and medicine.

One of the most important tasks you have ahead of you as a writer is to find and develop your own "voice," your own personal, unique style of written communication that is consistent with standards in the field, but also conveys your personality and vision. I had no idea that I had any talent as a writer until I took the same class you are now taking as a first-semester student and received support and encouragement from the instructor.

Teaching Tip to Reduce Stress

Conduct a class discussion on ways to overcome writer's block. Suggest that when a student is having trouble getting started on a paper, he or she might want to resort to an old composition trick. Go back to each research source and develop 3 × 5 index cards with facts gleaned from each source. Color code the information based on the areas to be covered in the paper. Arrange these cards to tell a story about the topic.

Teaching Tip

Encourage students to keep an academic as well as personal journal. Each day, students should record their personal impressions of their academic journey—searching for one new knowledge fact or application area for each class that became clear to them that particular day. Encourage students to review these journal entries before a test. In addition, these journal entries can help identify what areas are of most interest to them and provide valuable insight into their major and career selection.

Good writing, like painting, is about expressing yourself in an authentic way. At first, it is messy and awkward, but with self-discipline and practice you can learn to craft and polish your prose into a minor masterpiece, or at least something that you can be proud of.

7.1 FOR REFLECTION

Finding Your Writer's Voice through Journaling

To become a writer, you have to write—every day, even for just a half hour. Start with a journal in which you record your most intimate inner experiences and most interesting observations about what is going on around you. This is not a diary in which you merely record events, but rather a reservoir for your ideas and inspirations, a place for you to develop your writer's voice.

As far as what you write about, you will find limitless possibilities, including the following:

1. Observations about others around you, how they behave, and meanings you attach to their behavior
2. Honest assessments of your own behavior, including strengths and weaknesses, fears, and apprehensions
3. Exploration of unresolved issues in your life that keep cropping up again and again
4. Ideas from class and readings you want to remember and hold onto, explore in further depth, and apply to your own life
5. Work through conflicts you have with others, and rehearse things you'd like to say differently
6. Plans and goals for the future, including commitments you want to make and intentions you want to follow through on
7. Things you have learned about yourself that you want to remember
8. Ideas for future projects you might begin
9. List of books you want to read in the future
10. Dialogues with yourself about things you don't understand, or want to understand better
11. Creative expressions, including drawings, poetry, rants, stories, and dialogue
12. Documentation of your growth and progress

Remember, this is only a *limited* sample of possibilities.

Write your first entry below:

You may not have the freedom to express yourself as you would like in many class papers, but you still have the opportunity to communicate in your own authentic style. Instructors have to read stacks of papers every semester, and most of them are predictable and boring. It is so refreshing to read something wholly original, or at least offering a new perspective, or written in an imaginative way.

Writing is primarily about making ideas come alive. It persuades readers about your point of view. It stimulates them to see things in a new or different way. And it describes things in such a way that readers are influenced and affected by the prose.

You don't have to be a budding poet, or even to think of yourself as particularly creative, to find your own writing voice. But you do have to trust yourself enough to communicate what you have to say in your own words.

Writing and Rewriting

Less than half of freshman (47 percent) admit that they rarely, if ever, revise or rewrite their papers prior to handing them in, and only 21 percent ever use any scientific articles or resources (versus websites) to support their ideas (Higher Education Research Institute, 2008). The quality of this work is obviously reflected in the low grades assigned.

Harper Lee, author of *To Kill a Mockingbird,* spent almost three years writing her autobiographical novel about racial strife during the Depression in the South. Although her first novel is considered one of the greatest masterpieces of the twentieth century, Lee was never able to produce another work that met her high standards.

AP Photo/The Tuscaloosa News, Robert Sutton

Don't turn in any paper until you have written at least two, and preferably three, drafts. It isn't only the content of what you write that determines how it is viewed and graded, but also the style in which it is written. Even with spell-check and grammar-check embedded in word-processing programs, students still turn in work that is filled with mistakes and oversights in which it is obvious that the papers had not been carefully proofread.

Some of the greatest writers were perfectionists and compulsive rewriters. Ernest Hemmingway wrote and rewrote the ending to his great novel *A Farewell to Arms* twenty-six times. J. D. Salinger took ten years to write *The Catcher in the Rye* (only 180 pages). Tolstoy rewrote *War and Peace* twelve times before he thought it was ready. After writing *Call It Sleep*, Henry Roth required another fifty years before he was ready to publish his next book. Thomas Pynchon labored for seventeen years to write *Vineland*, and Joseph Heller took thirteen years to complete *Something Happened*. After writing *To Kill a Mockingbird*, Harper Lee never wrote anything else that came close to her exacting standards. The point of these examples? Good writing takes time, patience, and diligent crafting. You may not have ten years to turn in a paper that meets your highest expectations, but surely you can rework it a few times before submitting it for review.

When reviewing your first draft, go through the manuscript carefully to make sure that it is organized properly, that transitions connect paragraphs and sections, that you have included headings that are descriptive, and that the prose flows well. Read the draft as if you are a critical reviewer, checking punctuation, cutting out repetitive material, abbreviating sentences that are too long, and filling in gaps when points don't seem clear. Check to make sure that you have included citations and references for any material you have used from other sources; also check that you have listed them in the correct format. Finally, make sure that you have

Group Activity

If your campus has a writing center, ask one of the staff members to meet with your class. Ask him or her to talk about what issues are commonly seen with papers and share how students can write their best papers.

Classroom Discussion

Open it up: What process do you use to write and revise papers? How early do you start? Do you create outlines? How many times do you revise?

© Istockphoto.com/Catalin Petolea

Even among corporate executives, more than one-third report that their computer malfunctions at least once per month. Add to probable mechanical meltdown the threat of computer viruses and worms, plus inevitable human error (including loss, theft, and spilled coffee), and you can see the importance of protecting your work by backing up computer files in multiple ways.

addressed *all* the assignment's requirements—the first question the instructor will ask when grading it is "Did you complete the requirements?"

Get Help with Your Writing

Once you get your paper back with a grade, and hopefully detailed comments (this varies according to the size and purpose of the class as well as the instructor), you should consider ways to improve your writing for future assignments. Even if you didn't get as much feedback as you had hoped, you can bring the paper to the writing center on campus and review it with a tutor. The goal is to improve both your technical mastery (grammar, construction) and your prose.

Here is a summary of the most common mistakes that beginning writers make:

- Failing to meet the requirements of the assignment (not reading instructions carefully, or neglecting to cover all the required elements)
- Poor grammar and sentence construction
- Making statements without support, evidence, or examples
- Doing sloppy research and presenting inaccurate information
- Using improper citation style, or failing to provide needed references
- Rambling on and on, using far too many words to make your points
- Repetition and redundancy covering the same points over and over
- Disorganized and chaotic flow that doesn't appear logical and sequential
- Confusing common word usages (who, whose, and whom, or there, their, and they're)
- Stilted prose in simple sentences: *"This paper is about the Romantic era in poetry. It will concentrate primarily on Shelley and Keats. It will review their contributions. It will also discuss criticisms."*
- Waiting until the deadline looms and time pressures sabotage a quality effort

Chas:
Consulting the Instructor

❝ There's this one teacher who everyone says is so hard in her grading. She kept telling us in class that she was willing to go over our papers beforehand with us during her office hours. At the time I thought, "Yeah, right, like I'd really go to your office to have you chop up my paper." Then I tried to actually write the paper over the weekend, and I found that I was clueless. I had no idea what she was looking for. I decided right then that I would swallow my pride, suck it up, and go to her with my first draft. So I worked on it for a few days, knowing it was not very good at all. I was so nervous when I sat down with her, but she was actually really encouraging about it. She looked over my entire paper quickly, then sat and discussed with me my strong ideas and areas that needed more work. She even helped me with the format so I wouldn't get docked points on that. Though it took a lot of courage and guts for me to enter that office, I'm so glad I did.

Writing E-mail

While we are on the subject of writing skills, you will also need to master the intricacies of writing e-mail in a college setting, which is different than the informal messages you send to friends. Your college will offer both basic and advanced training in learning how to work the system, control spam, and, most critically, construct messages that are professional and appropriate. It is one thing to write any way you like to your friends, but any e-mail you send to an instructor should be written in a way to make the best possible impression. This means that instead of dashing off an impulsive message, you want to make sure the spelling, grammar, tone, and style convey what you wish (see Figure 7.3).

Some other suggestions to keep in mind for proper e-mail etiquette:

● Always put a meaningful descriptor in the subject line. This gives a preview of what the e-mail is about and also allows the reader to find it again more easily.

● Be selective with what you send. Most people are tired of getting forwarded e-mail with jokes, articles, announcements, and other things that clog your inbox.

● Identify yourself with descriptors and the class you are attending since your instructor likely has hundreds of students.

● Be brief. Many people, and *all* your instructors, already get way too much e-mail. Keep your messages brief and get to the point. Don't ramble endlessly.

● Don't ever, *ever* send an e-mail when you are upset or angry. Impulsive communications often lead to regrets and escalating problems.

● When you think you are sending attachments, make sure they are attached.

Classroom Discussion
Open it up: What would you change about this e-mail to an instructor? Rewrite this e-mail in a more appropriate style.

Figure 7.3   An E-mail to an Instructor

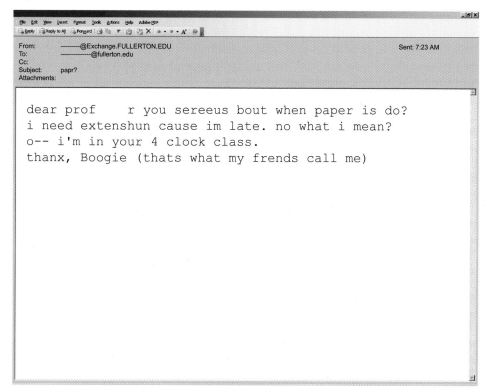

```
dear prof     r you sereeus bout when paper is do?
i need extenshun cause im late. no what i mean?
o-- i'm in your 4 clock class.
thanx, Boogie (thats what my frends call me)
```

- Learn to manage the storage of e-mails in your Inbox, in Deleted Files and Drafts folders, and in files on your hard drive. Be selective about what you retain, and make sure you can find it again.

- Edit your messages before you send them. Each communication you send is a reflection of who you are.

- Check your e-mail daily. Instructors get very annoyed when students don't respond to queries in a timely manner (the same holds true for instructors who don't respond).

- Reply promptly to e-mails. Taking weeks, or even days, to respond to someone is not acceptable.

- Remember how easily e-mail messages can be misconstrued. You may think you are saying one thing, but it can be interpreted very differently by the person receiving it. When misunderstandings arise, try to work things out on the phone or in person.

E-mail and text communications are both convenient and instantaneous, but they are often constructed impulsively, without much reflection and editing. Spontaneous is fine when talking to your friends, but be very careful when sending e-mails in which it is important to make a good impression.

Group Activity

Take a library tour and/or assign groups to brainstorm questions beforehand (e.g., "Is Wikipedia a credible source?") and interview librarians. Another option is for teams to go to the library and find specific things—like a scavenger hunt.

Searching and Re-searching Sources

Many of the papers you write are going to involve some degree of research. On the most basic level, it might involve integrating class notes and textbook readings with a theme that you are exploring. If you are asked to write reactions papers or thematic studies of books or articles you read, then you will be connecting source material to your own commentary. Regardless of the class and discipline, you will need to develop solid research skills to give your papers sufficient credibility and scholarly support. This goes *way* beyond a simple Google or Wikipedia search that is likely already familiar to you.

After you select a topic (or one has been chosen for you), begin every paper with research. This can involve reviewing the literature in the area, consulting with experts in the field, interviewing prospective firsthand sources who have experienced the phenomenon or know about it, or conducting your own surveys or observations in the field. The main idea is that before you can write about something, you have to have some breadth of knowledge about it.

Narrow Your Topic

One of the most challenging and important strategies for completing a research paper is to make sure the focus is narrow enough that you don't feel overwhelmed with all the material that already exists. Let's say you had an interest in researching something related to stress and you typed the term "stress" into one of the search options like Academic Search Premier or PsycINFO. Since you will get more than 100,000 possible hits, you need to narrow the topic further, so you add "college students" as another search term combined with stress. Now you've got 5,000 entries, which can be reduced further to less than 1,000 if you specify articles only in English and limit the search to the previous ten years. But that's still way too many sources to explore, so you review the possible "subject headings" that are offered and click on "coping behaviors" because you are interested specifically in strategies for dealing with stress in college. Good news: Now you are down to only sixty articles, which can be cut down further if you specify the kind of publication you prefer (article, book, etc.) and/ or set a shortened time span (previous five years).

Even with previous experience searching online, it takes practice using databases to find relevant material you can use for a paper. Consult with a librarian to help you with the process and teach you some tricks for working with the system.

Consider Your Sources

Although it is easiest just to do a Google or Yahoo! search on the Internet, the quality of information you get is often suspect, and sometimes inaccurate. Many of the websites listed are compiled by amateurs with extra time on their hands, or else they have their own agenda to sell something. So although doing a quick web search is a good starting point to get the lay of the land, you will not want to rely solely on this content for your paper. You will find excellent source material on some better-quality academic sites, but be critical of all sources.

Specific journals cover the academic discipline of your class, as well as a collection of books that are written about that subject. You can also find valuable information in popular media like magazines and newspapers. Of course, journalistic standards differ greatly between the *New York Times* and a supermarket tabloid like the *National Enquirer*.

When considering the quality of any source, regardless of where it was found, ask several questions:

- **Who is (or are) the author(s)?** What are their qualifications in this specific area? Is this person considered to be an expert in the field who is well recognized as an authority?

- **Where and how was the information published?** Even academic journals show tremendous variety in their quality and standards. Some online journals will publish almost anything an author submits (and pays a fee to have published), whereas others are subject to *peer review* (critically evaluated by other experts in the field) in which only a small fraction of those papers submitted are actually accepted for publication. Consider the quality and reputation of the publication.

- **If you consulted a book, how good is the publisher?** Academic journals are published by very competitive and reputable scholarly publishers such as university presses and well-known companies. Some books may be published by small, lesser-known publishers that may or may not have high standards for scholarship. And then in the case of "self-published" books, the author has paid to put his or her work in print. Self-publication does not disqualify the volume from being worthy and useful, but it just needs to be considered when evaluating how reliable, accurate, and up-to-date the information might be.

- **How old is the source?** In many fields, even five years is sufficient time for obsolescence. Be suspicious of any source that does not rely on reasonably current references for its own work.

- **What kind of resource is this?** A long-term experimental study that appeared in a first-rate, peer-reviewed academic journal versus an "opinion" essay that appeared in a professional newsletter will have great difference in stature. You have to assess not only who said it and what was said, but also on what basis the information was presented. Is it based solely on one person's experience? Based on a small sample of interviews? Based on a large-scale study of 10,000 people in multiple countries? More is not necessarily better, but it is just one more factor to consider.

Improving Your Abilities

Students talk about ways they improved their writing and speaking skills by getting the help they needed. (www.cengagebrain.com)

Teaching Tip

Encourage students to become familiar with your college library staff. These trained professionals are there to help students with research needs. Once a student has declared a major, the library staff can help him or her identify online databases and other resources that are developed for that particular discipline. Encourage students not to be afraid to seek the assistance of these "teaching" professionals. Their ability to share valuable knowledge on researching tools and techniques can have a tremendous positive impact on student development.

● **Exercise even more caution on the Internet.** It is much more challenging to assess the quality of a source you will find on the web since almost anyone can "publish" their ideas in a blog or personal web page. Even journals that may seem legitimate can be secret outlets for marketing products.

If you have not completed an extensive tour of research services at your library, or need a refresher, you would be well advised to consult with a reference librarian who can give you an orientation and introduce you to the possibilities.

Although each field has different styles of referencing, for most papers you will be required to support your points with sources that will then be listed in the reference section. One of the things your instructor will consider when grading your paper is whether you have adequately provided evidence for your themes and just how strong it is. If, for instance, you state that too much work and no play lead to neurological deterioration, the reader will be wondering what source supports that assertion. If you found a recent research article (or three) in a reputable journal like the *New England Journal of Medicine*, that carries a lot more weight than if you found it on the blog of some doctor promoting his or her practice.

Doing Research Online

The web, which contains more than 150 million sites, has just about anything you'd ever want to find, plus so much garbage interspersed with the rest that it is difficult to sort out what is useful and true from what is false and misleading. The two most important decisions to make when doing research online are, first, choosing the source and, second, creating the best *search terms* to find what you are looking for. Table 7.1 mentions several things to keep in mind when doing searches.

TABLE 7.1

Strategies for Electronic Searches

▶ Define the terms that best capture the essence of your topic.

▶ Clarify how deep your research must go: whether you can use popular media (magazines and newspapers) that are easier to digest, or whether you must use scholarly journals.

▶ Decide which databases are most appropriate for your search.

▶ If initial searches aren't providing what you want, use different terms or databases.

▶ Use AND to connect multiple terms (social justice AND volunteer vacations).

▶ Use OR to search for one term or the other (volunteer vacations OR volunteer tourism).

▶ Use NOT to narrow the search and eliminate possibilities (volunteer tourism NOT vacations).

▶ Use "quotation marks" to limit the search to that exact word order.

▶ Decide whether you want to search for terms in the title only, as a subject, or mentioned anywhere in a document.

▶ Specify time parameters, requesting more recent sources be listed first.

▶ Request eliminating from the search those materials that are not appropriate for your research (dissertations, videos, government documents, patents, and languages other than English).

7.2 FOR REFLECTION

Becoming Familiar with Search Resources

If you haven't already done so, go to the library or access some search databases online. Let's say that you have a curiosity (or assignment) about why wars seem to be going on continuously around the world, especially in poverty-stricken areas like the Middle East. How could you research this question?

If you go to the search databases of your library and select "history," you'll be offered a choice of a dozen or more options, or can combine all of them in your investigation. Type in "causes of war" and see what comes up—it's likely you'll get 150,000 or more articles because the subject is so broad. But if you limit your search to the title only, and add "poverty" to "causes of war," you'll get 100 articles. If this is still too many, you could limit your search to the "Middle East," adding that to the search under title, along with the other terms. In that case, you'll get a very manageable number of less than two dozen sources.

After you've tried a search or two through library databases, compare the results to what you can find on Google Scholar (www.googlescholar.com). If you put "causes of war" in quotation marks (meaning that all words have to be in this sequence) and combine it with "Middle East" and "poverty" as additional search terms, again you'll get a reasonable number of articles on the subject, especially if you decide to limit the search to articles in the last decade. Once you make these adjustments, you get a manageable number of possibilities to read and review.

Several all-purpose websites are excellent sources of academic information (like www.googlescholar.com, www.ipl.org, and www.doaj.org). In addition, every discipline has its own specialized research sites that are considered to be more useful than others. Your instructor can assist you in choosing the best options, but a few examples of the possibilities for you to check out include biology tutorials (www.biology-online .org) and a site that conjugates verbs in almost eighty languages (www.verbix.com/webverbix/index.asp).

Even better than these open sources are those databases and resources that are available through your library. As a registered student, you are entitled to log on to your system and then access hundreds of different search resources. They are organized by subject, allowing you to click on a discipline and see at least a dozen sources you may consult online. For instance, if you are interested in doing a search in anthropology, you will be given a choice to investigate (1) biological anthropology, (2) cultural anthropology, (3) linguistic anthropology, (4) archaeology, or (5) all sources.

Once you decide which aspect of the field you want to explore, and click on that link, you are supplied with a list of databases and given the choice to search any one of them, or all of them. If you want to search geology databases, for example, you can use GEOBASE or GeoRef, as well as a dozen other general science sources that also include geology in their sources. If you are doing research in psychology, then you could go to PsycINFO or PsycARTICLES. If studying education, you can go to ERIC or Education Full Text. Each field has its own sources, plus general ones that search newspapers and magazines (ProQuest, Lexis-Nexis) or academic sources (Academic Search Premier). If you feel lost, don't hesitate to consult with a librarian (in person, by phone, or via the Internet) to help you pick the right database to do your research.

Among all the staff available on campus, librarians are among the most cheerfully helpful. They really enjoy assisting students to find what they are looking for and especially seem to relish special challenges that push them to learn new things. Since the preceding discussion was only the briefest of overviews, it is now up to you to get the training and assistance you need to do effective research.

Citing Your Sources

Different academic disciplines have their own ways of referencing a paper's sources (see Table 7.2). Websites such as www.knightcite.com will assist you in formatting references for the appropriate discipline once you supply the reference information. Some of the most common styles such as APA (social sciences and education), MLA (humanities and liberal arts), and Chicago (nonscientific works) all contain the same basic information but in slightly different sequences and formats.

You will be expected to learn one or more of these systems and to apply them rigorously when you include citations and references. In the beginning, your instructor may be lenient and forgiving, but eventually you will be accountable for following precise guidelines. The reasoning behind what might seem to be extremely rigid attitudes is that this practice will prepare you for future work if you decide to participate in research and writing projects on a more advanced level.

Plagiarism and Academic Dishonesty

With so many politicians, writers, athletes, and business leaders caught cheating, some people believe that it is okay to play the system any way you can, as long as you don't get caught. A culture has emerged in which cheating not only is tolerated but is condoned (see Table 7.3 for a list of common excuses).

Every college has in place very strict policies regarding plagiarism, which refers to presenting someone else's work as your own. The word originates from the Latin word meaning to "kidnap," and in a sense that is exactly what is taking place when a dishonest student steals someone else's work. Lest you protest that this would not cross your mind, consider that 80 percent of college students admit to having cheated in school, close to 98 percent confess they have let others copy their work, and half admit to having copied material from the Internet without giving proper credit (www.plagiarism .org). The latter lapse in conscience, that is, copying content from a web page and pasting into a paper or presentation, is particularly tempting because it is so easy to do.

Teaching Tip

If you use an online teaching tool, such as Sakai or Blackboard, include a link to an online citation guide. Guides are often found on the campus library page.

Group Activity

Ask groups to discuss "horror stories"—things they've heard on campus from friends or others about cheating or plagiarism. Give groups a copy of the college's student handbook or catalog and ask them to find all areas in which cheating and plagiarism appear, as well as the consequences of the behavior. Review with students the campus academic honesty policy.

TABLE 7.2

Citation Styles in Different Disciplines

Style	Disciplines	Example
APA	Psychology, social sciences, education	Expert, I. M. A. (2010). The college student, alcohol consumption, right or left-handedness, and potential for success as an astronaut. *Journal to the Center of the Earth, 20*(1), 77–100.
MLA	Literature, humanities, arts	Spear, Shake. "The Great Plays of the Sixteenth Century." *Playwright Quarterly* 11.4 (2002): 1–12.
AMA	Sciences, medicine, health	Doctor, MD. Finally, a cure for cancer. *Medical Journal of Intergalactic Studies.* 2011; *12*: 21–22.
Chicago	Nonscientific books, magazines	Oriented, Dis. 1990. How do you get where you're going if you don't know how to get there? *Studies in Geographical Confusion* 4 (3): 108–?.
Turabian	All subjects in college	Oriented, Still Dis 1991. How do you find your way back if you don't where you started? *Studies in Geographical Confusion* 5 (July): ?–108.
Electronic media	All (with slight variations)	American Psychological Association, Electronic references. *APA Style.* Retrieved June 10, 2010, from http://apastyle.apa.org/elecmedia.html

TABLE 7.3

Excuses Students Tell Themselves (and Others) When They Cheat

Students who cheat on tests, or who plagiarize other people's work by pretending it is their own, justify their actions so they can sleep at night. They offer a number of excuses, all of which are still immoral:

▶ I didn't know that there was anything wrong with what I did.

▶ It was an accident. I didn't mean to do it.

▶ I didn't think it was that big a deal.

▶ It's not really cheating. I just took advantage of the situation.

▶ Everyone else was doing it, too.

▶ I didn't have a choice. It was either this, or I would have flunked.

▶ It hardly made any difference.

▶ How do you think all those bigwigs in politics and business get ahead?

▶ If the class (or instructor) wasn't so hard (or unfair), then I wouldn't have had to do it.

▶ I've done this before, and nobody ever said anything.

▶ The devil made me do it.

Whether plagiarism occurs accidentally or intentionally, the penalties can be harsh. In the case of some inadvertent case in which you may have neglected to include quote marks or a citation for a quotation you included, your grade could be lowered or even considered failing. For intentional efforts to be deceptive or dishonest, using someone else's material without acknowledging their authorship, you could flunk the class or even be kicked out of school. Having your transcript stamped that you were "dismissed for academic dishonesty" can make it difficult to gain entry into another institution and, in many cases, can ruin a person's life.

Students might commit such an offense for many reasons. They may feel time pressure and take a shortcut. They have "holes" in their conscience and feel entitled to operate under different rules. They enjoy challenging authority and the excitement of breaking laws that apply to others. They think of school as a game in which they are allowed to do anything they want, as long as they don't get caught. They think they are smarter than everyone else and therefore *won't* get caught.

To avoid inadvertent plagiarism, make sure that you have carefully checked your work. In general, avoid direct quotations from a source unless you can't think of any way to say it in your own words. Even with proper citations, don't rely too much on the same source(s) as it conveys laziness. When paraphrasing someone else's ideas, you must still properly cite your sources. This also allows readers to consult that reference if they want to know more about that topic.

The purpose of college is not just to accumulate credits and get a degree, but also to increase wisdom and learn skills that lead to success in the world at large. When shortcuts are taken, especially those that occur outside the boundaries of appropriate conduct, students degrade themselves. It may appear as if they got away with something in the short run, but it came at the expense of their dignity and morality.

Giving Speeches and Class Presentations

So far we have talked about communicating via written reports, either research papers or exploratory essays. Besides taking tests and writing papers, the other common form of demonstrating what you learn is in the form of either a speech or group presentation. Rest assured that as you begin college, nobody expects you to be very good at these skills, and most students feel anxious at the prospect of standing up in front of a large (or even small) group to talk.

You might find it interesting that more people fear public speaking than they fear dying (Sprague and Stuart, 2005). The idea of getting up in front of a group of people, heart pounding, hands sweating, and having to talk for five, ten, or even more minutes, seems terrifying to about 40 percent of the student population. Among first-year students, the rate is closer to half (so if you feel that way, you are not alone).

In spite of any fears or apprehensions you might feel, you will find few more supportive audiences than a group of students listening to another student speak publicly. While you are standing up in front of the room, each of the others present is identifying with you, rooting for you to do well. They know their turn is coming up next (or has already occurred), so they tend to be sympathetic to your plight. The audience will give you a break that they would never give the instructor.

Even if you escape the requirement of doing some kind of public speaking your first year of college, it will become increasingly important in later classes and in the workplace where employers value communication skills above all other personal qualities. At various times you will be called upon to give brief or extended talks in front of the class, participate in group presentations, debate with classmates, or perform in other public venues. Whether you are being graded specifically on your performance or not, the audience does have some hopes, if not expectations. And what will they (and your instructor) be looking for?

- **They want to be informed.** Your job is to teach something, or at least present what you have learned. There has to be solid content so that your listeners think afterward, "Gee, that was interesting. I didn't know that."

- **They want to see excellence.** They want a presentation that is polished, well rehearsed, and seamless.

- **They want to be involved.** It is hard to sit still for very long, so figure out ways that you can get the audience more actively engaged. Ask for audience responses. Create brief group and partner interactions.

Tiffany:
Getting the Hang of It

" I've always been afraid of class presentations. All those people looking at me, which I don't like anyway. I hate thinking about it even now. I just get so nervous. Then I start talking too fast because I just want to get the stupid thing over with. It's so weird because it's like I'm watching myself in slow motion and I get really self-conscious.

To make things worse, usually these presentations are not even fun or interesting. How am I supposed to present something I don't even care about? I don't know . . . I've always dreaded presentations. In high school, I would totally get sick before presenting anything in front of the class. The thing is, we have to do so many of these presentations in college that you eventually start to get the hang of it. I think I'm better at this now than I was a couple of years ago.

- **They want to be surprised.** Students (and instructors) get tired of the same old thing. Nothing delights more than being surprised by the unexpected.

- **They want to be entertained.** Use humor, visual aids, music, and a lively pace to keep people engaged.

- **They want to be stimulated.** Move your audience in some way. Tell a story that sparks emotion.

- **They want it short.** Never go beyond your allocated time limit and, if possible, let the audience out early for good behavior.

The single most common complaint that students make (besides grading being unfair or too hard) is that their classes are boring. Yet when given the opportunity to take the stage themselves, student presentations can be even more tedious than anything your worst instructors could ever do. Style isn't everything, but it certainly enhances what you do.

Limit Your Scope

A common mistake in any presentation, whether given in a class or in a meeting, is to cover too much ground in too short a time. An audience can digest only so many ideas before they start to tune out. When using visual aids, many presenters (students and teachers alike) use way too many slides, rushing through them as time runs short, as if the point of the whole exercise is just to run through the material at breakneck speed. It is far better to cover less material, using fewer slides, so you can present and develop each point and drive it home.

Beginnings and Endings

As general rule, you want to start your presentation by grabbing the audience's attention, to put them on notice, so to speak, that what they are about to experience is worth their effort. Standard procedure is to begin with a joke or personal story that is either humorous or endearing, or that illustrates a main theme you will discuss. You

Good presentations are not only informative but also engaging. As much as students complain about their instructors being boring, their own presentations can often be even more dry. Try to figure out ways to keep your audience actively involved, if not entertained.

can challenge the audience with a question that stimulates their curiosity: "Have you ever considered why you don't get more of what you want in life?"

The creative possibilities are unlimited. Just keep in mind that within the first minute of any meeting or presentation, people form an initial impression that is difficult to alter. You want to begin your talk in a way that is as dynamic and engaging as possible.

When giving a speech about conflicting theories and how they contradict one another, I begin by telling a story about going on a hiking trip and getting a dozen different pieces of advice about what I should do if I encounter a bear—crawl into a fetal position, climb a tree, back away slowly, run down a slope, and so on. One guide told me to carry "bear bells" that scare away any potential predators, whereas another guide laughed at that, saying they're called "dinner bells" because they actually *attract* the bears. The point of the story is that it illustrates the main theme of my presentation, yet does so in a way that gets the audience laughing and nodding their heads knowingly.

Since you tend to be most nervous while waiting for your turn to begin, your apprehensions can be eased if the most rehearsed part of your talk is the opening. You might also prepare a short overview of what you will cover and how you will proceed, highlighting key points. Once you get rolling with those, you will most likely feel yourself loosen up.

When you close, don't just abruptly end with a sheepish smile, "Well, I guess that's it. I'm done." End on a flourish, since it is the last thing that people will remember. You are also welcome to do a brief summary of key points covered, with useful applications.

Practice and Rehearsal

The best single antidote for stage fright before a performance is preparation. The more you can do to get ready, to practice your role (hopefully before a live audience of willing friends or relatives), the more confidence you will feel during the actual event.

You want to rehearse to the point that you can glance at notes as cues, but not have to read them. They should be talking points rather than complete sentences, similar to any slides you use. Your presentation will come across as much more engaging if you explain things in your own words rather than reading someone else's words.

One of the best tools for rehearsing, and improving your presentation, is to use an audio or video recorder to record a practice session. At first you may feel self-conscious watching or listening to yourself, but it will help to sensitize you to habits, nonverbal behaviors, speech patterns, or glitches in your delivery. This also helps you to see and hear yourself as you are viewed and heard by others.

It's About the Relationships

The best lectures or talks you have ever attended were those in which it felt like the speaker was talking directly to *you*. Many speakers make the mistake of thinking that their job is to cover information, get through material, and run through slides, as if merely talking about them necessarily ensures that anyone is really listening and learning.

Good presentations always begin with audience personal contact. This is most easily attained through eye contact—engaging as many people as you can with your eyes and your smile, conveying your interest in them. If you are looking only at your notes, or the slides behind you, then you are ignoring the audience (which is not much appreciated). It is as if you are saying to them, "You aren't important. Only my information is important. Here it is: Take it or leave it." Most of the time, they will leave it.

Rehearsal Helps

You may be surprised to learn that quite a number of well-known performers such as actress Scarlett Johansson and singers Rod Stewart and Beyoncé struggle with stage fright when asked to speak in front of audiences. Yet they have found a way to deal with their fears so that they can function onstage, mostly by *pretending* they feel more confident than they really do. You might follow their lead.

Research has shown that you just can't think straight or speak well when you are extremely anxious. The part of your brain that controls speech (Broca's area) shuts down during times when you are aroused (Cozolino, 2008). That's why it is so hard to get your thoughts together and express yourself the way you want when you are really upset. Yet you can control those overreactions by remaining calm and rehearsing your presentation ahead of time. Most of what you imagine can go wrong—such as losing your place, freezing, forgetting your lines, saying things that are stupid, and being humiliated—represent either minor, insignificant incidents or else exaggerated outcomes. It is important to challenge your irrational fears. It also helps to practice what you can do if you lose your place or forget where you are going next—such as ask a question of the audience to give yourself time to regroup and figure out where you want to go next.

One more suggestion: Don't *ever* start a presentation by telling your audience that you are nervous—that only ensures that you draw more attention to a situation you would rather minimize.

If you feel a lot of apprehension about giving presentations, consider taking an acting, communication, or public speaking class to turn your weakness into a strength.

During your scans of the audience, you will notice certain people who have expressive faces. Identify them early in different parts of the room so you aren't looking only in one direction. Watch their faces to see how you are doing. Notice when they are frowning, or amused, or puzzled. Take your cues from them as to whether you are going too slow or too quickly, and whether they are following where you intend to lead.

Presentations as a Performance

Chapter 4 on classroom excellence mentioned that the average person can pay attention to a talk, lecture, or speech, for only a little more than twenty minutes without concentration and learning diminishing significantly. You know this lesson well since you can easily track how fleeting your own attention can be.

Unless you can figure out a way to capture and maintain your audience's attention, whatever you say in a speech or presentation will be lost. Now maybe all you are thinking about is getting through the ordeal, getting up in front of the class, doing your thing as quickly and painlessly as possible, and sitting down. Yet this is another one of those life skills you learn in college that will serve you well in so many other aspects of life and work—from speaking at a meeting to giving a toast at a wedding.

Anything you can do to engage your audience is helpful. Rather than "hiding" behind a podium, try walking to different parts of the room to make contact with as many in the audience as possible. Use your body, as well as your voice, to vividly act out points you are making. Don't talk in a monotone or remain glued to your notes. Change the volume, pace, and pitch of your voice to emphasize certain points or create a sense of drama.

Burl:
Finding My Voice
as a Performer

" If someone had told me that I would be a stand-up comedian when I got older I would have laughed. As a child, I was painfully shy and I would often cry if I had to speak in front of the class. I was very sensitive to whatever a person said to me. If I was told simply to be louder, I would cry and go to my seat. I did not like being up in front of people at all.

One of my reasons for being so shy was I was embarrassed by my voice. I had seizures as a child and needed to go through four years of speech therapy. The other children would make fun of me and tell me that I sounded like a robot. It hurt to feel singled out because of my voice. Eventually, I began feeling more comfortable being myself in front of the class and even though people would still laugh at the way I talked, I was beginning to be all right with that. Now people tell me that I have a unique delivery.

The turning point for me was in college, when I finally started to get more comfortable with myself and being in front of an audience. Only a few things in life are more fun for me than making people laugh.

Freedom to Improvise

In spite of all your preparations and rehearsal, some of the greatest highlights of a presentation can arise from spontaneous insights. If you are paying too close attention to your notes and your intended plan, then you can't take advantage of spontaneous opportunities that might arise, leading you to improvise in response to how people react. If you aren't watching your audience and noting their responses, you can't make adjustments in the direction you are heading.

One of the greatest mysteries of the universe is how a teacher or presenter can stand before a room full of people who are half-asleep (you can tell because they are yawning, staring into space, writing notes to each other, or even laying their heads on their desks) and yet still continue what he is doing with no change. Even from where you are sitting in the back of the room, you can tell nobody is listening and nobody cares to hide it. Yet the teacher in the front of the room has an even better view of bored, blank faces, and still persists with the original agenda. You have to admit: This is a spectacular example of obliviousness. In the face of overwhelming evidence that what he is doing is not working, he still keeps doing the same thing! Don't make the same mistake.

If what you planned is not grabbing the audience like you hoped, then change the plan. Sounds simple, doesn't it? But you would be amazed how reluctant people are to change direction, even when they know they are lost. They just keep blundering onward, unwilling or unable to adapt to new circumstances. The worst thing you could ever do is to plan a presentation, make an outline with note cards (and slides), and follow the agenda in spite of obvious signs that what you are doing is not getting the expected responses (awe, laughter, and enthusiastic applause). In spite of all your preparations it may be time to pause for a moment, adapt your agenda, and try something else. This could involve asking the audience a question, sharing a personal example that just came to mind, or commenting on some observation that just occurred in the room. Some of the most magical moments in any presentation often take place when the speaker capitalizes on what is happening in the moment.

Using Technology in Presentations

It seems as if using slides, overheads, and PowerPoint has become obligatory in doing any kind of presentation these days. In some ways, that's a pity because many of these visual aids are either useless or distracting. They get in the way of engagement between

Teaching Tip
Discuss the importance of a backup plan for any presentation, regardless of the type of technology being used. What if the PowerPoint file fails to open or the jump drive fails to read? Discuss the value of coming prepared with multiple file storage options (e.g., on a CD-ROM, on a jump drive, on the computer hard drive, or even attaching the file to a self-addressed e-mail). Discuss other options when technology totally fails (power loss or machine malfunction) such as backup transparencies or even markers or chalk for putting information on the board.

Jo Hale/Getty Images

Nowadays, an overemphasis on flashy technological bells and whistles can easily overwhelm the content of a presentation (or concert). Remember that the single most important thing about any presentation is the relationship you develop with your audience.

the speaker and the audience—if everyone is looking at your slides, then they aren't making contact with *you*.

It's not that visual aids can't enhance public speaking, because they do. However, most people are either so unskilled at using the technology, or so dazzled by it, that they forget what they are up there for in the first place—to inform and entertain.

Here are some of the most common mistakes that speakers make when constructing their presentation slides:

● **Using too many words.** If you have too much content on your slides, then people in the audience will be trying to read and digest the material instead of listening to you. Slides should have talking points, a few at a time. Use them as starting points to develop, describe, illustrate, or tell stories.

● **Being too ambitious.** Most presenters are far too ambitious—and unrealistic—when it comes to planning what they can do within the time available. Use about one-third the number of slides that you think you'll need. You come across as frazzled, confused, and overwhelmed when you start rushing through your slides just to get through them all.

● **Reading from your slides.** Never turn your back on the audience. The single most effective goal of a presentation is to make contact with listeners, create a relationship with them, and engage them as personally as possible. If you've got information that you believe your audience must have at their disposal, then distribute it as a handout.

● **Providing handouts before the end.** What happens when you distribute something to read? People stop listening to you and read what you gave them. If you want to keep audience attention, then don't distract them.

● **Getting too fancy.** Student presenters often put an extraordinary amount of work into preparing their slides, complete with streaming video, music, sound effects, artistic effects, and so on. Sometimes simpler is far better. Any visual or auditory effects you use should augment and support what *you* are doing, not distract from it.

7.3 | FOR REFLECTION

Practicing Visual Presentations

If you have never used PowerPoint (or similar slide presentation software) before, sign up for a training session through your college technology department or complete an online course (such as http://office.microsoft.com/en-us/training for PowerPoint). You can also find books in your library or bookstore that introduce you to the software and teach you the basics. Alternatively, a friend or classmate who is already proficient and experienced would need only about thirty minutes to get you started.

Design a simple, six-slide presentation on some topic of interest.

Print out copies of the slides, and ask experienced experts for feedback on how you could make them better.

Group Activity

Brainstorm the pros and cons of group work: Why do instructors assign group projects? What structures and guidelines should be put in place to make sure it is an optimal experience for participants? Include things like making sure that everyone gets equal time and staying on task.

For Community College Students

What are the pros and cons of group work for commuter students? What strategies can a working student employ to actively participate in a group project?

Teaching Tip

Group projects require a more demanding deadline schedule than individual work. Encourage students to become leaders within their groups by scheduling meeting times well in advance of the project due date. Impose individual deadlines that are well ahead of the overall project due date. Take advantage of individual strengths within the group. Encourage students to schedule sufficient time for synthesizing individual contributions into the group effort as well as schedule multiple rehearsals before the group presentation.

Doing Group Presentations

Most of the same principles apply to group presentations as those previously described for individual presentations. The main difference is that your team has to function cohesively and your performance is only as good as the group effort. This is far more difficult than it seems since everyone in your group may have different ideas and personal agendas.

If presentations are evaluated, it is usually the case that everyone receives the same grade. This means that the most important thing to consider when planning what you'll do, assigning roles, and structuring the presentation is that the final product is the best that all of you can do—as a team.

Most groups have leadership inequities in that one person may try to take over and others may feel marginalized. This leads to feelings of resentment and anger, which do not produce the best possible performance. For any group project, each member should take responsibility to make sure that everyone feels heard, everyone's ideas are honored, and decisions are made in a democratic rather than autocratic manner. The reality is that this takes more time and effort to do. It is much easier for one person, usually the one who is most assertive and verbal, to jump in right away and say, "Hey, I've got a great idea. How about if we do this?" Then others may agree because either they don't want to challenge the person with such a strong personality, or they just don't care much one way or the other. The best presentations are those in which everyone has a role in creating the final product and everyone contributes their strengths to the project.

Look for More Ways to Practice

Honestly assess your skills as a speaker, regardless of your drive, ambition, and determination to be exceptional. If this area is problematic for you, and if you'd like to become more proficient, you have plenty of opportunities to get advanced training. A number of classes across campus are designed specifically to help you build your public speaking skills.

1. The communications department offers classes in public speaking, persuasion and argumentation, interpersonal communication, and intercultural communication.

2. The drama department may offer classes in acting for nonmajors, voice and movement, and improvisation.

Stephanie: A Horror Story

"You want to hear a horror story? I was in charge of doing the final polishing of our group's class presentation that counted for something like one-third of our grade in the class. It was on a figure that embodied what we considered the best traits of leadership. We picked Mustafa from "The Lion King," which we thought was pretty creative. We spent weeks working on this thing. It had photos, music, streaming video from the movie, sound effects—you name it, we put it in. So I go to do one more run-through the night before our presentation and I still don't know what I did wrong. But it was just not there anymore on my computer. I don't know if I forgot to save the file or I somehow deleted it. I don't know.

No big deal, right? Just go to the backup and redo the final changes. What backup? I guess I'd been lucky up until that point because I never backed anything up; it just seemed like too much trouble.

What happened with our presentation? Well, we were a pretty creative group anyway so we just put our heads together (after they almost beat me to death) and came up with an option in which we just acted things out. We were the only group that didn't do a Power-Point, but that just made us stand out more. Anyway, I always back up everything now."

3. English and foreign language departments offer courses on oral literature.

4. Leadership courses are offered by a number of departments, such as political science, women's studies, human services, business, and military science.

5. The forensics team on campus offers opportunities to learn and practice debating skills.

6. The student government has opportunities for learning leadership and public discourse skills.

7. Student organizations and clubs provide training in public speaking for those members who wish to improve their skills.

SUMMARY

Writing papers and doing presentations are similar in that they involve doing systematic research and demonstrating what you learned. Both are also structured in similar ways: an overview of what to expect, solid content that is supported by evidence or examples, and a closing synthesis with some implications and meaningful interpretations.

Students often have strong preferences about whether they are better skilled at writing or presenting in class. This is not surprising considering that they rely on different kinds of communication skills. Regardless of which type of research project you prefer, you are going to be required to do dozens (if not hundreds) of these assignments, depending on your major.

Writing coherent papers and making persuasive presentations will likely be an important part of any job in the future. You will frequently be asked to write reports that are descriptive and accurate. You will also be required to present your ideas in the most convincing and effective ways possible. That is why it is so important that you devote the time and energy to becoming the best communicator in writing and in speech that you can.

QUESTIONS FOR REVIEW AND FURTHER EXPLORATION

1. Without looking back on the chapter, quick: What are some of the organizing principles of constructing any paper or presentation? Your answer should be logical and intuitive, following the principles that were introduced.

2. How does keeping a journal help you to discover your writer's voice?

3. The chapter encouraged you to start research projects with your own experience. What are the dangers of such an approach in terms of biasing what you discover in the investigation that follows?

4. What are some questions that perplex you enough that they would make an intriguing research study? How would you approach this project in terms of finding relevant literature and other useful sources?

5. Very few students actually admit they cheated or plagiarized—and they actually appear to believe excuses that they just made a stupid mistake or didn't know it was wrong. What are other ways that students justify to themselves (and others) why they cheat or plagiarize?

6. Surveys consistently report that public speaking is one of people's greatest fears (right up there with snakes). Why do you think that it is anxiety-provoking for so many people?

7. Technology is so much a part of all aspects of life today, including public presentations. How can PowerPoints, audience response systems (clickers), slides, and videos actually detract from a presentation? Think of presentations you have attended where you felt lost, distracted, or annoyed.

Go to www.cengagebrain.com for an online quiz that will test your understanding of the chapter content.

Making Lifestyle Choices

KEY QUESTIONS

▸ **Why is it common for first-year students to gain weight?**

▸ **Why don't most diets work for very long?**

▸ **What are the benefits of regular exercise, and why don't most students stick with their exercise plans?**

▸ **Why is use of drugs and alcohol so prevalent in all human cultures?**

▸ **How do coping mechanisms turn into self-destructive habits?**

▸ **How does sleep deprivation affect school performance?**

▸ **Why is open communication so important to a mutually satisfying sexual relationship?**

▸ **Why does satisfaction with the amount of money or possessions you have depend on what others around you have?**

▸ **What are the most important strategies for staying within a budget?**

Teaching Tip
Introduce health topics with poster board signs around the room asking questions such as "Do you eat a healthy diet on a regular basis? Why or why not?" and "How many hours do you sleep per night?" and "What do you do when you're stressed out?" Have students write anonymous responses with markers. More questions can be found in Table 8.1 and For Reflection 8.1.

A ttending classes, studying for exams, taking tests, writing papers, and giving presentations are only a part of college life. Important learning experiences happen during your leisure time, in your social interactions, during work and play, and when you are alone.

This chapter has all the "fun" topics, plus a bit of the forbidden. It covers eating, sleeping, drinking, exercising, spending money, having sex, doing drugs, leisure activities, and other things you may do for relaxation and enjoyment. This chapter also addresses adjusting to your new environment in terms of healthy lifestyle issues. How should you manage your life to keep yourself in top physical and emotional shape?

The way you structure your lifestyle—how you take care of yourself with regard to eating, sleeping, socializing, managing stress, and dealing with daily pressures—is critical to preventing future problems. It is normal, if not expected, that you will face emotional as well as academic challenges your first year of college with all the adjustments and transitions that take place (see Table 8.1). This reality is not meant to frighten you, but rather to reassure you that such problems are part of the journey and that you are not alone with your struggles. You can reduce the intensity and frequency of personal difficulties by making yourself more aware of how lifestyle choices affect your functioning. It also helps to talk about these issues with others you trust.

For Community College Students
Conduct a discussion to answer the question "What does being healthy in college mean to you?"

TABLE 8.1

Percentage of Freshmen Reporting Emotional Problems during the Year

▶ "I feel emotionally exhausted."	82%
▶ "I feel overwhelmed by everything I have to do."	87%
▶ "There are times when I feel very sad."	64%
▶ "I feel very lonely."	60%
▶ "There are times I feel overwhelming anxiety."	49%
▶ "Sometimes I feel so depressed it is hard for me to function."	31%

Source: American College Health Assessment (2009).

Eating Healthfully

Classroom Discussion
Open it up: What do you think causes of freshman weight gain? How can you avoid freshman weight gain?

Group Activity
Divide the class into small groups, assigning each group to teach the class and facilitate discussion about a topic from this chapter: eating, sleeping, exercise, drinking/drugs, tobacco, sex, behavioral addictions. You could add additional topics such as caffeine or video gaming.

You've probably heard of the "freshman fifteen," referring to the common number of pounds of weight gain associated with being a first-year college student. This does not exaggerate the reality considering that the average student gains more than four pounds during the first semester of college alone (Levitsky, Halbmaier, and Mrdjenovic, 2004). And this only adds to the existing problem of more than one-third of students arriving at college already obese or significantly overweight (American College Health Assessment, 2007).

Eating on the run, overindulgence at fast-food outlets, candy machines, all-you-can-eat cafeterias, crazy sleep patterns, lack of exercise, poor food choices, and chronic stress all contribute to gaining weight. Although this is common knowledge, you've already been warned a dozen times before, and you resolve it won't happen to you, the probability that you will gain weight is still pretty high.

This subject of weight gain does not just relate to your appearance and body image because nutrition directly affects the way you function mentally and psychologically. This includes energy levels, ability to concentrate, moods and emotional states, sleep patterns, stress levels, and performance on tests and in class.

It isn't just *how much* you eat that counts, but also *what* you choose to put in your mouth. Poor eating choices that lead to excessive weight gain occur when you eat for reasons other than physical hunger. When you crave comfort foods because you are lonely, stressed, depressed, or just plain bored, you are not so much feeding your stomach as taking care of an *emotional hunger*.

A Guide for What to Eat

Classroom Discussion
Open it up: What snacks are in your rooms right now? What snacks did you bring with you to class? Get them out and let's talk about the nutritional value of each.

Here are suggestions for what to eat, when to eat, and how to eat to stay healthy.

● Eat something for breakfast, even just a granola bar, yogurt, or piece of fruit. As much as you might be tempted, skipping breakfast sets you up to eat even more throughout the rest of the day.

● Avoid fast-food restaurants whenever possible (sure, you think, like that's really possible for a student). If you must frequent such establishments, make informed food choices that include salads with low-fat, low-calorie dressings and vegetables.

● Do not fill up your plate at all-you-can-eat dining halls and cafeterias, but instead pretend that you are ordering off a menu. If you go back for seconds

Ben Edwards/Jupiter Images

The typical college student gains weight during the first year, despite dire warnings that this is likely to occur. The main reason is making poor food choices, such as eating what is most easily available rather than what is nutritious.

(or thirds), fill up on foods that are higher in nutrition and lower in fat and calories.

- Watch your consumption of sugar-saturated sodas and alcoholic beverages. Whenever possible, drink more water and diluted juices.

- Don't begin any diet that you aren't capable of sticking with for the long haul.

- Allow yourself to indulge in your favorite foods, but in moderation.

- Eat slowly. Enjoy every mouthful. Taste and savor every bite. Chew mindfully. Rest between bites, then take another, one at a time.

- Eat as many fresh vegetables and fruits as you can.

- Replace snacks that are high in sugar (cookies, cake, and ice cream) and fat (potato chips, burgers, and french fries) with those lower in sugar and fat.

- Don't eat at the same time you are doing something else like watching television, talking on the phone, or reading, as you won't pay attention to how much you are eating.

- Don't eat right before you go to bed.

- Avoid foods that increase stress such as excessive caffeine, sugar, and refined carbohydrates.

- Keep healthy foods available in your room or house, rather than those that lead to feelings of regret.

- Take a multivitamin every day.

- Eat a balanced variety of foods, including carbohydrates, fats, protein, and fiber in each meal.

Mitchell:
*Losing and
Gaining Weight*

> When I started going to college, I lost a lot of weight. Man, I was thin! The deal was that I wasn't eating much at all, I was just kinda drinking a lot of beer, partying like crazy, and sleeping just a couple of hours here and there. I wasn't anorexic or anything, but I wasn't healthy either. Then I decided to cut back on all the partying and all the beer because my grades were starting to suffer. That's when I put on a lot of weight. I was hanging out at home, studying, and trying to go to bed at a decent time during the week. The problem was that when I was studying, I was eating a lot.
>
> I'm still a little over my normal weight and I don't know what to do. I lost some, but I don't have time to work out all the time. This whole weight thing has depressed me a little bit. I had heard that college students usually put on some weight, but for me it was the opposite at first and that wasn't healthy either. I just never expected to get fat from studying.

Eating Disorders

The term "eating disorder" is a misnomer because the condition is really an *emotional disorder* rather than a problem related to food consumption or its avoidance. It is actually a form of mental illness that is considered among the most dangerous because of its high mortality rate. Many college students engage in purging (vomiting and use of laxatives) to control their weight or to make up for a food binge. Compulsive exercising is another way that students may attempt to control weight (or manage stress), sometimes working out several hours each day.

Anorexia nervosa is a form of deliberate self-starvation caused by excessive feelings of guilt and self-punishment and a *distorted body image* in which people see themselves as fatter than they really are. It also represents an attempt to exert excessive restraint over one part of one's life when so many other areas feel out of control.

Bulimia occurs when someone binges on certain foods, almost never associated with actual enjoyment, and then vomits or uses laxatives to purge afterward. This leads to a repetitive cycle, often stimulated by some kind of disappointment, perceived failure, or feeling of emotional upset.

Connie:
Eating Disorder

> I've always worried about my weight, but it was never that big a deal. I remember my friends and I even making fun of another girl we knew who was throwing up in the bathroom. But as soon as I got to this place, I just knew I didn't really belong here. The other girls have so much stuff—so many clothes, so many things, and it seems like all they do is talk about clothes and looks and guys. I thought it would all be okay if I just concentrated on my studies but when I got a C on my first exam, I just fell apart. It's like this whole thing was one big mistake.
>
> I walked to the grocery store after I got my exam back and bought a box of donuts—I started eating them in the store before I even paid. The guy behind the counter just started laughing. I felt so ashamed. But then I staggered out of there and into the Jack in the Box next door. I ordered four burgers, and tons of fries, pretending to talk with friends on my cell phone as I ordered food for them. I got back to my dorm room and sat in my closet—worried that my roommate would come in. I ate everything. When I finished I felt like it must feel when people do drugs. The funny thing is that I actually felt better 'cause I wasn't thinking about the test grade anymore. But I also felt sick, so I went in the bathroom and made myself throw up. And that's how it all began for me.

Binge eating is similar to bulimia, but without the purging that occurs afterward. Each of these three disorders may not occur in isolation but can be alternated or combined. For instance, a student might eat a whole half-gallon of ice cream, stick her finger down her throat, and vomit it in the toilet. Yet she might stuff herself with mashed potatoes and gravy, eating four helpings, but not purge afterward. Then some time later, she might begin a stage of slowly starving herself, not eating much of anything at all (but often disguising the behavior so to not alarm friends and family).

If you engage in any of these behaviors, or know somebody who does, it is imperative that you (or they) seek immediate help at the college health center, which has very experienced experts for dealing with these problems. Counseling, combined with nutritional interventions (more serious cases may require hospitalization), help victims of eating disorders find alternative ways to deal with emotional distress, as well as control their impulses.

Exercise

Exercising regularly—and moderately—in college is important not only to control weight but also to manage stress. So much of college life involves stimulating your mind with activities such as studying, attending class, reading books, writing papers, and having conversations that all occur while you are sitting. There are lots of good reasons why you can rationalize that you don't have time to work out on a regular basis ("too much work to do" sound familiar?), but the fact remains that regular exercise helps to stabilize everything else in your life. This includes your sleep, eating habits, stress levels, and ability to concentrate (see Table 8.2).

▶ VIEW IT

Campus Food Options
This video gives a tour of the typical eating choices available on a college campus and describes how challenging it is to make good food choices that maintain health and reduce stress. (www.cengagebrain.com)

© Cengage Learning

TABLE 8.2

What Regular Exercise Will Do for You

- Control weight.
- Burn calories so that you can enjoy the foods you like.
- Help you sleep better.
- Reduce stress.
- Stabilize moods.
- Improve cardiovascular functioning.
- Improve endurance and stamina.
- Increase capacity for pain tolerance.
- Increase self-discipline.
- Improve body image.
- Increase self-confidence.
- Improve strength and flexibility.
- Reduce high blood pressure and cholesterol.
- Reduce risk of diseases.
- Increase your life expectancy.
- Improve mental focus and concentration.
- Provide periods of solitude.
- Improve sex (yes, really).

Radius Images/Jupiter Images

Working out with friends makes exercise more fun and helps keep you committed to a regular schedule. It doesn't matter whether you run, bike, swim, work out with weights, do yoga, practice tai chi, or play soccer or basketball, as long as you build regular exercise into your schedule for at least thirty minutes three times per week.

It doesn't matter what you do, whether you work out in a group (aerobics class, team sports, cycling, etc.) or alone (running, weight lifting, stationary bike, etc.), as long as you can find an activity that you can commit yourself to doing at least three times per week for a minimum of thirty minutes.

Ideally, an exercise program has three components:

1. **Aerobic training** improves your cardio functioning and overall fitness and stamina. This involves some type of activity that pumps up your heart rate and keeps it up for at least a half-hour, three times per week at a minimum. The most common examples include running, swimming, cycling, basketball, soccer, rowing, cross-country skiing, aerobic dancing, or even walking at a fast pace.

2. **Weight training** develops strength and keeps your muscles toned. This burns calories in a different way, converting fat into muscle. Weight lifting with free weights or machines is recommended under supervision to get you started. Pilates and some forms of yoga develop resistance strength as well as flexibility.

3. **Stretching** increases your flexibility, helping your joints. Yoga is the best example of a form of exercise that seeks to improve your core strength and limberness.

The main challenge to maintaining an exercise program is similar to that for controlling weight. Most people do not follow through with their initial intentions and lose interest when they allow themselves to get distracted. Make exercise fun, and make it a part of your daily life.

Drinking and Drugs

Nothing can sabotage your career as a college student quicker than overindulgence in alcohol and drugs. You've gotten enough scolding from parents, lectures from school administrators, and informational handouts to write your own book on the subject.

Legal drugs (alcohol, tobacco, caffeine, prescription medications) and illegal drugs (marijuana, speed, downers, Ecstasy, cocaine, heroin) are commonplace on any college campus and at any social gathering you might attend. All of them impair decision making to a certain extent and produce side effects on your body and mind.

Aside from illicit drugs, prescription medicines like painkillers (Percocet, Vicodin, and OxyContin), uppers (Adderall), and downers (Xanex) are becoming increasingly common on campus as a way to manage stress or provide a boost of energy. Use of either illegal or prescription drugs has the potential to escalate into serious addiction.

Tanya:
Free of Drugs

"I'm a senior now, but when I first started college I was smoking a lot of pot to deal with stuff. I was smoking before class to make things more interesting. And then I started doing cocaine just so I could stay awake to cram because I was working a lot of hours, going to school full time, and trying to spend time with my boyfriend. And then it got to the point I was wasting all my money on drugs that I should have been saving. I just kinda snapped eventually.

I started doing meditation and yoga to do what the marijuana did for me and then I started exercising, which pretty much helped me with what the cocaine was doing. Now I've been completely drug-free for almost six months and I'm so appreciative that I got out of that stuff.

Alcohol is the most common "drug" of choice on college campuses. Students use it not only to get high but also as a form of "self-medication" for stress and other emotional problems. If you are feeling disturbed or distressed about something in particular, or just fearful, lonely, anxious, depressed, angry, frustrated, confused, rejected, or upset, it seems like an easy enough solution to have a few drinks or beers to make the trouble go away, at least temporarily.

Because alcohol and drugs use are so prevalent in our culture (in most cultures, for that matter), it would be a waste of time and utterly out of touch to warn you to refrain from *any* indulgence. Asking someone "Why do you drink or get high?" is likely to produce the obvious answer: "Because it's fun" or "Because it makes me feel good." And indeed it does. Responsible consumption of alcohol—having a glass of wine or beer on occasion (although it is illegal for those under twenty-one)—is not the problem, but rather binging to the point where you are (and feel) out of control. In case you are wondering, "binging" is usually defined as having five or more drinks in a sitting, but depending on your size and tolerance, it can mean as few as three consecutive drinks within a short period.

You may have seen research reports indicating that drinking red wine in moderation actually *prevents* a number of health-related problems in adults, but we are concerned here with drinking behavior that crosses the line, and impairs your thinking and decision making to the point in which you would do things that could be dangerous to yourself and others. This can range from driving while intoxicated to engaging in unprotected sex.

Classroom Discussion

Open it up: What makes alcohol expensive for students who are not of legal age, besides the cost of the alcohol itself?

8.1 FOR REFLECTION

Do You Have a Drinking Problem?

▶ Have you passed out, or blacked out, as a result of a drinking binge?
▶ Do you drink more than three drinks or beers in an evening, more than once each week?
▶ Do you have trouble controlling the amount you drink even when you have the best of intentions?
▶ Do you spend a lot of time thinking about drinking?
▶ Have family members or friends expressed concern to you about your drinking behavior?
▶ Have you skipped a class, missed work, or not shown up for a commitment or appointment because you had a hangover?

Alcohol and drugs are often used as "social lubricants" in college to reduce inhibition and anxiety while boosting confidence. They also lead to risky, inappropriate, and de-structive behavior when used in excess. Forty-four percent of college students admit to indulging in binge drinking which has led them to pass out or fall into a drunken stupor (Hales, 2006).

© Mark Peterson/CORBIS

Tobacco

Cigarettes and other tobacco products are also drugs. They happen to be legal be-cause they generate so much income for state and federal governments. They are just as addictive and habit-forming as most other drugs, and just as detrimental to your health when used chronically. You've heard all this before and maybe you're even tired of hearing all the warnings. The good news is that the messages are working because the number of people who take up smoking in North America is decreasing.

Even though tobacco use is diminishing nationwide, about one-quarter of college students smoke at least on an occasional basis—when drinking, when they're with friends who smoke, or when they are feeling anxious (remember: it *is* a drug). Since nicotine is classified as a stimulant, it has the desired effect of temporarily boosting energy. It is also used as an appetite suppressant and mood booster, and gives you something to do with your hands when you're feeling nervous.

Besides the expense for this drug habit, costing more than $2,000 per year for a pack-a-day habit, there are literally hundreds of detrimental effects on your body, most of which you may be aware of. In addition to the increased risk of lung cancer and heart disease, you also need to worry about being at risk for high blood pres-sure, bronchitis, emphysema, asthma, infertility, miscarriages, premature wrinkling of skin, loss of eyesight, ulcers, stroke, heart attack, gum disease, and cancer of the pancreas, kidneys, bladder, and cervix. Oh, yes: and sexual disorders like erectile dys-function and impotence. You have to admit: That is an impressive list of bad things that happen from smoking.

The problem with stopping the addiction is that there are cues everywhere that spark the craving—advertisements, actors looking cool in movies, and others who smoke around you. That means that to kick the habit, you'll have to remove as many of those temptations as possible, including perhaps changing friends and where you hang out.

Intention to quit is usually not nearly enough. The average person has to try a half-dozen or more attempts before finding the right combination of strategies that work. There are some prescription aids that are often useful, including patches and medications that help with withdrawal effects.

Flynn:
My Addiction to E

"I've been addicted to E [Ecstasy] since I started in high school. I didn't really think about how it affected my health or anything; it just felt good, real good. I felt like I was in a whole new world, although once it started to wear off, I would get muscle spasms, blurred vision, and even hallucinations. Eventually, I started getting real depressed afterward and I couldn't sleep.

I started doing E again in college even though I promised I would stop once I got here. I know it's a problem because I have these memory lapses and still get pretty depressed. The last time I did it with friends a week ago and my ears started to hurt. I slurred my words. I got so cold and then I just blacked out. But the craving is getting worse, I can tell. I woke up in the middle of the night screaming and I thought I was going to die. I'm trying to fight the urge, but I don't think I can do it on my own. I need help.

Behavioral Addictions

One of the temptations of the college lifestyle, which combines greater freedom with greater potential for stress, is the attraction to indulge in addictive behaviors as coping mechanisms. After a period of time, they become part of your daily lifestyle, dangerously distracting you from work and responsibilities.

As mentioned earlier, addictions can be considered either the *result* of stress or a *causal influence* that makes stress far worse. In the short run, various forms of self-medication like drugs and alcohol help to soothe an aching spirit and provide some relief from pressure. So, too, do *behavioral addictions*, in which students become overly attached to certain activities that they can lose themselves in.

Common examples of behavioral addictions among college students include the following:

● **Internet.** In its various forms, this involves spending hours and hours in front of a computer playing around with YouTube, Facebook, or MySpace; surfing the web; shopping online; reading; and sending e-mail.

James Woodson/Jupiter Images

Because of the relative freedom of college life and the pressures that students must manage, various addictions become attractive ways of reducing stress. While illicit and prescription drugs and alcohol are common outlets, students also seek relief through behavioral addictions. College students are particularly vulnerable to excessive use of the Internet, television, exercise, video games, music, gambling, and other means of escaping from pain or responsibilities.

- **Gambling.** Addicts lose more money than they can afford and spend more time than they can reasonably devote, all for the thrill.

- **Video games.** Five or six hours, and even whole nights, can be lost to those who play the games not just for enjoyment or diversion but because they are hooked and can't stop.

- **Role-playing fantasy games.** There are dozens of these—such as World of Warcraft, Dungeons and Dragons, Star Wars, Final Fantasy, and World of Darkness—all of which can become *very* seductive.

- **Television.** Watching a few of your favorite shows every night is thoroughly enjoyable, as long as it doesn't interfere with getting work done or isolate you from others. But many college students spend up to six hours a day or more watching television, and not quality programming but game shows, third replays of *Sports Center*, soap operas, *Jerry Springer*, *Antiques Roadshow*, reruns of *Hee Haw* or *My Mother the Car*, the Shopping Channel, the stock market ticker along the bottom of MSNBC—anything.

- **Exercising.** Surprised to see this on the list? Anything that someone can do for health reasons can also be done to an extreme. It is one thing to work out for a half-hour several times per week, or even an hour per day; but people may run for hours each day, lift weights in the gym for hours, or otherwise work their bodies ragged in a compulsive effort to control their anxiety.

- **Eating.** Eating addictions are so common in college that they deserve to get mentioned once again. This category includes the eating disorders that have already been described, plus any weird, compulsive rituals you have around food that give you an illusion of control. This also includes *comfort eating*, when you "medicate" yourself with certain favorite foods (chocolate, ice cream, donuts, potato chips, etc.) during periods of stress.

- **Shopping.** Whether compulsive shopping is done at malls or on the Internet, this can be a very expensive addiction. Before you whip out that credit card, ask yourself whether you really, really need this thing after all. The shame is that whatever enjoyment you get from buying something to make yourself feel better doesn't last much longer than the buzz from other addictions.

- **Workaholism.** People bury themselves in their work as a way to hide from the world, their loneliness, empty relationships, or even themselves. Unfortunately, this addiction may show rewards in higher grades or work performance, but it comes at the expense of a balanced life.

- **Sex.** People with this addiction become predatory in their sexual behaviors to the point where they are out of control. It isn't any longer about intimacy, or even enjoying physical pleasure; it is about conquest and escape. Another variation of this theme is addiction to online porn sites in which fantasy sex replaces the possibility of a healthy relationship with a real person.

- **Risk taking.** Like gambling, this addiction is about ratcheting up intensity to the point that a person engages in dangerous activities for the thrill of cheating death. There is a compulsive quality to the behavior where the risks become progressively more reckless and the thrill lasts only as long as planning the next caper.

Technically speaking, a true addiction involves some sort of *physiological dependence* such as what happens when the body develops cravings for additional quantities of heroin, tranquilizers, or alcohol. Nevertheless, psychological addictions to substances like marijuana or behavioral addictions to video gaming or gambling can be almost as difficult to control. And eventually the body and mind do become accustomed to the physiological changes (rush of adrenaline and serotonin) that take place during the activity.

© Cengage Learning

▶ **VIEW IT**

Partying, Drinking, and Drugs
Students discuss some of the temptations and difficulties they faced during their freshman year, in some cases losing control. (www.cengagebrain.com)

The true test of whether you are addicted to self-defeating behavior is whether several of the following apply:

1. You have *lost control* over the frequency in which you engage in this behavior. You can set goals for yourself but find you are powerless to control the amount of time.

2. You spend an inordinate amount of time thinking about or anticipating the behavior, even when you aren't engaging in it.

3. There is a noticeable *negative impact* on the rest of your life. The behavioral addiction isolates you from others, interferes with getting sufficient rest and sleep, costs more time and money than you can afford, compromises your academic performance, and limits your engagement with the world.

4. You get high from the activity, an actual buzz that lasts for a period of time; then you crash. A good example is the behavior of a compulsive gambler who doesn't care as much as you'd think about whether he wins or loses; he just loves the action. But once the binge is over, there is a depression hangover.

5. You can't stop. Even though you may say you can stop anytime, the excuse is that you don't feel like it. The truth is that you can't stop because you have nothing else to substitute for the behavior that will help you keep things together.

6. You develop *tolerance* to the behavior, just like with a drug. This means that you need more and more of it to get the same effect—more frequency, intensity, and variability.

7. You experience *withdrawal symptoms* when you attempt to stop or even cut back. This can included irritability, mood swings, depression, and anxiety.

8. You encounter relapses. During those times when you do resolve to quit, you find you can't do it because of the dependence that has developed, unless you find something else to replace it.

Sleeping

Close to three-quarters of college students have problems sleeping, and only about one in ten report that they sleep well on a regular basis (Bulboltz, Brown, and Soper, 2001). Nearly 12 percent of students experience significant sleep disruptions that affect their ability to concentrate during the day (Vail-Smith, Felts, and Becker, 2009). First-year college students have even more troubled sleep because of all the additional adjustment challenges that they face (Tsai and Li, 2004).

It may appear as if stealing extra hours from your sleep is a good strategy to build in more study time, but in fact students who sleep six hours each night (average for college students) have lower grade point averages than those who sleep nine hours (Kelly, Kelly, and Clanton, 2001). This means that putting in extra hours studying late at night may not be advantageous in terms of the actual quality of work that is produced. Other studies have found that getting more sleep improves your memory and recall, ensuring that you do better on tests and schoolwork (Stickgold and Wehrwein, 2009). There are even instances in which landmark scientific breakthroughs occurred during sleep, such as the case of chemist Dmitri Mendeleev, who awoke from a dream with the idea for developing the periodic table of elements.

Generally, there are a number of behaviors associated with poor sleep (Vail-Smith, Felts, and Becker, 2009), many of which will not surprise you. Worrying at night, especially about things outside of your control, is guaranteed to keep you tossing and turning in bed; the same goes for reliving conflicts that occurred or rehearsing things you want to say to people who have been annoying you. Smoking cigarettes,

Teaching Tip

Ask students to keep a sleep log for one week and a log of classroom performance. As a journal Activity Option, ask students to analyze their sleep: Did oversleeping make them late? Did they sleep during any class? Do they repeatedly hit the snooze button? Do they nap? How much do they sleep at night, and when do they go to bed? Next, ask students to reflect on sleep changes that might be warranted. How can the student implement these changes?

Sleep disruption presents one of the greatest obstacles for first-year students to effective learning, productivity, and enjoyment of their college experience. The average student sleeps less than six hours each night. Seven out of ten feel drowsy when studying because they are so tired.

Digital Vision/Jupiter Images

consuming caffeinated beverages, and drinking alcohol also tend to affect the quality and quantity of sleep. See Table 8.3 for tips on improving the quality of your sleep.

Leisure Activities

What do you do for fun and diversion? With all your other responsibilities and commitments, places you have to be, and assignments you have to complete, what do you do to take care of yourself?

You've probably heard adults tell you this so often you're sick of it, but your college years are (or can be) the best of your life. College is a time for freedom, exploration, and phenomenal growth that is unprecedented throughout the life span. The stated purpose of college is education in all the realms that make a person wise, productive, and balanced. Academics are only a part of that journey.

For Community College Students

Tap your nontraditional students in class to discuss what they have learned about the importance of leisure activities. Ask students whether they have time for such activities and if they don't think they do, ask them what they think the consequences are for ignoring "down" time.

Sex

Just what you need: another sex talk.

Every stage in life presents a series of developmental tasks that are required before progressing to the next stage in a satisfactory way. For the past tens of thousands of years, the main task of early adulthood has been finding a life mate. Because once upon a time human life expectancy was less than twenty-five years, the human body was designed to kick into gear its maximum sex drive during late adolescence. Even though many young people are now postponing marriage or living together until well after college, and even into their thirties or older, the biological equipment you have inherited still reaches its peak during your late teens and early twenties. That is one reason why sex may be on your mind, not to mention romantic fantasies involving one or more partners.

TABLE 8.3

Tips for Better Sleep

▶ Limit the caffeine in coffee, tea, or cola beverages that you drink, especially after lunch.

▶ Exercise on a regular basis.

▶ Don't get in bed until you are really tired.

▶ Stick with a regular sleep schedule as best you can, going to sleep and waking at the same times during weekdays.

▶ Don't take long naps, especially if they are used to make up for poor sleep the night before. You'll get into a cycle that will be difficult to break.

▶ Avoid excessive stimulation before you go to sleep. Resist the impulse to check e-mail, exercise vigorously, talk on the phone, play video games, or do anything that gets you worked up and thinking too much.

▶ Use deep breathing, visual imagery, or meditative-type exercises to help yourself relax.

▶ Drinking alcohol may initially help you to fall asleep (pass out), but often you will not remain asleep throughout the night.

▶ Avoid eating big meals close to bedtime, especially anything with a stimulant such as chocolate which has caffeine.

▶ If something is nagging at you or worrying you, write it down on a pad next to your bed so you can deal with it in the morning.

▶ If you are bothered by intrusive noises, get good ear plugs or a "white noise" machine that blocks sound.

▶ If you can't fall asleep after twenty minutes, don't continue to toss and turn. Get out of bed and read a little in your textbook; that will put you to sleep for sure.

▶ Chronic and long-term sleep disturbances can lead to serious health problems and interfere with academic performance. Visit the health center or your doctor for a consultation.

▶ If medication is used to aid sleep, it can quickly become habit-forming or addictive. Such drugs are only intended for short-term use.

Personal Choices Grounded in Your Moral Beliefs

Sex is a very personal matter. In spite of what others are doing around you, the choice to become (or remain) sexually active is a private decision, one that is influenced by your family upbringing, culture, religious affiliation, moral beliefs, and, frankly, the opportunities that come your way. Whether to engage in sex, and to what extent, also depends on the person with whom you are involved.

Some students (both men and women) feel it is important to remain a virgin until marriage, or at least until involved in a permanent love relationship. Others see sex as the most pleasurable way possible to share time with someone else with whom they feel an attraction. What is right and what is wrong are beside the point since each person has to make his or her own choices and live with them afterward.

Sex, and especially *good sex*, is always a negotiated process. It takes a long time to teach a partner what you like, and what you don't like. This applies not only to intercourse but to kissing, holding, touching, or any limits you choose to set. A good physical relationship requires continual verbal and nonverbal communication to teach someone how to touch you, how to make you feel good and meet your needs.

Constructing a Perfect Day

Even with all the obligations, responsibilities, and stressors you face, there are still ways you can build more joy into every day regardless of your financial situation. During a perfect day, what are all the things that you would include? What are all the things that are most important to you, that keep you satisfied and functioning optimally?

_____

_____

_____

_____

List the activities that give you the most pleasure and that, if possible, you would do every day.

1. _____

2. _____

3. _____

4. _____

5. _____

6. _____

7. _____

Given your personal limitations of time and money, it may be unlikely that you can do *all* of these things every day. Circle the ones that you are absolutely committed to including as part of your daily life to keep yourself happy.

Kathy:
Fear of Losing Control

"Okay, so there are a few things in college that everyone else does that I'm not doing. Mainly, I don't really drink, and I don't have sex. It's hard because I never really feel normal, not doing those things. I mean seriously, is there anyone else not doing them? I always feel like a complete dork and like everyone is making fun of me behind my back. I know I stand out at parties because I drink soda, and it's really, really embarrassing when I'm dating a guy and I have to tell him that I won't have sex with him. Sometimes the guy is nice; sometimes he just looks at me funny.

The reason I don't drink or have sex is because I'm just really busy with school and completely focused on my major. At least, that's what I tell myself. To be honest, I really think it's just because I'm scared. I mean, what happens when you get drunk? How much control do you lose? I don't want to lose control. And sex ... what happens if you get pregnant? What then?

Meghan:
I Was Raped

"I am a rape victim. I know that something like one out of six women have had such experiences and, like me, most of them have never told anyone.

I was fifteen and out with my boyfriend, who was two years older than me. I was crazy about him and we did everything together. He was the first guy to say I was beautiful and that he loved me.

One of the times we were out together, he became very aggressive. We were sitting in his car kissing a little, but this time it was different. He began to push me back until I was lying across the seat. He locked the doors. I was trapped. He kept saying how he wanted me and how he knew I wanted him too. I screamed at him to leave me alone, but he didn't listen. He said it would be better for both of us if I stopped fighting. There was nothing I could do. And I never, ever told anyone about this until now.

It takes a degree of trust and safety with a partner to feel comfortable enough to talk about your preferences, as well as what you don't want to do. This refers not to the pleasure and satisfaction of sex but also to protecting yourself against unsafe practices.

Safe Sex

The first line of defense is *celibacy*, or at least masturbation. That is about as safe as you can get, at least from the perspective of avoiding a *sexually transmitted infection* (STI) or *sexually transmitted disease* (STD) or getting pregnant. However, it isn't nearly as fun or fulfilling as having sex with a partner.

Abstinence is also a choice in which you and a partner deliberately choose to limit your sexual involvement within agreed upon parameters. Such a choice requires the consent of both people to work, and a certain amount of self-discipline.

Monogamy is often the preferred option if you are involved in a committed relationship with someone you care about deeply. As long as both of you are free of STIs, and are respectful and sensitive in your responses to one another, this is often an ideal choice for some couples. Since an exclusive relationship does not, by itself, prevent unwanted pregnancy, it is important that both partners take responsibility for ensuring that sex remains safe.

Birth control methods vary tremendously in terms of their relative effectiveness. None of them is foolproof, but you can anticipate that if you are sexually active and using no method at all, or predicting periods of fertility, the chances are pretty good that at some point, there will be a miscalculation. Even using contraceptives like condoms or diaphragms results in failures 15–20 percent of the time.

Some methods of birth control, like condoms, may not be as effective as oral contraceptives for preventing pregnancy, but they certainly do a better job of protecting you against STIs. No matter how careful you intend to be, 25 percent of college students end up with one kind of sexual infection or another, and a much higher percentage will contract an STI before the age of twenty-five. Table 8.4 reviews the most common infections that put you at risk. Basically, women should seek medical help if they have unusual vaginal discharges, burning sensations during urination, itching, or sores anywhere near their genitals. Men should also remain alert for discharges or pain during urination, as well as warts or blisters. Unfortunately, by the time you notice symptoms you are already infected with an STD that may be with you your whole life.

TABLE 8.4

Common Sexually Transmitted Infections

STI	Symptoms	Treatment
Chlamydia	Painful urination in men; vaginal discharge in women; sometimes no apparent symptoms	Antibiotics
Genital warts	Warts in genital area or around cervix, also in mouth	Topical medications, laser surgery, burning, freezing
Gonorrhea	Sore throat, discharge, pink eye, painful urination	Antibiotics
Hepatitis B	Nausea, fatigue, jaundice, changes in urine and bowel movement appearing a few months after infection	No cure and minimal treatment except diet and rest
Herpes	Blisters or sores in genital area that may be painful or itchy	No cure but medications reduce outbreaks
HIV	Weight loss, fatigue, unexplained sweats, chronic and persistent flu-like symptoms	No cure but medications treat some symptoms and prolong life
Syphilis	Genital sores, flu-like symptoms, rash, swollen glands	Antibiotics

You can greatly reduce your chances of contracting an STI if you use prophylactics (condoms) during sex, or at least be very selective about your sexual partners. But don't wait until you are in the advanced throes of love-making to "interview" a partner. Imagine ripping clothes off one another and then you stop to say, "Wait, before we go any further, can I take a sexual history? Have you been blood-tested recently for HIV or any other STI? Can I see your medical history in case you might be lying?

If celibacy or abstinence is out of the question, it is important to talk openly with your partner about issues related to birth control, sexually transmitted infections, and mutual consent for all sexual activities. Even the idea of "consent" is difficult when one person pressures the other to engage in sex with threats or emotional blackmail ("I thought you loved me").

Dorgie Productions/Photographer's Choice/Getty Images

TABLE 8.5

How Do You Know if You've Crossed the Line?

If you want to initiate sex with a partner, how do you know if you've gone too far?

▸ You can't know … unless you ask. If you aren't sure, ask permission to go further.

▸ It is never okay, under any circumstances, to force yourself on another person without his or her explicit, clear consent.

▸ If you've had anything to drink, or taken any drugs, assume you can't trust your best judgment.

▸ Don't make assumptions about what you think your partner really wants, even though you may sense ambivalence.

▸ Forcing yourself on another person constitutes a crime in the form of assault or rape, which is punishable by time in prison.

▸ Victims of unwanted sex are often traumatized by the experience, not just for one bad night but also for many years thereafter.

Can I have a list of your previous sexual partners so I can check them as references? Would you mind if my physician does a genital exam to make sure you are healthy?"

Obviously that strategy won't work very well, but it is entirely appropriate to have a conversation with your prospective partner *before* you get too far into things. This may indeed feel a little awkward, but usually your partner will also feel relieved that you broached the subject. And if he or she doesn't feel concerned or curious, perhaps you should wonder if this person is truly a wise choice for you to become physically intimate with.

In addition to the risks of STIs or pregnancy, safety also relates to preventing unwanted sexual advances. Putting yourself in a situation that could result in sexual harassment, date rape, sexual assault, or disrespectful behavior is an experience that can take years to recover from. Commonly, such transgressions occur when excessive alcohol or drugs are in play, but just as often, it can result from miscommunication in which signals are misread. Be selective about who you spend time with and under what conditions.

Money

Of critical relevance to your lifestyle choices are the financial realities that dictate what you can afford to do, and what you cannot, especially when financial aid is limited, jobs are tight, and the economy is weak. In conversations with first-year students about their major concerns, a prevalent theme is concern about securing enough money to finance education, pay for current expenses, and get a solid return on the college investment (Franklin et al., 2002). This is true whether you are being totally supported by parents or putting yourself through school via part-time jobs, loans, and/or scholarships. Campus counselors have reported significant increase in stress and depression among students as a result of money problems they are currently experiencing or foresee in the future (Bushong, 2009).

One of the rites of passage when beginning college is becoming the target of credit card companies promising you untold riches "available at low, low interest rates and affordable monthly payments." Ah, such a deal. This glittering but treacherous principle already permeates the rest of our culture, proposing that you can have most anything you want, and have it now, with no money down and the obligation of paying for it put off into the indeterminate future.

Classroom Discussion

Open it up: How much do you value your education? Calculate the cost of each college course. Divide this cost by the number of class sessions for the semester. Relate these per-class costs to skipping class: How much money is wasted for each missed class period? Ask yourself, "How is going to class an investment in a better financial future for myself?"

Teaching Tip

Introduce the topic of money with several statements which you can ask students to place on a continuum from *strongly disagree* to *strongly agree*. Statements could include "Credit cards are good for college students," "Money really can buy happiness," and so on.

Group Activity

Introduce the topic of money with questions that students can answer on poster paper anonymously. Questions could include "How much do you plan to earn in your first career after college?" "Where did you get this number?" and "How much is enough?" To bring perception closer to reality, provide information from the National Association of Colleges & Employers (NACE) Salary Survey.

Money doesn't really make the world go around, even if it seems that way from watching how the lifestyles of the famous and powerful are portrayed in the media. Studies show that what best predicts happiness are friendships, stable love relationships, grounded spiritual beliefs, and control over emotional states, while things that you might think would be associated with happiness—income, health, or even ideal geographic location—have minimal or no effect (Seligman, 2002).

How rich you feel is always relative to those around you. If you have a ten-year-old clunker of a car, but none of your friends has any transportation, then you are pretty well off. Interestingly, however, the person who owns a brand-new Porsche 911 doesn't feel that fortunate when he sees a turbo convertible model race by him. Consistently, studies have found that people who are fabulously rich, living in mansions, and driving a Mercedes or Rolls Royce are not significantly happier than most other people (except those living in abject poverty). Even more interesting, citizens of Japan, who have ten times the purchasing power and standard of living of those living in China, have lower life satisfaction. So the old saying really is true that money doesn't buy happiness.

Even knowing this usually doesn't change people's attitudes or behavior. You can be absolutely positive, beyond a doubt, that making gobs of money will not improve the quality of life, and yet you'd still like to give it a try. You might take the job offer with the highest salary, even though it is not a career path you'd prefer to take.

Look at those who live a life you would someday like to emulate. What is it about their lifestyle that most appeals to you? If it is the size of their house, the cost of their car and clothes, and the obscene amounts of money at their disposal, in all probability they are no happier with their lives than you are now. Someone who lives in a one-room flat aspires to have a one- or maybe two-bedroom apartment. But someone who lives in a 20,000-square-foot mansion also yearns for one twice as big and feels just as disappointed when she or he can't have it.

One of the most persistent sources of stress for students is concern about money, especially during difficult economic times when financial aid and jobs are in short supply. It is important to remember that higher education represents an investment in your future, and that sacrifices must be made for long-term gains.

There are some things within your control such as reducing spending, keeping expenses within reason, earning extra income if possible, and applying for additional financial aid, but there are other factors beyond what you can do at this time. Worrying about money issues, without taking action, doesn't change things.

Credit Cards

Many students who are financing their education with loans can expect to graduate owing tens of thousands of dollars. Adding to the burden are credit card balances that exceed $5,000 or more, a predicament that creates a never-ending cycle of debt. The majority of college students have at least four different credit cards in their possession (Stephey, 2009). Given that the interest rates on credit cards can rival those of loan sharks (often 18 percent or higher), it is challenging enough just to make the minimum monthly balance that does nothing to reduce the amount owed.

Let's look at an example. Some friends invite you to go to a resort in Mexico during semester break. "It's a great deal," they tell you, "so good it's ridiculous to pass up." Of course you're interested, but you are broke, flat busted, with little savings except what you have budgeted for next semester.

"Just charge it," your friends tell you. "Live a little. What are a few extra bucks added to the bill with everything else that is adding up? We'll all be making the big bucks when we graduate, so you can pay this off in no time."

Makes sense, you agree. Besides, it was a tough semester and you really do need a break. It's really not a vacation anyway, you tell yourself; it's a kind of mental rejuvenation. Just think how relaxed you'll be when you return.

You add up all the expenses and figure it will cost about $1,000, including airfare, hotel, meals, alcohol, and incidentals. And, oh yeah, you'll need to buy a few things

Teaching Tip

Assign students to write down everything on which they spend money for a week. Were there any times they felt they wasted money?

for the trip, say another few hundred dollars. The total bill will be about $1,300, a pretty good deal for eight days of hanging out in a resort. Even though you don't have the funds, you can try out your new credit card. Heck, they don't even charge interest until the bill comes thirty days later.

You return from Mexico relaxed and refreshed. You open up your credit card statement and see the $1,300 balance, plus interest tacked on that seems higher than you thought it would be. You read the fine print and see that the interest rate is 14.9 percent annually. Since you weren't planning on starting to pay this off until the summer at least, you now realize that it's going to be several hundred dollars higher before you can start chipping away at it. You do some quick calculations and now realize that by the time you can pay off the debt from this trip, it will take you two years and end up doubling the price.

The lesson from this example? Even the best deals come with a cost.

Signing up for a credit card is actually a good idea, as is using it on occasion. In fact, this is one way to start building your credit history so that someday you will more easily qualify for a home mortgage or some other major purchase. But be smart about avoiding the problems that occur when you can't pay off the balance and the exorbitant interest starts kicking in.

So here is the plan for using credit cards:

1. Sign up for a credit card that offers the best deal. That means with the absolute minimum annual fee (preferably zero) and the lowest possible interest rate. You will be surprised how much the plans vary.

2. Use your credit card for making small purchases that you *know*—that you are absolutely *positive*—you can pay for when the bill comes at the end of the month. Never, ever, under any conditions or circumstances make the minimum required payment when the bill comes and let the balance remain intact. If you pay off the balance every month, then you will never be charged interest and never accumulate debt. The reward for this self-discipline is that you can take advantage of the convenience of buying and enjoying something immediately, but not have to pay for it until several weeks later. But this only works if you do pay off the balance each month—and if you study the terms of the contract to make sure you aren't charged hidden fees. One other advantage of using a credit card carefully is that it helps you to establish also a good credit history for the time you may wish to borrow money for a home or car.

Group Activity

Do some math in class. Exactly how much interest will accrue between the student's trip at spring break and the end of August? What difference will minimum payments make?

RandFaris/Corbis/Jupiter Images

One of the most overwhelming sources of stress for college students is financial debt, a lot of it accumulated through impulsive spending for things that are really not needed. Learning to manage money and control spending are life skills for which few people receive solid training.

3. If you don't think you can resist the temptations to buy more things than you can comfortably pay off at the end of the month, then don't sign up for a credit card in the first place. Instead, use a debit card that deducts purchases from your bank account. That way you can never spend what you don't have.

4. In spite of this warning and advice, if you ever find yourself in the predicament in which you have not paid off the balance of your credit card for two months in a row, take that as a dire sign that you are on the way to financial trouble. Since you are paying astronomical interest rates for use of this money, you must now figure out an alternative way to beg, borrow, or earn sufficient funds from someone or somewhere else to cancel this credit card debt. Otherwise, you are going to be in hock for years.

5. Save all receipts from credit card and ATM purchases and check them against your monthly statements. Identity theft is a real possibility in which someone will use your credit card number to charge items that you may not notice. In more serious cases, your whole identity can be "stolen" in which someone applies for credit under your name and social security number. For that reason, you will want to keep all your financial papers in a secure place and destroy any documents that have your identifying information.

College occurs during formative years in which you are learning good habits to maintain throughout your lifetime. If you start charging things you can't afford now, what do you think is going to happen later in life? You may have more discretionary income, but that won't change the pattern of spending more than you can afford.

Making a Budget

Classroom Discussion

Open it up: Let's brainstorm ways to spend less money. List your responses on the board. Which ones sound most workable?

A budget is a necessity for making sure that you stay within your means. It doesn't have to be complicated, but it should be as detailed and complete as possible. In one column, list all the sources of income that you can count on. Don't include anticipated lottery or gambling winnings, possible inheritances, or other wishful thinking! Income includes not only money that you earn, but also contributions from family, loans, scholarships, grants, and stock or bank interest. Add up all the funds coming your way to see what you've got to work with. Decide on a time frame as to whether this budget will cover a week, month, academic semester, or year. Most students prefer to average things out per month, so that means adding up all annual tuition, fee, and book costs and dividing by twelve months.

In a second column, list all your anticipated expenses. Here is where you have to be as precise, realistic, and comprehensive as possible. Doing a budget doesn't work very well if you forget to include expenditures that can throw predictions out of whack. You don't have to make wild guesses in planning for the future because you have some data already available. For instance, you know which bills are due and you can estimate how much they might be (and how they might change throughout the seasons). It can require a degree of skill to forecast expenses in the social and entertainment arena. Make sure you include anything that you *might* spend.

The budget format in For Reflection 8.2 will get you started but is by no means complete. It will be up to you to revise and refine the items listed according to your own spending practices. For instance, if you have haircut and grooming expenses, dry cleaning, or child care costs, you'll want to add those to the list. Take out the items that don't apply to you, and add others that are part of your lifestyle.

Add up the income column and also the expenses column. If your expenses exceed your income, you must either figure out a way to earn more money, or else reduce your planned expenses. The second option is preferable since your time as a first-year college student is so limited, and your first priority should be staying focused on your studies.

"After completing this exercise," one student reported, "I started keeping track of my expenses on an Excel spreadsheet. It was just an experiment. After a few weeks of keeping track of my spending, I was amazed at where my money was going, things

I didn't even think about. Now I've become a lot more disciplined and I think twice before I buy something that I really don't need. It just really helps!"

Tracking Your Money

It is one thing to plan how you will manage your finances and quite another to follow through on your intentions. Each year our government plans a budget in which expenditures exceed costs, leading to extravagant debt and interest payments. The reasoning goes that some future generation can deal with the debt, but for now we want what we want. Unfortunately, you can't print your own money and the consequences for you borrowing more and more money are likely to be more immediate and more crippling.

Group Activity
Make an overhead of the budget form, or ask students to write in their books. During class, share costs of room, board, tuition, and fees at your institution. Discuss the difference in price for in-state versus out-of-state students. Share the amount of fees and, if available, where the various fees go.

8.2 FOR REFLECTION

Making a Budget

Income		Expenses	
Job	_____	Tuition and fees	_____
Parents' contributions	_____	Rent/room and board	_____
Student loans	_____	Meal plan	_____
Scholarships	_____	Snacks/eating out	_____
Other sources	_____	Groceries	_____
		Books	_____
Total Income	_____	School supplies/lab fees	_____
		Gas	_____
		Car payments	_____
		Health care	_____
		Car insurance	_____
		Car maintenance	_____
		Parking/public transport	_____
		Computer	_____
		Clothes	_____
		Phone	_____
		Cable/Internet	_____
		Utilities	_____
		Taxes	_____
		Interest payments on debt	_____
		Entertainment	_____
		Vacations	_____
		Miscellaneous	_____
		Savings for emergencies	_____
		Total Expenses	_____

8.3 FOR REFLECTION

Making Money Last

Short of cash? Try this experiment to see if you can make $50 last ten days.

1. Put your credit card in a drawer because you won't be using it.

2. Take out $50 from the ATM machine or bank.

3. Tell everyone you know what you are planning so you can't back out or change your mind.

4. Think of this as a game, a challenge that few people you know could complete.

5. Since food in restaurants and fast-food establishments is beyond your budget, buy inexpensive grocery stables (rice, ramen noodles, etc.) that will last. Use coupons you find in the paper.

6. Since you can easily blow your whole budget on a daily $3 cup of coffee from Starbucks, drink something you make yourself.

7. If possible, take public transportation or else limit your driving.

8. Find free entertainment. Use the park and library. Go for walks, runs, and hikes. Play with friends.

After the week is over, reflect on how you did. What new habits do you intend to use on a regular basis?

Source: Based on an idea from Turk (2004).

The best way to keep track of how you spend your money is to keep track of every receipt, ATM withdrawal, check purchase, electronic bank transaction, and cash purchase. Keep all of the receipts together in a file so you can reconcile your account balance. Not only is this important on a monthly basis for reviewing and revising your budget, but to monitor for unauthorized activity in case of identity theft.

You should have both a checking account for funds that you will eventually disperse and for automatic deposits of any paychecks, as well as a savings account where you can squirrel away money for long-term purchases and emergencies. Once you have more than a few thousand dollars saved, consider working with a stockbroker to invest your money for a higher rate of return. Just as you would do when you sign up for a credit card, shop carefully for your bank services as there are big differences in the fees that are charged for checks, ATM cards, and stock transactions. Find out exactly what type of minimum balance you must maintain to avoid such fees.

If you do feel the increasing burden of financial pressure and building debt, and you can't figure out a way to reduce expenses (which is unlikely), then consider reducing your course load and working more hours. But under no circumstances should you drop out of school. As difficult as it might be now to manage money issues, it only gets harder as you grow older and acquire more responsibilities.

Saving for the Future

One additional incentive for being frugal with your finances is the money you will need for the future. Even though you may not be able to imagine it now, there is a possibility that your undergraduate education will only be the beginning; looming over the horizon could be law school, business school, medical or dental school, or other graduate programs. And if you think college is expensive, wait until you get a handle on how much advanced education will set you back. The cost of law school for three years could be as high as $150,000 (of course, that's close to the annual starting salary). Other graduate programs can cost just as much, if not more.

You will want to save money to purchase your first home someday or to buy a car without having to go deeper in debt. Even more important, you will want to give yourself the freedom to take the job you really want rather than one you feel pressured to accept just because the salary is attractive.

If You're In Over Your Head

If you find that you are too far in debt and unable to pay your basic expenses, the worst thing you can do is to just keep it to yourself and hope the problem will go away. It won't.

Here are some constructive steps that you can take to get your financial situation back under control:

- If the emotional price is not too much to pay, ask your parents and family for help. Be prepared to pay *some* price for this assistance (like listening to a lecture, being scolded, and making requested changes).

- Get a part-time job or participate in work-study on campus (unless you are already working).

- Cut expenses. Drastically. Maybe you don't need a car, or the most expensive cell phone plan, or a single room, or the other indulgences you have allowed yourself. It's time to make hard choices and some sacrifices, at least in the short run.

- If you are in trouble with credit card debt, retire the card until you can demonstrate greater financial discipline.

- Consult with your school's financial aid office to learn what packages you might be eligible for. Scholarships or grants may be available that you hadn't considered when you first applied to college.

- Apply for student loans with deferred interest until after you graduate.

- Talk to a counselor in financial aid to get help consolidating your debt, reducing interest penalties, and developing a repayment plan.

SUMMARY

Most of college life is spent outside of the classroom, dealing with all the realities that affect your daily functioning. While effective classroom and studying behavior are critical to doing well, such skills can easily become compromised by poor decisions or habits with regard to lifestyle management. If your sleep is disrupted, if you have financial problems, or if you "medicate" yourself with excessive drugs or alcohol, you can easily sabotage your progress.

It is important that you establish healthy patterns related to eating and exercise, as well as other aspects of your lifestyle. This includes monitoring carefully how you feel on a daily basis, assessing your physical, emotional, psychological, and spiritual satisfaction. If you are not functioning at your best in these areas, your academic performance can suffer, not to mention your enjoyment of college life. It is important to find a balance between work and fun, obligations and leisure, and indulgence and self-restraint, establishing sound habits that you can follow for the rest of your life.

QUESTIONS FOR REVIEW AND FURTHER EXPLORATION

1. What are some of the most important things to keep in mind when eating healthfully?

2. What are the reasons why the effects of dieting, or any life change, don't always last very long?

3. Why are eating disorders actually considered *emotional* disorders? How is eating behavior linked to your feelings?

4. When structuring an exercise program, what optimal things do you want to keep in mind?

5. Why is there a distinction made between drug *use* and *abuse*? What are the factors that separate them? If you take drinking as an example, what do you think distinguishes casual social drinking from alcohol abuse?

6. Evolutionary theory proposes that gender differences might explain why men and women have different mating strategies to perpetuate their genes and, therefore, engage in different sexual behavior. How would you use this model to explain why rape is such a serious crime in all cultures? Hint: In almost all cultures, women are the choosers of sexual partners because they have limited opportunities for procreation (capable of carrying only about twenty possible fertilized eggs in their lifetime versus unlimited sperm production for men). In the case or forced sex, a woman is not only subjected to violence, humiliation, and physical harm, but also has twenty years of her life "stolen" if there is a pregnancy in which she will be left to take care of the unwanted child with a partner she never would have chosen.

7. Why do you believe that wealth or material possessions are not good predictors of happiness and life satisfaction?

8. This is one of those chapters that you might read and nod to yourself that the advice and guidance would definitely improve your life. The bottom line, however, is that you probably won't follow through on many of the suggestions even if you agree they would be useful. What would it take for you to put the ideas into action?

Go to www.cengagebrain.com for an online quiz that will test your understanding of the chapter content.

Thinking Critically and Solving Problems

KEY QUESTIONS

▶ **What's the difference between creative and critical thinking?**

▶ **How do you evaluate the credibility of an information source?**

▶ **What's the difference between expert and celebrity opinions?**

▶ **What are the barriers that impede critical thinking?**

▶ **How do you balance intuition with reasoning?**

▶ **Why do people keep trying the same things over and over again even though it is clear they aren't working?**

A student is in a discussion (read: disagreement) with an instructor over her grade on a paper. She makes the following case for a grade change but is unsuccessful in her effort. As you read through her plea, note as many errors as you can in her reasoning that led to the disappointing result.

"I want to talk to you about this B – you gave me on the paper. Is this a good time?"

"Not really, I ..."

"Good. See, here is the problem. You *definitely* made a mistake."

"I made a mistake?"

"Yeah, you see I tried my hardest on this assignment so it should've been an A for sure."

"Because you tried your hardest, it deserves an A?"

"Uh-huh. And besides, you gave a friend of mine a B+ and my paper is definitely better than his."

"I should trust your judgment on this?"

"Sure. Why not? What about freedom of speech? Doesn't my opinion count for anything?"

"In general, yes, but not in this case."

"See, there you go again. I'm very offended by your attempt to marginalize me. Is it because of my gender or my religion?"

"Actually I don't know what your religion is."

"There you go. You don't even care."

"You don't think I care? Besides, what does that have to do with the grade on your paper?"

"Okay, then, how about this? I really need a better grade on my paper, at least a B+ or I'll never get into graduate school. Can't you see how important this is to me? Can't you give me a break?"

Presumably you can see how this student doesn't have a prayer of getting her grade changed—regardless of her religious beliefs. She has violated almost every rule of critical thinking in the book. She *externalizes blame* ("You made a mistake"). She states *opinions as facts* ("I tried my hardest"). She makes *illogical assumptions* ("Because I tried my hardest, I deserve an A") and *illogical connections* ("What about freedom of speech?"). She makes *invalid analogies* ("You gave my friend a higher grade") *based on inexpert sources* ("Isn't my opinion as important as yours?"). She bases her argument on *emotional appeals* ("Don't you care about me?"). Personally, if I heard this appeal I'd be so appalled I'd *lower* the grade on the paper.

What Critical Thinking Means and What It Will Do for You

One purpose of college is to learn to think more critically. Math courses teach you to apply logic and sequential thinking. Philosophy teaches you how to examine meaning. Science classes teach you a method for testing hypotheses. History teaches about trends in the past. Social sciences teach you about behavior. The arts teach you to appreciate aesthetics and intuition. The accumulative effect of this education is that you internalize certain principles and processes that will become second nature over time, a part of the way you make sense of the world.

As a relative newcomer to academic life and critical thinking, in some ways you have an advantage over those who are far more experienced. Sometimes experts get in ruts, at least as far as pursuing familiar patterns of solving problems and thinking critically about issues that concern them. Having a fresh perspective, with limited experience in certain areas, can actually lead you to come up with alternatives that have not yet been considered (Hutson, 2008). In one study, chess masters easily spotted a common five-move checkmate strategy but missed a more novel, three-move solution that beginners would have recognized if they took the time to figure it out (Bilalic, McCleod, and Gobet, 2007). Take heart—if you devote the time and energy to thinking systematically, strategically, and persistently about problems, even with limited experience, you can still discover some very exciting things.

Thinking refers to the internal mental process that takes place when you attempt to process information, understand something, solve a problem, or make a decision. It comes in two varieties: (1) *creative thinking*, when you generate new ideas or solutions; and (2) *critical thinking*, when you assess information as to its usefulness and merit (Ruggiero, 2007). In both cases, this is the reasoning process by which you make sense of almost anything you encounter in life, sorting out the best course of action.

Critical thinking doesn't mean taking a negative or judgmental approach but rather *evaluating* what you read, hear, observe, and experience. It is a process of analyzing information in such a way that you determine its relevance, accuracy, and usefulness. It helps you to decide what to believe and what to question further. It helps you to take charge of your own mind instead of being a victim to what others tell you.

Critical thinking is a skill that can be learned through rigorous and disciplined practice. It sharpens your mind, allowing you to think more clearly about issues that concern or puzzle you. You can find better solutions to problems and be more effective in convincing others about what you think is most important. As mentioned in Chapter 3 regarding the payoffs of procrastination and other puzzling patterns, being a critical thinker helps you to make sense of behavior, both your own and that of others around you.

How to "Do" Critical Thinking

Critical thinking is not a magical process; you already know how to do it even though you may only apply it selectively. The method can be broken down into three basic steps.

1. Explore the full nature of a situation, problem, or phenomenon. This means collecting all data and evidence that could be relevant and useful, investigating things deeply and widely enough that you have sufficient information to proceed further. If, for instance, you are trying to determine whether you should take a course in cultural anthropology versus forensic anthropology next year, you cannot make an *informed decision* unless you know enough essential facts, such as: What are the prerequisites for each course, and can you meet them? What is the content of each class? Who is teaching them? What time does each class meet? How big are the classes? What are the required assignments? What do others say who have taken these courses previously?

2. Sort through all the information you've collected and make sense of it—interpret the data. This stage involves discriminating between what is useful and what is not, as well as the relative importance of various bits of information. How reliable and accurate are the reports you collected from previous students, and do you trust their opinions? How consistent are the class schedules and instructor assignments from one year to the next?

3. Finally, make an informed and critical judgment about what you believe is best based on the information available. Although such decisions often involve gut feelings and intuition, at least you are now prepared to balance emotion with facts to proceed toward optimal solutions. For instance, your heart may tell you that you want to know more about forensic anthropology (studying skeletons), but logically it makes more sense that you take other courses first to get a better background.

Following are some of the main procedures that lead to critical thinking in a variety of contexts, whether you are attempting to discover a new path, collect information of interest, evaluate information at your disposal, make an important decision, or persuade others of your position.

Gather Relevant and Useful Information

You will find no shortage of information to consider in your decision making. The problem is finding material that is accurate, reliable, grounded in solid data, replicated by others, and actually relevant to the issue you are exploring. Too often people rely on information that is inadequate or inaccurate.

Image Source/Jupiter Images

Critical thinking allows you to systematically consider situations that present multiple options, to sort out available choices, and then to make the best selection based on the data.

Group Activity

Organize students in small groups and ask them to brainstorm for acronyms for the three-step critical thinking process. Have each group report its deliberations and acronym. Determine a class acronym that will be used throughout the semester to recall the critical-thinking process (e.g., IED for investigate, evaluate, and decide).

Strongly held beliefs, such as the claim that aliens live among us or visit us regularly in their spacecraft, may or may not be true. But such beliefs are shaped by something less than critical thinking, instead relying on the opinions of a few individuals rather than an examination of compelling evidence that meets the demands of scientific scrutiny.

TOSHIFUMI KITAMURA/AFP/Getty Images

For example, you can find sources that absolutely *prove* that aliens live among us. Some individuals claim to have irrefutable evidence that they have been kidnapped to their spaceships, gang-raped, and tortured, and then released to tell the world about their captivity. Others have provided sworn testimonies that they have killed aliens on their property. Others offer photographs, alien artifacts, or messages from other planets to convince you of their sightings and experiences. Now, does that mean you are going to accept these claims at face value? Or will you also take into account conflicting facts and explanations before leaping to judgment?

Evidence can be collected in a number of different forms that vary in their accuracy, reliability, and usefulness.

● **Published research in peer-reviewed academic journals.** These studies have been subjected to accepted standards of the profession and review by qualified experts. You would have to evaluate the relative merits of the particular journal, as well as judge for yourself whether the study was conducted in a suitable manner. Unfortunately, the latter requires considerable training, so often you will be dependent on others' interpretations of these findings.

● **Media reports.** Newscasts, newspapers, magazines, radio, and Internet news sources are the most common sources of information.

● **Blogs.** Because these are neither peer reviewed nor accountable to any professional standards for accuracy, they often include unsubstantiated rumors, fabrications, exaggerations, and outright lies. However, they can also be on the cutting edge of investigative reporting compared to traditional news agencies. Evaluate critically.

● **Expert opinions.** You see these people in the media all the time making claims about anything and everything. You have to decide whether their statements are informed, and whether they are qualified enough to make them.

● **Celebrity opinions.** Popular figures often appear in advertisements to claim that certain products or political views are better than others. The question you have to ask yourself is what qualifies them to hold views that are any more legitimate than your own.

Classroom Discussion

Open it up: Give examples of celebrities marketing products or opinions on television or Internet advertising. Does this type of selling work for you?

- **Personal experiences.** Based on what you have observed, lived, thought, and felt previously, what can you reasonably expect or predict will happen in the future? To make that determination, you have to decide whether your experiences are truly representative of similar cases or are exceptions to them.

- **Eyewitness reports.** Just like a jury, you must decide whether what people say they witnessed is, in fact, what transpired. Given that observations are notoriously untrustworthy, colored by biases, distortions, memory lapses, and blind spots, you have to judge their value as a reliable source. After all, tens of thousands of people absolutely swear they have seen alien spacecraft—and, indeed, maybe they *have*—but so far that's all the evidence available.

Read with a More Penetrating Perspective

College teaches you to question what you read, or at least it should. A skeptical mind-set is one in which you ask critical questions like "Who says?" "Where did that come from?" "What are the underlying assumptions of those conclusions?" "Where is the evidence to support those claims?" and "How good is the data that is presented?"

Skepticism must also be balanced with a degree of open-mindedness to ideas that conflict with your own assumptions or those that you might find threatening. Most people read or listen to content wanting to confirm what they already know and believe. After all, it takes hard work to reorient your thinking. If what you think is true is not really the case, then you've got to figure out a way to reconcile your prior beliefs and behavior with what you've now learned.

For instance, you have particular eating habits that you prefer to keep. It doesn't matter whether you are a vegetarian or a meat eater, whether you favor chocolate, coffee, brown rice, or rutabagas. You will tend to pay closer attention to claims that confirm that you are on the correct path, and you will resist statements that say what you are doing is unhealthy. The problem, of course, is that science is always revising the current "wisdom" based on new studies that are completed. Coffee used to be bad for you. Then it was good for you, then bad again, and now good again (at least in moderation).

In a Woody Allen movie of long ago, *Sleeper*, the protagonist wakes up from a several-hundred-year sleep understandably malnourished and disoriented. His doctors are overheard planning a high-potency diet of sugar-laden foods for him, shaking their heads at the "primitive" beliefs that the medical establishment once held in the twenty-first century that vegetables were good for you. Now, they say, everyone knows that they cause cancer. While intended to be funny, that scene captures the dilemma you face when evaluating information and research to guide your behavior. It is not enough to hear experts (including and especially me) tell you things unless you evaluate them for yourself. On one hand, you should exhibit healthy skepticism toward ideas that conflict with what you think you already know, or what has been grounded in your experience. Yet, on the other hand, you should force yourself to remain open to new ideas that may actually be more accurate and useful.

Challenge Biases and Prejudices

A prejudice is exactly what it sounds like, a prejudgment based on prior experience and learning. In spite of the shame associated with being prejudiced, it is both natural and sometimes useful. During ancient times, human beings were often faced with making split-second, life-or-death decisions about whether a person approaching was a friend or an enemy. In some cases, you had just a moment to determine whether you should prepare for battle, run away and find some of your tribe for support, or greet the person enthusiastically. This snap judgment was based on prior experiences you had with others who resembled the person who approached. That is one reason why we are suspicious

Group Activity

Ask students to raise their hand if they are biased. Most students won't raise their hands because of the negative connotation of the word "bias." Praise those students who were honest enough to recognize that every person has his or her own biases. Emphasize that bias only becomes problematic if it interferes with making fair judgments and seeing others' perspectives.

of strangers and why often many people prefer to hang out with their "own kind." At first glance, you can notice this on any college campus: People tend to congregate with others who they see as part of their "tribe." While this can be (and often is) based on race, ethnicity, gender, or religion, it can also be grounded in shared interests and values. Thus, members of the volleyball or debate teams may hang out together because their interests and goals transcend their skin color or religious affiliation.

For Community College Students

Ask students in class to talk about if or when they have challenged any stereotypes they or others have about community college attendance.

You not only hold prejudices about certain people who have helped or threatened you in the past, but also about prior associations with objects or ideas. For instance, I drive a small car and in the past I have had a few close calls in which large pickup trucks, often black and with elevated suspensions, almost ran me off the road. Now when I see one of those things on the freeway, I feel an immediate visceral sense of anger and fear. I find myself not liking the person driving it even though we have never met. Is this rational or evidence of critical thinking? Hardly. It represents an illustration of one way that prejudices are formed. And it is particularly difficult to change these biases once they are established.

So it is with things you read, hear, and are exposed to. You shut down your willingness and ability to consider alternative perspectives because you believe your mind is already made up. There could be no possibility other than what you already have come to believe. End of story.

Even the most brilliant scientists can be uncritical in their thinking when trying to prove what they want to believe or to be the first to discover something. Margaret Mead, one of the most influential cultural anthropologists of the past century, had her groundbreaking work as a graduate student eventually discredited. She did not learn this during her lifetime, but later researchers discovered that the foundation for her first book on Samoan sexual behavior was based on interviews with two girls who later admitted that they had made up all their stories. In doing any research, or considering any information, it is absolutely critical that you confirm the data by checking additional sources. When someone tells you something that sounds unbelievable, it often is untrue. For example, how do you know *this* story is really true? Check the sources yourself (see Cote, 1994; Freeman, 1983, 1999; Miller and Kanazawa, 2007).

9.1 FOR REFLECTION

Loosen Yourself Up to Consider Alternative Perspectives

Here is a list of issues about which many people feel strongly; having made up their minds, they resist seeing the possibility of another point of view. For each of these controversial issues, make a strong, persuasive case for the position that is the *opposite* from your own opinion.

As one example, if you think the death penalty is wrong, then argue why you think in some circumstances it could be a legitimate punishment (for instance, a mass murderer who shows no remorse). Alternatively, if you think capital punishment is justified in certain situations, then make a case for why it is immoral and should be prohibited.

▶ Death penalty: right or wrong?
▶ Global warming: myth or reality?
▶ Prostitution: a crime or a victimless act between consenting adults?
▶ Health care: individual responsibility or universal right for all?
▶ Illegal immigration: create a path to citizenship or continue enforcing penalties for breaking the law?
▶ Terminally ill patients: a right to die or obligation to do no harm?
▶ Abortion: murder or a woman's choice about her own body?
▶ Gay marriage: legitimate lifestyle or unnatural union?
▶ Legalization of marijuana: harmless indulgence or path to addiction?

In so many cases, large groups of people have subscribed to mass hysteria because they failed to question the accuracy of reports and rumors. Such episodes have included not only the famous 1938 radio "news bulletin" by Orson Welles of a Martian invasion on Halloween, but also the belief among thousands of men in Singapore, Thailand, and China that their penises were shrinking as a result of having contracted a rare disease (Bartholomew and Radford, 2003). This gullibility makes it possible for certain businesses to sell you things you don't really need or that don't really work as advertised.

Recognize the Barriers That Distort Your Thinking

In addition to biases you hold that prevent you from attending to all useful information and making objective decisions, you must monitor other barriers carefully (see Table 9.1). Most of them result in lapses in memory or logic, or demonstrations of naïveté.

Appreciate Deeper Meanings and Complexities

Every day you read and hear hundreds, if not thousands, of ideas that you may take at surface value. You don't have the energy, or the inclination, to look at the deeper meanings of most of them. Yet many actions have some motives that appear obvious while others are unconscious or deliberately hidden from view. Many writers seem to treat a subject on one level when they actually intend speaking at other levels that may not be readily apparent.

Most of the lyrics of your favorite songs are interesting precisely because of their deeper meanings. Most of your cherished movies have appeal on multiple levels because of the complex messages they convey that go beyond the obvious. Classic literature abounds with examples of stories within stories. J. R. R. Tolkien's *The Lord of the Rings*, Jonathan Swift's *Gulliver's Travels*, and L. Frank Baum's *The Wizard of Oz* appear to be simple fantasy tales, yet they also represent social commentaries about greed, social class, and other troubling issues of their day that still have relevance for readers now.

Classroom Discussion
Open it up: What are some current examples of outlandish reports that people are prone to believe? Have you ever used websites such as Snopes.com to verify stories (especially those forwarded through viral e-mail)?

Group Activity
Have students in groups list and discuss what products are specifically marketed to college students. Possible answers may be credit cards, beer, cigarettes, and hookah bars.

TABLE 9.1

Barriers to Critical Thinking

Confirmation bias	Leads to looking only for information that supports a favored position
Attribution bias	Believing that good things happen to you because of what you do but bad things are the result of others' actions or events outside of your control
Trusting testimonial evidence	Believing what someone tells you without questioning its accuracy or validity
Memory lapses	"Forgetting" critical information
Accepting expert opinion	Not cross-checking facts, assumptions, and conclusions
Generalizing	Applying conclusions based on too small a sample to larger cases
Ignorance	Lacking knowledge about a subject but being unwilling to admit it

Source: Pinder (2007) and others.

The most popular songs and movies are often those that offer complexity and deep meaning on multiple levels. *The Wizard of Oz*, one of the most popular movies of all time, on the surface seems to be a children's fantasy about a lost girl trying to find her way home. Yet volumes of scholarly analyses have discussed the political, economic, and social conditions of America at the end of the nineteenth century symbolically depicted in the original book. You don't have to look very far or deep to recognize the issues of prejudice, social class, and marginalization.

Copyright © Everett Collection/Everett Collection

The things you study in class, the books you read, and the assignments you complete usually have multiple levels of complexity, just like most of your conversations. One of the things that a college education teaches you is how to look beyond the surface to examine what might be operating beneath what is within view. Likewise, you learn to go beyond the obvious to the deeper meanings of behavior, or to find the hidden, disguised, or subtle nuances of interactions you have with others.

Distinguish between Facts and Opinions

Consider several things when examining a piece of information:

1. Is it a *fact* with only one possible right interpretation? Facts can be objectively verified, and people almost universally agree on the correct meaning.

> *"The boiling point for a liquid (when it begins to turn into gas) is 212 degrees Fahrenheit."*

Even this fact could be disputed because it depends on what type of liquid you are speaking about. Alcohol boils at a lower temperature than water. It also depends on the altitude at which you boil the liquid. Boiling a liquid in New Orleans (sea level) is different than in Denver (the "Mile-High City").

2. Is it a *matter of degree* that makes some statements true?

> *"A Porsche is a better car than a Toyota."*

This statement could be verified, but in terms of several different variables. Which models of these cars are we speaking about, and for which years? What is meant by "better"? Are we talking about 0-to-60 acceleration, customer satisfaction, or value for the dollar? In this case, the quality of the answer is based not on the choice that one car is better than the other, but rather on the quality of the evidence used to support the answer.

3. Is it an expression of *personal opinion*? This is a statement of belief, based on someone's feelings, preferences, and experiences. All such statements are therefore considered equally valid.

> *"A Starbucks macchiato is the only legitimate coffee worth drinking."*

Often such opinions are expressed by supposed experts who are really elitists. Who is to say that a nonfat decaf cinnamon dolce frappuccino with an extra shot isn't the preferred choice?

Imagine a Completely Different World

This is where creativity comes into play. Critical thinking means not only unraveling the intentions, meanings, and interpretations of what other people say and do, but also inventing something quite new. Albert Einstein was able to imagine a world in which a different set of physical laws might be operating. Mark Rothko was able to picture a world in which images could be portrayed as abstract impressions of innermost feelings. Steve Jobs was able to conceive a world in which ordinary people would have personal computers on their desks, laps, or in their phones.

When Igor Stravinsky's most famous work, *The Rite of Spring*, debuted in Paris in 1913, a riot broke out because members of the audience were so incensed by the "savagery," violence, perceived chaos, and radical rhythms of the music. Fistfights, brawls, and outright duels ensued between different groups, some of whom were appalled by this radical departure from accepted musical style, and others who were absolutely delighted. By intermission, police squads tried to break up the riot, but by that time Stravinsky himself had fled in tears. Throughout history, it has not been unusual for radical thinkers who push the limits of convention to encounter considerable resistance. Other examples include Alfred Wegener's theory of tectonic plates (continental shifts) or Louis Pasteur's proposition that disease was caused by germs. For every dreamer there is a Charles Duell, commissioner of the U.S. Patent Office, who pronounced in 1899 that "everything that can be invented has already been invented."

Whenever you read or hear something in which the main premise begins with the assumption that the world must be a certain way—such as filled with war, violence, poverty, or inhumanity—imagine a world that could be different. Whenever you are exposed to certain rules about the way things must be, picture how things would be different if they were changed. Whenever you are told that things must be a certain way, imagine if this were not the case. Such rebellion, resistance, creativity, and critical thinking are responsible for most of the advances in science, art, music, literature, and politics.

What leads a gambler to assume that just because he didn't get the preferred roll of the dice ten times in a row, he is due for just rewards on the next one? This flaw in reasoning, called "gambler's fallacy," occurs when people discard actual probabilities in lieu of faith.

Recognize Errors in Logic and Reasoning

The title of Joseph Heller's World War II novel *Catch-22* refers to one of the more amusing examples of *circular logic* invoked to preserve the status quo. Since the beginning of time, representatives of authority have conceived of ways to maintain their power and stifle unrest among the masses. In

Jupiterimages

this case, the rule went something like this: Only a sane, rational person would want to escape flying more combat missions in which death was a high probability. One of the crew members was clearly insane and erratic in his behavior. But if he asked to be excused from flying, that proved he was really quite sane. See if you can follow the circular logic as explained in the book: "If he flew them he was crazy and didn't have to; but if he didn't want to he was sane and had to." This "Catch-22" is now used to describe situations in which you are in a no-win situation no matter what course of action you take.

Interestingly, the novel's Catch-22 was never an actual military rule, but was only an invention of the high command to keep personnel in line. Yet nobody had the wherewithal to challenge the rule; they just assumed this crazy logic made a kind of sense.

Critical thinkers question why things are a certain way and attempt to uncover errors in logic and reasoning, especially their own. Besides circular logic, there are several other common types of faulty logic:

- **Invalid assumption.** You base an argument or decision on a premise that isn't true in the first place. A parent declined to immunize her children against hepatitis B, a very contagious, incurable disease, because "only adults get that from dirty needles and promiscuous sex." In fact, one-third of people who are infected (including infants and children) contract the disease from unknown causes.

- **Logical fallacy.** You can find hundreds of these everywhere—in advertisements, debates, arguments, and articles—all based on some flaw or weakness in thinking. This can include overgeneralizing, appealing to some authority or evidence that doesn't fit, or making a poor analogy or illogical conclusion: Students who flunk out of school don't study; you didn't study this chapter as you were required; therefore, you will flunk out of school.

- **Pseudoscience.** People often use experts to bolster their ideas, just as you will do in your papers and presentations. The problem occurs when the so-called expert is, in fact, a fraud, or at least less than qualified. What determines whether evidence is legitimate? The accepted answer is whether it originates from "the established body of knowledge," defined as the consensual agreement among leaders in the field as verified through empirical methods. For example, although there has been much debate in the scientific world, as well as among the general public, whether global warming is real, 99 percent of earth scientists, climatologists, and other *recognized* experts agreed that the phenomenon is occurring. But that doesn't mean you can't find other experts with equally recognizable credentials for the alternative position. Your responsibility as a critical thinker is to consider *all* the evidence and use the *best* authorities that are available.

Classroom Discussion
Open it up: Give examples of each type of faulty logic that you have found in current news or advertising.

- **Unsupported assertion.** This occurs when the person you are arguing with asks with a laugh, "What orifice did you pull that out of?" This means that in papers, presentations, debates, or discussions, you make certain dramatic statements ("The main problem with the world today is that people don't get enough hugs") without offering compelling proof or evidence. That is why you are asked to provide citations and references for your work.

- **False analogy.** This is when you try to make comparisons that don't fit. You are talking to someone about problems of racism on campus and you make the statement, "Calling someone a derogatory name, or even thinking those words in your mind, is the same as murder." As important as your argument might be that racism cannot be completely eradicated until we deal with our internalized, most private prejudices that are hidden from view, you lose credibility through exaggerations that don't fit.

9.2 FOR REFLECTION **AND ACTION**

Viewing Advertisements Critically

Following is a list of pain reliever slogans that have appeared in the media over the years. Each one makes claims that contradict one another; they can't all be true. Using logic and reasoning, consider how these claims might be deceptive.

▶ "The medicine in Anacin is recommended by doctors four to one over substitutes like Tylenol."
▶ "Tylenol. The pain reliever hospitals use most."
▶ "Nothing acts faster than Anacin."
▶ "Bayer aspirin is recommended by doctors four to one over substitutes."
▶ "Tylenol is recommended by doctors more than any brand of aspirin."
▶ "Four out of five doctors surveyed recommended Excedrin's formula."
▶ "Bufferin works better than any other pain reliever tested."
▶ "Bacardi and cola. They get the job done!" (I just thought I'd sneak that one in to see if you were paying attention.)

While you are watching television or listening to the radio this week, find several advertising claims you see or hear that appear deceptive.

Test Assumptions against Outcomes and Realities

"Thoughts are but dreams till their effects be tried," said William Shakespeare. Rather than just assuming that certain beliefs are true, test them out for yourself. It is much easier to make a persuasive argument when you have direct experience, verified from personal trials and checked against literature on the subject. For example, you read in an article that enzymes in warm milk are supposed to help you fall asleep. It sounds good and you try it—without success. In fact, in your case, it seems to even keep you up at night. Does this mean that the claim is unfounded? Not necessarily, but it does lessen the likelihood you will suggest this method to others.

Using Critical Thinking to Solve Problems

The material in the previous section is hardly just theoretical and academic. It goes to the core of intelligent, informed, persuasive communication that you will use in every facet of your life. If you are going to get your needs met, if you are going to have any influence with those around you, you must have the ability to marshal points of view that are both well founded and convincing.

Another way to apply critical-thinking methods is not only in the arena of public communication but also in solving problems that plague you. The same methods that help you to analyze data, process information, evaluate situations critically, and proceed strategically are also useful when making decisions.

You can classify problems in several ways, such as tough versus easy, or simple versus complex. But that only begins to describe how challenging a particular situation may be.

Most decisions you will face have far more than the limited options in this photo. Sometimes the most challenging part of finding an acceptable solution is to figure out what the real problem is in the first place. Maybe the important issue for this person really isn't to return home by one of these roads, but rather to consider other possibilities.

© Blend Images/Alamy

Simple problems are the kind in which it is clear exactly what you are dealing with and equally clear how you will fix it. You are walking and you stumble; you look down and see your shoelace is untied. You bend down, retie the lace, and voilà—you are on your way again. Of course, there could be simultaneous problems as well. Say you had trouble walking not because your shoelace had unraveled but because you stepped on a nail. The untied lace just drew your attention to the real cause.

Next on the list of complexity are *problems with limited solutions*. This is like a multiple-choice test. You know that the correct answer is one of the options you've identified. For instance, you are walking in a strange city at night and lose your way. You attempt to retrace your steps and come to an intersection with three different streets. You can't recall offhand which way you came, but you know one of the streets will get you back to your hotel.

Far more frequently, you will face *problems that have undetermined numbers of solutions*. You have a choice about how to proceed, but you're uncertain of which way to go or even unsure if you should move forward. A good example is what you are facing now in settling on a major in college. Literally hundreds of possible choices are available, plus combinations to blend them. Nobody knows for sure which is the "correct" solution. Whichever way you choose, you could wonder if another path would have suited you better.

Finally there are *problems without any answers*, or any way to know what the best answer might be. These are the most challenging of all and deal with bigger questions like "What is the meaning of life?" This is also the kind of personal problem that produces the most anxiety and frustration, often because you aren't sure what the "real problem" is in the first place.

Overview of the Problem-Solving Process

With the grounding you already have in critical thinking and logical reasoning, it will make sense to you that good decision making follows a sequential process. First, you have to accurately define the problem before you can hope to figure out what to do about it.

Define the Problem

In some ways, it may not be helpful to use the word "problem" since it implies a solution, which may not exist. Many of the *issues* that you will struggle with are familiar to you because you have faced similar challenges in the past—and you will again in the future. What concerns and frustrates you the most are often part of an ongoing pattern. This could mean getting yourself in the same dicey situations, unsatisfying relationships, or frustrating predicaments that you have encountered previously—and thought you'd put behind you. You may find yourself in conflict with someone you've just met, and yet it reminds you of what you've dealt with in the past. Or you might find yourself making the same mistakes you've made before. These are the kinds of issues that are difficult to get a handle on, or even to give a proper name.

Much of the time you'll find that you are unable to define exactly what the "real" problem or central issue might be. You are aware of how things are affecting you in a negative way but still unsure what the cause might be. Until you can make this determination, it is hard to figure out a way to address the problem. For example, Albert Einstein, one of the most successful problem solvers in history, experienced his fair share of disappointments and failures. Yet he found a way of "reframing" those as mere setbacks, allowing him to persist toward eventual solutions to the problems that concerned him most.

Not only can it be difficult to put your finger on what is wrong, but it can be equally challenging to deal with problems that have been defined in ways that prevent you from finding solutions. Consider the following problem statements:

● "I'd like to control myself better, but I just have a bad temper. I'm Irish and it runs in my family. My father was like that too."

● "I know I'm overweight, but that's because I have bad genes. Everyone in my family is like this."

● "I've just gotten some bad breaks. That's why I haven't done very well so far."

How do you fix a problem if its cause is inherited anger, bad genes, or bad breaks? In each of these cases, the problem has been *externalized*, meaning that the person doesn't accept responsibility for it, preferring to blame factors outside of his or her control. When problems are defined in this way, it is virtually impossible to resolve them. The individuals have provided themselves with ready excuses to remain the way they are.

When any problem or issue appears difficult to resolve, the first level of intervention is to redefine it so it *can* be addressed successfully. The person with the bad temper can reframe it as difficulty controlling his anger, acknowledging that he could learn to exhibit more control. The person who believes herself to be overweight because of bad genes can reframe it as a difficulty in making sensible food choices, also something that can be learned. And the person who believes himself to be a victim of bad luck can reframe it as "I haven't made the most of my opportunities."

Define the Goals

What is your desired outcome? Is action necessary, and is now the right time? Sometimes the best solution is to let things ride for a while, or not do anything at all. This is not procrastination, or putting off action that is required, but rather allowing things to unfold further until the most opportune moment to intervene. And then some problems just improve on their own.

Apply what you already know about setting goals. Your goals should be as specific and detailed as possible. They should be realistic and attainable. And they should be related to what you want most.

▶ **VIEW IT**

© Cengage Learning

Overcoming Problems
Students talk about some major problems they faced and how they struggled with them. Ultimately, determination and motivation helped them to overcome their difficulties. (www.cengagebrain.com)

Ask yourself what you want most in terms of a satisfactory outcome. What would that look or feel like? Change often begins with a focus on future possibilities. In some cases, solutions might even arise from such imagination.

One standard procedure that therapists often use to help people set goals, and at the same time find possible solutions, is called the *miracle question*. Rather than describing what it can do, it might be interesting for you to experience its power.

Settle on a problem.

Think of a problem or issue that you are facing right now in your life. This could be something that has been bothering you for some time, something that hasn't gone away on its own. This problem may be especially annoying and perplexing because you've tried a number of strategies to deal with it, none of which have proven successful. You feel stuck. Got one of those in those in mind?

Travel into the future.

Now, imagine that a miracle has occurred and—poof—magically your problem has been resolved. Close your eyes and picture yourself going forward in time to where your problem is no longer bothering you. It is gone, vanished. Think about how your life is different now with the problem no longer pressing on you. Consider what that feels like.

Take a wild guess.

This last step is the most challenging: Using your imagination during your time travel into the future, what did you *do* to fix things? Problems don't actually go away magically, so something must have happened: What did you stop, start, or change to resolve your problem? Even though you may feel the inclination to just shrug and say, "I don't know," take a wild guess. If you had to make up some explanation to account for this dramatic change, what do think could have happened?

Use the clues. This fantasy exercise may point you toward the solution that has seemed just out of reach. Even though its focus is on setting goals for *what* you want, you may also find that it delivers suggestions for *how* to proceed.

What Have You Already Tried?

Prior to exploring options for solving problems or addressing issues, it helps to first catalog what you have already tried that hasn't worked so far. When people are stuck in a situation it is often because they keep doing the same things over and over, even though it is clear they don't work very well.

A parent is frustrated with her child, who keeps talking back in a disrespectful way. She tells her daughter, "Please don't speak to me that way."

The daughter ignores the request and continues a tirade against her mother.

"I TOLD you to stop talking to me that way. Are you DEAF? Don't you LISTEN?"

Obviously not, because the teenager keeps going on her rant.

Finally, the parent really loses her cool and this time raises her voice to a level intended to *really* make her point. In each case, she tries the same exact solution, increasing the level of intensity each time, but with equally dismal results.

This would seem comical if it wasn't such a common scenario. Lest you shake your head at this stupidity, consider how often you do the same thing. Most people, when they are stuck, try the same thing they are already doing, only harder and more persistently.

Usually if you try the same thing twice, or three times at most, it is a good bet that it won't work the next time either. If, for example, you have trouble getting up in the morning, and set your alarm three days in a row yet still oversleep, it's a pretty good prediction that this strategy won't work the fourth day.

People often remain stuck in situations because they keep doing the same things over and over, even though they don't work. The key to breaking the frustrating cycle is trying new, alternative strategies. Even if these experiments aren't as successful as hoped, they open up the possibility for more creative, flexible options in the future.

©Istockphoto.com/Joey Boylan

Why do people persist in doing things over and over even if they don't work? Because they are familiar. People will continue to stay in unhealthy relationships or do the same self-defeating things, in the face of compelling evidence that they aren't getting anywhere, because they are used to it. It is really, really hard for people to let go of such strategies because they are afraid of trying the unknown (or unwilling to surrender the payoffs).

What *will* work after you abandon what you've already tried but doesn't work? That's hard to know. You may not know what will work, but you sure know what will not. That's why making a list of such ineffective strategies, and committing yourself not to do those anymore, frees you up to try other things that *might* work. After all, you have nothing to lose.

Looking for Exceptions

You might feel discouraged at times when all you do is focus on problems, that is, when things are going wrong or you have failed in some way. But nobody screws up all the time, and very few problems persist in every situation. You will always find exceptions.

Instead of constantly examining weaknesses and failures, balance this tendency by studying those situations that have gone well. Someone who says he is shy can't possibly be that way in every situation, with every person he knows; sometimes and in some situations, he can be assertive or outgoing. Someone who thinks of herself as a procrastinator has exceptions to this as well. Someone who feels lonely, depressed, or anxious doesn't feel that way all the time; again, exceptions to this abound.

Examine those times when you *don't* have the problem, when you have managed to function quite well. How is it that someone who procrastinates about reading assignments for class always finds a way to meet deadlines while working on the school paper? How can someone be so uninhibited when hanging out with his childhood friends but so withdrawn in the presence of college classmates? And someone who complains of always being depressed surely has some situations (probably the majority of the time) when she doesn't feel that way.

Stop Doing What Isn't Working

Stress often arises from a sense of helplessness that no matter what you do, you have no hope for resolving a problem or situation. The best rules of thumb when trying to get unstuck from a situation or problem are as follows: (1) If you are doing something and it doesn't work, do something different; and (2) if what you are doing is working, do more of it.

Think of an ongoing problem that you have in some aspect of your life. Make a list of all the things you've tried to resolve this situation that have *not* worked.

_____   _____

_____   _____

_____   _____

_____   _____

_____   _____

Put a line through any approaches that you have tried several times—meaning you are absolutely certain they won't work, no matter how often you try.

Promise yourself you will boycott those behaviors in favor of others that are more creative or unusual.

It is interesting that one way to take pressure off yourself and instill hope is to feel like you have multiple options, even if they don't work initially. Make another list below of things you *might* try, even options that may seem out of the ordinary.

_____   _____

_____   _____

_____   _____

_____   _____

Make a commitment to follow through on trying out these new options, crossing those off your list that don't prove useful or effective. Remember the goal is not necessarily to find the single, right solution to the problem, but rather to open up the possibility of becoming unstuck once you abandon strategies that are clearly counterproductive.

9.3 FOR REFLECTION

Looking for Exceptions

Think of something that you don't consider yourself very good at. This could be in the area of academics (writing papers or taking tests), communication (speaking in front of groups, expressing feelings, or articulating thoughts), relationships (developing intimacy, working through conflicts, or shyness), or sports. Maybe you think you stink at math or art. Everyone has some areas of their life in which they label themselves as hopeless.

Now think of an exception to this self-label. Consider a few times when you had, in fact, been able to perform without this problem in evidence. You might have to dig deep, but surely you did just fine at some point.

How does this change the absolute labels that you bestow on yourself (or were bestowed on you by others) as being a particular way if you also have the capacity to be different?

Exploring Options

After you have settled on what you want as an outcome, defining the problem in a way that it can be solved, it is now time to consider your options. *Brainstorming* is a technique invented in the business and advertising community to encourage greater creativity when solving problems. All too often, people are restricted in their thinking because they limit themselves to traditional solutions or are too stressed to feel free to play with new ideas.

The main strategy focuses on maximizing the quantity of solutions, rather than worrying about whether they are practical. Silly, far-out ideas are encouraged. Criticism is withheld (so postpone your critical-thinking skills at this juncture). The goal is to generate as many options as possible. Interestingly, even if most of the possibilities are not easy to implement, you feel a greater sense of power just knowing you have so many choices.

Brainstorming works best in group settings. So if you are feeling really stymied, gather together a few friends or classmates. With the stated purpose to list as many options as possible, have a designated recorder write down all the ideas that are mentioned. Suspend all criticism and judgment about whether they are good ideas; just keep the suggestions flowing. Encourage ideas that might be considered crazy as they often lead to more practical solutions. Many important inventions and discoveries result not so much from individual achievement as from collaborative brainstorming in which a team works together to generate novel solutions to problems. For example, Wallace Hume Carothers was a brilliant but emotionally unstable chemist who headed DuPont's polymer fiber project in the 1930s. He worked with a group of scientists, sharing ideas and refining their process of manufacturing a kind of synthetic silk that became known as nylon. That first manmade synthetic fiber revolutionized the fabric and clothing industry.

During the process of generating options for yourself, it is important to collect all relevant and useful information that may be helpful. Miko was having trouble keeping up on all her assignments. Working a part-time job and caring for her ailing parents cut into her available time to study and do schoolwork. In spite of her efforts to study more, she still fell further behind.

Miko reframed her problem as one of confused priorities. Her schoolwork would often come last on her list of things to do. She would get distracted by things at work or at home, and by the time she concentrated on schoolwork, she was already either out of time or too tired to concentrate. She had already tried a number of solutions—changing her work hours and talking to her parents about getting them additional help. Neither strategy made much of a difference.

Group Activity

Practice brainstorming in class. Ask students to choose one thing they would like to improve about the campus. In groups of four to six students, get them to brainstorm ten ideas to improve the campus, without regard to how much the improvement costs or how practical the idea is. Then have them go back through the list, decide which one of the ideas is most feasible, and explore options for making it happen, such as submitting the idea to student government or school administrators.

Group Activity

Give students index cards and ask them to write a personal problem on their card (without their name). Collect all the cards, break the class into groups, shuffle the cards and redistribute them among the groups. Have groups brainstorm solutions according to the brainstorming rules in this section and write solutions on the back of the index cards. Ask groups to share one problem and their brainstormed solution with the class. At the end of class, put all index cards out for students to pick up if they choose.

Miko began talking to other people she knew who also had financial and family hardships and found that she was hardly alone in her struggle. This exploration process actually made her feel better already, just knowing that this was not such an unusual challenge. But she also learned that other students were far better at organizing their time than she had been. They may have lived with lots of responsibilities, but their grades were not suffering. She wondered what they were doing differently.

The main difference, Miko discovered, was that others were setting limits that she had been unable or unwilling to do herself. Because of her cultural background, she felt a strong obligation to put her parents first, and also to reduce their financial burden by working more hours than she could reasonably manage. She realized that if it was her intention to remain in college, she would have to set limits on what she could do. This led to a host of alternatives.

Choosing a Course of Action—or Two

Having too many alternatives can feel as frustrating as not having any at all. With a staggering array of options it can often feel that no matter what you decide, you didn't get to choose so many others. In some countries where I work, stores have only one kind of shampoo; in contrast, I counted hundreds of choices during my last visit to a local drugstore trying to pick out a product. I felt so bewildered I didn't buy any at all.

Our lives are now so saturated with choices that it is often difficult to decide anything. And whatever choice you make, you can ruminate endlessly about what you could have had instead. So whatever selection you make, it's time to move on and try it out. Make the best of it and don't look back.

Among the (hopefully) many options that you have developed, which one will you select first? I want to emphasize that this is just the primary option but hardly the only one. If you try something and it doesn't work, this just means that you move down your list until you find the right combination for the desired result.

In Miko's case, she talked to her parents about getting some outside help but they refused, saying that this was not the job of a stranger, but a family obligation. Next she spoke to her siblings about working closer to share the burden of caring for their parents. This was a great idea in theory, but her siblings had long ago figured out a way to extricate themselves from these inconvenient responsibilities. After some soul-searching, Miko realized that her own future was at stake. As important as it was to take care of her parents, she also had to take care of herself; nobody else would

Billy:
A Major with Interests in Common

"I tried so many different majors. How was I supposed to know what major to pick? And I didn't want to go to a school where I had no friends! I kept changing my mind about what I wanted to do and where I wanted to be. I would pick a major and then realize I had nothing in common with the other people in my class. Plus, sometimes the class was just too boring. It was so freaking frustrating. At one point I thought of just dropping out and doing something else with my time. You know, I really like exercising and stuff, so I thought of getting a job at a gym or something.

It took me a while to understand that just because I didn't like one class, it didn't mean that I wouldn't like that major. I was impatient ... I still am [laughs], but now I realize that I'm just not going to like some classes and there's nothing I can do about that. I started talking to other people and I saw that they were having some of the same experiences with their classes and majors. That was when I realized I wasn't the only one feeling that way and that helped me a lot. I guess in the beginning we all have to go through some classes that aren't really what we signed up for. Now that I'm taking some classes I really like, I've even found some new friends—people that actually have a lot in common with me.

do it. This helped her to make some important decisions about what she was willing to do and not willing to do in the future. Her chosen strategy was one in which she would (1) reduce her hours at work, (2) visit the financial aid office to see about scholarships and loans, (3) designate two days per week in which she would be available to assist her parents, (4) notify her siblings of her new schedule, and (5) turn off her cell phone during planned study periods so she would not allow herself to be distracted.

When making a decision, any decision, you'll want to consider the pros and cons of the choice you make. It isn't just a matter of whether a choice is good or bad in absolute terms, but also *how* good or bad. You can thus weight each factor according to whether it is extremely important (rated a 3), moderately important (2), or minimally important (1).

Let's say that a student is trying to decide between remaining an undeclared first-year student and taking her time to settle on a major, or declaring engineering, which would mean immediate enrollment in required courses. She feels torn and can't make up her mind, so she makes a list of pros and cons, weighting each point as to its relative importance to her.

Should I enroll in the engineering program?

PROS	CONS
Will make my parents happy. (2)	Restricts my freedom to study other things of interest. (3)
It'll take pressure off to make a decision now. (3)	A lot of math classes required. (1)
Will have an easier time getting a job. (3)	It's really hard, so I'll have to study a lot more. (2)
I'm interested in building things. (3)	I'm interested in a lot of other things. (2)
I'll earn a good salary. (2)	I'll get stuck in an office. (1)
Could create future options for law or business. (1)	I don't like engineering students I've met. (2)
Lots of guys in class, which should be fun. (1)	It's expensive buying all the books and material. (2)
Total pro score: 16	Total con score: 13

In a close decision like this, the difference between the two scores may not be significant or meaningful, but it does help to sort out the variables involved and what's at stake. Sometimes even with critical thinking and logical decision making, you still go with your gut—you listen to the voice inside your heart and mind that tells you to follow your dreams. Perhaps in this case, although the student says that making her parents happy is only moderately important to her, she likes the *idea* of being an engineer, because that's what her father and uncle do—but she'd really like to explore other possibilities as well.

Given this added information, if you think she is in danger of making the wrong choice, she almost always has opportunities to reassess the situation. If she should find

Group Activity
One big decision many students make in their first year in college is whether to remain in the residence halls or move off campus. In small groups, have students form pro–con lists for living on campus and moving off campus. Ask the groups to share their thoughts with the larger group.

For Community College Students
To meet community college students where they are at, change this table of pros and cons to something related to transferring schools.

that the appeal of making a decision now is washed out by disliking her engineering classes and classmates, then it is easy enough to make a switch. Sometimes the worst decision of all is sticking by a choice no matter what, even when compelling evidence says that it isn't what's best.

Implementing the Plan

It is one thing to make a plan, but quite another to put it into action. Most resolutions aren't followed through, and most changes don't last. It is both surprising and disappointing how often other people will actively sabotage your efforts to make constructive progress. Friends who say they want the best for you will still try to meet their own needs. Those who are closest to you may feel threatened by changes you want to make. And others don't want to be inconvenienced in any way by things you decide to do differently.

Although it sometimes feels daunting to put a plan into action, the good news is that a small change in any aspect of a problem begins the process of solving it. Any small step you take to make a difference gets the momentum going.

Evaluating the Results

Putting your decisions into action isn't the final step in problem solving. Believe it or not, there really is no final step, rather there are periods of assessment in which you make a thorough and honest evaluation of where things stand compared to where you'd like them to be. Since moderate forward progress is a most likely outcome, at times you will need to cycle back to the beginning and figure out how next to proceed to deal with the problem.

Apply this concept to a conflict you were having with a friend. You had decided to confront the situation rather than (1) ignore it, (2) do nothing, or (3) end the friendship. You are delighted with the results of this decision and have now been able to renegotiate a new relationship. But does the problem really end there? What if this disagreement with the one friend was actually part of a larger problem in your life? What if it was one component of a pattern that you have encountered before and are likely to experience again?

In this situation, you would want to take what you learned from the mini-solution and reformulate new goals and plans to avoid making the same mistakes in the future.

SUMMARY

Critical thinking means exploring a situation thoroughly, weighing evidence in terms of its value and appropriateness, and controlling biases and emotions to evaluate the situation clearly. Such a process involves following several sequential steps that begin with data collection and end with forming logical conclusions.

When making important decisions, critical thinking and logical thinking are important, but so is trusting your intuition. Don't let yourself get forced into making an impulsive decision without exploring the situation thoroughly, weighing the evidence, considering the choices, and predicting the consequences. Good decision making always begins with framing the problem in a way that it can be more easily solved. It is usually a good idea to generate multiple alternatives before narrowing them down to one or a few that seem most viable.

QUESTIONS FOR REVIEW AND FURTHER EXPLORATION

1. What pitfalls can lead you to rely on sources of information that may be biased, inaccurate, or unreliable?

2. Consider a recent argument or debate you were having with someone. Looking back on the conversation, how do you differentiate between facts and opinions?

3. Think of a problem you have faced for some time and feel stuck in. What ideas from this chapter might help you to break through the impasse?

4. How does looking for exceptions to a problem help lead to a solution?

5. You have been encouraged to think critically about material you read, challenging assumptions and claims that are not supported by convincing and legitimate evidence. What are some claims or ideas in this chapter that you could refute with solid, defensible support from reliable evidence?

6. Even though people understand the rules of probability and logic, they still ignore the likely outcomes. Explain, for example, why a gambler who flipped a coin five times in a row and landed on "heads" would bet a huge amount that the next time the coin would come up "tails" because it was "due."

Go to www.cengagebrain.com for an online quiz that will test your understanding of the chapter content.

Stress Management and Prevention

KEY QUESTIONS

▶ Why is it normal to feel considerable stress in college, even to the point of sometimes feeling overwhelmed?

▶ How is it that the body and mind sometimes overreact dramatically to a situation that is not life threatening?

▶ What are the ways that brief, moderate stress can be useful and enhance performance?

▶ How do relaxation strategies work to counteract chronic stress?

▶ How do people make themselves upset and stressed?

▶ How can you change disturbing feelings by altering your interpretations of what you experience?

▶ How can you take control over what you choose to feel upset about?

▶ How does talking to yourself differently produce dramatic mood changes?

▶ How do you know when you need to ask for help?

You have already learned that the college years are among the most stressful periods in anyone's life, a time when you are attempting to not only master vast academic material and sort out career goals, but also create a social support system, find a potential mate, separate from parental influence, and make great strides in your moral, intellectual, social, and emotional development. For older, returning students, college stimulates a different set of stressors—financial, familial, and so many others. This is why college students suffer a disproportionate number of psychological problems ranging from homesickness, loneliness, and stress to severe depression, anxiety, and self-destructive behavior (Dyson and Renk, 2006).

As many as 40 percent of college students admit that at times they feel so depressed they can barely function, and as many as nine out of ten admit that stress sometimes or frequently becomes a problem for them (Associated Press, 2009); one out of ten students have felt so despondent that they seriously considered suicide

PHOTO: Image copyright Yuri Arcurs, 2009. Used under license from Shutterstock.com.

229

(McGinn, 2007). Suicide is, in fact, the third leading cause of death among college students (after car accidents and homicide). Just as disturbing is that when students do feel so out of control, they rarely ask for help (Gallagher, 2005).

Whereas adult working students have considerable life experiences and maturity that help to immunize them against some of the pressures faced by those coming right out of high school, such returning students also deal with many "inter-role" conflicts trying to juggle work, family, and civic responsibilities with their schoolwork (Giancola, Grawitch, and Borchert, 2009). In fact, for many older students, academic-related stress pales in comparison to what they must face at home or on the job.

So it is normal to feel overwhelmed at times, especially during the stressful time that takes place during the first semester of college. With increased economic challenges and financial pressures, the burden to cope with limited resources and an uncertain future are leading a record number of students to seek counseling to manage their stress (Bushong, 2009). In some ways, if you aren't feeling pressure, then you aren't paying attention.

One of the unique features of this book is the focus devoted to stress management and prevention throughout every chapter, and related specifically to the topics covered. In this chapter, we look more deeply at the nature of stress and how it affects you, as well as additional ways that you can act proactively to reduce the tension and challenges you face.

This chapter contains several different video segments—more than in any other chapter in the book—that teach you strategies you can put to use right away. Yet for these techniques to become part of you, you must not only watch the demonstrations but also start practicing them every day.

For Community College Students
Conduct a conversation with your class about whether they think stress is higher, lower, or the same for community college students versus their four-year university counterparts.

Sidney:
Too Much Stress

"I have an ulcer, thanks to all the stress of going to school and working at the same time. It's like I need to work so I can pay for school, but if I work and go to school, my health gets all screwed up. Working takes so much of my time, I usually feel like crap after working all day and then going to class. I get headaches, back pain, and that awful stomach pain because of my ulcer. I wish I could just do one thing at a time. My friends are always hanging out and going to parties, and I can never go anywhere with them because I'm always busy. I mean, I could go if I wanted to, but then I wouldn't have time to study. Damn, I'm paying for my school and I'm not going to start throwing my money away.

Anyway, it's not like I have an option, so I can't really do anything to change this. Maybe I could learn to relax or something, but it's hard to relax when you have so many responsibilities, you know what I mean? I'm hoping I can take some time off soon so I can, like, enjoy things a little more. I don't want to miss out on all the college experience either.

What Is Stress and How Do You Know When You've Got It?

Stress is both an internal assessment and a physiological reaction to a perceived threat. It is nature's way of equipping you to deal with emergency situations, whether real or imagined. When faced with what is believed to be a dangerous situation—a stalking predator, an enemy with a weapon, an earthquake, a final exam, being called on in class, or approaching someone you really like—your body kicks into gear everything you might need to survive the situation.

As originally designed, this *fight-or-flight reaction* was intended for either doing battle or running away. Thus, the familiar sensations you associate with fear such as a fluttery stomach, sweaty palms, a racing heart rate, and accelerated breathing are all the results of your body diverting blood away from the extremities, shutting down systems you won't need for the next critical minutes, and pumping more oxygen into your muscles so you can run fast or fight hard. The problem, of course, is that your mind sometimes confuses real from imagined dire threats. It may seem like taking a test or asking someone to go out with you is a life-or-death matter, but it is really an exaggeration that still ignites your emergency sympathetic nervous system. Stress becomes a real problem when it is chronic and unremitting, when you are constantly living on the edge, easily upset about the smallest thing. It is as if your crisis management system is running on overdrive.

Given this close connection between the mind's interpretation of trouble and the body's subsequent response, it is often difficult to separate physical pain and discomforts from those that are actually the result of psychological problems. It has been estimated that close to 75 percent of all visits to the doctor are really the result of stress-related difficulties and are linked to the six leading causes of death in North America (heart disease, cancer, stroke, respiratory disease, accidents, and diabetes) (Kottler and Chen, 2011).

©Istockphoto.com/Sandra O'Claire

How do you know this person is stressed? Notice the look in the eyes, the facial expression, and the posture, all of which signal a sense of helplessness and feeling overwhelmed. Adjustment to college is one of the single most stressful life transitions, forcing you to juggle academic, personal, relational, financial, and family pressures and yet still perform at a high level.

TABLE 10.1

Common Stress Reactions

Physiological	Cognitive	Behavioral
Heart palpitations	Impaired memory	Crying
Sweating	Imagining disasters	Withdrawal
Insomnia	Blaming others	Impulsiveness
Appetite gain or loss	Suicidal thoughts	Substance abuse
Nausea	Obsessions	Phobias and fears
Fatigue	Blaming self	Aggression
High blood pressure	Illogical thinking	Rambling

Symptoms of Stress

People say all the time that they are feeling anxious or stressed, but what exactly does that mean? Stress has a set of common responses associated with the condition, including physiological, cognitive, and behavioral indices (see Table 10.1). In particular, you may notice signs of sleep disruption, repetitive worry, appetite disruption (or overeating), and difficulty concentrating. They all signal that your body has activated its fight-or-flight arousal system because it misperceives life-threatening danger.

Whereas short-term stress reactions are to be expected—that is, temporary spikes in your nervous system to deal with crises—it is *chronic stress* that causes the most concern. Getting worked up over an upcoming exam, feeling pressure prior to an assignment that is due, and worrying about an impending conflict are all normal and even constructive to a point. They mobilize your energy so you can devote your full attention and resources to the job at hand.

Chronic stress, the kind that sticks with you even after the crisis is over, destroys your health and takes years off your life. When cortisol and other stress-related chemical reactions continue to circulate within your system, with the on-button stuck in the open position, every system in your body is affected and worn down. Your arteries begin to deteriorate. Your digestive system rebels, presenting eating problems or constipation. You feel constant muscle tension, maybe even teeth grinding or jaw aches during sleep. Your immune system breaks down, making you more vulnerable to sickness and stress-induced diseases like colitis (stomachaches), psoriasis (itchy skin), and asthma (trouble breathing). Your sexual functioning is also affected, and you often lose the interest or ability to respond the way you want. And then additional burdens appear when you attempt to *self-medicate* these problems with drugs, alcohol, and other addictions.

Sources of Stress

Classroom Discussion

Open it up: What are common sources of stress for you in this class?

Regardless of what developmental stage you find yourself in—late adolescence, young adulthood, or middle adulthood—college life tends to intensify the effects of transitions because of the continual emphasis on processing and analyzing experience. Life transitions thus lead to periods of temporary instability. Relationship conflicts occupy a significant amount of your time, such as worrying about family members, friends, and romantic partners. Pressures related to career decisions and planning for the future lead students to wonder what will happen after they graduate.

Returning students and minority students face additional challenges related to fitting into an environment that had been traditionally designed for young people of the privileged classes. The same diversity on a campus that makes for such rich learning experiences also presents a bewilderingly complex culture to negotiate.

Copyright © Tony Freeman/Photo Edit

Students with children have the added pressure of trying to meet the rigorous academic demands they face, plus taking care of family and work responsibilities. While they have the advantage of more life experience, they also face additional stressors that come with age and parental roles.

For some unfortunate students, the stresses of college come to a breaking point. College-aged students are particularly vulnerable to developing the first major symptoms of emotional problems like depression and anxiety. That is why early recognition is so important so that students get help before things feel out of control. It is also why you have to become aware of the greatest sources of stress in your own life (see Figure 10.1).

Figure 10.1   Most Common Sources of Stress for College Students

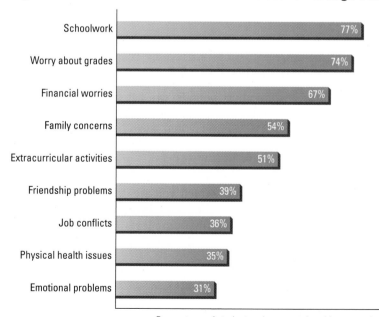

Source	Percentage
Schoolwork	77%
Worry about grades	74%
Financial worries	67%
Family concerns	54%
Extracurricular activities	51%
Friendship problems	39%
Job conflicts	36%
Physical health issues	35%
Emotional problems	31%

Percentage of students who report that this source has a significant impact on their stress levels on a daily basis.

Source: Associated Press Poll, 2009.

Group Activity
Have groups of four to six students list all coping mechanisms they can think of and then decide which ones are healthy and unhealthy. Report findings on a dry-erase board for all groups.

Anxiety disorders can be either *acute reactions* to some normal or expected challenge which eventually disappear within a period of weeks after the crisis has been addressed, or *chronic conditions* that are potentially health threatening. Some people you know are just generally nervous all the time, always overreacting to any situation. This stress-saturated style eventually wears down the nervous system and can significantly interfere with the ability to function at high levels. The good news is that there are many strategies covered in this chapter that can help anyone bring anxiety and stress under better control.

10.1   FOR REFLECTION

Favorite Coping Mechanisms

When you are feeling overwhelmed and stressed, how do you seek immediate relief? How do you typically "medicate" yourself?

_____

_____

_____

Think of a time recently when you were feeling out of control in some aspect of your life. You were feeling down, but not exactly sure why you were upset or how to go about fixing the situation. What did you do to soothe yourself?

_____

_____

_____

Classroom Discussion
Open it up: Think of a situation where stress has helped you improve your performance.

Teaching Tip
As a follow-through on the discussion of stress, ask students to keep a log for one week regarding anxiety levels and responses. Ask students to identify anxiety-producing situations, and reflect on their feelings and innermost thoughts at the time (e.g., "What was I feeling or saying to myself?"). Students should analyze the data to determine what courses or situations produce the most stress. Ask them to develop appropriate and realistic responses to the stress.

Preventing and Managing Stress

Stress, within reasonable limits and for short periods, can actually *enhance* performance in a variety of tasks. It helps you focus better, access additional resources, and thus bring out your competitive drive (Carmichael, 2009). Even traumas and extreme crises can actually strengthen people's resources and lead to growth rather than debilitating effects (Calhoun and Tedeschi, 2006; Joseph and Linley, 2008). But that is only when the stress response is activated temporarily and for a relatively brief period of time. Think, for example, about a situation in which you are driving in traffic and someone suddenly cuts in front of you. Your almost instantaneous stress response can save your life by heightening senses and quickening your reflexes. But once the danger is averted, if you remain aroused for hours afterward, you will have a problem returning your system to standby mode.

The best way to manage excessive stress is to prevent it in the first place. If you follow healthy lifestyle practices, exercise and sleep regularly, keep up with your workload, and manage your time effectively, you won't allow yourself to become overwhelmed. Yet even with the best intentions, motivation, and skills, you are still likely to encounter periods of intense pressure that feel beyond what you can comfortably handle.

Any successful stress management strategy has the following components:

1. **Identify chronic stressors**. What is it that gets to you most easily? What are the challenges that you struggle with the most? It is critical that you get an accurate and comprehensive assessment of your areas of vulnerability.

2. **Check interpretations**. Your perceptions of events are what determine their effects. In Chapter 11, Negotiating Relationships, you'll learn a lot more about the power of changing the way you think to change negative feelings.

3. **Select responses**. If you can slow down the process of responding selectively to stressful situations, you are in a position to make different choices in your behavior.

4. **Evaluate consequences**. As a result of your response to a stressful situation, what happened? Are you satisfied with the outcome, or might you wish to make some adjustments?

These next sections will introduce you to several strategies that can help you not only reduce the existing stress in your life, but also prevent future problems. Some of the methods involve things you can do inside your own mind, while others help you react to critical incidents or other people in calmer and more controlled ways.

Relaxation Strategies

The opposite of feeling stressed is feeling … *relaxed*. Imagine yourself starting to lose control as you are about to take a test for which you don't feel ready, or find yourself in an argument with someone who is bent on attacking and humiliating you, or walking on stage to give a speech in front of an audience that appears bored if not downright hostile. Throughout your life, you will continuously face pressure situations in which you can feel your blood pressure rising and panic starting to set in. You must develop ways to bring yourself back under reasonable control so you can think clearly and respond effectively.

Relaxation methods are those designed to turn off the emergency fight-or-flight responses going off inside your nervous system. The adrenaline is pumping, the cortisol is flowing, the muscles are tensing, and you are breathing so hard it feels like you are going to pass out. In no way are you going to function very well under these conditions. Until you can calm yourself down, you are destined to struggle.

Deep Breathing

The first line of defense, among the most effective and easiest-to-learn strategies, is called *deep breathing*. You already know how to breathe since you have done it every few seconds since the moment you were born. But you don't do it very well when feeling pressured. Breathing becomes shallow under stressful conditions. As much as your diaphragm is working overtime, you still can't seem to catch your breath. You feel dizzy, on the verge of passing out.

Learning deep breathing is part of meditation and yoga, as well as a relaxation technique practiced on its own. You have probably heard others say to take a deep breath before beginning a performance. The rationale behind this advice is that if you take the time to slow things down, to concentrate on only one thing—breathing—you can regain a semblance of control. This is especially important when your mind is cluttered, distracted, or otherwise overstimulated. The bad news is that your mind completely controls your body. The good news is that your breathing controls your mind. When you can slow down and deepen your breathing, making it more conscious and deliberate, you increase the oxygen flow to all the systems of your body, as well as reduce stress, provide more energy, and have better cognitive functioning (Lee and Campbell, 2009).

Group Activity

Assign a relaxation strategy for small groups to discuss and try before the next class, at which time they will teach that strategy to the entire class.

Classroom Discussion

Open it up: What are some unhealthy and healthy ways that you attempt to reduce stress?

Teaching Tip

Ask someone from your campus counseling center to lead a session on relaxation and deep breathing during class. Or, have an expert teach you this skill so you can teach others—and practice yourself.

© Cengage Learning

Progressive Relaxation

This video shows you how to practice a technique for systematically reducing stress by relaxing every muscle in your body. When practiced regularly, it can be used in any situation when you feel under pressure or are unable to relax. (www.cengagebrain.com)

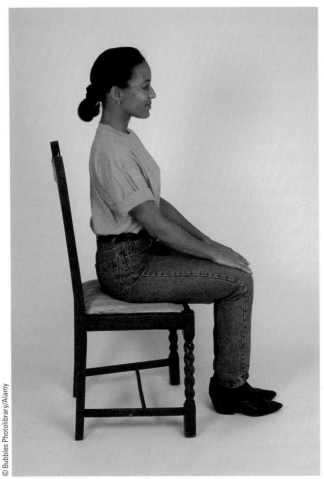

© Bubbles Photolibrary/Alamy

Mindful breathing uses all your concentration to focus on the moment. The relaxation begins with perfect posture to take a perfect breath. Your feet should be on the floor, your back erect, and shoulders back. Hands can rest comfortably on your lap or on your belly to feel the inflation, or you can entwine fingers. Each complete breath from inhalation to exhalation should last a minute. With diligent practice, this technique can be invaluable in any stressful situation you face.

Anytime you notice that your breathing is labored, ragged, or shallow, or your heart is pounding anxiously, you can literally will yourself to relax through deep breathing. It helps to follow the "View It: Progressive Relaxation" video segments that demonstrate this method in action. But for now, just try the experiment given here:

1. Regardless of where you are reading this—stretched out on a couch, hunched over a desk, lounging on the floor, laying in bed, or sitting in the library—reposition yourself so that you are sitting upright, feet flat on the floor, back straight, and posture erect. *Do that now.*

2. Your posture is *very* important to access the deepest breathing within your lungs, belly, and chest, and then out through your mouth and nose. Sit as straight as you can, neck and head centered over your body, shoulders, and back, with your arms resting comfortably on your lap. *Check your position before reading further.*

3. Okay, now take a minute or two to just pay attention to your breathing. Soon you're going to close your eyes, remain in this mindful sitting position, and concentrate *only* on your breathing. You should concentrate on feeling the breath originating deep in your belly and then slowly, deeply moving into your chest. Feel your shoulders rise as you take a deeper breath. Then exhale. S-l-o-w-l-y. Take three breaths like this with your eyes closed, each one taking a full minute. *Do that now.*

Interesting, wasn't it? If you were doing this correctly, that is, breathing with intention, then you weren't thinking about anything else. That is the primary object of this technique, to take your mind off everything except breathing. Just breathing. Only breathing. It sounds simple, but it actually takes a lot of practice to breathe without doing or thinking about anything else.

With practice, this technique can become nothing short of miraculous. Take five breaths in five minutes and you are totally grounded, no matter what chaos rages around you. Nervous before you approach someone? Take a few deep breaths. About to take an exam or give a presentation? Calm yourself with a few deep breaths. Trouble sleeping? Practice deep breathing.

Wherever you are, whatever the situation, and no matter how anxious you feel, restore a measure of tranquility by piloting your nervous system back to a quiet landing.

Meditation

Meditation makes use of deep breathing along with other techniques designed to promote relaxation. In all its hundreds of different forms, it achieves a state of intense concentration and inner stillness in which your mind is completely absent of thought. A *mantra* (a sacred word), *mandala* (geometric design), or image is used to help focus attention (deep breathing is also a form of meditation). Moving meditations involve *mindful walking* or the practice of *tai chi*, which is a kind of slow-motion martial art form. *Yoga* also makes use of meditation as part of its focus on developing greater body control.

The mechanics of meditation can be deceptively simple, although it can take many years to become proficient in the method. For instance, one common approach called *mindfulness meditation* merely requires that you focus concentration on a single object (leaf, flower, or symbol), word (mantra), or task (breathing). If you think this

" Of everything I learned in this class—and I learned a lot—I think the one thing that totally changed my life was learning that breathing technique. I remember that day we learned how to do it in class and I thought it was pretty stupid at first. I mean, give me a break, teaching us how to breathe! But that same afternoon, I was upset about something—I can't even remember what it was now—and so I thought, what the heck, I'll try the breathing thing. It was amazing! It was like a switch turned off. I've been using it every day since then, and it has made such a difference.

is easy, try a simple counting meditation: Close your eyes and count slowly, beginning from the number "one." What's the trick? Well, as soon as any other intrusive thought, image, or idea pops into your head other than the number you are saying, you must begin again. Close your eyes and see how far you can get.

If you made it to "two," that is pretty darn good. Most students of meditation could take months to reach "three" without a distracting thought. The fact is that your mind is always racing, flitting from one thing to another, rarely concentrating on any one idea, thought, or image at a time. The goal of meditation is to teach you to turn off your mind, to find the place of perfect tranquility where you totally lose yourself in the moment.

I can describe meditation to you, but if this appeals to you at all, I'd urge you to attend a workshop or class on the subject that is offered on your campus or in your community. Watch the "View It: Stretching Meditation" video segments to see meditation in action.

VIEW IT

Stretching Meditation
This video shows a brief "class" teaching you how to learn meditation and a stretching exercise to reduce stress. (www.cengagebrain.com)

Flow

Flow is a word that describes meditative-like states in everyday life (Csikszentmihalyi, 1975, 1997, 2008). It was originally coined by a graduate student who was doing research on why college students chose to engage in certain activities that seemed to have no external rewards. At his East Coast college, hockey and football were the prestigious men's sports. It was no mystery why guys would compete to play for the teams because they enjoyed lots of attention, privileges, and status. But why, Csikszentmihalyi asked, would anyone want to play soccer? Hardly anyone showed up to watch games. The team barely had uniforms or space to play. Obviously they were enjoying the activity for some internal reward. He heard stories of other people who would lose themselves in their activities—playing chess, rock climbing, and dancing. *Flow* was the word he heard again and again as the best way to describe the experience.

You experience flow almost every day. It is not about daydreaming or drifting off; rather, it is about concentrating so totally on a task that you enter into it. The best sex or dancing or athletic activities take place in a flow state where you lose yourself totally in the experience. The best meals are those when you slow down the pace of your eating and savor every sensation. Watching clouds float by, gazing into a fire, walking outside, washing dishes, listening to music—*anything* can become a flow experience.

Flow takes place in a zone between boredom and anxiety. If you are engaged in an activity that is too easy, or matched against an opponent who is not challenging you, then you feel boredom. On the other hand, if the task or your opponent is too far beyond your capability, then you feel anxious. That is why video games offer different levels so players can adjust the challenges to best meet their skill levels. If the game is too easy, you get bored; if too difficult, you become frustrated and give up.

10.2 FOR REFLECTION AND ACTION

Practicing Flow

Flow means slowing down the pace of *anything* you do to lose yourself in the experience and to practice total "mindfulness." You already know this feeling when you listen to music, play a sport or video game, or totally immerse yourself in an activity.

You can practice flow more often by deliberately concentrating on anything you do with full concentration. An easy way to practice this is with something very simple that you take for granted like walking (s-l-o-w-l-y) or even eating an ordinary cracker. Place a watch or clock before you and see how slowly and consciously you can savor a single cracker, studying it, smelling it, taking tiny, little bites, and resting in between each one.

The goal of any flow experience is just to enjoy ordinary moments with greater appreciation and awareness.

Teaching Tip

Ask students to develop a guided imagery for success on a test in their most difficult subject. Instruct them to develop these thoughts so completely that they appear as a motion picture in their minds, including frame-by-frame pictures of what they do to ensure success. Instruct students to practice "seeing" this movie multiple times as they prepare for the exam. Students should play this same success video in their mind during future testing situations.

▶ **VIEW IT**

Positive Imagery

This video demonstrates ways you can use deep breathing and imagery exercises to reduce stress and keep yourself focused during times when you feel under pressure. (www.cengagebrain.com)

© Cengage Learning

Once you are more aware of the possibility of flow in your life, you can create more opportunities to enter into this meditative state. It is a fabulous cure for stress because you can't feel *anything* when your full attention is captured by a calming activity. Flow provides rejuvenation and recovery because it allows you to turn off your brain for a period of rest. It increases your confidence because you can resume functioning at optimal levels.

Guided Imagery

This technique for training your mind to control your stress levels involves visualizing particular images that help promote positive thoughts and feelings. Imagine, for example, taking one of your pressing problems and shrinking it to a tiny, insignificant object. Or recast the image of someone you fear as a harmless gerbil.

Visualization is a favorite technique of professional athletes who have learned how to imagine positive outcomes as a result of their best efforts. Watch a sprinter before a big race. You'll see her stretching, limbering up, and shaking her muscles, but you'll also see her looking inward, picturing every moment of the race before it begins. Watch a golfer before she hits a difficult shot, and you'll see her pausing for a moment, looking inward, and visualizing the ball rolling perfectly into the hole. Observe a baseball player before he steps up to the plate. He is not just taking practice swings but also picturing the image of the ball striking his bat. After all, he has only a fraction of a second to decide whether to swing or not, what kind of pitch is coming, and whether it is a ball or strike. What are these athletes doing exactly? They are rehearsing in their heads what they intend to do when the pressure is on.

You do this quite naturally already. Whenever you anticipate having a difficult conversation with someone, you first rehearse it in your head—practicing what you want to say, imagining how the other person will respond, and trying out your counterarguments to see how they might work. Once the actual event arrives, you feel better prepared because it seems like you have already lived it before (and you have).

As one example of this, a student on the wrestling team found himself becoming increasingly nervous before matches. "I would get this overwhelming feeling of apprehension and dread that I was going to lose. It just washed over me. But lately, before a match begins, I visualize myself as vividly as I can taking the guy down. Now when I warm up, I not only do my stretches but also my visualizations."

10.3 FOR REFLECTION

Finding Solace in the Spiritual

Many people find comfort and relief from stress through communion with a higher power, association with a religious community, the practice of prayer, or relying on individual spiritual beliefs. Think of when you drew on some aspect of your spiritual life to provide support during a recent time of trouble. What do you see as the most important elements of this experience?

Prayer and Spiritual Support

Whether you believe in a higher power or not, there have been all kinds of research about the effects of prayer and spiritual practices on reducing stress and improving well-being, leading to higher self-esteem and greater life satisfaction (Hayman et al., 2007). Although such rituals are not for everyone, and come in a wide variety of practices that take place in religious institutions, nature, and personalized settings, many students report a sense of peace that results from communing with powers outside themselves.

Some evidence reveals that prayer, as well as regular religious service attendance, can prolong life and even help cure disease, not to mention reduce stress (Koenig, 2008; Kluger, 2009; Newberg and Waldman, 2009). While the results have been inconclusive, many people claim that prayer is one of the primary supports in their lives (50 percent of Americans report they pray every day). Indeed, belief in a supreme being or higher power can offer tremendous relief. The rituals associated with prayer and religious or spiritual practices provide comfort and security, especially during difficult times. Prayer often helps people to let go of things they can't control, as well as to practice forgiveness and greater tolerance.

Prayer can take an infinite number of forms, whether worshipping a deity, fortifying moral beliefs, meditating in solitude, seeking communal sustenance, or finding spiritual solace in nature. All of these forms of prayer may prove helpful to those who are looking outside themselves for support during times of reflection or crisis.

Changing the Ways You View the World

The next set of strategies is designed to help you reduce or prevent stress not so much by what you *do*, but rather by how you *interpret* and *think* about what you are experiencing. Some circumstances or events happen to you that you cannot control; the good news, however, is that you *can* change how you choose to react to them.

For example, Kyle gets out of class and finds a message waiting for him on his voicemail. It is from his girlfriend, telling him that she has decided to end their relationship; she has moved out of the place they were sharing and taken their Sony flat-screen TV. Choose the way you predict that Kyle responds to this situation:

Athletes train themselves to use imagery in order to rehearse situations that are extraordinarily stressful. Golfer Jack Nicklaus once said that a successful shot is only about 10 percent related to the actual swing; 40 percent is related to setting up and planning the shot, and the other 50 percent to visualizing the ball going into the hole. The same use of visualization is effective for anyone who wants to function better under pressure.

Stephen Dunn/Getty Images

Using Imagery

Think of an upcoming situation that you dread or feel apprehensive about. It could be a test, performance, debate, conversation, confrontation, or anything else that provokes instant stress in your mind.

Imagine the situation unfolding in the greatest possible detail. Picture exactly where you are, who else is around, the day and time, and even what you might be wearing. Set the scene in your mind as accurately as you can.

Picture yourself performing and responding with the utmost poise and confidence. See yourself in control of the situation, utterly prepared for anything that might arise.

Now imagine that you are caught off guard in some way. Something unexpected arises, something that you didn't anticipate. You are surprised at first, but then picture yourself adapting to the situation and regaining your tranquility.

Practice this as often as you can prior to the actual event that you *used to believe* would be difficult.

▶ VIEW IT

© Cengage Learning

Imagery in Action

This video segment teaches you how to use imagery to reduce stress and improve concentration. It only takes a few minutes of practice each day to make this strategy part of your natural reaction to stressful situations. (www.cengagebrain.com)

1. He is devastated and depressed, feeling lost and alone.

2. He is anxious about what happened and confused about how he missed the cues.

3. He is frustrated that he didn't get a chance to talk this through and feels sad about the loss.

4. He is relieved and excited because he didn't have to be the one to end the relationship and he has his freedom again.

5. He is annoyed by the surprise announcement and especially the loss of the TV.

6. It's difficult to say without knowing what Kyle was thinking.

I hope you chose answer 6. Although any of these responses to the ending of a relationship are possible, what decides the reaction is *not* the event itself but rather how Kyle chooses to interpret it. If you imagine yourself in his shoes, you could conceivably think any of the following:

1. This is the worst thing that ever happened to me. I can't believe she did this to me. I'll probably never recover from a tragedy like this. And I'll never meet anyone again. I'll probably end up alone for the rest of my life.

In reviewing this internal thinking, you can readily identify a number of exaggerations ("the worst thing that ever happened," "never recover," and "never meet anyone") and distortions ("she did this to me"). It is no wonder he feels depressed with this sort of interpretation, in which he chooses to be a victim, wallows in his suffering, and imagines the absolute worst.

2. How could I have been so stupid to not see what was coming? I'm such an idiot. If I couldn't tell this relationship was so bad, I must be screwing up everything else too.

This thinking isn't quite as distorted as the previous example, but it is still full of self-pity and illogical reasoning. Although it might be useful to consider how he missed evidence that his girlfriend was unhappy, it doesn't necessarily mean that he has messed up all his relationships. It also doesn't mean he's stupid or an idiot just because he didn't anticipate the breakup. This could be constructive for him if he takes the time to learn from the experience.

People do not necessarily react to disasters in the same way. Whereas some individuals become traumatized by the events, others show remarkable resilience, recovering quite quickly. The deciding factor determining how people react to failure, disappointment, or even tragedy is how they choose to interpret the situation. More than anything else, how you think about a situation determines your subsequent emotional reaction.

3. Wow, this hurts. I will miss her and miss the relationship, even with the problems we were having. The fact that she walked out without even choosing to talk about it, or at least negotiate our split amicably, tells me that she has some serious problems. I don't blame her for that, but it would have been nice to talk this through so we could both have closure.

This is probably the most measured interpretation of all. He is owning his sadness rather than denying his feelings. After all—how could he have been in a serious relationship if he doesn't feel some degree of loss now that it has ended so abruptly?

4. Whoopee! This is fantastic! I had been planning to end this relationship myself for weeks, but I didn't want to hurt her feelings. This lets me off the hook. I don't even have to feel the least bit guilty either.

Lynn:
Talking to Myself

" I've felt pretty helpless to control how I feel most of my life. I guess you could say I'm pretty emotional. That's not something I want to change either. I like the way I react strongly to stuff—at least most of the time. But I sure wish I could stop letting some people get to me, you know, like really messing with my head.

There's this one guy who is always teasing me about stuff. He thinks he's being funny or something. He probably likes me, but he's so immature he doesn't know how to show it. Instead he calls me names and embarrasses me. I've told him to stop it but the more I complain, the more he does it.

What I've tried to do lately is to just say to myself that he's not trying to hurt me; he's just too immature to express himself. I've found that reminding myself of that, I start to feel sorry for him instead of angry. Now I notice that when I don't react so strongly, he gives up and leaves me alone. That's the thing with these kinds of people—they are so annoying because they're after a reaction.

Internalized Language

Externalized language blames factors outside of yourself for your emotional reactions. *Internalized language* accepts responsibility for choosing your own reactions. In the examples below, substitute internalized language that communicates greater personal control and choice.

Externalized Language	Internalized Language
"This job has really got me down."	
"I hate it when it is dreary outside like this."	
"I always get nervous when a paper is due."	
"She drives me crazy with her complaining."	
"He did this to me, and it's all his fault."	

Compare your answers with classmates to make sure you understood the concepts. Possible answers are listed at the end of this chapter.

Pretty interesting, huh? This response demonstrates most clearly that how a situation looks from the outside may not reflect the real feelings of the people on the inside. Rather than despairing or self-pitying, this reaction is relieved and joyful, illustrating the diversity of ways people can react to an identical stimulus.

5. Well, this is a bit of a pain, isn't it? I've got to go shopping for another TV, and a girlfriend too! Oh well, it really wasn't that much of a loss. And if she doesn't want to be with me, that's her loss.

In this case, you can probably see why his girlfriend left, if he is really so cavalier about the relationship and only cares about his television. This example is included not because it represents a mature, desirable response but because it demonstrates the possible variety of interpretations.

Any situation you face in college, or in life, does not necessarily dictate an automatic response—even if it sometimes feels that way. You make choices based on how you perceive the event. In other words, *you* are the only one who ultimately determines how you feel about what happens to you. Anytime you are unhappy about anything, you can transform that feeling by interpreting it differently. Any instance in which you are feeling stressed or disappointed, *and you don't want to feel that way any longer*, you can learn to think differently. For example, compare the difference between someone who says, "This traffic is driving me crazy" versus "*I'm driving myself crazy* over this traffic." Or, as another example, "He made me so upset when he did that" versus "*I made myself* so upset when he did that."

What changes because of these two different ways of expressing the situation? In both cases, the second statement more accurately identifies that the crazy, upset feelings are self-inflicted; the power remains with you to choose how you react to most situations.

Teaching Tip

Ask students to journal on the prompt, "What was the most difficult academic experience of your life?" Ask students to reflect on inner thoughts they encountered during that period, and identify negative or self-defeating thoughts that enveloped them. Each student should develop a repertoire of positive self-management thoughts that help in this kind of situation. Ask students to analyze how they could apply these same positive thought processes in a current difficult academic situation.

Changing Negative and Self-Defeating Thoughts

Learning to better control your emotional reactions involves several sequential steps, a few of which you have already learned. Being able to recognize the most common forms of irrational thinking, *as they are occurring*, is a critical part of managing stress.

Identifying Troublesome Thinking

Once you understand that the negative feelings and stress responses you are experiencing result mostly from your thoughts, you can change how you feel by changing how you think. Let's say, for example, that you are feeling frustration, confusion, and stress associated with reading material in this book. The critical question to ask yourself is, "What are you telling yourself, internally, about this situation?"

You have already learned that almost all emotional reactions, especially unpleasant ones, are not really *caused* by the circumstances themselves, but rather by your interpretations of these events. Even though it may seem like the reactions are automatic, some internal processing almost always happens first. This processing often involves your irrational beliefs, so called because they are exaggerations and distortions, leading to extreme emotional reactions such as feeling really upset just because you can't understand the content of this chapter as well as you would prefer.

In the example related to feeling frustrated and confused about the chapter, you might say something like the following to yourself that makes things far worse than necessary: "I should be able to get this," "I'm stupid," or "This isn't fair." You don't have to be a genius to figure out that you can make things so much worse for yourself when you are magnifying and twisting the significance of what is often a minor annoyance or inconvenience.

Challenging Irrational Beliefs

When you were a young child, you heard the rhyme "Sticks and stones may break my bones, but names can never hurt me." Stopping names (and other perceived attacks) from hurting you is the core of this next section.

Now that you are able to name the thoughts with which you hurt yourself (notice the internalized language), the next step is to challenge the beliefs underlying these statements to examine their validity and rationality. Pay attention to how this process applies to the case of not understanding a reading assignment.

- **I'm dumb because I can't learn this.** Where is the evidence that just because you happen to be having some difficulty with this one chapter, *therefore* you are stupid? In fact, there are lots of areas that give other people trouble in which you can learn things quite easily.

- **This is way too hard.** It isn't way too hard; it's only hard. The difference is that life is full of tasks that are challenging, which means that you must rise to the occasion (or not). Saying that something is "too hard" means that it is beyond your

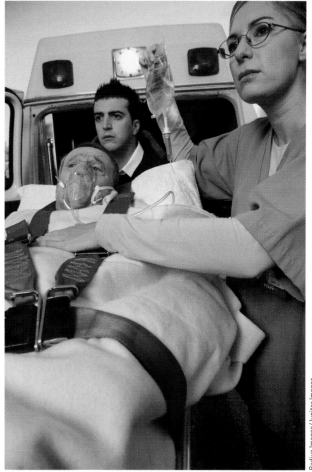

Radius Images/Jupiter Images

Events or circumstances themselves do not *cause* you to feel upset; rather, it is your interpretations of those experiences. Even during emergencies, you have the power to remain calm and collected through internal self-talk. This is a critical skill for anyone who must operate under pressure.

Group Activity

Put the six examples of self-talk on slips of paper in a hat or bag. Break the class into six groups, which draw out one slip and develop new phrases that change the negative self-talk to positive self-talk. Groups can then share their ideas with the entire class.

VIEW IT

Changing Self-Talk

This video segment shows how distorted, irrational, and exaggerated thinking is challenged in a conversation, teaching a student to reduce stress by substituting different interpretations of events. (www.cengagebrain.com)

capability, but no evidence exists to support this absolute judgment just because you have some trouble learning new concepts.

● **I should be able to do this easily.** Who said that? The answer is *you*. If you tell yourself that it should be easy, then you set yourself up for a fall. Just as easily, you can change that thinking to a more rational expectation: "I wish this was easy but I can only expect to struggle when learning something new."

● **This isn't fair that I have to work so hard.** Who says life is fair? In a perfect world, you wouldn't have to work at all—everything would be delivered to you on a silver platter. Alas, in this life you've got to work hard for the things that are most important and useful. Who said college would be any different?

● **This is terrible that I can't learn this.** Terrible? Like on a par with the world ending? Like finding out you have terminal cancer? Like being imprisoned for a crime you didn't commit? Now *that* is terrible.

● **Because this is hard, I should give up.** The "should" is the clue to a common assumption that just because something is hard, one should surrender. That is certainly an option, but other interpretations include "Because this is hard, I have to work harder if I want to master it."

Talking to Yourself Differently

In the beginning you will find that it takes several minutes, perhaps as long as a half hour, to go through the various steps that have been introduced. Like any new set

10.4 FOR REFLECTION

Analyzing Irrational Beliefs

What is irrational about the following statements, and how might you dispute them?

1. I'm an idiot because I can't figure this out.

_____

_____

2. This isn't fair that I have to work all night to get this project done just because others didn't do their part.

_____

_____

3. I should be able to handle this better than I'm doing.

_____

_____

4. I can't stand this situation any longer.

_____

_____

Possible answers are listed at the end of this chapter.

Stopping the Little Annoyances

Sometimes you feel annoyed about minor things because *you* convert them into major sources of frustration. You know you can't do much to change other people's behavior, at least in the short run, yet you still allow these incidents to get under your skin. For each of the following common annoying situations, how could you reframe them in your mind so as to reduce your irritation?

1. Someone is speaking loudly on a cell phone in a public space.

_____

_____

_____

_____

2. A person on the freeway is driving slowly in the express lane, blocking you from driving faster.

_____

_____

_____

_____

3. Someone is standing in line in front of you, chatting to the cashier as if he has all the time in the world.

_____

_____

_____

_____

4. A teacher in one of your classes is giving a particularly boring lecture.

_____

_____

_____

_____

of skills, these require practice and perseverance. Also, because you will most often be doing this when you are already upset, it takes considerable resolve to follow through.

Probably several times this very day, you have been disturbed about something, however minor. One way to minimize the effect of these situations is to talk to yourself differently. Become more aware of the thinking inside your head when you feel negative emotions. Check your underlying thoughts for exaggerations and distortions.

Group Activity

Divide the class into groups of two to four students to discuss their results after the activity "Stopping the Little Annoyances." Ask small groups to report back to the class.

I WISH MY DAD WOULD GET OFF MY BACK! IT'S ONLY BEEN NINE YEARS AND HE WANTS TO KNOW IF I'VE PICKED A MAJOR YET!

www.CartoonStock.com

Substitute alternative, more rational interpretations. Revel in the power to change at will how you feel.

Some Final Thoughts about a Sense of Humor

Much of the stress you feel results from taking life far too seriously. You feel overwhelmed most when you exaggerate the significance of a challenge, when you let the wave that rocks your boat become a tsunami of utter doom and disaster. You can easily fall into the trap of thinking you might as well just give up because something didn't work out the way you hoped.

It turns out that first-year students who use humor to cope with stressful situations adjust much better to college—not to mention have more fun (Hickman and Andrews, 2003). As important as college may be to foster wisdom and prepare you for a career, it is also about enjoying the process of learning and growing in a multitude of ways. It is critical to find ways to giggle and laugh at the ironies and absurdities of daily life, play with friends, and appreciate the many delights that are available on campus.

SUMMARY

Stress is an inevitable part of college life, yet it doesn't have to be incapacitating. In some situations where you experience moderate levels for short periods, stress can actually help you focus your attention and perform at the highest levels (think of athletes). When stress becomes chronic and sustained, however, you must take active steps to control the symptoms and prevent the situation from becoming far worse.

Initial attempts to deal with stress often involve forms of self-medication that may bring with them their own additional problems. Forms of self-talk and internal coping strategies can be used to change undesirable negative emotions, but they require consistent practice. Since college life takes place in a community, reach out to others for help when you feel like you are in over your head.

QUESTIONS FOR REVIEW AND FURTHER EXPLORATION

1. What are symptoms of fight-or-flight stress reactions that you have experienced in the past week?

2. How is it that some forms of self-medication for stress can make initial problems so much worse?

3. Why is feeling distressed more a matter of choice rather than circumstances? What are some ways that you have "chosen" to be upset about something?

4. You receive a disappointing grade. What might be your immediate reactions, and how could you combat those that were counterproductive?

5. Even when people have the skills and ability to counteract negative thinking, they still persist in making themselves miserable. Why do you suppose that people don't want that sort of responsibility and self-control if it really could help free them of negative emotions?

6. Among all the different strategies for reducing stress that were presented in this chapter (deep breathing, medication, positive imagery, self-talk, etc.), what are you prepared to commit yourself to *doing* every day?

ANSWERS TO FOR REDUCING STRESS: INTERNALIZED LANGUAGE

Externalized Language	Internalized Language
"This job has really got me down."	"I'm getting myself down over this job."
"I hate it when it is dreary outside like this."	"It looks dreary outside, but it is still a beautiful day to be alive."
"I always get nervous when a paper is due."	"I *sometimes* get nervous when a paper is due."
"She drives me crazy with her complaining."	"I drive myself crazy over what I see as complaining."
"He did this to me, and it's all his fault."	"He did some things that I don't like."

ANSWERS TO FOR REFLECTION 10.4

What is irrational about the following statements, and how might you dispute them?

1. I'm an idiot because I can't figure this out.
   This is a ridiculous assumption that because you can't figure one thing out, therefore you are an idiot, an absolute label implying that you can never figure anything out. This exaggeration leads to greater frustration, decreasing the probability that you will ever understand it.

2. This isn't fair that I have to work all night to get this project done just because others didn't do their part.
   Sure, it would be nice if people would "do their part," but they are free to do whatever they please, even if you don't like it. They may face consequences, of course, but that is their problem. It is natural to feel disappointed that you have to do more work than your "fair" share, but wallowing in self-pity wastes precious time.

3. I should be able to handle this better than I'm doing.
   You should be able to handle this better? Who says? And even if you, or someone else, genuinely believe that you are not performing at your best, aren't you allowed to be less than perfect at times? Maybe you'll handle this better in the

future, maybe you won't. But regardless, that does not reflect on your worth as a person.

4. I can't stand this situation any longer.
   You will die any moment? You have reached the absolute limit of what you can tolerate and will soon just implode? It may feel that way, but only because of what you're telling yourself at this very moment. This situation is merely difficult, maybe very difficult, but will you even remember this moment a year from now? You can stand it even if you don't like it.

Go to www.cengagebrain.com for an online quiz that will test your understanding of the chapter content.

Negotiating Relationships

KEY QUESTIONS

▶ **Why do existing relationships with friends and family often change so much when students begin college?**

▶ **What can you do to make sure you don't leave loved ones behind or neglect your most important relationships?**

▶ **Why are family conflicts so common, if not inevitable, when students begin college?**

▶ **What are the best ways to deal with disappointment when someone doesn't respond to you the way you hoped?**

▶ **What are the danger signs of an unhealthy relationship?**

▶ **What are the functions and benefits of conflict?**

Group Activity
Ask students to depict their relationships with support people like a solar system. The student is in a center circle like the sun and then draws other circles for friends and family members either close to them or far away, depending on the importance of the relationship and level of current support. Convene groups to talk about how their constellations might have looked different six months ago, before they came to college. Has college changed some relationships? Why or why not?

Relationships aren't just important; they are *everything*. Research studies point again and again to the quality of relationships as the best predictor of happiness, satisfaction, and successful adjustment to college (Pittman and Richmond, 2008). First-year students often report that what most facilitates their adjustment to college are close supportive relationships with peers (Dennis, Phinney, and Chuateco, 2005) and connections with faculty who appear approachable and caring (Donahue, 2004). The operative word in the previous sentence is *approachable*, as in: *you* are the one who must initiate the contact.

So far this book has covered many skills related to academics and personal control, yet it is the interpersonal arena where you will flounder or flourish (or likely end up somewhere in between). You can achieve the best grades you ever imagined, but if you are feeling lonely and isolated, an exceptional grade point average becomes a hollow victory. You could win the lottery but still be absolutely miserable. In fact, many people who do win the lottery find their lives going down the tubes afterward because of relationship problems that develop from their suddenly changed situation.

In this chapter we review many of the relationship issues that you will face in the coming years, both the positive and the gut-wrenching. You will be introduced to ideas that can help improve your interpersonal skills and increase satisfaction in all your relationships with family, friends, roommates, classmates, and instructors. These will allow you to develop far more intimate and satisfying relationships with those you care about, as well as to negotiate far better outcomes in conflicts that arise. In addition, solid and satisfying relationships will improve your academic success through the support system and networks you create. Just as with the other chapters in this book, you must practice these skills for them to become part of you.

PHOTO: Christopher Robbins/Jupiter Images

Friendships

More than anything else, the affiliations you develop with classmates, neighbors, and roommates, and within various social contexts, will determine how well you do—and how good you feel about your accomplishments. Frequently, college acquaintances become lifelong friends. It is not out of the realm of possibility that the networks you develop will lead to future jobs and opportunities. Whatever you learn in the next few years about making new friends with many different kinds of people will likely serve you well throughout the rest of your life. This not only will lead to an assortment of career options that might not otherwise be possible, but also enrich the quality of your life by exposing you to alternative lifestyles, cultures, and ways of being in the world.

Leaving People Behind

When you attend college, you face a real danger of leaving some friends and loved ones behind. This doesn't mean purely in the physical sense, that you are off to campus while others stay at home or at work, but emotionally and psychologically. A few years from now, you will be a very different person than the one you currently see in the mirror. Because the stated objective of college is to encourage your growth in all possible dimensions, you will be learning more than ever before. Your values and interests will change. Your priorities will become realigned. These changes will also impact all of your current relationships. Some will grow stronger, but others will end.

Classroom Discussion

Open it up: What issues or interests might be on a list of things that cause people to grow apart?

Any relationship has a hard time surviving when the participants are growing at a different pace or direction. If you are challenging yourself, learning new things, and developing new interests while your friends or family members are doing the same old things they've always done, an unbridgeable gap can open up between you. "I came to college with one of my closest friends," Amy shared with real sadness. "We made so many plans together about what we were going to do, but we just drifted apart. I don't know what happened, really. I guess once we got here, we realized that we didn't have as much in common as we thought."

It is the nature of life that as you move on to new opportunities, some old relationships will fade while others will blossom. During the first year of college transition, students commonly attempt to hold onto and nurture their friendships from home. After all, you haven't yet built a new support system, a new tribe, to watch your back and assist your survival in this unfamiliar environment. Yet even with the highest motivation and best intentions, it is still difficult to freeze the past and keep things as they were.

Research on the role of past friendships in adjustment to college is interesting. It turns out that while remaining in close contact with high school friends helps a lot during the first few weeks of college, such friendships can actually hinder adjustment throughout the rest of the year (Swenson, Nordstrom, and Hiester, 2009). Ongoing and frequent contact with old friends, however comforting and familiar, may prevent you from investing the time and energy to make new friends on campus who might have more in common with your new roles and responsibilities.

Many existing friendships do survive, and even flourish, during the college years, but primarily that results from a cooperative effort by both parties to make their connection a priority. For romantically involved couples who are attending different colleges or pursuing different career paths, it is even more critical that you communicate openly and regularly, bringing one another up to date on what is happening. This can be done on the phone, and via texting or e-mail, but must also involve face-to-face quality time.

Online Relationships

I was walking across campus one day, stopped at a traffic light before crossing the street, when I overheard the conversation of two students standing right in front of me. A woman was talking to a friend, sharing a story that was obviously quite intimate and emotional for her, as evidenced by the catch in her voice. I could see her friend occasionally nod his head and even glance over at her, but the whole time she was talking he was sending an e-mail or texting someone else! What struck me as most remarkable about this interaction is that this limited attention didn't seem to bother the woman at all; she had become used to conversations with people in which they were only partially present. In fact, most college students today report that it is perfectly fine with them if someone they are speaking to on the phone or in person is simultaneously e-mailing, texting, tweeting, Facebooking, playing a computer or video game, or engaged in some other activity.

Classroom Discussion
Open it up: What online social-networking tools do you use most? Has this changed since you came to college? How well do these tools actually connect you to others?

Negotiating relationships with people electronically presents different challenges because it limits the cues you normally use to communicate. In some ways, you feel freer to be honest when people are not present, but in other ways it is much easier to misunderstand one another. Just think about how often you have sent a text or e-mail to someone and found your intention wildly misinterpreted, or received a message from someone else that you found rude, hurtful, disrespectful, or confusing, only to discover later that it wasn't meant to be taken that way at all.

Recognizing these risks, you should resist the urge to be impulsive out of concern that your message will be corrupted by the messenger. Misunderstandings can occur quite easily when you fire off a question to an instructor without thinking about how it might be received or write something to your parents, a friend, or a family member before considering how they might react. Before you hit "Send" on an e-mail, for instance, take a minute to reread it as if it might be forwarded to the president of the college. Does the message make sense by a potential reader who is not your friend? Is there anything that could be misconstrued, especially exaggerations or implied threats? You may be joking, but the reader may not see it that way.

In some ways, however, communicating with others online is much easier. You can say things that might be more difficult to express in person. You can talk on your own terms, when it is most convenient, and when you are in the mood. Nevertheless, special care should be taken with all your online relationships since the potential for confusion, misunderstanding, and hurt feelings is so much greater than when you are actually with someone and you can assess his or her reaction and respond before any real damage is done.

Initiating Friendships

It isn't how many friends you have, but rather the quality of these intimate connections. As incredible as it may seem, surveys of adults have found that the average person has only two close friends with whom she or he can confide "important personal issues." Furthermore, one-quarter of those surveyed admitted that they had nobody with whom they could talk about intimate matters (McPherson, Smith-Lovin, and Brashears, 2006). This represents a significant

So many relationships today are not conducted face-to-face but rather via e-mail, texting, phone, Facebook and Twitter. As satisfying and convenient as these communications might be with family and friends, it takes special care to frame your messages in such a way that their meaning is understood the way that you intended.

In a landmark study, Robert Putnam (2000) found that people in the industrialized world were becoming increasingly isolated because of the popularity of television, the Internet, video games, consumerism, and workaholism as substitutes for close, intimate relationships. Attendance at religious services, clubs, social poker or bridge games, and bowling leagues is down considerably in recent years, hence the name of Putnam's book, *Bowling Alone*. Subsequent surveys show this trend continuing, with the average adult admitting to only two close friendships (down from three two decades ago). On the other hand, web-based communities like Facebook and MySpace have flourished. More than 100 million people log on to these social networks, satisfying their need to belong to a tribe.

Juan Silva/Jupiter Images

drop in friendships from twenty years ago and is believed to be the result of technology that is increasingly taking over our social lives.

If you can develop two or three close friendships while in college, you are doing pretty well for yourself. "Friendship" doesn't just mean acquaintances with whom you exchange pleasantries or engage in superficial conversations—although these interactions are also satisfying and important. Real friendship means the kind of close, trusting relationship in which you feel comfortable talking about the most intimate matters—confusions, fears, apprehensions, joys, failures, successes, love, sex, money, *anything*.

Friendships are not all-or-nothing experiences. You have different kinds of friendships for different purposes. Some friends are fun to party with, and others are great for serious, intellectual discussions. Some friends you like to talk to every day, and others you might speak with a few times each semester. You have friends you would trust with your life and others whom you would be reluctant to have hold your wallet. There are the kind of friends who help you feel better about yourself, while there are others who instigate competition with you. Some friends you shake hands with upon greeting, some you peck on the cheek, and others you embrace. To some friends you can tell anything, and with others you would only talk about certain matters. Yet they are all friends and serve important purposes in your life.

If you wait for potential friends to approach you, it could be a long, lonely wait. The usual reluctance to initiate relationships is based on the fear of rejection. But that should no longer be an issue for you, right? After all, now you are equipped with the skills to counteract negative thinking. Based on what you learned in Chapter 10, you can talk to yourself differently if someone doesn't respond as you had hoped.

If this very day, you were to walk up to five people on campus whom you didn't know and strike up a conversation with the intention of getting to know them better, what would the outcome be? One might give you a strange look, ignore you completely, and continue walking as if you were invisible. Another might smile but decline politely. A third might give you a lame excuse—sounds great, but just no time right now, maybe later. A fourth might show some initial interest but really isn't available at that moment (but is still interested). And the fifth might say yes and accept your invitation.

Dugan:
Being Selective with Friendships

" I kept dropping classes because they weren't interesting to me. The teachers were boring and I couldn't get good grades. Hanging out with my friends was a lot more fun, so I just stopped going to class. I mean, I would still show up once in a while, but I really hated going. At the end of the semester, I was only taking one class because I had dropped all the other ones. Even then, my grades were still crap.

I was about to flunk out, so I decided to give it one more shot. I realized that if I flunked out, I would have to go home and get a job because my parents were paying for school and all my stuff, but they wouldn't keep paying if I dropped out. So, I got motivated [laughs] and started going to class. I made some new friends who helped me bring my grades up. We studied together and we helped each other make it to class on time. I started hanging out more and more with these new friends, and we now pick our classes together so we can help each other get through the tough ones.

Learning to summon the courage and openness to initiate friendships will prepare you for what it takes to build the sort of relationships and support systems that you will want and need throughout life. It may feel good to have people pick you as a friend, but that puts you in the helpless position of hanging out only with those who made the first move. This could work out just fine, but it could also lead to spending time with those who may not be a good influence or share your most important interests or values.

Cutting Your Losses

You only have so much time and energy and can hardly afford to waste time with people who not only don't add much to your life but actually deplete you. These individuals are difficult for you (and perhaps others) to be around. They are toxic and frustrating for you.

Difficult people sometimes can't help the way they are. They either get rewarded too much (remember secondary gains?) for their behavior, or they just operate in a particular way that makes them annoying. In some cases, they may have *personality disorders*, that is, predispositions to be unusually manipulative, self-centered, and abusive. They may not have a conscience or abide by commonly accepted ethics and morality. Or, in some cases, the difficulty may not arise from their quirks or shortcomings, but rather because of the way they push your buttons.

People who are challenging to spend time with may include classmates, friends, neighbors, coworkers, or family members. Regardless of whether the conflict and anxiety you experience results from their behavior, your own reactions, or a combination of both (which is often the case), you should be prepared to set limits and even end relationships that are distracting you from your goals or, worse case scenario, threaten to make you the victim of abuse. No matter how reluctant you are to hurt someone else's feelings (remember that people hurt their own feelings), or how uneasy you are with asserting yourself, you must make smart choices about friends or you will squander a lot of emotional energy that could be better directed toward healthier relationships and happier times.

Family Relationships

Your family is the unit into which you were born (or perhaps chosen), and it remains the foundation for much of what you have already learned about life. There may have been considerable benefits to this upbringing, but also legacies

Teaching Tip
Challenge students to approach five people before the next class meeting and then report on the results. Ask them to share not just their relative successes in these encounters but also whatever reluctance they felt, any negative thinking, or fears of rejection.

For Community College Students
Since many traditionally aged commuter students live at home while going to college, discuss whether their situation at home seems the same as when they were in high school, such as with home rules, curfews, and the like.

that still haunt you. Sometimes you can't wait to see your family members; other times, you feel the need to put some distance between you.

Going to college represents a huge milestone, not only in your life but also in the lives of your family members. If you are leaving home for the first time, it represents a statement of your independence and achievement. If you are a parent yourself, it may mean sacrificing time with your children to create a better future for all. If you are a returning student, you may have to choose between a night out with your family versus being holed up in the library to study. Going to college certainly involves adjustments for you, and for everyone else who must come to terms with this new stage of your life.

As proud as they might feel of your achievements, many parents have a hard time letting go of their children (no matter how old they are). Campuses are designed as insulated environments surrounded by ivy-covered walls (or perhaps parking structures) to foster detachment and autonomy. The goal is to allow you to explore and experiment beyond your parents' influence, or at least help you develop your own views about the world. Those students who remain "tethered" to their parents through constant communication via e-mail, texting, and twice-a-day phone calls tend to be much less satisfied with their college experience *and* their relationship with their parents (Hofer, 2008). In other words, one purpose of this stage in life is to establish new boundaries with family that allow you to widen your contacts and relationships with others.

Conflict is inevitable between college students and their families. You are a child to your parents, and you will always be their child—no matter how old you are. I have a grown son myself, and yet my father still treats me like a little boy. He still doesn't think I'm capable of making sound decisions without his input, still believes I am misguided and immature in my choices, and never fails to caution me about how I spend money or what I do with my free time. I used to argue with him about this, remind him that I am a professional in my own right, but all to no avail. I thought a college degree might earn some respect, then a master's degree, then a PhD, a professorship, and even many books published, but alas I am, and will always be, a little boy to him. Does this annoy me? You betcha.

There is a difference between healthy disagreements and toxic, ongoing conflict. Regardless of your cultural or family upbringing, if you feel like your family is meddling too much in your life, constantly trying to control you and undermine your progress, then one of several outcomes can result. First, if you continue to take what feels like abuse, then you will feel more resentful and angry. Second, if you try to assert yourself but do so while feeling angry and threatened, then the conflict can

Classroom Discussion

Open it up: How has your relationship with your parents changed since you began college? Have you or your parents "picked your battles" over certain topics? If you were to talk to your parents about the ways your relationship has changed, and will change in the future, what might you say?

Myles:
Renegotiating a New Relationship

" The first semester I commuted to campus, which was only a half hour from school, but my parents just kept getting on my nerves like I was still in high school or something. They wanted to know what time I'd be home and where I was going. A real pain in the butt. So then I moved into the dorm and that was better but they still called me all the time.

I used to go home on Sundays, do laundry, and have dinner with everyone, but still it was like the third degree or something. Who am I going out with? What are my classes like? How am I getting along with my roommate? Stuff like that. I knew they just wanted to know how I'm doing and all but it really started to bug me. I tried to answer their questions but it was never enough. I could tell they were disappointed and that only made me feel guilty.

We had some rocky times that first year. I wouldn't call them back and I stopped coming home on Sundays. I know they worried about me and I know it was hard for them. But it was just something I had to do. Now that I'm a sophomore, we kind of laugh about it.

Yeah, I do still come home on Sundays, most of the time anyway. My mom cooks me a good meal, and I just get tired of eating that crap in the dorm.

escalate to the point of estrangement. The third possibility, and the preferred one, is to understand the difficult time that some family members may be having, just as you are struggling with your own adjustments. Even while you are tapped into some compassion, you can still enforce boundaries of what you are and are not willing to do and communicate in ways that won't exacerbate the problems between you. Studies show that freshmen who are able to maintain reasonably good connections to their parents or other family members experience significantly less stress and emotional problems than those who feel estranged (Hiester, Nordstrom, and Swenson, 2009).

Here are some other things to keep in mind:

- **Among the various demands and expectations family members make of you, choose your battles carefully.** Some are not a big deal to you, but others are extremely important.

- **Decide on what is most important and communicate clearly what your boundaries are.** You have the power to control access by limiting when you answer phone calls, respond to messages, and sit down for conversations.

- **If you accept financial support from your family, you are accountable to them in certain ways.** Taking money or other kinds of support (such as medical insurance, an allowance, or use of a car) almost always comes with strings attached. If this bothers you enough, you can declare emancipation and arrange your own finances. If you are going to accept their help, negotiate with them exactly what that means in terms of your responsibility or repayment.

- **Once you set limits, enforce them—consistently and without exception.** Otherwise, you lose credibility.

- **Avoid predictably difficult situations.** Just stay away from those situations that most consistently result in negative outcomes for you. If you consistently do and say things to get approval and validation from a parent or authority figure, yet always get disappointing results, then stop. (I know this is much easier said than done since I still fall into this pattern with my own father.)

- **Make time for your family.** Remember that what you are doing is important not only to you, but to them as well. It takes so little time and effort to check in on a regular basis and fill them in on what is new in your life.

- **If you are having trouble dealing with your family, get some help.** Solicit the support of other family members if you can do so without escalating the struggle. Seek counseling, either for yourself individually or for all of you as a family.

Working adult students have an entirely different set of challenges. In fact, recruiting the support of family and coworkers may be the single most important factor that reduces stress in college for those who are returning to school after a significant period of time raising a family or working on a career (Giancola, Grawitch, and Borchert, 2009). This is why it is so important to communicate openly with coworkers and family members about the difficulties of managing all of their responsibilities now that they are college students.

Michael Cogliantry/Getty Images

Renegotiating relationships with parents and family members is both expected and completely normal during your first year as a college student. You are an adult, yet in some ways still treated like a child. You yearn for respect, autonomy, and independence, yet also depend on your family for reassurance, encouragement, and advice.

Teaching Tip
Conduct a class discussion on the role of gratitude in personal happiness and in adult relationships. Emphasize that gratitude can play an enormous role in developing a healthy adult relationship with parents. Suggest that students send parents (or an influential adult role model) a thank-you card during the semester (preferably during the early weeks). In this card, the student should express gratitude for all the parents have done to help him or her develop into a responsible adult. The student should explain how this has helped with a successful transition into adulthood.

Romantic Relationships

One of the "jobs" or developmental tasks of young adults is to find a prospective mate. This doesn't necessarily mean you should expect to find a life partner while you are still in college, since marriage often doesn't take place until after graduation or well beyond. But you will still feel a strong emotional urge, not to mention physical desire, to connect with someone in an intimate relationship. Regardless of your age and stage in life, as well as your marital status, most people are interested in enhancing romance in their life—with a current partner or a new one.

Depending on your age, sexual orientation, religious beliefs, family upbringing, culture, gender, intensity of sex drive, prior experience, and other factors, you may experience the romantic urge as a gentle prodding or a full-blown obsession. Expect romantic relationships to be one of the most popular subjects for conversation.

People grow (rather than fall) in love for a variety of reasons. You meet someone who fits your ideal image, or what you believe that to be. Or you feel uncontrollable infatuation and lust to possess someone. Or you develop a friendship initially based on mutual respect and admiration that later blossoms into something else. The latter description actually fits arranged marriages, which are common in many parts of the world.

Finding Someone to Love—Who Will Love You Back

Not everyone is interested in being involved in a romantic relationship at this stage of life but many students make it a priority. Even if affairs of the heart are not on your radar screen with everything else you are trying to manage, there will come a time when connecting with someone will be important to you.

Everything said earlier about initiating friendships applies to prospective romantic relationships, only more so. Because the stakes are greater (both the risk of rejection and intensity of pain), you need even more courage to approach someone who is attractive or interesting. Nevertheless, if you are serious and committed to finding someone with whom you can share romance (anywhere from recreational sex to a committed relationship), you are going to have to put yourself on the line—again and again. You will definitely experience rejection. You will face excruciating pain. And, if you are fortunate, you will enjoy the greatest feeling known to humanity: true love.

To find a romantic partner, several tasks are involved. First, locate someone of interest (usually not the hard part). Second, determine compatibility beyond physical attraction (unless this is all you are looking for). Third, assess the other person's comparable interest in you as a partner. This last step is a tough one, frequently requiring you to express your own interest first and therefore risk that it won't be reciprocated. When this occurs, you must find ways to rebound from the disappointment without discouragement.

Of course, you don't want to accept just any relationship; insist on one that meets your needs in the areas that are most important to you. Too many people settle for unhealthy relationships because they fear being alone or don't know how to extricate themselves. How do you recognize the danger signs of an unhealthy relationship? Look for things like chronic jealousy, possessiveness, deception, lying, dependency, verbal or physical abuse, or poor communication.

How do you know if a relationship is a good one? Love is certainly important but not nearly enough. You can love someone with all your heart, that person can love you back, and yet you both drive each other crazy.

Healthy relationships usually have the following features:

● Open and honest communication

● Mutual trust

- Having fun together

- Respect for one another's interests, priorities, and goals, even (especially) when they are different from your own

- Care and support for one another

- Shared decision making

- Time and space available to pursue individual interests

- Physical responsiveness and compatibility

- Working through disagreements and arguments constructively

Patterns of staying in unhealthy relationships are forged early in life, usually by what you witnessed with your own parents. But they become more deeply ingrained during college, when you experience your own romantic encounters. If you want to find a partner someday who will greatly enhance the quality of your life, and remain at your side until death do you part, you will have to establish high (but realistic) standards in the coming years.

Breaking Up IS Hard to Do

The good news: you will likely develop a romantic relationship during your first few years of college. The more distressing news: close to one-third of first-year students experience a breakup, which is the single most frequent cause of depression among college students (Foreman, 2009). Whether you are the one who decided to end things, or the victim of heartbreak because it wasn't your choice, healing takes time.

Relationships end for all kinds of reasons:

- Infidelity or breach of trust

- One or both partners outgrow the other

- Physical infatuation wears off (usually after lasting a few months)

- Incompatibility of values, interests, and priorities

- Irreconcilable differences in viewpoints or goals

- One or both partners are not getting primary needs met

- Chronic misunderstandings and miscommunication

Whereas the ending of any personal relationship represents some kind of loss, you might be surprised to know that students often report significant personal growth after a breakup, even if it was not their choice. When students were interviewed after a romantic relationship ended, they were asked to describe all the changes that resulted. Almost everyone in the study reported noticing at least one positive change such as greater maturity, resourcefulness, resilience, shifted priorities, or a better sense of what they will look for in future relationships (Hebert and Popadiuk, 2009).

If you experience grief, depression, loneliness, and loss after a relationship ends, that is to be expected—especially if you weren't the one who ended it. You have a perfect right to struggle during this transitional period, which can last anywhere from a few weeks to several months. If you remain unhappy for longer than that, it is time to seek help. Unfortunately, only 5 percent of those who are suffering ever consult with a professional to help them out of their misery (Foreman, 2009). The point is not just to accept what happened and move forward, but also to learn from the experience so you don't repeat the same mistakes.

Group Activity
List the barriers to listening. Then bring the discussion alive by dividing the students into pairs and asking them to take turns talking about something while the listener exaggerates not listening (turning away, yawning, playing with the phone, and doodling). Then have them discuss what this was like and how often they are involved in similar conversations in which one or the other person is not really listening.

Group Activity
Pair up students and ask them to decide who is A and who is B. All A's talk for three minutes while all B's listen with eye contact and attending skills (and no interruption). The topic for discussion is to describe the two closest relationships in their life and why these people are important. Switch roles after three minutes. Next, bring the class together to discuss what it feels like to be *heard*—and understood.

Teaching Tip
Discuss with students the importance of eye contact in communication. Suggest that many students have extreme difficulty in maintaining eye contact with professors during office visits. Suggest that each student practice the principles of maintaining eye contact with a professor during a conference and report back to the class on the results.

Teaching Tip
Ask a member of the counseling center staff to visit class to give an overview of listening skills.

Relationship Skills

The subject of this section is rather unusual for a textbook on adjustment to college, which typically focuses only on academic issues. But because loneliness, interpersonal conflict, and lack of intimacy are frequently cited by new students as their most troubling challenges, it would be shortsighted to ignore the importance of relationship skills. Success in college—and in life—is determined by your ability to relate effectively to others. This is how you get your needs met, feel connected, and work cooperatively.

If you want to be more proficient in your ability to develop close, intimate relationships with others (and who doesn't?), you can try several effective strategies. I teach these exact skills to beginning therapists and counselors since they must be experts in establishing close, trusting alliances with their clients, and doing so in a very short period of time. This process isn't magical (well, a *little* magical) since it involves applying certain techniques and responding in certain ways, depending on what is required.

The Power of Eye Contact

You can learn the following relationship skills in a remarkably short period of time and notice dramatic changes in the ways that people respond to you. You can easily prove this by using one of the simplest, most basic skills of all: making eye contact. Although cultural, age, and gender differences may influence appropriate eye contact during conversations, no other behavior is more important to communicate interest, support, caring, and attentiveness.

If you pay close attention to the way most conversations take place around you, as well as those you participate in, you will observe that most people are not giving full attention to the interaction. Most of the time, they are multitasking or distracted. While someone is talking to you, he may be looking around, waving to others, flipping through papers, or even stopping you in the middle of a sentence to answer the phone. This happens so frequently that you hardly even notice. But it is a sign and symptom of how accustomed people have become to receiving someone else's minimal attention.

One of the first things that therapists learn to master is the art of comfortable but attentive eye contact. Gazing into someone's eyes in a comfortable, natural way is among the most intimate forms of engagement. Try kissing someone, or making love with someone, and keep your eyes *open*. You'd be amazed at the even greater intensity of the experience. So it is with any aspect of a relationship that your eyes should be communicating riveted attention to what the person is saying or doing. No other single thing more intensely transforms the intimacy that you experience.

This behavior is so enticing, so attractive, and so enveloping that most people would talk to me forever if I would allow it (but that requires other skills to set limits). But don't take my word for it—try this out for yourself. Take a day, or even just an hour, and experiment with making solid eye contact with those who are talking to you. Don't do anything else at the same time. Don't permit your phone to interrupt, which essentially communicates to the other person that he or she is not as important as whoever else might be calling.

Attending Skills

Eye contact is just one of several "attending skills," meaning behaviors that communicate your interest in what the other person is saying. If you want to develop trust and intimacy with others, make them feel heard and understood by you. The first step in

Peter Cade/Getty Images

Maintaining relaxed but attentive eye contact communicates interest, support, and respect during conversations. Yet we have become so used to talking with people who are only half-listening that we no longer think twice about it. One of the most powerful ways to take conversations and relationships to a deeper level is to concentrate on maintaining appropriate eye contact. You are literally peering inside one another's brains since eyes are actually the brain's primary sense organ.

that process is letting them know that you are fully present. It is actually so rare in people's lives to ever feel truly listened to that communicating complete interest is, in itself, incredibly therapeutic, if not seductive.

Although making good eye contact is a significant component of effective attending behaviors, there are other facets as well. This includes using your posture and body position (facing the person fully, leaning forward, showing interest) to communicate your intense focus on what the person is saying. This means ignoring all distractions, both internal (intruding thoughts) and external (phone calls and text messages).

Listening Actively

While your attentive body position communicates interest, you are also carefully listening to the other person's words. This includes not only the *surface messages* but also the *deep messages*, those beneath the surface. When people say things to you (or anyone else), they are often communicating on multiple levels. They are saying one thing but meaning quite another, or sometimes not aware of what they really think and feel (see For Reflection 11.1).

While you are listening to someone speak, you are *decoding* what is really being said. Besides the spoken words, what is the person communicating right now? Pay attention not only to the words but also to the nonverbal behavior to figure out the deeper messages.

Every conversation has undercurrents. People don't often say what they really mean. If you are fully attending and listening carefully, you will be amazed at the hidden and disguised meanings you can uncover. For that to occur, however, you have to *listen actively* during the conversation.

● **Suspend judgment.** Quiet that critical voice inside your head that is distracting you and also expressing your biases.

● **Wait to respond.** Don't be in such a hurry to talk. Most people want to be heard. The one exception is if you are unusually quiet and reserved, in which case you should make an effort to talk more or others will wonder what you are thinking (and assume you are being judgmental).

▶ VIEW IT

© Cengage Learning

Active Listening
This video demonstrates two students learning how to use active-listening techniques to deepen their conversation.
www.cengagebrain.com

11.1   FOR REFLECTION

Listening for Deep Meanings

In the following examples, decode the likely meaning of the message beyond what was spoken:

● A five-year-old child pointing at a big dog coming toward him on the street: "Mama, MAMA, does that doggy bite?"

● A friend rubbing his eyes and looking down, speaking in an uncharacteristically soft voice: "Yeah, she broke up with me. But I don't really care."

● An instructor pacing back and forth across the room, gesturing dramatically: "This probably isn't very important, but I'd like to mention one other thing...."

Possible answers are listed at the end of this chapter.

● **Decode what you hear.** Ask yourself what this person is really saying. Look for the deeper messages. For instance, if someone says to you, "Did you study for the test?" he probably isn't really asking a question but is expressing apprehension and anxiety. Decoding that statement allows you to respond with more than just a "yes" or "no," but with "You're feeling anxious about that test." Such responses open up conversations to a deeper level.

Responding with Compassion

So far in your attentive conversation all you've done is listen and nod your head. Now comes the time to respond and say something appropriate. Therapists use a particular mind-set when they are talking to people they are helping. It is an attitude, a *way of being*, that communicates not only the hovering interest mentioned earlier but also a deep level of empathy.

"Empathy" is the ability to crawl inside someone else's skin and sense what he or she might be experiencing. When things are humming just right, you can actually seem to read the other person's mind, or at least have a pretty good idea of what is going on.

Empathy takes place when you feel compassion, respect, and caring for another person. You have temporarily put your own needs and feelings aside, those that would clutter your mind and heart. Instead, you are trying to really feel what it is like to be the other person.

Although sensing someone else's thoughts and feelings allows you to have a deeper, more accurate resonance of their experience, it doesn't contribute much to the relationship unless you are able to express this understanding. You must be able to communicate what you've heard the other person say and what you've sensed they really mean. Reflective listening like this has a number of advantages over other ways of responding in conversations:

1. You let the other person know that you are listening carefully to what is being said. It is pretty lame to say to someone, "Yeah, I understand what you mean." You can *prove* this by showing your understanding through a reflection of what you heard.

2. You can check the accuracy of what you heard. The beauty of this skill is that even when you aren't exactly on target, the person will still keep talking to clarify what was meant.

Almost everyone wants to feel heard and understood, yet it is relatively rare in our lives. Everyone is so busy and distracted by other things going on that we don't often enjoy someone else's undivided attention. Offering compassion and caring to others not only can make a huge difference in raising their spirits but also provides a significant boost to your own feelings of self-worth.

3. By helping the listener hear what is being said, it helps him or her to explore more deeply what is being experienced: "So what you are saying is that you don't feel very good at all about what happened."

4. It keeps the conversation going and keeps the focus on the other person. If your goal is to develop greater closeness with another, help the person to feel understood by you.

5. Most amazing of all, these skills lead the conversation to a deep, intimate level. Since you are choosing to reflect back what you think is most significant, you can keep the discussion from becoming trite and superficial.

Reflections of Content

Reflections can be framed in two basic varieties: those that focus on the *content* of what is being expressed, and those that bring out the underlying *feelings*. Both are considered important parts of communication.

Another way to think of reflection of content is *paraphrasing*. You listen to what the person says, and you respond by feeding back the essential content of what you heard. It looks something like this at its most basic level:

Myra: "I can't decide whether to drop this class or stick with it."

Fred: "It's a tough choice."

Myra: "The class is so hard. I don't have a clue what's going on."

Fred: "You can't keep up with the work."

Myra: "Keep up with it? Are you kidding? I don't even know where to start."

Fred: "You're so far behind, that's why you're thinking of dropping it."

Myra: "Yeah, but if I drop it, it's too late to add another class and then my load would be reduced to part-time status and I could lose financial aid."

Fred: "So you're in quite a bind. You can't keep up with the class, but you don't think you can drop it either."

Paraphrasing is not that difficult to do but it does require a certain amount of discipline and practice. You have to resist giving advice, refrain from getting into your own issues right away, and concentrate completely on listening and then reflecting back what you hear the person saying.

Whereas this might seem rather simplistic, this basic relationship skill is so crucial that it is at the core of what therapists do when they teach couples to improve their communication. Most of the time people fight or don't get along because they don't understand one another and don't feel understood. This addresses those concerns.

Reflections of Feeling

This relationship skill is even more powerful than paraphrasing because it gets at the core feelings that someone is experiencing, some of which may be beyond his or her awareness. In the conversation between Fred and Myra, Fred did a good job of reflecting back the content of what he heard her say. This let her know that he was hearing her accurately and was truly interested in what she was saying, while perhaps even helping her to clarify what was at stake. But it didn't get at the deeper feelings at the heart of her fears and apprehensions.

Here is how the conversation would unfold if, instead of honing in on the content of the conversation, Fred went after the feelings:

Myra: "I can't decide whether to drop this class or stick with it."

Fred: "You're really confused because it seems like a tough choice."

Myra: "Yeah, the class is so hard. I don't have a clue what's going on."

Fred: "You just feel so lost because you can't keep up with all the work. You feel overwhelmed."

Myra: "That's for sure. I just don't know where to begin and I don't know how to catch up even if I wanted to."

Fred: "You just want to give up, and that's why you are thinking of dropping the class. But a part of you also wants to see if you can recover somehow. That's why you haven't dropped it already."

Coby:
Learning Reflective Listening

"As soon as I got pregnant, I started to freak out that I was going to be this terrible, neglectful mother like mine was when I was growing up. There's all these birthing classes you take but I also wanted to get the jump on being a perfect mom so I took this parenting class. They taught us active-listening skills, like how to talk to your kids so they open up instead of close down like kids usually do.

The class met for, like, six weeks in a row and I never missed one. They had us practice with each other but also try the skills out with, you know, our friends and family. So I couldn't wait to practice with my husband, but he would kinda laugh at what I was doing because I guess it was pretty obvious. The teacher told us this would happen until we got comfortable and all, so I kept trying it out, you know, like with the cashier at Piggly Wiggly, or this neighbor who lives downstairs from us. And you know what, it really worked! People started talking to me like they never had before. Even my husband stopped noticing what I was doing, or maybe he was just giving me a break.

Myra: "I guess that's true. Besides, if I drop the class, it's too late to add another one. Then my load would be reduced to part-time status and I could lose financial aid. I just don't know what to do."

Fred: "So you're just really anxious and uncertain about what to do. If feels like whatever choice you make is a lousy one. I sense you'd really like to figure out a way to make this class work, but you're uncertain how to approach the problem."

The hardest part of the relationship skills that Fred demonstrated was being able to figure out what Myra was feeling within the second or two that he had during the natural pauses in their conversation. Have no doubt about it: This takes practice. You can also benefit from receiving feedback from someone who has some degree of proficiency in these skills. This is another one of those strategies that is good to be exposed to in a book such as this, but really requires advanced training. If you are so interested, your college may offer courses to help you improve your relationship skills.

11.2 FOR REFLECTION

Practicing Conversational Reflections

To learn the relationship skills presented in this chapter, it is crucial that you find ways to practice them and get some feedback on ways you can improve.

Whether you do this with classmates or friends, in class or on your own, find someone who is willing to talk to you for a few minutes about something of interest. Record the conversation so you can review it afterward and critique what you did best, as well as what you need to improve.

1. For the first round, practice attending behaviors—lean forward, nod your head, show appropriate facial expressions, and communicate intense interest. During the conversation, you are allowed to do only one other thing—paraphrase or reflect content. That means that when you respond, you do so by repeating back the content of what you hear.

2. The second round is much more challenging, so you'll need to be patient with yourself. Have the person continue talking, but this time you are going to concentrate on reflecting the feelings underlying what is communicated.

After you are done, listen to the recording to note ways to improve your skills. Be realistic—you will not be very good at first. It takes many weeks of diligent practice to become reasonably proficient.

If you have the opportunity, ask someone who already knows these skills to listen to your recording and give you some constructive feedback.

Conflict in Relationships

So far we have been talking mostly about how to deepen good relationships. The other side of the story is how to reduce the negative effects from interactions that are already too deep and intense. During your college years (and afterward), you will face disagreements with friends, family members, roommates, and others, interactions that take an emotional toll and eat up a lot of time and energy. It is well worth learning more about what conflicts mean and how they can be more effectively resolved—or else how to live with them in such a way that they aren't nearly as disruptive to your life.

Functions of Conflict

As much as you might complain about conflicts or disagreement in your life, they actually serve several useful purposes. This is related to what you learned previously about how all behavior persists because it is rewarding in some way. For one thing, conflicts bring your attention to things that must be examined more deeply. This often relates to issues of power and control in which negotiations are taking place. As such, conflicts can often promote further growth and reflection, and regulate distance between people. In other words, ongoing arguments are a way to keep people you don't fully trust at a safe distance.

For some people, conflicts release tension and then may even promote greater intimacy. When you consider how much time you spend thinking about someone with whom you are fighting, you must admit that they are living very close to your heart and soul (see For Reflection 11.3).

Until you can figure out what you are really fighting about, it is very difficult to resolve the struggle so that it doesn't flare up again. Consider the following examples:

- Someone is angry at her roommate for borrowing clothes without asking, but the struggle is really about reciprocating equally in their relationship.

- A mother frequently criticizes her son, as if he can do nothing right. He retaliates by doing things to deliberately provoke her disapproval. Both are trying to renegotiate a new "adult" relationship.

- Two friends fight continually about what they are going to do when they go out at night. Sometimes it gets so bad that they end up separating. They are actually still in disagreement about an incident that happened long ago that they have been unwilling to talk about.

- A couple constantly fights over sex, but what is really under dispute is whether their relationship has a future.

In each of these cases an *interactive effect* takes place, meaning that both parties have a role in the conflict. Each one has some responsibility for the ongoing misunderstanding and subsequent problems. Each person's behavior exacerbates (worsens) the other's reactions, creating a never-ending cycle.

Although in most cases conflicts are the result of both parties playing a role in the disturbance, in some situations you really feel abused by someone who is unusually insensitive, neglectful, or hurtful. In these situations, as in so many others, it is important to be flexible in the strategies you employ. If one thing doesn't work, keep trying until you find the right combination.

11.3 FOR REFLECTION

Living Inside Your Head

An expression says that when you are in an ongoing conflict with someone who continues to upset you, you are allowing that person to live rent-free in your head. What do you think that means? Who are you currently letting reside in your head (and heart) without paying rent?

_____

_____

_____

Conflicts with Roommates

Among college students who live away from home, either on campus or in off-campus housing, conflicts with roommates are often reported as one of the greatest sources of stress. In some cases, your whole well-being depends on the quality of that relationship and how well you are able to settle disputes and disagreements (Stern, 2009).

"My roommate drives me absolutely crazy," one freshman admitted during a discussion about most annoying problems. "He leaves his dirty dishes in the sink—*my* dishes I might add. But the worst thing is that he actually eats my food in the refrigerator! I had to resort to putting signs on the orange juice, 'Don't touch,' but he ignores them anyway."

"Yeah," another student chimed in, making this the single most animated conversation we'd had all semester, "my roommate sleeps until noon, stays out until ungodly hours, then wakes me up when she comes in early in the morning. She actually turns on the light in the room as if I'm not sleeping."

"You think that's bad?" still another student added. "My roommate just piles all his clothes in a big heap by his bed. It's now spilling out all over the floor. Then when he runs out of clean clothes—I don't think he ever does laundry—he starts taking *my* clothes and then just throws them onto his pile. It's disgusting."

In each of these examples, and many others that were shared, communication between roommates was marginal. They could complain to others, but something blocked the person's willingness to talk about these problems with the roommate in such a way that some mutually agreed-upon solution could be found. Whether you are living on campus or off campus, conflicts with the people who share your space are among the most common sources of frustration. Yet once personal preferences are negotiated, and open communication is facilitated, there can be nothing more satisfying than having companions with whom you can debrief and share the day's events. Avoiding conflict over things that start out small and inconsequential can later lead to much bigger sources of difficulty.

Strategies for Managing Conflict

Just as you learned in previous chapters, the best strategy for managing conflict actually takes place inside your own head. Regardless of how the other person behaves, and what you do to try to change his or her behavior, it is still totally within your control what you tell yourself to remain calm in the face of adversity (see Table 11.1).

▶ VIEW IT

Conflict Resolution
This video shows someone addressing conflict in a relationship.
www.cengagebrain.com

© Cengage Learning

TABLE 11.1

Things to Say to Yourself in the Midst of Difficult Conflicts

1. This is *only* difficult, but not impossible.
2. What doesn't kill me will make me stronger.
3. This isn't about me, but about the other person.
4. Take a deep breath.
5. In ten years this won't matter—and I probably won't remember it.
6. This person is just doing the best he can.
7. What am I missing?

Looking Inward Rather than Outward

Think about an argument, fight, or conflict you are having with someone in your life. This could be with anyone you feel is giving you trouble.

One way to reduce stress is by focusing on what you can change, instead of that which is outside of your control. Whether you like it or not, you can't control someone else's behavior, but you can manage your own reactions to what happens. With that in mind, put aside all blame and attention on the other person(s). What is *your* role in initiating or maintaining this conflict? In other words, what are you doing, or failing to do, that is making this conflict worse than it needs to be?

_____

_____

_____

What could you do differently in the future to avoid getting involved in similar struggles?

_____

_____

_____

For Community College Students

This section provides an appropriate place to ask nontraditional students in class and/or student parents about the necessity of active listening skills. Ask for examples of when they have tried it and when they haven't but wished they had.

Using Active-Listening Skills during Conflicts

All the skills previously reviewed are effective in not only deepening relationships, but also diffusing conflict situations. This implies that you have enough control of yourself to not respond defensively or aggressively. The same strategy is used by consumer relations specialists who are accustomed to dealing with complaints and angry customers.

Basically, don't take the bait that is offered—don't respond as you usually do. Instead, stay cool, calm, and collected, reflecting back what you hear the person saying. This is remarkably effective in cooling down tense, potentially explosive situations when the other person is infuriated and on the verge of losing further control.

Megan: "I can't believe you acted like such a slut."

Carole: "I can tell you're really angry with me right now." *Imagine the usual response that would take place: "I did NOT act like a slut. How dare you call me names!"*

Megan: *"You're right I'm upset! Who wouldn't be? You screwed me big time when you didn't support me when I needed it the most."*

Carole: "You're feeling disappointed that I didn't stand up for you the way you wanted." *Notice the careful way this is worded. The feeling of disappointment is acknowledged, but it is framed conditionally as "the way you wanted." Also picture how much more effective this response would be than the usual one: "What do you mean I didn't support you?*

I always support you. I'm sick and tired of it, too. It's exhausting trying to please you all the time. I've had enough."

"I" Messages

If reflective or active listening is designed to help someone else feel heard and understood, then it is also necessary at times to have effective ways that you can assert yourself and get your own needs met. If angry, aggressive behavior escalates rather than diminishes, then it is time to try something else. Regardless of the situation, you never have to suffer abuse in any form. This includes being subjected to screaming, swearing, verbal threats, racism, harassment, or disrespectful behavior.

Being assertive is *not* the same as being aggressive, which stomps on other people's rights and feelings. It involves standing up for yourself, yet doing so in a way that is both direct and sensitive.

The use of *"I" messages* involves "owning" the problem in such a way that you are clear about what you want and what you'd like to happen. People often make the mistake of using "you" rather than "I" when confronting an issue, with the regrettable result of a big misunderstanding.

For example, somebody cuts in front of you in line and you say to him, "What's *your* problem, buddy?" Of course, the person is now thinking to himself: "Hey, I don't have a problem. *You* do." And he's right. The problem is yours since you are the one unhappy with his behavior. A more genuine way to confront this breach of appropriate behavior would be to say: "Excuse me, but I have a problem with you cutting in line in front of me and others behind me." This may not necessarily lead to a resolution of the problem. Anyone who is rude enough to cut in line may not care much what you or anyone else thinks. On the other hand, this direct approach may force him to back down.

"I" messages are indicated during those times when you are unhappy with the way someone is behaving or something is proceeding. Such declarations may not necessarily lead to the situation changing, but they are at least more honest in owning the problem as yours.

▶ **VIEW IT**

© Cengage Learning

"I" Messages
This video demonstrates how someone involved in a conflict uses "I" messages while expressing the most important points in a way that "owns" his reactions and doesn't put the other person on the defensive. www.cengagebrain.com

Group Activity
After viewing the video, divide students into groups of three. Give students a list of "you" messages. One student in the small group will convert a "you" message into an "I" message, one student will be the designated listener, and one will evaluate the "I" message. Have the students switch roles after each "I" message is delivered.

Miriam:
Altering Expectations

" I guess I am learning the hard way that I expect a lot from other people—maybe too much. I get upset a lot because friends, they just—I don't know—they just don't seem to want the same things I do.

You want an example? Okay, so I'm always on time when I agree to be somewhere. I just think that's the polite, considerate thing to do. If we agree on a time to get together, say at 2:00 o'clock, then I will be there at five minutes to two. I am never late. Never, never. I just think that's important. So I always show up on time when we schedule a group meeting or if a friend and I make plans.

But it's been this huge problem for me because most of the people I know are late a lot. They show up five, ten, even twenty or more minutes late. And it drives me crazy. By the time they show up, I'm already upset. They can tell, I know, because they feel like they're always letting me down—which they are. So after a while I think it makes people not want to be around me because they think I'm so demanding all the time. I guess I am.

That's just one example, but there's more. It's just I'm learning that I've got to stop trying to make other people be like me. They resent the hell out of it. And soon I'm not going to have any friends left.

Jupiterimages

Some people are so abusive, violent, disrespectful, or socially inappropriate that they repeatedly behave in hurtful ways. You have the right *never* to be subjected to such behavior. If asserting yourself does not make a difference in setting limits, and if taking constructive action to confront the inappropriate behavior does not have an effect, then minimize damage by avoiding contact with that individual.

Be Careful What You Expect from Others

You are destined to become disappointed if you expect others to live up to your expectations. Remember that other people live by their own rules that don't necessarily jibe with your own. Not that you shouldn't hold high standards for those people you live and work with, but just don't be surprised when they don't or can't measure up. It is one thing to be selective and another to be unrealistic.

If others are consistently letting you down, or you get upset frequently with people who don't meet your standards, maybe it is time to examine your expectations. Conflicts often occur when two people have different agendas and desires for their interactions. Mutual interests must be negotiated.

Tit for Tat

Many years ago, researchers were conducting war games to make predictions about how to respond effectively to armed conflict or aggressive behavior by other nations. They set up computer programs to calculate the optimal responses to various scenarios, depending on who initiated an attack and what happened afterward.

Among the various solutions that were tested, the best strategy was called "tit for tat," in which (1) you start out trusting the other person (or nation), expecting to be treated fairly; (2) if you are betrayed in some way and discover that the other party is not trustworthy, don't make the same mistake again; and (3) you respond with swift, decisive action that matches the behavior of the other party.

What this research shows is that trusting other people is worthwhile, and even desirable. But once someone behaves in a hurtful manner, don't keep setting yourself up for continued mistreatment. This might not seem very profound, but you'd be amazed how often people allow themselves to be hurt over and over again. If people have already shown themselves to be untrustworthy, *then don't trust them.*

Walk Away

Simply leaving may seem like an obvious solution when dealing with someone who is out of control or abusive, but it is remarkably difficult for many people to do. As discussed elsewhere, you are entitled to be treated with respect and caring from everyone you deal with on a regular basis. If you have friends and acquaintances who treat you with less respect than you deserve, then "fire" them. Walk away from these relationships or, at the very least, minimize your contact with these individuals.

Some people won't change no matter what you—or anyone else—might do. The best you can hope for is to reduce your potential exposure to the damage they can do.

SUMMARY

Relationships are at the core of your college experience, for better or for worse. An extraordinary amount of your time will be spent thinking about relationships, as well as talking about them to others. This includes the best of times in romances, friendships, and constructive collaborations, and it includes the worst of times in destructive relationships that eat at your heart and soul.

Relationship skills can be improved with a little training and practice. These help you to become not only a better friend and lover, but also a better person. You can learn to become more compassionate and responsive to others, and yet also become more assertive in getting your needs met. One key is to be honest with yourself, and with others, as to your needs, expectations, and hopes.

QUESTIONS FOR REVIEW AND FURTHER EXPLORATION

1. Why are supportive relationships so critical to college success and satisfaction?

2. Why do you think that the number of quality friendships is diminishing when compared to past decades?

3. By what standard would you determine if a relationship is toxic and unhealthy? Since it is highly probably you are involved in such a relationship, how do you propose to get yourself out of it?

4. Why do people stay in destructive relationships even though they know they're so bad?

5. What are the most important things to remember when listening actively to someone?

6. Why are issues of power and control at the heart of most conflicts?

7. How is being assertive different than being aggressive?

ANSWERS TO FOR REFLECTION 11.1

In the following examples, decode the likely meaning of the message beyond what was spoken:

● A five-year-old child pointing at a big dog coming toward him on the street: "Mama, MAMA, does that doggy bite?"
  This really isn't a question at all but a statement of apprehension and fear.

● A friend rubbing his eyes and looking down, speaking in an uncharacteristically soft voice: "Yeah, she broke up with me. But I don't really care."
  He cares a lot but is uncomfortable admitting how much he is hurt.

● An instructor pacing back and forth across the room, gesturing dramatically: "This probably isn't very important, but I'd like to mention one other thing...."
  This is VERY important. Pay close attention to what I'm about to tell you.

Go to www.cengagebrain.com for an online quiz that will test your understanding of the chapter content.

Diversity and Appreciating Differences

KEY QUESTIONS

▶ How does diversity apply to cultural groups beyond race, religion, and ethnicity?

▶ How are people strongly identified with multiple cultural affiliations?

▶ What are the special challenges faced by minority students?

▶ How do prejudices develop and persist?

▶ What are the ways that you can expand your cultural horizons?

One stated purpose of attending college is to expand your vision and breadth of experience. You are deliberately introduced to a variety of disciplines and points of view that are intended to increase your knowledge, stretch your flexibility, and improve your ability to deal with a wide range of situations. To be educated means that you are far more worldly and wise.

Because much of the significant learning that takes place in college occurs *outside* the classroom—through friendships, informal conversations, social interactions, extracurricular activities, and relationships, it is crucial that you expand your interests and experiences as much as possible through the interactions you will have with those who are different from you.

Group Activity
Introduce this chapter by asking small groups to design their "perfect" college campus on a large poster board. Ask each group to do a show-and-tell with their picture for the entire class. Conduct a class discussion about the similarities and differences in the perfect college campuses while tying in this chapter's diversity topics.

Teaching Tip
Schedule a class visit to your campus's multicultural center to meet the staff and learn about programs and activities.

PHOTO: Reggie Casagrande/Jupiter Images

Misunderstandings about Cultural Affiliations

Many people associate cultural diversity with issues of race or ethnicity, yet the term actually applies to all kinds of ways that people are different. Cultural groups are defined by their shared beliefs, values, traditions, characteristics, and rituals. Although the most common categories are based on religious practices (Christian, Jewish, Muslim, Hindu, etc.), race (black, white, etc.), and ethnicity (Mexican American, American Indian, etc.), people express their cultural affiliations in dozens of other ways (see Table 12.1).

The idea that each person identifies with only one primary cultural group is a myth. The verb form of "to be" is often used for such descriptions, like "I *am* Vietnamese American," "He *is* Catholic," or "We *are* Marines." It is as if being a member of one group is the single, defining characteristic of who you are. While in some cases this might be true, most of us are made up of quite a few different cultural identities that compete for dominance, depending on the situation and who we are with.

Another misunderstanding related to this subject is that you can easily tell what someone's cultural identity is by appearance. You look at someone who is Asian or Latino or black and make assumptions about them based on what you see, the first of which is that they must identify primarily with their ethnic or racial features. But if the person is strongly religious, might that not trump ethnicity? What if the person

Group Activity
Write group identifiers, such as small town or big town, musical tastes, racial background, and the like, on large sheets of paper and post them around the room. Ask students to sign their names to the appropriate sheets. Discuss how these identifiers contribute to the class's diversity.

For Community College Students
Clans are sometimes prevalent at community colleges based on academic majors such as radiologic technology, fire science, law enforcement, surgical technology, medical assisting, and more. Mention this to students and solicit class feedback.

TABLE 12.1

Examples of Cultural Groups

▸ Race (black, white, Asian, Latino)
▸ Ethnicity (African American, Chinese)
▸ Country of origin (Mexico, Cuba, Chile)
▸ Language (Gaelic, Spanish)
▸ Gender
▸ Living situation (widowed, divorced with children)
▸ Sexual orientation
▸ Club (Harley Davidson, sorority, rave)
▸ Hobby (gun collecting, fantasy baseball)
▸ Physical characteristics (tattoos, blondes, short people)
▸ Physically challenged (hearing impaired, dwarfism, wheelchair-bound)
▸ Afflicted (HIV, multiple sclerosis)
▸ Socioeconomic class
▸ Profession (athlete, construction worker, police)
▸ Religion (Mormon, Orthodox Jewish, Southern Baptist)
▸ Church or temple affiliation
▸ Age (baby boomer, Gen-X, newly retired)
▸ Family lineage
▸ Clan (extended family, Marines, Peace Corps)
▸ Institution (university, boarding school)
▸ Geography (New Yorker, farming town, Texan, southern Californian)
▸ Victimization (incest survivor, Holocaust survivor)

ORNCHAI KITTIWONGSAKUL/AFP/Getty

All of us are made up of multiple cultural identities rather than just a single affiliation based on skin color, origin, or religious preference. If you were to ask the person in this photograph which culture he most strongly identifies with, would he say the Army unit to which he belongs, his race, his disability, his religion, the small town in the South that he is from, or the college he is currently attending? The answer is that you don't know. The same blending of different influences is also part of your dominant cultural identities, and those of most of the people you know.

is gay or lesbian? Don't you think that might have a potentially strong influence? Or what if the person is a Marine or a member of any other "tribal" group? You might find it interesting, for instance, that socioeconomic status is often a better predictor of a person's core values and interests than race or ethnicity. In other words, a black person from the upper middle class living in suburbia may have more in common with whites from the same social position than blacks from lower socioeconomic strata. Likewise, sexual orientation, physical disability, generational age, or affiliation with a group that was forged under battle conditions (Army, Peace Corps, athletic team, etc.) may easily become more important to someone rather than race, religion, or ethnicity.

You can walk around campus and see plenty of evidence of cultural affiliations. Students wear T-shirts and hats proclaiming identification and pride associated with their college. These feelings can develop so strongly that you can see evidence of this cultural identification among alumni who advertise their college on a bumper sticker or license plate. So, if you asked someone the question, "What *are* you?" you might very well get the answer, "I'm a [University of Iowa, Harvard, or University of Alabama] graduate." Cultural identities forged with colleges can become so strongly entrenched that they remain intact for life.

Expanding Your Cultural Wisdom

You may feel a tremendous temptation to hang out with your own kind, however you define that. This can mean spending time with only those of your race or religion, as well as those of your fraternity or sorority, neighborhood or dorm, major, or athletic team. The most natural instinct for human beings is to seek out and associate with others who are "like me" and avoid those who are perceived as "not like me." We are conditioned to mistrust those who are not of our "tribe" and who therefore pose a potential threat to our safety. Although such suspicions and *xenophobia* (fear of foreigners) once had a survival value, they are no longer useful in a society in which diversity is the rule rather than the exception. Most schools and colleges

Group Activity

Share diversity statistics from your institution's admissions office. Ask students to brainstorm ideas for ways to promote interaction between the various groups on campus.

Teaching Tip

Ask students to develop a *private* list of individuals in their classes who they think are "different," and identify why these people are "different." Ask students to proactively overcome their stereotypes by making contact with one of these individuals in class. Suggest that they try to learn more about this individual by listening to his or her story, interests, or problems. Have them reflect in their journals if this encounter had any impact on their previous perceptions of the individual.

12.1 FOR REFLECTION

Dominant Cultural Affiliations

Your particular values, interests, and priorities in life are strongly influenced by those cultures with which you identify most strongly. These are your "tribes," the people with whom you share the most interests and common values. Often this is based on skin color, but it could also include religion, hobbies, geographical origins, political convictions, sexual orientation, and many other groups mentioned in Table 12.1.

What are the cultural groups to which you feel the strongest ties?

Among those that you have identified, which one would you identify as the most dominant in terms of how it has shaped your interests and values?

When meeting someone new who you'd like to get to know better, what are some of the most important things for them to understand about you in terms of your cultural affiliations?

today have a student body speaking dozens if not hundreds of different languages. In some states like California, English is now the minority language in students' homes. Everyone comes from a different place, with a different background, creating a complex mix of groups sharing common interests and goals.

It is challenging to figure out ways to learn about various cultural groups, some of which may be difficult for an "outsider" to break into. Even if you are especially inquisitive, assertive, and highly motivated, how far you can go still has limits. The goal is not just to gain more information about different cultures, but also to identify those prejudices and biases that compromise your ability to feel empathy and compassion toward others who represent cultures very different from yours.

Challenges Faced by Minority Students

Minority status can be defined in several different ways, most obviously in statistical terms of being a member of a group that represents less than 50 percent of the population in a given setting such as a college campus. Indeed, on some college campuses Asian, Middle Eastern, Latino, or African American students are the majority and whites are the minority. Even whites can be marginalized in such places if they don't hold positions of power and influence or are subject to discrimination because of their skin color.

Although being the subject of prejudice or bias is undesirable in any situation, the term "minority student" usually applies to those members of ethnic, racial, and religious groups that have been subjected to injustices in the past. Let's explore more deeply the experiences of being a member of a minority group that has suffered greatly as a result of this status.

In almost all regions of the world, the group that is in power attempts to suppress the rights and privileges of those minority groups that have been pushed to the fringes of society. In addition, concerted attempts are made to hoard resources. This is actually the most natural human impulse to provide the best opportunities for one's own kin and exclude those who are not from your tribe. Throughout the world, history is littered with examples of different tribal groups engaged in feuds and conflicts that last through multiple generations: Union versus Confederacy, Bloods versus Crips, Hatfields versus McCoys, Sunnis versus Shia, Croatians versus Serbs, Hutu versus Tutsi, Turks versus Armenians. In the past half-century alone, there have been over thirty documented cases of systematic genocide in which one group of people attempted to wipe out another group. It is important to understand that while it may be natural to resent or mistrust other groups of people "not like you," the college experience is about learning greater acceptance and tolerance of differentness. This isn't just about bending to political correctness but rather preparing you to work cooperatively, respectfully, and sensitively with a wide range of people with whom you will likely come into contact throughout your life.

Jeremy Woodhouse/Jupiter Images

This journey toward embracing people who are from different cultural groups begins with a greater understanding of what *we all* are facing.

Behind Before They Begin

Studies of first-year minority students, especially those who are the first in their families to attend college, indicate that they are disadvantaged from the outset. They lack firsthand knowledge of what to expect on campus and therefore hold unrealistic visions. They are less prepared to negotiate the college system. They tend to work more hours and have more family responsibilities than those in the majority. As if that is not enough of a challenge, they also have poorer academic preparation and take longer to complete their degrees—meaning more financial burden and time commitment (Dennis, Phinney, and Chuateco, 2005). Only about 18 percent of African Americans and 10 percent of Latino students receive their baccalaureate degree before they are thirty years of age, compared to 33 percent for Caucasians (Cutolo and Rochford, 2007).

All colleges offer additional resources and support to minority students to aid in their adjustment to campus life. Whether such services are utilized or not, the most important thing to keep in mind is that success in college, as in life, is based on not just individual ability and motivation, but also the support network that you have created. Regardless of the personal challenges you face, they are a lot easier to manage when you realize you are not alone and that others struggle with similar issues.

If you do identify as a minority student on campus (in *any* dimension), it is critical that you are honest with yourself about the areas in which you feel most unprepared. This could be in *academic skills* such as doing research, using the Internet, writing papers, or reading assignments; in *interpersonal skills* such as speaking in public, expressing yourself, initiating relationships, or asserting yourself; in *personal skills* such as organizing your time, managing stress, working through conflicts, or taking care of yourself physically, emotionally, psychologically, and spiritually. Even more so than a student from the majority culture who may have had certain privileges and opportunities, it is absolutely critical that you learn the things that you need to

Since the beginnings of our species, humans have preferred to congregate with those of their own "tribe," mistrusting those who are "not like us." Yet the college campus has evolved into a place where traditional boundaries of race, religion, gender, and socioeconomic background are collapsed, or at least partially dissolved. Some of your most trusted friends and closest confidantes may very well come from backgrounds quite different from your own, especially if you remain open to learning about other cultures.

▶ VIEW IT

© Cengage Learning

Appreciating Differences
Students talk about their struggles to reconcile their family and cultural backgrounds with the new people they met on campus.
www.cengagebrain.com

12.2 FOR REFLECTION

Watch a Movie

Other than direct experience with representatives from different cultural groups, the next best option for expanding your exposure and perspective is to read novels and watch films that have strong cultural themes. Better yet is to watch the movies with friends or family so you can discuss them afterward, especially what thoughts or emotions were stirred up or what triggered new awareness of ignorance, biases, or prejudices that you hold. Below is a selected list of such films.

- *Black Robe*: A violent but powerful portrayal of how missionaries tried to convert the Huron Indians to their religion and values without anticipating the unintended consequences.

- *Hoop Dreams*: A documentary about the culture of inner-city youth who see playing professional basketball as the only way out of the ghetto.

- *Once Were Warriors*: A New Zealand film about life among urban Maoris, the indigenous people, and also about domestic violence.

- *Brokeback Mountain*: Academy Award–winning film about two cowboys struggling with their sexual identities.

- *Best in Show*: Satirical window into the culture of dog shows and the neurotic competition that takes place behind the scenes.

- *Borat: Cultural Learnings of America*: A simultaneously disturbing and hysterical look at the dark side of prejudices.

- *God Grew Tired of Us*: Tells the story of Sudanese refugees who come to America and struggle to make sense of the world we take for granted.

- *Crash*: Academy Award winner about the mistrust between people and the clash of cultures that so often lead to prejudice and racism.

- *Murderball*: A film about the culture of paraplegic men who play wheelchair rugby as a way to regain their sense of dignity.

- *Lost in Translation*: A look at Japanese culture (or any foreign culture) through the eyes of lost souls.

- *City of God*: A glimpse into the violent, chaotic world of street kids in the slums of Rio.

- *House of Sand and Fog*: Tells the story of an immigrant Iranian family that struggles with adjustment to their new culture in America.

- *Babel*: Takes place in four different countries, telling interconnected stories that are based on miscommunication.

- *In America*: An Irish immigrant family tries to survive and adjust in a strange new world, encountering experiences that are both joyful and tragic.

- *Thirteen*: Highlights the culture of a particular age group, in this case, that of young adolescent girls who are dangerously precocious.

- *Friday Night Lights*: This movie (not the TV show based on it) shows the culture of small-town football and what it means.

- *Hotel Rwanda*: Although this story happens to be about genocide in one African nation, it highlights the nature of oppression everywhere.

- *Slumdog Millionaire*: Academy Award–winning film about life in the slums of India.

- *The Kite Runner*: The story of two Afghan boys, each from a different caste, who try to forge a friendship in a culture that prohibits such affiliations.

- *District 9*: Aliens who come to earth are segregated in refugee camps—in South Africa, of all places, where apartheid once marginalized all minorities.

© Jeff Greenberg/Alamy

compete on an equal footing. This begins with being honest about what you don't know and then asking for help and support from those you trust.

I once had a colleague, a new faculty member in our department, who had recently completed his advanced degree to begin his academic career. He was African American and had grown up in a rural area of the South, the first in his family to ever graduate college. Even though he had excelled in his studies and completed a doctoral degree, he had managed to hide, disguise, and deny a number of basic skill deficiencies because he was so reluctant to ask anyone (especially a white person) for help.

We were collaborating on a research study together when I glanced at his computer screen and noticed that it was littered with hundreds of files practically covering the surface. When I asked him why he didn't organize his files into folders, he just shrugged and smiled, changing the subject. Once we shared more trust in our relationship, he confided that he didn't know how to use folders—or practically anything else related to his computer—but had been reluctant to ask anyone for help for fear they would realize how clueless he felt most of the time. Eventually he felt comfortable enough to come to me with many other questions that nobody had taken the time to explain to him, nor had he been willing to ask. Everyone needs a mentor, but a minority student (or professor!) most of all.

Prejudice and Racism

The graduation rate of African American students is significantly higher when they attend predominately black colleges. Such institutions educate approximately 80 percent of all black federal judges, physicians, army officers, and PhDs (Lucas, 1993).

With all the other challenges that must be navigated on campus, new immigrants, international students, and minority students must also deal with pressures to fit into the dominant culture while trying to hold on to their ethnic identities. It is precisely this diversity in a student body that makes a college campus so rich, yet provides complex challenges for everyone to get along and learn from one another.

Teaching Tip
Assign students to watch one of the movies listed and then write a paper describing their reaction to the movie, including what they learned from watching it. Alternatively, ask them to talk about their reactions in class.

12.3 FOR REFLECTION AND ACTION

Who Are Your Friends?

It isn't a coincidence that most people prefer to hang out with "their own kind," however that may be defined. While this often refers to race, religion, or ethnicity, it could also mean that your social group is composed of those who are from your high school, athletic team, fraternity or sorority, or club. How diverse is your friendship circle, including members who are from different religions, races, cultural backgrounds, sexual orientations, geographic regions, and socioeconomic backgrounds?

It should be a priority in the coming years for you to expand the range of your social contacts to include those from groups about which you are less familiar. What will you do to make this happen?

Teaching Tip
Share the percentage of first-generation college students on your campus. What are the challenges that first-generation students face?

Classroom Discussion
Open it up: Share (or write about) a time when you have been in the minority. How did it feel? How did you respond?

Among the reasons for the higher success rate than at predominately white institutions is that minority students don't feel so isolated.

What it means to be a minority in *any* situation (and surely you have felt that some time in your life) is being different from everyone else. Whereas "different" can sometimes be a good thing if it brings positive attention and status, most minority students don't find their status to be an enjoyable privilege. Many students report incidents of racism and prejudice that sparked intense feelings of fear, anger, and resentment. How easy is it to feel confident about your ability to succeed if you receive both direct and indirect messages that you are inferior?

Jay:
Experiencing Racism

"This white girl asked me if I wanted to hear a joke, so immediately I was on edge, 'cause nobody tells a good joke when they start like that. But maybe my Malcolm X radar was just on high that day and I was overreacting in my mind. Besides, if I said no then I would come off as a douche bag, and nobody wants to be that as a freshman.

My worst fears were confirmed when the girl's joke included the standard racism trifecta—black people, slavery, and drug dealers. Needless to say I was not delighted with the punch line, but offered a courtesy chuckle to save face. Some others were listening, and I noticed that they seemed uneasy as well. To this day, I don't know if they were genuinely offended or just waiting for me to unleash my rage on this poor girl. That's kind of funny when you think about it. I mean, because of a racist joke the rest of the group seemed to be waiting for me to react in a violent manner, thereby reinforcing their stereotypes and prejudices. You can't buy that kind of irony. To break the tension, she offered me the offensive language consolation prize by telling me her boyfriend was black. I shrugged it off and went to my room to think about a few things.

Why did this girl think she could tell me this joke? I mean she kind of asked for permission, but deep down I think we both knew I wasn't going to object. Was I some Uncle Tom, so caught up in this Ivory Tower that I would laugh at any nigger joke that came my way? The black community has an adage that if white people are not afraid of you, then you're not doing your job. Then, as weird as this sounds, I started thinking about black men in prominent positions—Barack Obama, Colin Powell, Thurgood Marshall, Clarence Thomas—and realized what it must be like for them to try and strive for some kind of excellence while listening to all their white colleagues. Yet somehow they persevered. I figure that I can do the same.

When You Are Subjected to Abuse, Aggression, or Anger

At one time or another, whether you are a member of an identified minority group or not, you have been the victim of some kind of abuse, aggression, or oppression. You know what it feels like to be subjected to discrimination because of something about yourself that is difficult, if not impossible, to control.

You must not remain passive and withdrawn in the face of aggressive or abusive behavior; even if you can't change the other person's behavior, it is within your power to change your reactions to it. After all, stress results from feelings of helplessness, so you need to take some kind of self-protective action.

- Don't ignore the problem and "turn the other cheek," as this is often taken as a signal to continue the abuse, if not toward you then toward others.

- Asking for an apology may be futile since chronic bullies feel little remorse or guilt.

- Assert yourself in a firm manner, announcing that you will no longer tolerate such behavior and stating the consequences.

- Rather than blaming or attacking back, state clearly what you want and need in the future.

- If you can't approach the abuser on your own for fear of retribution, then bring someone for support to act as a mediator.

- Get support from the women's center, the dean of student affairs, or other offices on campus that have the role of protecting student rights.

- Take detailed notes of exactly how your rights were compromised, where and when it happened, and who else was present.

- If this was not the first time that you have been a victim, seek counseling to explore what you can do in the future to prevent more incidences.

Aggression, anger, abuse, and hostility continue because the perpetrators are permitted to continue their behavior. Whether you are a victim of such behavior, or a witness to it, the only way it will stop is if you and others take a stand against injustice, abuse, and aggression (see For Reducing Stress).

Loss of Cultural Identity

To fit into the majority culture, minority students are often required to abandon their own heritage. They are expected to speak like everyone else, dress like everyone else, and behave like the majority, or they risk ostracism. This *acculturation process* involves reconciling one's own background with that of the dominant culture, often producing conflict and tremendous stress (Paukert et al., 2006). As just one example, students from *collectivist cultures*, those that emphasize interdependence and family responsibility, stand in marked contrast to the kind of independence, autonomy, and self-centeredness that are part of the American majority culture. Thus, students from Latino or Asian families (depending on their level of acculturation) may experience confusion and anxiety trying to come to terms with expectations in college versus those they deal with at home. Native American students try hard to preserve what little remains of their heritage, yet realize that their ability to gain jobs and success in society at large depends on their ability to dress, talk, and act like whites. Women also can feel they must sacrifice their cultural upbringing as nurturers and caregivers if they expect to succeed in traditionally male-dominated professions like business, law, science, and medicine.

Charles: Black—but Not Like Me

" My first Black Student Association meeting was an experience I will never forget. I came from a small town in West Texas with only a handful of black people. To make matters worse, that minority of blacks was generally relegated to the poor side of town, affectionately known as "the Southside." Needless to say, when I arrived at a university with a Black Student Association I was giddy. I was ready to be around my people, people who knew what it felt like to be black like me.

After some introductions we were supposed to mix with one another, and I started to learn that these people came from a different world than I did. I was at this elite college because I played basketball, but the rest of these kids had money—and lots of it. They charged their tuition on Visa or American Express. Meanwhile, here I was, no doubt the only kid on an athletic scholarship, mingling with these "aristoblacks." Besides the obvious wealth disparity, I listened in utter disbelief as this group of kids talked about their respective private schools from back East. They all had their class rings and jackets with various crescents proclaiming their stature. Meanwhile, here I was, a kid born and raised on public school education and government-assisted lunches since kindergarten.

I realized that none of these people in the Black Student Association knew what it was like to be me at all. None of them knew what it was like to pawn jewelry to get money to pay a light bill. None of them had friends named Smurf, Pudgy, and Chico—guys who were more likely to be in the local police blotter than in *Who's Who*. That was my last meeting with the Black Student Association.

I went back to my dorm room that night and hung out with my roommates who were white, but from more modest beginnings like me. As we talked, I realized that despite color I was much more like these guys than most of the BSA members. We were a melting pot of diverse interests, backgrounds, and talents from all over the country. Over the years, I formed friendships with those guys that remain to this very day. I cannot say for certain that would not have happened with members in the BSA—I mean, they were genuinely nice people. But I am happy with my choice and my relationships with my lifelong friends.

Homophobia

Among various minority groups, students who are gay, lesbian, and transgendered may suffer the worst of all. Not only are they subject to discrimination, prejudice, and hate crimes from the majority population, but they can suffer as minorities within minority groups that are intolerant of homosexuals.

Gays are subject to constant slurs, including using the term "gay" in the most derogatory way imaginable. What is one of the worst things you can call a guy who you think is behaving "less than manly"? The answer is "gay," "queer," or "faggot."

"Homophobia" refers to extreme hatred and fear of the gay and lesbian lifestyle. This "reaction formation" is a kind of defense mechanism in which you overreact to something or someone, way out of proportion to reality, because it triggers something in you that you fear. The biggest homophobes are often those who worry the most about their own masculine or feminine identity.

Sexual identity is not an all-or-nothing phenomenon but more reflective of a continuum of attraction to both genders. Although true *bisexuality* is actually rare—that is, equal sexual attraction to both men and women—all of us feel at least a mild degree of attraction to those of our same gender, even if it is only an admiration for another's inner or physical beauty.

Dave: " When I first started college, I decided that maybe it was time to live more in the
Hating Myself   open. I was excited that I could finally come out of the closet and that the world would
embrace me with open arms. At least that's what happens in the movies. Some people tried
to be supportive, but I could tell that I was their token gay friend. I wanted to reach out, but
I didn't want people who didn't know I was gay to know I was gay. Try figuring that riddle. I
was left feeling more alone and more disconnected than I did when I was living in the closet.
A part of me hated the fact that I was gay. I was ashamed and believed the worst about
myself. I was a sinner, molester, sodomite, effeminate sissy—a faggot. I hated myself and
who I was. Do you know how hard it is to live with that?

If you find yourself feeling a strong aversion—not just discomfort or mild distaste
for something that is different from your experience—you might examine what this is
all about for you. The reaction could come from religious beliefs that lead you to make
judgments about one group of people who act in ways that you find unacceptable. You
could be influenced by values ingrained from your family upbringing. Regardless of
the origins of your beliefs, you are entitled to make whatever choices you want related
to your own sexual preferences. Homosexuality, however, should not be considered a
"preference." Overwhelming evidence indicates that sexual orientation is genetically
determined, just like left-handedness. Condemning someone because of their inherited characteristics is just like what happened in World War II, when Jews and other
non-Aryans were systematically exterminated.

Hate Crimes

Approximately 1 million students are the victims of prejudice-driven abuse, slurs,
or physical assaults each year. Literally every day, almost every hour, a hate crime
is reported on a college campus in which a minority student is subjected to vicious
intimidation and violence. In a representative inventory of such incidents during one year, the Southern Poverty Law Center (2001) mentioned the following
examples:

- Two gay students, one black and the other white, were walking across campus at
  the University of Kentucky when they were assaulted and beaten by ten white men.

- At one of the State University of New York (SUNY) campuses, an Asian American
  student suffered a fractured skull when he was beaten by three other students.

- At another SUNY campus, twenty-one Arab students left campus after they were
  repeatedly subjected to harassment and assaults.

- A black student at Brown University was beaten by three other students after being
  told she didn't belong there and was only a "quota."

- A white head resident at the University of Mississippi had his door burned down
  and rocks thrown through his windows with notes attached threatening his life
  and calling him a "godforsaken nigger-lover."

- A student from the Congo ran for student body president at the University of Alabama, only to find his posters had been defaced with messages warning that he
  would be hung from a tree.

Marc:
Victim of Oppression

" I was in this political science class when the subject of gay marriage came up as an issue. At the time, I was coming to terms with my sexuality—"out" in some places, where I felt safe, and "in" in others, where I felt insecure. One of my fellow classmates stood up, moved to the front of the class, and gave a soapbox speech essentially talking about how despicable and disgusting gays were and that they shouldn't have any rights at all. I could feel my stomach churning. A surge of energy was rushing to my ears—are they noticing my reaction? Will they soon come to know my secret? Will I get beaten up in the parking lot, or will my professor grade my papers harder than my colleagues'? I was scared, mad, and fragmented in a way that literally felt debilitating.

At the class break, a student asked me to sign a petition banning gay marriage. I declined, and in that moment I found a part of my voice—at least enough of it to feel my pride hadn't completely dissolved away. He went on to ask me if I was a faggot. Hatred can be so intimidating. I knew he already knew—I had the laugh of a faggot and the strut of a queen. It wasn't a matter of being genuinely interested if I was a faggot or not. He wanted me to feel like the hunted—powerless, less than human, afraid, hopeless. As I searched for an answer to his question I realized, again, what it feels like to be seen as less than human.

I suppose you're wondering how I answered my classmate's question. I lied.

- Forty instructors with Latino surnames at California State University, Los Angeles were sent e-mails that read, "I hate your race and want you to die."

- A neo-Nazi group held a rally on campus at the University of Connecticut.

- At Olivet College, 90 percent of all the African American students left the school because of repeated harassment and racial violence.

Neo-Nazi and Holocaust denier groups regularly pay for inserts in campus newspapers and send e-mails to students recruiting them to join their efforts. Fraternities at several colleges have organized "slave auctions" as fundraisers, worn Ku Klux Klan robes at costume parties, or burned crosses on their campuses. The victims of these insensitive acts and hate crimes are not just those directly subjected to the abuse, but also every member of the group being targeted. It is difficult to concentrate, study, and perform well in classes when you feel such hostility and fear for your safety.

Hate crimes and oppression of minorities can only take place if members of the campus community tolerate behavior that stems from a combination of ignorance, irrational fear, and intolerance. You can take action in several ways (Willoughby, 2004):

- **Your voice and actions matter.** Rather than standing by as a silent witness to racial or otherwise biased slurs, you can intervene to stop such behavior, as well as report it to authorities. Apathy and indifference are often interpreted as acceptance of the status quo.

- **Support the victims of abuse.** Communicate your caring and compassion for their plight. Offer your help and ask what you can do.

- **Teach acceptance of differences and practice what you preach.** Live your life as a model of acceptance of others who are different. When you become aware of areas in which you are ignorant or misinformed, take that as a valuable lesson to promote further growth.

12.4 FOR REFLECTION

Lingering Effects of Oppression

Think of a time in which you experienced some form of oppression or marginalization because of your personal or cultural characteristics.

_____

_____

_____

Recall how that felt for you, as well as the ways this experience has since influenced and affected you.

_____

_____

_____

What are the difficulties you have faced since that experience whenever you've met someone who resembles your oppressor?

_____

_____

_____

Confronting Prejudices and Stereotypes

- Blondes are dumb.
- Jocks are stupid.
- Asians are good at math.
- Professors are absentminded.
- Blacks have large penises.
- Californians have breast implants.
- Jews are good with money.
- Irish people have bad tempers.
- Computer science majors are nerds.
- Native Americans are drunks.
- Muslims are terrorists.
- Gays are swishy, and lesbians are butch.
- Lawyers are scum suckers.

Group Activity
Arrange students in groups to discuss answers to this exercise.

For Community College Students
Conduct a discussion about community college stereotypes: Where do people get them? What can be done about them?

A stereotype is a perception that people who are similar in one regard (race, religion, ethnicity, etc.) also share other characteristics. These groupings of traits can be either positive or negative. You might assume someone is lazy or smart based on his membership in a group. Stereotypes are developed around any possible way that people are categorized, but are most common around status ("Freshmen are lost and clueless"), race ("Japanese take photos of everything"), religion ("Mormons only want to convert you"), gender ("All that men want is sex"), age ("Old people are only worried about saving money"), professions ("Politicians can't be trusted"), and even places ("There's nothing to do here").

Many stereotypes have a basis, or at least a beginning, in personal experience (usually secondhand), and hold a semblance of accuracy with some people, in some situations, some of the time. Many Muslim students, for example, suffered horribly because of assumptions made by others that anyone who resembled a terrorist in the media must be dangerous. While it is true that a few groups of terrorists are Muslim, instigators of violence exist in every race and color, such as Latino and black terrorists (gang members) and white terrorists (Ku Klux Klan).

Stereotypes represent overgeneralizations based on a limited amount of data, which is bad science and poorly predicts accurate outcomes. Such typing of individuals developed for use in situations where you had to make an instant judgment about whether you were facing a friend or foe. Based on appearance, behavior, speech, and other signs, you made a quick assessment whether to hold out an open hand or make a fist. The remnants of this strong survival tendency still remain—it's almost impossible to stop yourself from seeing someone and forming an instant opinion of what she is like based on her accent, clothes, haircut, or gestures.

The main problem with stereotypes, besides the tendency to view people inaccurately, is that they are so resistant to change. Once you have formed a strong opinion about what a group of people are supposedly like, you will look for ways to reconfirm your bias time after time, no matter how an individual of that group behaves. You tend to ignore examples of behavior that are exceptions to your established rule and notice only those instances when your prejudices are reinforced.

Classroom Discussion

Open it up: Describe a time when a stereotype you held was different from reality. How did this affect the way you felt about the group of people you had previously stereotyped?

Experiencing Other Cultures

To succeed in today's increasingly diverse world, you must be able to work (and play) well with others, regardless of their background. This isn't something you can fake by pretending that you like everyone and hold no biases or prejudices. You are more transparent than you think. People who have already been subjected to discrimination are often extraordinarily sensitive at reading others who may pose a threat or danger. They are looking carefully for any cues that might give away latent or hidden prejudice.

Becoming more culturally competent is a consequence of attending college, in which you are required to interact with people who come from very different places in life. As already mentioned, the first step involves increasing your awareness of personal biases and prejudices you hold, and working to combat them as much as possible through exposure to new cultural situations. Through attending classes and socializing with people who are dissimilar from you, new friendships and alliances are formed that cross racial, religious, and cultural boundaries. Incidental contact will increase your knowledge about other cultural traditions, but the most direct and lasting way to do so is through immersion experiences.

Knowing that permanent change takes place only through active learning, the best way to explore different cultures is to immerse yourself into them, not as an observer but as a participant. It isn't necessary to spend a semester abroad or even travel to a foreign country to increase your knowledge of other cultures. You will do that vicariously through the books you read, the films you watch, and the interactions you have with others. However, I have had students investigate the cultures of

Vietnamese, Persian, Hindu, Mexican, and other immigrants by making links to these communities, attending their religious and social functions, and participating in their feasts, rituals, and traditions. Students have also taken advantage of opportunities in college to explore other cultures that they found interesting but never had the chance to examine closely.

One student who was a passionate antiwar advocate decided to "join" the Army for a few weeks, training with them, participating in ROTC activities, and talking to recruits about their goals and aspirations. Another student who was uncomfortable around gays had the courage to confront his apprehensions by spending time in gay and lesbian bars and attending rallies and social functions. Another student spent several nights in a homeless shelter to learn about the experiences of children living on the street. Another student felt ignorant about Jewish culture, so she made plans with several others to attend religious services and participate in holiday festivities. In each case, the goal was to learn about a culture from the inside.

During the coming years you will have many opportunities to learn more about the traditions of hundreds of cultures different from your own, if you take the initiative to show interest and curiosity to those who can guide you. It doesn't matter who you choose because the skills of exploring a culture, *any* culture, are basically the same:

1. **Do your homework**. Before you visit a new place, prepare for your visit by familiarizing yourself with the traditions, rituals, history, customs, and behaviors that you will encounter. You will have no chance of being accepted if you make a complete fool of yourself because you don't have some rudimentary knowledge.

2. **You have to open your heart and mind to what you will encounter**. Almost by definition, people in other cultures do things differently than what you are used to. They may drive on a different side of the road. They may have foods and styles of dress that are unusual for you. They may have unique speech patterns. They may value certain things that do not appeal to you. Rather than judging this behavior as "weird," consider their alternatives as interesting.

3. **Don't just observe the culture from the outside; join it**. To truly get a taste of what life is like in other places, do your best to fit in as much as possible. As long as you are seen as an outsider, you will not be trusted or treated as anything other than a stranger. So often when people travel to other places, they revert to those habits that are most familiar. You see tour buses full of people who stay with their own kind, eat their own foods, and stay at places that are exact re-creations of homogenized hotel and restaurant chains back home.

4. **Be inquisitive**. Most people enjoy talking about where they live and what they do. Watch any college sporting event on television, and you see students who are fiercely proud of living in Florida, Nebraska, Iowa, Utah, Idaho, Connecticut, or anywhere else. Whether the place is in the mountains or the plains, north or south, east or west, the people who live there think of it as their own slice of heaven. Spend time talking to people about why they love where they are (or why they don't). Ask what is unique about the place. Learn as much as you can about their traditions and history.

5. **Pay attention**. Notice everything around you—the sights, sounds, and smells. Being in a new environment heightens all your sensations. So many things look unusual. If you doubt this, think of a time a visitor came to where you live and how often he or she remarked about things you take for granted and hardly notice at all.

6. **Get lost**. Some of the best things happen when you wander off the beaten track. I interviewed hundreds of people for a research project about travel experiences that changed their lives forever. More often than not, these powerful experiences occurred during times when people were lost, literally and figuratively. It is when they missed the tour bus, meandered into a strange neighborhood, and became separated from their friends that the most growth and learning occurred.

Group Activity
Present a ten- to fifteen-minute shock lesson in another language. (Do this yourself, or ask someone else to give this lesson.) Choose a simple topic, such as U.S. geography or simple nutrition information. Conduct the whole lesson in a foreign language, including questions to the students. After the lesson, ask students for their reaction to the feeling of not understanding what is being said.

The best way to become more culturally sensitive and aware is to travel to foreign lands where the traditions and rituals are different from what you are used to. This can even happen in your own country in any environment that is novel. Travel experiences give you the opportunity to look not only at different parts of the world, but also at yourself in new ways. This is especially the case when you wander off the beaten track and immerse yourself in the new culture.

© Heide Benser/Corbis

Respect and Civility

One of the best potential outcomes of college is breaking down cultural barriers that pervade many aspects of life. So many conflicts, wars, gang rivalries, political disputes, and territorial battles are about not just competition for resources and economic rewards, but also intolerance for differences.

Most colleges try to instill within the student body, as well as among staff, an atmosphere of civility. This policy is not intended to restrict freedom of expression, but rather to guide interactions in the direction of mutual respect and collaboration. The world already has enough violence, abuse, and domination, so each of us can do our part to promote greater cooperation.

I don't mean to sound like a Pollyanna or naïve about inevitable disputes and disagreements that take place within any human arena. It is highly likely that you will find yourself in conflict with others now and in the future, just as you have in the past. But you can engage with these individuals and still maintain your own dignity and integrity, standing up for your own rights without needlessly hurting others.

SUMMARY

Employers are looking for graduates with not only academic, technical, and professional skills, but also the ability and track record of being able to get along with the most diverse groups of people possible. The more experience you can gain interacting with others who are different from you, the better prepared you are to function optimally in a diverse world.

The first step in this journey is being honest in confronting your own biases and prejudices, and working to overcome them by getting outside the groups that are most comfortable for you.

QUESTIONS FOR REVIEW AND FURTHER EXPLORATION

1. Why do people generally prefer to hang out with others whom they perceive as their "own kind"?

2. Based on discussions in the chapter, why do you suppose conflict and war are so universal across cultures?

3. Why is "losing" one's cultural identity a potential problem? Isn't it a good thing to fit in with the majority culture?

4. How are stereotypes formed and maintained?

5. What does it mean that the best way to learn about a foreign culture is to "lose" yourself in it?

6. What are some cultural groups (broadly defined) that you have an interest in exploring further?

Go to www.cengagebrain.com for an online quiz that will test your understanding of the chapter content.

Planning for the Future

KEY QUESTIONS

▸ Why must you prepare for not just one profession, but also multiple career paths that may unfold in the future?

▸ Why is a declared major less important than most people think?

▸ Which jobs will have the highest demand in the next decade or two?

▸ Which jobs will have the least growth and opportunities?

▸ What are the factors that most contribute to job satisfaction?

▸ Why are mentors so important in developing career choices and opportunities?

▸ How do attitudes toward work become so important in career satisfaction?

▸ What are the skills that will be important to you in *any* career you pursue?

▸ Why aren't motivation and commitment enough to make changes last?

▸ How do you plan for setbacks and relapses that will inevitably occur?

▸ Why is it important to be able to generalize or transfer new skills to other situations?

You aren't just planning for one future, but for multiple lives. In all likelihood, you will move through a number of different careers during your working life. As technology changes, as your interests evolve, as you develop new skills and gain experience, and as opportunities come your way and others close down, you will change jobs a half-dozen or more times. That means that even if you think you know what you want to do now, you can be certain this will change over time.

My career history is certainly diverse and checkered, but hardly that unusual. When I was a first-year student I had no idea the twists and turns my life would take, all the different jobs I would work, and all the experiences I would have. Although I hadn't planned it as such, I am so grateful that I had a truly "liberal" education that covered so much ground, preparing me for everything I wanted to do as a writer, teacher, administrator, consultant, and psychologist.

You would be wise to plan your college curriculum so that you prepare not only for a single job, but also for a lifetime of different careers. The truth is that you really have no idea what you'll be doing twenty, ten, or even five years from now.

PHOTO: BananaStock/Jupiter Images

13.1 FOR REFLECTION

Plans Change

One of the biggest challenges about making a plan for the future is overcoming the feeling that this is a commitment that you have to stick with, no matter what. During the era of your grandparents, it was common to choose a trade for a lifetime. Yet in today's (and the future's) rapidly changing world, it isn't unusual that people change careers three or more times during their working lives.

When you were a kid, what did you want to be when you grew up?

_____

_____

In high school, your career aspirations likely changed as you became aware of more options (other than a professional athlete, an actor, or what your parents do). You also became more realistic about your abilities and interests. What did you want to become in high school?

_____

_____

What is your current best prediction of what you want to do with your life?

_____

_____

It is ten years in the future. What are you doing now with your life? Even if the future is cloudy, take a wild guess about what you might be doing.

_____

_____

Considerations When Planning Your Future

College students hold a number of misunderstandings and misperceptions about career preparation. These can lead to misguided choices about how you can best prepare yourself for a lifetime of productive and satisfying work.

Your Major Is Less Important Than You Think

Choosing your major can be associated with so much stress. It is the one question that you are asked most frequently by family members and others who you first meet: "Oh, you're in college. What's your major?" It is as if your answer will unlock the secrets of your soul.

Although some undergraduate majors do prepare you for specific jobs (nursing, journalism, engineering, education), many are designed to provide you with a basic education that allows you to go in many different directions. Even among those who do choose career-tracked majors, many end up in jobs only tangentially related to their initial training. Nursing graduates may find themselves doing quality assurance assessments for a health care organization. Engineers may end up in business or public policy. Journalism majors could find themselves working in advertising or marketing. Education students could very well teach for a few years and then move on to something else. In the job market you are likely to face, it is critical that you have some solid skills that can be adapted and transferred to a variety of settings and career options.

So take a deep breath. Relax. Pick a major, *any* major for now, since you don't have to declare it officially for a few years (although exceptions are fields like engineering, education, pre-med, nursing, etc.). Make up something that sounds good to those who ask. Meanwhile, give yourself some space to do the kind of rummaging around you need to eliminate some choices and consider others.

A College Degree Will Not Guarantee You a Job

You know more than a few college graduates who are working as taxi drivers, waiters or waitresses, security guards, or clerks in retail stores. These jobs are fine, but they may not be the careers that these folks imagined when they invested their time and money in an education. Many of these individuals may have actually *chosen* these jobs over other opportunities and find them fulfilling, but many others feel stuck in dead-end jobs and have abandoned hope of pursuing their dreams.

Because wealth and income (above minimal levels) are not good predictors of life satisfaction and happiness, it is important that you find meaningful and productive work that is enjoyable and where you feel like you are making a difference. This can be defined in a number of different ways, depending on your values, interests, and personality.

For Community College Students

Community college requires a student to decide from the outset if he or she wants to transfer. Discuss the differences between associate of arts (AA) degrees, associate of applied science (AAS) degrees, and other types of certifications in your state which may require a student to make very early choices regarding future plans.

Courtesy of Jeffrey Kottler

Having a solid grade point average and good recommendations is certainly important in finding a good job upon graduation, but not nearly enough. Employers and graduate schools look for applicants who have far more than a good academic background, including previous work experience (internships, volunteer service), research experience, and a record of serving in leadership roles. Even in your first year, you can start networking and making contacts that will provide opportunities for you to develop such experiences.

You can do many things to increase the probability that your college education will provide not only enlightenment but also marketable skills for finding a satisfying job once you graduate. For one thing, concentrate on getting as much practical experience (field studies, internships, and volunteering) as you can to build your résumé, make valuable contacts, and supplement classroom learning with work in the field. Second, research areas of interest to explore which careers are likely to grow in the future (see Table 13.1). Finally, finding worthwhile employment is based on not only *what* you know but also *who* you know: make as many contacts as you can during college with your instructors, as well as prospective employers who might be in a position to help you.

Your Degree Is Based on Where You Complete Your Studies

Whether you attend a community college or four-year institution, at some point you may wish to transfer to another school. Many students attend a local college for their first two years to save money, then move to another university that will confer the final degree. More than half of all college graduates have attended more than one institution (Schoenberg, 2005).

Although it is challenging to go to a new place and learn your way around all over again, some students elect to make this choice because (1) the current college doesn't offer a concentration they are most interested in, (2) they want to pursue more advanced studies beyond what the previous college offered, (3) the new institution may be more prestigious and the degree more marketable, (4) they want to move further away from home to create more freedom and independence, or (5) they are just unhappy and unsatisfied where they are.

The application process for transferring to another institution usually takes place after you've completed your first year, so you want to make sure that you give your current college a fair chance before you abandon ship altogether. Although it is indeed challenging to begin the adjustment process once again, many students consider the inconvenience worth it to obtain a marketable degree. After you graduate, nobody will ever ask you where you attended for your first two years, only where your degree was conferred.

If you are planning from the outset to transfer to another college, make sure you take courses that will satisfy the requirements at any other institution. An advisor can help you to choose those classes carefully to ensure that all your credits transfer.

Is There More Education in Your Future?

You've got your hands full right now just surviving your first year, but it is never too early to think about how far you want to go in your education. Many of the technical and specialized professions (law, medicine, business, research, public health, academia, etc.) require an advanced degree to secure viable employment. In many other cases, students elect to continue their education later in life to retrain for a different career.

The Global Economy and Job Market Are Ever-Changing

Pity those people who used to work as switchboard operators or phone receptionists, now replaced by voice-activated services. What about elevator attendants who used to open and close the doors, or milkmen who used to deliver dairy products to the door, or projectionists who used to run the movie machines? All gone. Vanished. Kaput. Just think: What jobs are people training for today that will become obsolete, or at least changed beyond recognition, in the coming years?

Zack:
Finding a Place in the World

"I had it all. I was making good money from commissions, working hard, schmoozing clients, driving a nice car. I was, like, just a few years out of college and I had made it big time. Yet I was spending every penny I was making on clothes and crap. I still don't know where all the money went. And I was miserable, to tell you the truth. It just felt like—I don't know—that I wasn't really doing anything that mattered. I was good at my job, and that part felt good, but really, who cares if they bought what I was selling or from some other competitor?

My friends thought I was crazy that I quit and went back to school to be a teacher. And I have to tell you, there are days now when the kids drive me crazy, or when I get frustrated because of all the stuff going on in schools these days. But all in all, I love what I do even though I'm paid half what I used to make. It's all about finding a place for yourself in the world—and I found mine."

Several trends can help you make some reasonable predictions about which jobs will be in greatest demand by the time you graduate (Nemko, 2007). You have probably noticed that our health care system is considerably stretched beyond reasonable limits and changes are on the way, creating more jobs for health care professionals like doctors, nurses, and medical technicians, but also health systems analysts. Similar changes are under way with regard to environmental studies and global warming, creating new jobs for those in the renewable energy field. Increased globalization will create a huge demand for bilingual professionals in a variety of fields, especially those who can speak Chinese, Japanese, and Spanish. Then, of course, technological innovations will continue to create demand for those who have expertise with computers. Another prediction is that by the year 2019, close to half of all employees will be independent contractors, yet you will be expected to work collaboratively with others across the globe (Fisher, 2009). Other jobs with a strong future are listed in Table 13.1.

TABLE 13.1

Jobs with a Future

According to predictions made by the U.S. Department of Labor, here are some careers with the highest demand potential:

▶ Pharmacy

▶ Gerontology (working with the elderly)

▶ Software design and computer programming

▶ Data communication analysis

▶ Medical and health professions

▶ Dental hygiene

▶ Teaching (all levels)

▶ Environmental engineering

▶ Customer service

▶ Recreation and hospitality

▶ Real estate

▶ Public service

▶ Armed services (Army, Navy, Air Force, Marines, and Coast Guard)

▶ Technical consulting

▶ Biotechnology and nanotechnology

▶ Skilled trades (carpentry, plumbing, electrician, etc.)

▶ Hospitality

▶ Entertainment and creative enterprises

▶ Law (specifically entertainment, patent, real estate, and technology)

▶ Product development

Photo by Lambert/Getty Images

For the past 600 years, ever since Johan Gutenberg invented the printing press, skilled tradesmen who could set type had stable employment and an unlimited job market. Family businesses flourished for generations. Then, within a matter of a decade, advances in computer technology wiped out the industry, making mechanical typesetting completely obsolete. The whole printing industry is now in jeopardy, with more publications and marketing campaigns going online. What jobs today will vanish in the next decade or two?

Much of What You Will Learn in College May Be Obsolete within a Decade

Facts and theories that were popular a few years ago are being constantly updated and revised in light of new research. My most distressing example of this comes from the folklore of my childhood, when the prevailing parenting theory was that you could absolutely not go in the water after eating or you would die a most horrible death from stomach cramps. All moms had a precise formula for calculating exactly how long we had to wait before we could go swimming on a hot summer day. This has since been refuted, and now divers are required to eat before going in the water to prevent hypothermia.

Education is not about learning information that remains constant but rather learning strategies for teaching yourself whatever you will need in the future. Although Tables 13.1 and 13.2 list jobs with the brightest and dimmest futures, there will always be a market for someone who is well trained and experienced in any field, including fields that are expected to have reduced demand (like agriculture, ranching, etc.). In all sectors, information technology, problem-solving and communication skills, and especially knowing how to work well with others will serve you well regardless of your chosen field and the obsolescence of any specific knowledge (Altman, 2009).

You Won't Be the Same Person Ten Years from Now

You will have different interests and goals. You may have someone in your life whose priorities will have to be negotiated with your priorities. Whatever you now believe

> ### TABLE 13.2
>
> ### Jobs with Limited Prospects for the Future
>
> ▶ Farming
> ▶ Ranching
> ▶ Fishing
> ▶ Forestry
> ▶ Mining
> ▶ Secretarial (except legal, medical, and executive)
> ▶ Manufacturing
> ▶ Telemarketing (good news, huh?)

is most important, whatever tastes and interests you hold, will likely evolve. What brings you satisfaction today could easily become substituted by other preferences. Your age, life experience, relationships, opportunities, transitions, crises, disappointments, failures, accomplishments, and successes will all shape you into someone you would not likely recognize looking ahead a decade or two.

The changes we go through often occur so incrementally and gradually that we hardly notice them taking place. Yet look at photos of yourself from several years ago, talk to someone who hasn't seen you in a long while, or read journal entries you wrote in the past, and you'll get some measure of how you have grown and developed in new ways.

Anything you think you want to do now, any career you prepare for today, is based on who you are and what you value this minute. Your college education and curricular choices should be well rounded and broad so you can better prepare yourself for different paths you may take in the future, some of which are currently beyond your imagination.

Work Is Important, but Not Everything

You aren't just searching for a career, but a lifestyle. Some people *become* their jobs and they love every minute of it. They work fifty, sixty, seventy, or more hours per week but don't think twice about it because they so enjoy what they are doing (and sometimes don't have other diversions or interests). Other people are content to work twenty hours per week or less, at least for paid employment, and figure out ways to reduce their expenses so they can pursue other priorities that might include leisure—intellectual, creative, or athletic pursuits—or, more often, full-time parenting. More and more often, men are choosing "careers" as full-time parents that were only acceptable for women a generation ago.

Certain careers can be all-consuming, and are pressure filled and deadline driven. Others move at a slower pace that can be largely dictated by the individual doing the work. Think of the difference between a tax attorney working for a big firm during the weeks before the filing deadline versus an attorney in a small practice who works a forty-hour week doing wills and real estate transactions. Software designers and publishing editors may put in long, exhausting hours in company headquarters, working under constant pressure—and then some work at home and telecommute. Think about the difference between a physician who works a thirty-two-hour week for a clinic versus one who logs over sixty hours doing intricate surgery. Or, for that matter, think of the difference in lifestyle between a professional chauffeur who works for an agency versus someone who drives a solo cab.

Balance is what you need to consider. Finding a career you love is wonderful, but so is having time to enjoy your life with those you care most about.

© Cengage Learning

It Is Normal to Be Confused
Students talk about their confusion related to the choices they make for the future. www.cengagebrain.com

Begin Your Career Planning Now

Although you don't want to prematurely declare a major when you have just begun the college journey, it is never too early to begin checking out available resources and exploring options.

Teaching Tip
Invite a staff member from your campus's career services office to give an overview of the services it offers.

Do an Honest Self-Assessment (or Have One Done for You)

People end up in careers based on a variety of factors, some related to opportunities that arose, some due to random events, and others resulting from deliberate choices. If you want to choose a vocation rather than fall into one, it is important to have some idea of where you stand in a number of areas.

Mike Kemp/Jupiter Images

The reality is that many people don't like their jobs and live for their time away from work ("Thank God it's Friday!"). What would it take for you to find a line of work that not only pays the bills but also feeds your heart and soul?

Group Activity

Place six "career personality type" signs in different areas of the room. Tell the students they are at a party. Which personality type would they instinctively be drawn to? What group of people would they most enjoy for the longest time? Ask students to move to that corner. Ask one student in each group why he or she was drawn there. Then ask students to pick their second preference and move to that corner, and then ask one student in each group why he or she was drawn there. Discuss the entire activity after all are seated.

The first area to assess deals with your *interests*. What is it that you like, and perhaps have always liked, to do? Enjoying your work is difficult if you don't feel a strong affinity for what you do, one that can be sustained for many years. You can take tests at the career center that can help you clarify which jobs may appeal to you most and least.

A second related area is your *values*. While it is important that you like what you're doing, your tendency to remain invested in it over the long haul is related to whether it has special meaning to you.

It is all well and good that you may have a strong interest in a career and value the work, but neither of those qualifications will be very helpful if you have no particular talent in that area. You might like the idea of being a surgeon, but that won't work out very well for you (or your patients) if you have poor eyesight or eye–hand coordination. Being an engineer might appeal to you, but that isn't nearly enough if you have trouble with math and science. You might love to become an actor or musician, but the long-term prospects are poor if you have no dramatic or musical talent. Ditto with being a professional basketball player if you can't shoot, pass, and dribble. Motivation and interest are hardly enough when a certain set of *abilities* is required. If you're not sure what you're good at, or have potential to develop, college will help you to figure that out.

In addition to interests, values, abilities, certain *personality styles* are better suited to particular professions. Imagine someone who is creative and artistic but ends up working as an actuary (an insurance statistician), or someone who loves working with numbers more than people but ends up in social work.

According to one model (Holland, 1997), six basic personality types are compatible with certain careers. While it is rare that someone fits in only one category, you'll note in Figure 13.1 how some personality types are connected by shared characteristics while others appear to be polar opposites.

Realistic types enjoy mechanical, outdoor, or physical activities. They prefer working with things rather than people. They tend to be more comfortable working with their hands and tools rather than their minds, and enjoy constructing things. They tend to be very practical. Examples include construction contractors, engineers, and environmental scientists.

Figure 13.1 Career Personality Types

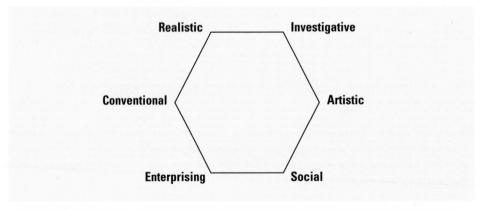

FOR REFLECTION AND ACTION

Ask People What They Think You'd Be Good At

You have surely been given plenty of advice already by family and friends, but now might be a good time to take a fresh look at how you are perceived by others. Ask ten people who know you in various contexts to describe what they picture you doing after graduation. Select some people who don't know you well at all, as well as others who know you intimately. You'll hear a cross-section of possibilities—some of which you may not have considered and others you may find quite disagreeable. No matter. The important thing is to get feedback from others in ways you might not have engaged with before.

Conventional types like predictability and control in their work. They prefer security and dependability over risk and adventure. They are efficient, responsible, and well organized. They often end up in middle-management positions, accounting, statistics, computer programming, banking, finance, and other careers in which they can control their environments.

Enterprising types fit the mold of the prototypical salesperson or business executive— persuasive, energetic, enthusiastic, assertive, and influential. They are ambitious and driven toward success, demonstrating leadership in several areas.

Social types are just like what you might think. They are people-oriented and gravitate toward jobs that allow them to interact with others on a regular basis (like teaching, counseling, and mediation). They like working in groups and as part of a team rather than on their own. They tend to have strong interpersonal skills and are good at expressing themselves.

Artistic types are found in creative professions such as art, drama, writing, music, and design. They tend to be more intuitive and abstract in their thinking rather than concrete and practical as are conventional and realistic types.

Investigative types are inquisitive, above all else. They want to make sense of things and solve complex problems. This fits the typical image of the scientist. Such individuals thrive on investigating new phenomena, predicting outcomes, and doing research. This category also fits police detectives or systems analysts.

You probably will not fit neatly into only one personality type, but you may immediately recognize that you share traits with a few of them. Likewise, you can eliminate some of the types as completely incompatible with your own style. You can take tests at the career center that can help you learn more about how your personality and interests fit best with certain vocations.

Talk to People about What They Do and How They Feel about It

Most people don't like their work as much when they have been doing it for ten years or longer. They become bored or feel trapped in their jobs. They look forward to weekends and talk about what they will do on their vacations or what they did during their last holiday. Wouldn't it be wonderful to absolutely love what you do for your career, to look forward to going to work every day?

Find people who love what they do and interview them about how they managed to locate themselves in such situations (see For Reflection 13.3). It is not that any particular job is the perfect match; it is more a matter of how you approach the work. This satisfaction depends on several factors that you can control such as finding a good match for your interests and abilities, the attitude you bring to the experience, and investing the hard work and energy it takes to walk away from a job that doesn't excite you and find (or retrain) for something more suitable.

13.3 FOR REFLECTION AND ACTION

People Who Love Their Work

Search out individuals in a broad range of fields, professions, and walks of life. Include not only those who work in white-collar jobs, but also those who work at every level of the economic ladder. Your interviewees should meet one major criterion: They must *love* what they do and show visible signs of this satisfaction. These people are passionate and take pride in their work. Regardless of whether they work in an office building, forest, shipyard, factory, restaurant, store, home office, car, truck, or wherever else, they are enthusiastic and excited about what they do and feel it is both meaningful and productive.

Ask these individuals how they ended up getting into their jobs and how they get enjoyment from what they do. At the heart of this investigation, you will discover that it is not just their line of work but their approach to work that matters most.

Love What You're Doing or Do Something Else

In a book called *Working*, Studs Terkel interviewed thousands of people about what they do for a living and how they feel about it. One of the most memorable conversations for me was the story of two brothers who both worked as paperboys in their neighborhood (Terkel, 1985, p. 161). The older brother, Terry, hates his job in every way possible:

> I don't see where people get all this bull about the kid who's gonna be president and being a newsboy made a president out of him. It taught him how to handle his money and this bull. You know what it did? It taught him how to hate the people in his route. And the printers. And dogs.

Terry's younger brother, Cliff, has the *exact same job*. He covers the same neighborhood, gets up every day at the same time as his brother, and has the same responsibilities. This is his view of his work:

> It's fun throwing papers. Sometimes you get it on the roof. But I never did that. You throw the paper off your bicycle and it lands someplace in the bushes. It'll hit part of the wall and it'll go booooongg! That's pretty fun, because I like to see it go booooongg!

So, what's the difference between two people who have the same work but feel so differently about it? The answer, of course, is their attitudes. You already learned about how important internal thinking is for perceptions of experience, and this is another example of that. Regardless of what they do, some people love what they do, some hate it, and some are roughly in the middle. This is true regardless of the job. Imagine whatever you think is the best job in the world (actor, judge, successful musician or artist, professional athlete, wealthy entrepreneur, research scientist, forest ranger, or FBI agent) and, guess what? Even some of these people wish they were doing something else. Imagine, as well, what you consider the worst job in your community; yet some people really enjoy that work. So the job itself does not intrinsically provide joy and satisfaction; as mentioned earlier, it is the way you approach it that counts most. By the way, the same thing is true for every class you take in college.

13.4 FOR REFLECTION

Rank Your Work Values

For each of the following career characteristics, rank them 1–16 in their order of importance to you. This will force you to choose what is most and least critical in a job since you can't have them all.

_____ High salary

_____ Good benefits (health insurance, retirement, etc.)

_____ Plenty of time off for vacations and long weekends

_____ Opportunities for advancement

_____ Variety of tasks

_____ Flexible hours

_____ Lots of responsibility

_____ Power and authority

_____ Status, prestige, and respect

_____ Physical activity

_____ Creative opportunities

_____ Supportive and caring supervisor

_____ Friendly cowokers

_____ Job security

_____ Independence and freedom

_____ Minimum of pressure

Depending on how you've ranked these work values, what are some examples of careers that are most likely to offer your top five priorities?

Explore Your Interests More Deeply

What is truly most important to you? Jobs that have some features versus others represent a trade-off. If you want to make a lot of money, then you may have to take risks that would not be required for a job where the premium is on security. If you like working alone, independently, and without direct supervision, then you will sacrifice other things like social interactions and a sense of community. If helping other people and making a difference in the world is important to you, then you will make other personal sacrifices not asked of those in business and industry. Each career offers its own distinct advantages and disadvantages. The most important question is "What matters to *you*?"

Classroom Discussion

Open it up: What are your two top work values and why did you chose them? Which jobs fit those values?

Create Multiple Options

Because you never know where you'll end up or how the job market will shift, plan for several different career paths in the future. If one choice doesn't pan out, you won't panic if you already have alternatives that are just as attractive. Here are a few things to keep in mind.

1. Regardless of your specific interests, certain skills will be valuable to you in any future career. These include familiarity and competence with any and all technology, as well as the willingness to learn upgrades that take place continually. If you are technophobic and avoid machines, software, and computers whenever possible, take on the challenge of redefining yourself in this area. Every field, from music composition and screenwriting to architecture and education, now demands a degree of technical expertise. Learn as much as you can about the major software programs.

Classroom Discussion

Open it up: Where do you work now, or where have you worked before? How are (or were) computers used in that workplace?

2. Another skill mentioned repeatedly is the ability to get along with a wide range of people. Extend your social comfort zone as much as possible. Spend time with classmates and others whose backgrounds are the most different from your own.

3. Read everything you can and everything you have time for—fiction, nonfiction, newspapers, magazines, and anything you can find that educates you about fields or subjects that are foreign to you. The goal is not to learn everything but to become comfortable with the process of researching and reading whenever you discover gaping holes in your knowledge.

4. Irrespective of the career you choose, you are still going to need to learn some business sense, how to write and speak well, how to get along with others in a productive and professional manner, and so on. That is why it is so important to diversify your class planning, making certain you take courses in a broad range of fields that might someday serve you well.

Check Out Resources on Campus

Visit the career center, the office that is devoted to helping you plan job options for the future. It has computer-assisted interest inventories and aptitude tests that can provide information about how your preferences compare to people who are successful in their chosen professions.

In addition to providing assessment services, the career center can help you develop a portfolio that includes your résumé, letters of reference, and other supporting documents that will be required by prospective employers. The staff can also help you with your job search, schedule appointments for potential jobs, and provide feedback on ways to best present yourself during interviews.

Although most of these services will become far more important as you approach graduation, it is a great idea to familiarize yourself with the career center so that you can make the best use of it when you are ready.

Make Time to Volunteer

Personal experience has no substitute. No matter how good a job sounds, the only way to find out whether you like it is to try it for yourself. Close to one-third of all college students volunteer their time each year to help others, a 20 percent increase over just three years ago.

As mentioned in Chapter 2 about service-learning opportunities, you can gain work experience in lots of ways and find out more about what you enjoy and what you'd prefer to avoid. Even if you can't find paid employment or don't have time for a part-time job, you can still volunteer a few hours each week to gain experience and broaden your perspective (see Table 13.3). If you are feeling more ambitious and motivated, the service-learning office on campus can help you arrange a more intensive experience during your spring or summer break. Organizations such as Volunteers for Peace, Orphanage Outreach, Cross Cultural Solutions, the International Volunteer Programs Association, WorldTeach, and Global Volunteers all specialize in helping college students find suitable matches.

I often take groups of students to developing countries to volunteer, working with neglected children in remote areas. One such project that we started in Nepal (www .EmpowerNepaliGirls.org) supports young girls in school who would otherwise be sold into slavery. I am fascinated not only by the power of caring and compassion to help marginalized children have a better future, but also by how students' lives are utterly transformed through their volunteer efforts.

For Community College Students

Smaller community colleges may not have a specific career center; possibly one member of the staff or faculty is also an academic advisor. Make sure students know where help is offered.

Teaching Tip

Ask students to reflect on the information given in the chapter and from other sources for identifying and narrowing down career options. Ask students to visit with current and past professors or high school teachers. During these visits, students should discuss their short list of career options and seek these trusted professionals' perceptions on the match of this career to the individual and his or her past academic performance.

Teaching Tip

Ask students to search the college newspaper or other media outlets for volunteer opportunities. Each student should decide which of these opportunities would best fit with his or her interests and future career. Encourage students to volunteer in one of these identified areas.

For Community College Students

Many community colleges do not have the resources to offer a service-learning office. Instead, students can seek out campus clubs with humanitarian missions and look to community groups in which to do service-learning projects for résumé enhancement and/or academic credit in partnership with a professor.

Courtesy of Jeffrey Kottler

If you make the effort, you can volunteer to help address problems of poverty, oppression, and neglect in unlimited ways. Pictured here is Ali (see "Ali: Volunteering Took My Breath Away"), a student who raised scholarship money for children in Nepal to attend school and then visited the villages to work with the children.

In considering such opportunities, make sure you find a cause or organization that is dear to your heart, one that you can feel passionate about. Otherwise, with all the other commitments and obligations on your plate, you will find it hard to sustain your effort. Pick something that is not only a good match for your skills and interests, but also a cause in which you will learn new things and develop new areas of expertise (make sure you won't be doing only busy work). Finally, make sure you are realistic in terms of how much time you can commit to this project. Be realistic with the organization—and yourself.

Classroom Discussion
Open it up: Which of you have served as volunteers? Where have you volunteered? How has that volunteering experience contributed to your life?

Ali:
Volunteering Took My Breath Away

❝ After being home for a while, there has not been one day that I haven't thought about our work in Nepal. It seems that everything I experience and learn now is different because the experience is always in the back of my mind. I feel like I know something more, like I'm in on a secret. Now, it is only a memory. I have so many mixed emotions about that. Some of the time I cry just thinking about it, because when I was there I felt more alive than I had ever felt before, and it's tough to not have that light anymore. Other times I smile and experience an overwhelming feeling of happiness. I could not be more grateful for the moments that I had, for the things that took my breath away, and for the people that I met. I experienced the secret, and that was enough for me to never forget. When I experience these emotions I think about my future. I either become very excited to go out and experience these things again in a new way, or I become upset because I don't believe I will have the chance to do so. What I am certain of for my life right now in this moment is that I have gone through something extremely special. My mind has been opened so big that it can never go back to the way it was.

My spirit has been so enriched by what I've seen, by the people I've met, by the things I've done. My heart sees clearly what I need to do next and I'm inspired to do what I can. Each smile from a child has been a blessing for me, a reward that will last a lifetime.

Teaching Tip
Assign students to research volunteer opportunities in the city where your college is located or in their home communities, including the requirements for the positions and the contact people.

> **TABLE 13.3**
>
> ## Organizations That Are Always Looking for Volunteers
>
> | | |
> |---|---|
> | ▶ Big Brothers, Big Sisters | ▶ Public schools (tutoring) |
> | ▶ Salvation Army | ▶ Prisons |
> | ▶ American Red Cross | ▶ Museums |
> | ▶ National Park Service | ▶ Homeless shelters |
> | ▶ Day care centers | ▶ Crisis centers |
> | ▶ Homes for the elderly | ▶ Battered women's shelters |

Start Networking

Like everything else in life, it is not just *what* you know that matters but also *who* you know. The friends you are making now, the associations you develop with your peers, and the connections with faculty and staff can pay off for you in the future. Many of your peers will end up in positions of leadership and influence. As an extreme example of this, note how often presidents of the United States end up hiring friends they made in college. The people you trust the most are those who have been most loyal over time.

Making Changes Last

This is it: the end of our journey. But it is really just the beginning. What do you do with what you've learned?

If this is like so many other classes you've taken, you just sell the book, throw away your notes, and move on to the next semester and set of challenges. You did what was asked of you, completed the assignments, and passed the tests, and now it is time to face the next set of tasks.

Yet, you were promised that this class was going to be like no other because you would learn things that would be immeasurably valuable for the rest of your life, not just for flourishing in college. However, most of the information and ideas are not going to stick with you very long *unless* you remain committed to practicing the skills on a regular basis and applying them in ways that are meaningful for you. Forgetting everything might be just fine with you for subjects you hope never to face again, but surely you can see that the majority of these chapters had material that will be extremely useful in the future.

Let's pretend (and this *is* an assumption) that you really want to retain a lot of what has been presented in this class. What would you have to do to make that happen?

Teaching Tip
Invite a few students who have already taken this course to visit the class and talk about information and ideas they learned that they are still using.

Realize That Motivation Is Not Enough

Feeling strongly committed to a course of action is certainly important, but such resolve often is not enough to sustain you. This is especially true when you get distracted, feel lazy, or lapse back into old, familiar patterns. People set themselves up for failure because they tell themselves that *this time* things are going to be different, naïvely believing that commitment is all it takes. If this were the case, just imagine how easy it would be to just say what it is you want and then, voilà, it appears before your very eyes.

Let Go of Expectations

All this discussion about planning for the future can create a lot of anxiety if you have no idea what you want to do (which most students don't). Think of dreams you or others have about your future. Whether you are completely "undeclared" or firmly convinced you've already found your calling, give yourself permission to let go of expectations that you and others have for your future, and explore as many different options as you can.

What options have you never let yourself consider because others might disapprove?

_____

_____

What things have you thought about but never talked about to others for fear of how they'd react?

_____

_____

What plans would you like to explore but seem unrealistic or beyond your current means?

_____

_____

If you were going to begin from scratch in your plans, what are new options you would explore?

_____

_____

What if your current weaknesses were strengthened and you developed new skills and abilities that are not currently within your repertoire? What would you do that does not now seem realistic?

_____

_____

If you were a different gender or culture, what are some opportunities you'd pursue that you aren't currently considering?

_____

_____

In spite of intentions and the best-laid plans, most students end up in a very different place than they ever imagined when they graduate college. When you surrender (even briefly) your previously held expectations, you may be surprised to discover what other possibilities might open up for you.

Most things worth doing in life are really, really hard. What makes them so challenging is that it takes a commitment every day, sometimes a dozen times each day, to keep the momentum going. You can say that it would be nice to change something about your life, and truly believe it in the moment, but will you also consider this a priority almost every waking moment thereafter?

Be Brutally Honest about What Is Working and What Is Not

You'll remember from an earlier chapter about how people get stuck because they keep doing the same things over and over even though overwhelming evidence tells them it isn't working. If you've tried strategies before to solidify gains you've made but they haven't served you well, it's time to abandon them and try something new.

This might seem logical, but it is very difficult to stop people from repeating the same mistakes. They get out of one destructive relationship and then enter another one exactly like it. They say they're going to stop drinking and partying so much, but then keep hanging out with the same friends who they know are a bad influence. They say they're going to the lounge to study, knowing full well they will see friends who will distract them.

You need to figure out for yourself what it is that you are doing (or not doing) that isn't producing what you say you want most. You probably know the answer but have been reluctant to change. The key question to ask, which you also learned earlier, is what payoffs are you enjoying as result of remaining stuck?

Plan for Setbacks and Relapses

It is an absolute certainty that at some time in the future you will lose some part of what you've gained. This doesn't have to be any kind of major problem—*if* you've planned for this ahead of time.

Trent had been trying for some time to get his head more into his classes and studying. He was finding this especially challenging because he had made some new friends whom he really liked to spend time with. Whenever they'd stop by or call, he'd have trouble declining their invitations to do things with them, even when he had to study for a test or complete an assignment. Since they were new friendships, he didn't want to disappoint them. Besides, he was having more fun than he'd ever had in his life.

Trent realized that if he didn't take constructive steps he'd be in real trouble with his grades, particularly since he was already on the cusp of screwing up. He had decided (with the highest level of motivation) that he would set aside three nights each week that were untouchable, three evenings designated for studying and reading no matter what else came up. He negotiated this with his advisor who had become concerned about his marginal performance.

So far so good: Trent stuck by his rule and was staying in his room to study on those three nights as he had agreed. His worst nightmare didn't occur (that his new friends would dump him or stop calling), however, they persisted even more. They'd even tease him about being so studious, sometimes with genuine ridicule.

Darrel:
When Setting Goals Doesn't Work

"I've been trying to give up coffee because it makes me all jittery and anxious. I'm already anxious enough on my own, thank you very much. So, as a New Year's resolution I decided the coffee needed to go. The problem is that I'm so used to having coffee all the time that I totally crash anytime I don't. Everyone bugs me now because I can't quit coffee. They tell me it's not healthy—at least drinking six big cups a day—and they tell me I'm not gonna be able to do well in my classes if I keep this up. I guess they notice I'm all hyper and stuff. Whatever.

I have a hard time sticking to my goals anyway. To be honest, I often don't finish things I start. I always pick these goals that are just way over my head. I know it sounds stupid, but I think that giving up caffeine is way over my head right now, and I just can't do it. At least while I'm in school, I can't do it. Is this an excuse? I don't know and I don't care. How am I supposed to study for my midterms and finish all my papers without caffeine to help me? I just don't know how people do it.

Sami Sarkis/Jupiter Images

If you ride on roads long enough, eventually you're going to take a fall. Regardless of the injury (often to your pride), mistakes or misjudgments don't have to be a big deal if you've planned for them ahead of time. The biggest obstacle to maintaining life changes occurs when people allow a single lapse to spiral out of control. Professional cyclists actually practice falling, even if it means losing some skin, so they can learn how to recover quickly, get back on the bike, and finish the race.

Trent feared giving into the pressure, making an exception to his new study rules that would cause him to fall back into his old pattern. He believed that if he gave in one time and went out on a night that had been set aside for studying, that it would be the beginning of the end. Trent's assumption was not unreasonable because this is exactly how people fall off the wagon, so to speak. They experience one lapse and then abandon all control.

Trent decided it was time to test his resolve and actually plan for a time in the future when he might be tempted to give in to some special situation. When his friends called him on a Wednesday night (one of his sacred days) to tease him because an amazing party was in progress and it was too bad he couldn't go—ha ha ha—he surprised them by agreeing to come along. Of everything he had accomplished so far, this was the hardest thing he'd done. He could feel his control slipping and feared that the rest would collapse after this "violation."

Fortunately, Trent deliberately planned for such a deviation from his plan by making an agreement with himself that if he went out on a Wednesday night set aside for studying, he would trade off for it by spending the following Friday or Saturday night at home no matter what else was going on. This flexibility helped him to maintain his resolve in the future since it allowed him to make an exception and yet still maintain his balance.

Reframing Failure

Failure is a state of mind more than circumstances. What one person considers a failure, another perceives as a learning experience. Failures present valuable lessons for those who are willing to pay attention to what worked and what apparently did not.

Meredith approaches a guy she likes and asks him a question about an upcoming test. He appears to blow her off, saying he can't talk and has to leave. Is this a failure on her part? Indeed, that is what she starts to think inside her head: "I just knew he'd do that! This always happens to me. I'm just not hot enough for guys like him. I don't know why I even try anymore."

Do you recognize the symptoms of irrational thinking, including exaggerations, distortions, and overgeneralizations? Meredith didn't fail—she just made an attempt that didn't work out as she had planned.

Classroom Discussion

Open it up: What suggestions do you have for Darrel as he tries to give up coffee? Have you ever tried to set a goal like this one? How successful were you?

Teaching Tip

Ask students to reflect in a journal entry on a past failure. Ask them to examine the reasons for the failure. What important lessons did they learn from it? How do they plan to use this gained knowledge to enhance future success? (Based on an exercise from Skip Downing's On Course Workshop.)

Confront Secondary Gains of Self-Defeating Behavior

It's time to test what you learned in previous chapters. What might be the payoffs for someone whose changes don't last even though he says they are important?

_____

_____

_____

_____

_____

Possible answers are listed at the end of this chapter.

So what does this mean? Whatever she wants it to mean. If she chooses to see this as a stunning and humiliating failure, the change she had started to initiate of becoming more assertive and less shy will not persist; she'll quickly give up and lapse back into the way she used to be.

Yet Meredith can view this encounter in other ways. The guy's behavior may not have anything to do with her in the first place—maybe he is even more shy than she is and was intimidated by her assertiveness. Maybe he is so nervous about the test he doesn't want to talk about it. Maybe he really was busy with something important and had to rush off, regardless of any possible interest he might have had in her. Or maybe he just plain didn't like her. So what? She can choose how to think about that as well, reflecting on her approach and perhaps making adjustments with the next guy.

The important part for Meredith is that she not allow herself to become discouraged because one or more situations don't work out as planned. Now, if she gets shut down repeatedly, then it would be time to seriously rethink her strategy, style, and manner. No matter how difficult and painful the process, it is absolutely crucial to her getting what she wants.

Surround Yourself with Positive Influences

Being your best is all about who you spend time with. These are the people who help shape your values and influence your behavior. To maintain the progress you've made during this semester, to learn from your mistakes and miscalculations, to improve your performance, and to increase your effectiveness, you must have support for your efforts. You just can't do it all alone, and even if you could, you must learn how to work well with others and share responsibilities and resources.

This book has emphasized the importance of various support groups to your efforts. This goes double if your goal is to hold on to the skills and strategies for the rest of your life, much less by the time you return for the next semester. People are inclined to do whatever others around them are doing. If your friends exercise regularly and study diligently every day, more than likely you will exercise and study as well. If the people you hang out with drink and get high every day, you are more likely to follow in their stumbling footsteps.

The semester is coming to an end, but learning is ongoing throughout your life, especially if you make such efforts habitual and a part of who you are. The last thing you might think you need right now is more homework and assignments, but as any class comes to an end, you have one piece of unfinished business that you should pursue. Before saying goodbye to your instructor, ask for a list of favorite books that have been most influential to him or her, or those that he or she believes you might enjoy the most. You aren't expected to read all of them over semester or summer break, but get in the habit of asking wise people for recommendations that you can grow with later.

© Photofusion Picture Library/Alamy

Many campuses offer counseling and advising services for free or at minimal cost. They provide you with a safe, confidential, and private place to talk about your innermost struggles, fears, and apprehensions, and to work through feelings that seem overwhelming. Often you will notice positive results within just a few sessions.

Seek Counseling

How do you know when you need help from a professional? Everyone needs help at times and could benefit from counseling. It doesn't necessarily mean that you have an emotional disorder but just that you could profit from talking to someone who is safe and objective, and can put your best interests first. Even when talking to your closest friends, you have to wonder if they are telling you what they really want rather than what you want. Also, friends don't often keep secrets as well as you would like.

Counseling is most often sought by those having a problem that they can't work out for themselves as quickly as they'd like. It feels good to have someone in your corner who can help you sort things out, offer honest feedback, and challenge you to explore new areas.

I have been in counseling a half-dozen times in my life for various concerns. The first time happened when I was in college and absolutely devastated about the breakup of a relationship. I felt totally abandoned and alone, and could barely get out of bed. I started skipping classes. I began to question my future. Clearly I wasn't thinking straight. Yet as desperate as I felt, I still wouldn't have gone to the counseling center unless a friend reminded me that it was an option. I had all but given up.

I don't remember much of what we talked about in those sessions because this first time was so long ago. But I remember she was a good listener. I got a kick out of telling her things just to see if I could get a rise out of her (I never could). I ended up seeing her for the rest of that academic year, moving on from my breakup to discussions about my dysfunctional family, my parents' divorce, and my uncertainty about what I wanted to do with my life. It is more than a little interesting that I was so impressed and inspired by what this counselor did for me that I decided counseling was what I wanted to do with my life as well.

Your problems don't need to be nearly as severe as mine (I was so depressed I could barely function) to seek counseling. If you start to feel overwhelmed or out of control, if you are having trouble dealing with things on your own, or if you just want an objective perspective on your situation, I would strongly urge you to try it.

Like any professionals, some counselors are good and others are not so good. You can tell the difference primarily based on feeling you can trust the person, sensing that he or she understands you, and, most importantly, seeing some improvement. Contrary to what you might have heard, counseling does not need to take a long time; often less than a half-dozen sessions is enough to make a difference.

The best place to begin your search for a competent counselor or therapist is the counseling center on campus. If they don't have adequate staff, they can refer you to someone in the community who specializes in seeing students for reduced fees. Depending on your health benefits, part or all of the sessions may be covered by insurance. Even if this is not the case, most practitioners have a sliding scale based on ability to pay. When you consider how much you spend for entertainment in a week, paying about the same to get your head and heart in shape isn't much at all. On many college campuses, counseling is free for a certain number of sessions.

Counselors and therapists have a number of different qualifications. Whether the professional is a social worker, psychologist, counselor, or psychiatrist is less important than how comfortable you feel with that person and how capable he or she seems. Unless you require medication (which is not often recommended as a first choice), any of these professionals would be fine.

To get the most from your counseling sessions, don't worry about how you tell your story—just jump right in. You'd be amazed how the important material comes out no matter how you begin or what you choose to share. The quality of experience depends on how honest you are and how much you share; the counselor can only work with what you provide.

Build Social Support

One of the most effective ways to calm down from stress is intimate contact with people you trust and feel comfortable around (Gold, 2007). When you are in the presence of soft voices, smiles, and familiar faces, your heart rate and breathing slow down, and your sympathetic nervous system cools off. According to a neuroscientist who has measured these changes, what the body craves most when you are upset is a familiar, predictable, and safe environment, in which you are surrounded by those you care for (Porges, 2006). This has been supported by other studies that examined the adjustment of first-year students, finding that stress is significantly diminished for those who have developed social support from friends (Friedlander et al., 2007). Interestingly, this does not apply to family during this critical year because one developmental task of beginning college students is to separate from older relatives.

Group Activity

As a wrap-up for the semester, give groups a set of markers and large paper or poster board. Ask them to draw a student *before* this class and a student *now*. Have groups share their before-and-afters with the class.

Your campus offers many kinds of support groups—through student affairs, disabled student services, the women's center, various clubs and organizations, as well as the counseling center. Not only do they provide great opportunities to meet people, but they also give you a chance to learn how others cope with challenges. In addition, you won't feel so alone knowing that others are struggling with similar issues.

Courtesy of Jeffrey Kottler

Most campuses offer support groups focused on particular themes. They can be offered by student services, the counseling center, the women's center, multicultural affairs, residence life, or other offices. They can deal with the general topic of personal growth or have a specific focus on test anxiety, study skills, addiction recovery, relationship issues, assertiveness, trauma, sexual abuse, grief and loss, depression, stress management, chronic diseases, and learning disabilities—almost any problem you can imagine. The best groups are led by professionally trained leaders, although self-help groups can also be helpful.

By participating in a group, you gain the advantage of learning from others who share similar concerns and thus not feel so alone. Groups can be especially powerful and transformative because of the opportunities to practice new skills and receive feedback from others. A few disadvantages might occur to you as well—confidentiality is more difficult to enforce, you get less time to talk about your own issues, and it might be more easy to become hurt if the leaders are not well trained.

Group Activity
As an alternative wrap-up assignment, give individual students pipe cleaners or Play-Doh and ask them to symbolically represent their experiences this semester, both in this class and in others. Then discuss in groups.

SUMMARY

Preparing for the future means giving yourself permission to enjoy fantasies of how you'd most like to spend your time and what you'd like to accomplish in your lifetime. Unfortunately, many people are unhappy or dissatisfied in their jobs but feel stuck doing the same things, counting the years until retirement. You not only deserve better, but also can make such dreams a reality—if you educate yourself for maximum options and continue to remain flexible as new opportunities arise.

Even in challenging economic times, most college students remain highly optimistic about the future. Close to 80 percent believe that they—or anyone—can succeed if they work and try hard enough (*Chronicle of Higher Education*, 2008). Indeed, in a study of what leads to the kind of extraordinary success that puts someone at the top of their field, it isn't so much intelligence or ability that matters as dedicated practice and persistence (Gladwell, 2008).

You have likely learned more during the past few months than during any other time in your life. I am speaking not only about intellectual and academic gains, but also about challenges you have faced and obstacles you have overcome. Multiply these effects tenfold in the coming years and you will have some idea of how much you will learn and how far you will grow.

Yet trials and tribulations lie ahead. There will be periods of doubt, times of disillusionment and encouragement, and feelings of frustration—perhaps even despair. These are part of the journey, no extra charge. You will be tested in ways that you can't predict and grow in directions that you can't anticipate. You will also experience unprecedented stimulation in so many areas of your intellectual, emotional, interpersonal, spiritual, and physical development—*if* you remain open to these experiences.

QUESTIONS FOR REVIEW AND FURTHER EXPLORATION

1. What changes are likely to occur that make it crucial to prepare for a variety of careers throughout a lifetime?

2. Which jobs today will become obsolete twenty years from now?

3. What can you do to begin your career planning right now?

4. What factors are most important when considering a good match between a person and a satisfying career?

5. Why do the things you learn not stick for very long?

6. How do you see yourself as different from the person who began this semester? What are some ways that you have already changed?

7. Looking back on this semester, what are the main messages that you predict will stick with you over time?

ANSWERS TO FOR REDUCING STRESS: CONFRONT SECONDARY GAINS OF SELF-DEFEATING BEHAVIOR

Possible payoffs for someone whose life changes don't last even though he says they are important include:

- You return to what is familiar and might even have sentimental value, even if it is self-defeating and hurtful.

- You don't have to invest the ongoing time and effort that are involved in getting unstuck.

- You get to feel like a victim, helpless and vulnerable, allowing you to make excuses for inaction.

- You get sympathy from others and permission to feel sorry for yourself.

- You can get others to take care of you.

- You can hurt, control, and manipulate other people who are invested in your progress.

- You get to be impulsive and self-indulgent because you are obviously out of control.

- You can blame factors outside of your control since it is not really your fault.

- Is the point of view convincing and persuasive?

Go to www.cengagebrain.com for an online quiz that will test your understanding of the chapter content.

References

Altman, A. 2009. High tech, high touch, high growth. *Time*, May 25, 39–40.

American College Health Assessment. 2007. *National college health assessment: Executive summary.* Baltimore: American College Health Association.

American College Health Assessment. 2009. *Reference group executive summary for fall, 2008.* Baltimore: American College Health Association.

Andrade, M. S. 2005. International students and the first year of college. *Journal of the First-Year Experience and Students in Transition* 17 (1): 101–129.

Andrade, M. S. 2006. A first-year seminar for international students. *Journal of the First-Year Experience and Students in Transition* 18 (1): 85–103.

Armstrong, T. 2000. *Multiple intelligences in the classroom.* Alexandria, VA: Association for Supervision and Curriculum Development.

Associated Press. 2009. "Financial worries, stress and depression on college campus: A survey." http://surveys .ap.org/data/Edison/APMTV%20Topline%20marginals.pdf (accessed March 13, 2010).

Bailey, H. 2009. Will the BlackBerry sink the presidency? *Newsweek,* February 16, 37–38.

Bartholomew, R. E., and B. Radford. 2003. *Hoaxes, myths, and manias: Why we need critical thinking.* New York: Prometheus.

Baum, S., K. Payea, and P. Steele. 2006. Education pays; Second update. From *Trends in Higher Education Series 2006,* College Board. www.collegeboard.com/prod_downloads/ press/cost06/education_pays_06.pdf (accessed March 13, 2010).

Bernstein, M. W., and Y. Kaufman, eds. 2006. *How to survive your freshman year.* 2nd ed. Atlanta, GA: Hundreds of Heads Books.

Bilalic, M., P. McCleod, and F. Gobet. 2007. Inflexibility of experts: Reality or myth? *Cognitive Psychology* 56(2):73–102.

Braskamp, L. A., L. C. Trautvetter, and K. Ward. 2006. *Putting students first: How colleges develop students purposefully.* Bolton, MA: Anker.

Buckley, W. F. 1994. Ka-Pow! He's famous: Graffiti artists seek fame through vandalism in Los Angeles. *National Review,* April 18.

Bulboltz, W. C., F. Brown, and B. Soper. 2001. Sleep habits and patterns of college students: A preliminary study. *Journal of American College Health* 50(3):131–135.

Burns, D. 1999. *Feeling good: The new mood therapy.* New York: Avon.

Bushong, S. 2009. Campus counseling centers react to recession-related stress among students. *Chronicle of Higher Education* 55(33):A21.

Calhoun, L. G., and R. G. Tedeschi, eds. 2006. *The handbook of posttraumatic growth: Research and practice.* Mahwah, NJ: Lawrence Erlbaum.

Campbell, J. 1968. *The hero with a thousand faces.* Princeton, NJ: Princeton University Press.

Carmichael, M. 2009. Who says stress is bad for you? *Newsweek,* February 23, 47–50.

Chaskes, J. 1996. The first-year student as immigrant. *Journal of the First-Year Experience and Students in Transition* 8(1):79–91.

Chronicle of Higher Education. 2008. This year's freshmen at 4-year colleges: A statistical profile. *Chronicle of Higher Education* 54(21):23.

Clark, M. R. 2005. Negotiating the freshman year: Challenges and strategies among first-year college students. *Journal of College Student Development* 46(3):296–316.

Cote, J. 1994. *Adolescent storm and stress: An evaluation of the Mead-Freeman controversy.* New York: Lawrence Erlbaum.

Cozolino, L. 2008. It's a jungle in there. *Psychotherapy Networker,* September–October, 20–26.

Csikszentmihalyi, M. 1975. *Beyond boredom and anxiety: The experience of play.* San Francisco: Jossey-Bass.

Csikszentmihalyi, M. 1997. *Finding flow: The psychology of engagement with everyday life.* New York: Basic Books.

Csikszentmihalyi, M. 2008. *Flow: The psychology of optimal experience.* New York: Harper.

Csikszentmihalyi, M., S. Abuhamdeh, and J. Nakamura. 2005. Flow. In *Handbook of competence and motivation,* ed. A. J. Elliott and C. S. Dweck, 598–608. New York: Guilford.

Cushman, K. 2006. *First in the family: Advice about college from first-generation students.* Providence, RI: Next Generation Press.

Cutolo, A., and R. A. Rochford. 2007. An analysis of freshman learning styles and their relationship to academic achievement. *College Quarterly* 10(2):1–17.

Day, J. C., and E. C. Newburger. 2002. *The big payoff: Educational attainment and synthetic estimates of work-life earnings.* Washington, DC: U.S. Department of Commerce, U.S. Census Bureau. www.census.gov/prod/2002pubs/ p23-210.pdf (accessed March 13, 2010).

Dennis, J. M., J. S. Phinney, and L. Chuateco. 2005. The role of motivation, parental support, and peer support in the academic success of ethnic minority first-generation college students. *Journal of College Student Development* 46(3):223–236.

Donahue, L. 2004. Connections and reflections: Creating a positive learning environment for first-year students. *Journal of the First-Year Experience and Students in Transition* 16(1):77–100.

Duffy, R. D., and W. E. Sedlacek. 2007. The work values of first-year college students: Exploring group differences. *Career Development Quarterly* 55:359–364.

Dunn, R., and K. Dunn. 1999. *The complete guide to the learning styles inservice system.* Boston: Allyn & Bacon.

Dunn, R., and A. Honigsfeld. 2008. *Differentiating instruction for at-risk students.* Lanham, MD: Rowman and Littlefield.

Dyson, R., and K. Renk. 2006. Freshmen adaptation to university life: Depressive symptoms, stress, and coping. *Journal of Clinical Psychology* 62(10):1231–1244.

313

Ellis, A. 2006. *How to stubbornly refuse to make yourself miserable about anything.* New York: Citadel.

Engberg, M. E., and M. J. Mayhew. 2007. The influence of first-year "success" courses on student learning and democratic outcomes. *Journal of College Student Development* 48(3):241–258.

Erickson, B. L., C. B. Peters, and D. W. Strommer. 2006. *Teaching first-year college students.* San Francisco: Jossey-Bass.

Fisher, A. 2009. When Gen X runs the show. *Time*, May 25, 48–49.

Foreman, J. 2009. Students, don't blame college for your misery. *Los Angeles Times* March 2, F3.

Franklin, K. K., V. Cranston, S. Perry, D. Purtle, and B. Robertson. 2002. Conversations with metropolitan university first-year students. *Journal of the First-Year Experience and Students in Transition* 14(2):57–88.

Freeman, D. 1983. *Margaret Mead and Samoa: The making and unmaking of an anthropological myth.* New York: Penguin.

Freeman, D. 1999. *The fateful hoaxing of Margaret Mead: A historical analysis of her Samoan research.* Boulder, CO: Westview.

Friedlander, L. J., G. J. Reid, N. Shupak, and R. Cribbie. 2007. Social support, self-esteem, and stress as predictors of adjustment to university among first-year undergraduates. *Journal of College Student Development* 48(3):259–274.

Gallagher, R. 2005. *National survey of counseling center directors.* Alexandria, VA: International Association of Counseling Services.

Gardner, H. 1993. *Creating minds.* New York: Basic Books.

Gardner, H. 2006. *Multiple intelligences.* New York: Basic Books.

Gardner, H. 2009. *Five minds for the future.* Boston: Harvard Business School.

Giancola, J. K., M. J. Grawitch, and D. Borchert. 2009. Dealing with the stress of college: A model for adult students. *Adult Education Quarterly* 59(3):246–263.

Gladwell, M. 2008. *Outliers: The story of success.* New York: Little, Brown.

Glausiusz, J. 2009. Devoted to distraction. *Psychology Today,* March/April, 84–91.

Gold, S. 2007. A higher road to relaxation. *Psychology Today,* July/August, 57–58.

Goleman, D. 2006. *Social intelligence.* New York: Bantam.

Gonzales, L. 2003. *Deep survival.* New York: Norton.

Goodman, K., and E. T. Pascarella. 2006. First-year seminars increase persistence and retention. *Peer Review* 8(3):26–28.

Greenberger, D., and C. Padesky. 1995. *Mind over mood: Change how you feel by changing the way you think.* New York: Guilford.

Hales, D. 2006. *An invitation to health.* 12th ed. Belmont, CA: Wadsworth.

Hayman, J. W., S. R. Kurpius, C. Befort, M. F. Nicpon, E. Hull-Blanks, S. Sollenberger, and L. Huser. 2007. Spirituality among college freshmen: Relationships to self-esteem, body image, and stress. *Counseling and Values* 52(1):55–70.

Hebert, S., and N. Popadiuk. 2009. University students' experiences of nonmarital breakups: A grounded theory. *Journal of College Student Development* 49(1):1–14.

Hickman, G. P., and D. W. Andrews. 2003. Humor and college adjustment: The predictive nature of humor, academic achievement, and authoritative parenting styles in the initial adjustment of male and female first-year college students. *Journal of the First-Year Experience and Students in Transition* 15(2):61–82.

Hiester, M., A. Nordstrom, and L. M. Swenson. 2009. Stability and change in parental attachment and adjustment outcomes during the first semester transition to college life. *Journal of College Student Development* 50(5):521–538.

Higher Education Research Institute. 2006. *The American freshman: National norms for fall, 2006.* Los Angeles: Higher Education Research Institute.

Higher Education Research Institute. 2008. *The American freshman: National norms for fall, 2007.* Los Angeles: Higher Education Research Institute.

Higher Education Research Institute. 2009. *The American freshman: National norms for fall, 2008.* Los Angeles: Higher Education Research Institute.

Hofer, B. K. 2008. The electronic tether: Parental regulation, self-regulation, and the role of technology in college transition. *Journal of the First-Year Experience and Students in Transition* 20(2):9–24.

Holland, J. 1997. *Making vocational choices.* Lutz, FL: Psychological Assessment Resources.

Howard, D. E., G. Schiraldi, A. Pineda, and R. Campanella. 2006. Stress and mental health among college students: Overview and promising prevention interventions. In *Stress and mental health of college students,* ed. M. V. Landow, 91–123. New York: Nova.

Hutson, M. 2008. Expertise: Creatures of habit. *Psychology Today,* November/December. http://www.psychologytoday.com/articles/200811/expertise-creatures-habit (accessed April 14, 2010).

Ishler, J. L., and M. L. Upcraft. 2005. The keys to first-year student persistence. In *Challenging and supporting the first-year student,* ed. M. L. Upcraft, J. N. Gardner, and B. O. Barefoot. San Francisco: Jossey-Bass.

Joseph, S., and P. A. Linley, eds. 2008. *Trauma, recovery, and growth: Positive psychological perspectives on posttraumatic stress.* New York: Wiley.

Kabat-Zinn, J. 1995. *Wherever you go, there you are: Mindfulness meditation in everyday life.* New York: Hyperion.

Kabat-Zinn, J. 2005. *Coming to our senses: Healing ourselves and the world through mindfulness.* New York: Hyperion.

Kadar, A. G. 2006. *College life 102: The no-bull guide to a great freshman year.* New York: Universe.

Karp, D. R., and T. Allena, eds. 2004. *Restorative justice on the college campus.* Springfield, IL: Thomas.

Kelly, W., K. Kelly, and R. Clanton. 2001. The relationship between sleep length and grade point average. *College Student Journal* 35:84–86.

Kluger, J. 2009. The biology of belief. *Newsweek,* February 23, 62–68.

Koenig, H. G. 2008. *Medicine, religion, and health.* Conshohocken, PA: Templeton Foundation Press.

Kottler, J. 1990. *Private moments, secret selves: Enriching our time alone.* New York: Ballantine.

Kottler, J. A. 1991. *The compleat therapist.* San Francisco: Jossey-Bass.

Kottler, J. A. 1996. *The language of tears.* San Francisco: Jossey-Bass.

Kottler, J. A. 1997. *Travel that can change your life.* San Francisco: Jossey-Bass.

Kottler, J. A. 2006. *Divine madness: Ten stories of creative struggle.* San Francisco: Jossey-Bass.

Kottler, J. A., and J. Carlson. 2002. *Bad therapy: Master therapists share their worst failures*. New York: Brunner/Routledge.

Kottler, J. A., and J. Carlson. 2007. *Moved by the spirit: Discovery and transformation in the lives of leaders*. Atascadero, CA: Impact.

Kottler, J. A., and D. Chen. 2007. *Stress management and prevention*. Belmont, CA: Wadsworth.

Kottler, J. A., and M. Marriner. 2009. *Changing people's lives while transforming your own: Paths to social justice and global human rights*. New York: Wiley.

Krause, K. L. 2007. Social involvement and commuter students: The first-year student voice. *Journal of the First-Year Experience and Students in Transition* 19(1):27–45.

Kruger, J., D. Wirtz, and D. Miller. 2005. Counterfactual thinking and the first instinct fallacy. *Journal of Personal and Social Psychology* 88:725–735.

Kuh, G. 2007. *Engaged learning: Fostering success for all students*. Bloomington, IN: National Survey of Student Engagement.

Kuh, G. D., J. Kinzie, J. H. Schuh, and E. J. Whitt. 2005. *Student success in college: Creating conditions that matter*. San Francisco: Jossey-Bass.

Lang, D. J. 2007. The impact of a first-year experience course on academic performance, persistence, and graduation rates of first-semester college students at public research universities. *Journal of the First-Year Experience and Students in Transition* 19(1):9–25.

Lee, A., and D. Campbell. 2009. *Perfect breathing: Transform your life one breath at a time*. New York: Sterling.

Levitsky, D. A., C. A. Halbmaier, and G. Mrdjenovic, 2004. The freshman weight gain: A model for the study of the epidemic of obesity. *International Journal of Obesity* 28(11):1435–1442.

Lucas, M. 1993. Personal, social, academic, and career problems expressed by minority college students. *Journal of Multicultural Counseling and Development* 21(1):2–13.

Malikow, M. 2007. Professors' irritating behavior study. *College Student Journal* 41(1):25–33.

Mark, G., D. Gudith, and U. Klocke. 2008. The cost of interrupted work: More speed and stress. In *Proceedings of the Conference on Human Factors in Computing Systems*, Florence, Italy, 107–110.

McGinn, D. 2007. After Virginia Tech. *Newsweek*, August 27, 70–74.

McKay, M., M. Davis, and P. Fanning. 2007. *Thoughts and feelings: Taking control of your moods and your life*. 3rd ed. Oakland, CA: New Harbinger.

McPherson, M., L. Smith-Lovin, and M. Brashears. 2006. Social isolation in America: Changes in core discussion networks over two decades. *American Sociological Review* 71:353–375.

Mezrich, B. 2002. *21: Bringing down the house*. New York: Pocket Books.

Middledorf, J., and A. Kalish. 1996. The change-up in lectures. *National Teaching and Learning Forum*, 5(2):1–7.

Miller, A. S., and S. Kanazawa. 2007. *Why beautiful people have more daughters*. New York: Perigee.

Minnick, T. L. 2008. Fourteen ways of looking at electives. In *Foundations: A reader for new college students*, 4th ed., ed. V. N. Gordon and T. L. Minnick. Belmont, CA: Wadsworth.

Morioka, S. 2009. Multitasking: Fact or fiction? *Michigan Alumnus*, Spring, 28–30.

Nathan, R. 2005. *My freshman year*. Ithaca, NY: Cornell University Press.

National and Community Service Corporation. 2006. "College students helping America." http://servicelearning.org/filemanager/download/CollegeVolReportFinal.pdf (accessed (March 10, 2010).

National Surveys of Student Engagement. 2007. *Student engagement: Exploring different dimensions of student engagement*. Bloomington: Indiana University Center for Postsecondary Research.

Nelson, A. P. 2009. What's your name again? Why low-contrast information fades. *Newsweek*, April 27, 57.

Nemko, M. 2007. Ahead-of-the-curve careers. *U.S. News and World Report*, December 19.

Newberg, A., and M. Waldman 2009. *How God changes your brain*. New York: Ballantine.

Outside the Classroom. 2009. "College students spend more time drinking than studying." http://www.outsidetheclassroom.com/images/PDF/NaspaRelease.pdf (accessed May 1, 2009).

Pascarella, E. T. 2006. How college affects students: Ten directions for future research. *Journal of College Student Development* 47(5):508–520.

Pascarella, E. T., and P. T. Terenzini. 2005. *How college affects students*, vol. 2. San Francisco: Jossey-Bass.

Pascarella, E. T., G. C. Wolniak, C. T. Pierson, and P. T. Terenzini. 2003. Experiences and outcomes of first generation students in community colleges. *Journal of College Student Development* 44(3):420–429.

Paukert, A. L., J. Pettit, M. Perez, and R. Walker. 2006. Affective and attributional features of acculturative stress among ethnic minority college students. *Journal of Psychology* 140(5):405–419.

Pinder, G. 2007. "Eight barriers to critical thinking." http://ezinearticles.com/?Eight-Barriers-to-Critical-Thinking&id=716694 (accessed March 12, 2010).

Pittman, L. D., and A.Richmond. 2008. University belonging, friendship quality, and psychological adjustment during the transition to college. *Journal of Experimental Education* 76(4):343–361.

Porges, S. 2006. The role of social engagement in attachment and bonding: A phylogenetic perspective. In *Attachment and bonding: A new synthesis*, ed. C. Carter, L. Ahnert, K. Grossman, S. Hrdy, M. Lamb, S. Porges, and N. Sachser, 33–54. Boston: MIT Press.

Putnam, R. 2000. *Bowling alone: The collapse and revival of American community*. New York: Simon & Schuster.

Reason, R. D., P. T. Terenzini, and R. J. Domingo. 2007. Developing social and personal competence in the first year of college. *Review of Higher Education* 30(3):271–299.

Regmi, K., and J. Kottler. 2008. An epidemiologist learns grounded theory. In *Qualitative journeys: Student and mentor experiences with research*, ed. V. Minichiello and J. Kottler. Thousand Oaks, CA: Sage.

Rollins, J. 2007. Students lacking education on healthy relationships. *Counseling Today*, September, 1.

Ruggiero, V. R. 2007. *Beyond feelings: A guide to critical thinking*. 8th ed. New York: McGraw-Hill.

Schoenberg, R. 2005. *Why do I have to take this course?* Washington, DC: Association of American Colleges and Universities.

Schutte, N. S., and J. M. Malouff. 2002. Incorporating emotional skills content in a college transition course enhances student retention. *Journal of the First-Year Experience and Students in Transition* 14(1):7–21.

Seligman, M. 2002. *Authentic happiness.* New York: Simon & Schuster.

Sergo, P. 2007. Fired up on sleep. *Psychology Today*, September/October, 26.

Shapiro, S. L., J. A. Astin, S. R. Bishop, and M. Cordova. 2005. Mindfulness-based stress reduction for health care professionals: Results from a randomized trial. *International Journal of Stress Management* 12(2):164–176.

Southern Poverty Law Center. 2000. "Hate goes to school." http://www.splcenter.org/get-informed/intelligence-report/browse-all-issues/2000/spring/hate-goes-to-school (accessed July 19, 2010).

Spradlin, S. 2003. *Don't let your emotions run your life: How dialectical behavior therapy can put you in control.* Oakland, CA: New Harbinger.

Sprague, J., and D. Stuart. 2005. *The speaker's handbook.* Belmont, CA: Wadsworth.

Stephey, M. J. 2009. A brief history of credit cards. *Time*, May 4, 16.

Stern, V. 2009. Sharing spaces. *Psychology Today*, March/April, 53.

Stickgold, R., and P. Wehrwein. 2009. Sleep now, remember later. *Newsweek*, April 27, 56.

Stith, S. 2005. Future directions in intimate partner violence prevention research. *Journal of Aggression, Maltreatment, and Violence* 13(3–4):233–248.

Strayhorn, T. L. 2009. An examination of the impact of first-year seminars on correlates of college student retention.

Journal of the First-Year Experience and Students in Transition 21(1):9–27.

Swenson, L. M., A. Nordstrom, and M. Hiester. 2009. The role of peer relationships in adjustment to college. *Journal of College Student Development* 49(6):551–567.

Terkel, S. 1985. *Working: People talk about what they do all day and how they feel about what they do.* New York: Ballentine.

Tsai, L., and S. Li. 2004. Sleep patterns in college students: Gender and grade differences. *Journal of Psychosomatic Research* 56(2):231–237.

Turk, E. 2004. "How to make $50 last 10 days." www.young-money.com/money_management/budgeting/040902 (accessed March 13, 2010).

Upcraft, M. L., J. N. Gardner, and B. O. Barefoot, eds. 2005. *Challenging and supporting the first-year student.* San Francisco: Jossey-Bass.

Vail-Smith, K., W. M. Felts, and C. Becker. 2009. Relationship between sleep quality and health risk behaviors in undergraduate college students. *College Student Journal* 43(3):924–930.

Wesch, M. 2008. "A vision of students today." www.youtube.com/watch?v=dGCJ46vyR9o (accessed March 13, 2010).

Willoughby, B. 2004. *10 ways to fight hate on campus.* Montgomery, AL: Southern Poverty Law Center.

Wolfe, M. 2007. Reaching my goal of having no life plan. *Newsweek*, June 25, 17–18.

Index